Running:

through the looking glass

As viewed by Dick Telford

ECHO BOOKS

First published in 2015 by Barrallier Books Pty Ltd, trading as Echo Books.

Registered Office: 35-37 Gordon Avenue, West Geelong, Victoria 3220, Australia.

www.echobooks.com.au

National Library of Australia Cataloguing-in-Publication entry

Creator: Telford, Richard D. author.

Title: Running : through the looking glass / Dick Telford (as viewed by)

ISBN: 978099455898 (hardback)

Notes: Includes index.

Subjects: Long-distance running--Coaching. Marathon running--Coaching.

Running--Coaching--Australia. Runners (Sports)--Australia--Anecdotes.

Dewey Number: 796.426

Book and cover design by Peter Gamble, Ink Pot Graphic Design, Canberra.
Set in Garamond Premier Pro Display, 13/17 and Worstveld Sling Bold.

Cover image: *The Canberra squad in 2010 on Doyle's Hill in the bushland behind the Australian Institute of Sport.*

Andrew Sheargold/Fairfax Syndication

www.echobooks.com.au

Foreword

Running: through the looking glass is an insightful, provocative, valuable book and a great read. The author, Richard (Dick) Telford and I go back a long way—to the very start of my international running career. He helped me enormously over those exciting and successful years.

The book, as it should be, is an expression of the author himself. What Dick shares is insightful and questioning, comprehensive and thorough. His entries indicate a generosity of time, thoughtful ideas, a willingness to help others, and a man with a quick and good sense of humour. It is filled with amazing and revealing stories and anecdotes that add richness and colour to key messages and insights.

The book highlights one of Dick's greatest talents—his ability to communicate.

As a pioneering and leading sports scientist, he certainly knows what makes us tick. Dick has the unique ability, as demonstrated in these pages, to present potentially complex physiology and science in a way that is easy to understand, and absolutely practical and applicable to any coach or runner.

Through the looking glass also goes into the realm of the artistry and 'magic' of coaching. This is an area in which some of the most successful coaches thrive; working with the emotions, psychology and personalities to get the very best out of their athletes.

It is in this fascinating space that the best coaches work, as the mind and emotions are perhaps the most important attributes of a champion. Getting fit in many ways is the easy part. Getting results when it really matters and coping with the multitude of setbacks and issues can be the most challenging thing for any coach or athlete. It is in this space that Dick has succeeded time and time again.

Dick is incredibly generous and open in this book, sharing his many insights and precious jewels of performance. Many of these treasures have been documented here for the first time.

Any coach, sports scientist, runner or lover of sport should read and digest these pages and, I am certain, will be richer and better for it.

Learn from his wisdom, enjoy the stories and read between the lines to understand the magic of this great man.

Rob de Castella AO MBE

Dick Telford was Co-ordinator of Sports Science and Medicine at the AIS in the early days.

Image: Australian Sports Commission

Acknowledgements

My father and mother encouraged me to play and run in the park, fed me plenty of good fresh food from the Vic Markets and made sure I was well educated. They set a scene of physical activity and academic curiosity that was to last for a lifetime. Melbourne University played a dominant role. I went to a small primary school in the corner of the university for six years and later studied as an undergraduate and graduate student for another eight, the solid scientific foundations of which I call on to this day. During early married life my world was family, teaching, studying then research and football and cricket. Sue and our children Nerilee and Rohan provided the all-important family and home-life buffer to the inevitable stresses of competition in sport and academia. My teachers, team-mates and colleagues taught me that our best work is not driven by the dollar but by the satisfaction and enjoyment of making a difference. I hesitate to single out any of my many mentors, but among them were my PE teacher at Northcote High School, Alec Weston, my PhD supervisor at Melbourne Uni, Mary Chennells, my RMIT Head of School Peter Reichenbach, my football coach at Preston Allan Joyce, and the first Director of the Australian Institute of Sport, Don Talbot. Each in their own way saw fit to give me unusual freedom to exploit any creative skills I may have possessed in academia and on the sporting field. Their style of leadership became a blueprint I was to adopt with my own staff in the physiology lab at the Australian Institute of Sport in Canberra, which turned out well. The first technician at the AIS was a young runner from Melbourne called Robert de Castella who had burst on to the world scene with a 10th place in the Moscow Olympics. 'Deek' of course went on not only to inspire me as a distance runner but the whole nation. I was glad I gave him plenty of flexibility at work to fit in his training in those very early days, because following his magnificent athletic career he came back to the AIS as its Director. Now the running shoe was on the other foot. It was his turn to approve my time out to train! We always had a lot of fun at the AIS and the pioneering collaboration of sports scientists, coaches and athletes in those formative years was a daily source of energy for me. It helped that Australia's Olympic medal count climbed from five in Montreal to 58 in Sydney. From these experiences an unplanned career as a running coach evolved; one who works from first principles, doesn't read coaching manuals and whose looking glass reflects back years of experiences. Sometimes that reflection comes back somewhat convoluted and inconsistent with expectations, a bit like seeing right through that looking glass.

Three final acknowledgements. Firstly, Hannah Walmsley (nee Flannery) whose ongoing enthusiasm for running and writing provided a timely reminder to apply my own training principles to my writing; to knuckle down and get this book fit for publication. Secondly, to my wife Sue for her creative contributions and proof reading. Thirdly, to Charles Lutwidge Dodgson, mathematician, artist, and cleric, whose intuitive words often fit in beautifully with what I'm trying to say, and in a way that puts this small contribution of mine into appropriate perspective. After all, when it's all said and done, I'm describing only how better to run in our world, not how better to run our world. Charles, by the way, was better known as Lewis Carroll and he introduced us to the adventures of an inquisitive young lady called Alice in a Wonderland she discovered through her own looking glass.

'What is the use of a book' thought Alice, 'without pictures or conversations?'

Contents

Chapter 1
Setting the Scene

'Tut, tut child!' said the Duchess. 'Everything's got a moral, if only you can find it.'

Lewis Carroll

You've opened up a book written in the style of a coach who happens to be a scientist, rather than a scientist who happens to be a coach. In this collage of distance running, I retrace the footprints of a running coach; reflecting on the people and experiences which have shaped my view of distance running. In no way do I, nor should I, try to tell you how you should train or coach, but I do hope my stories and experiences provide insights which help you hone your personal philosophy and practice of training and coaching. The art and science of coaching and a lot of its fun and satisfaction are derived from working by first principles. Discovering what works best for each individual runner requires an understanding of why and how things work. Cookbook instructions simply don't fill the bill.

My looking glass reflects those experiences indelible in my mind; experiences of running, runners and life in general. Sometimes though, it's been a case of seeing through the looking glass into a world where things don't always conform to the perspectives of popular wisdom. Now, in my fourth decade of coaching distance runners the learning curve might be flattening out a bit but its asymptote is still nowhere within reach. I continue to learn not just from my best-performed athletes, but also from my club and fun runners whose drive to produce their very best often matches that of the champions.

As I write these words I have spent exactly half my life in Canberra. The first half was in Melbourne, the home of the most fanatical population of sports fans in the country, some would say the world. A city of passionate Australian football and cricket fans, Melbournians come out in droves to support any sport played at the highest level. My father was certainly no exception, and it had rubbed off on me by the time I was six. I don't have to close my eyes to recall six decade-old flashbacks of footballers, swimmers, boxers, cricketers and runners doing magical things.

> British medical student Roger Bannister does the impossible and runs a mile in under 4 minutes and not long after our own Melbournian John Landy does it too. Vladimir Kutz looks over his shoulder, blonde of hair and barrel of chest, toying with the world's best 10,000m runners at the Melbourne Cricket Ground during the 1956 Melbourne Olympics. Betty Cuthbert, our own fleet-of-foot golden girl, gallops gracefully (that's the way I remember her anyway) to the tape as the fastest and most determined woman in the world. I read about our many great Australian distance runners in those days, and the names Dave Power, Alan Lawrence, Alby Thomas and the 'Flying Milkman' Dave Stephens sit alongside the household names of Landy, Herb Elliott and Ron Clarke. I rush out to the front porch of our inner city Parkville rented house (cheap rent in those days) to read with delight that skinny little boxer Jimmy Carruthers had won a world bantamweight title overnight. Australian Rules footballer and Collingwood Aussie Rules Captain Bobby Rose gets the ball on the half back line at Victoria Park and drills a stab pass onto the chest of free-flowing winger Thorold Merrett. I'll never forget gracefully fearsome English fast bowler Frank 'Typhoon' Tyson swaying back in his then classical side-on delivery position and cleaning up the Aussies at the MCG with the fastest out-swingers I have to this day ever witnessed.

My approach to coaching evolved from these Melbourne roots and playing and coaching cricket and football magically reunited and introduced me to many of my boyhood football and cricketing idols, as did my later role at the Australian Institute of Sport. Putting the icing on the cake was the cornucopia of sporting greats I was to meet within a gathering of inductees to the Australian Sporting Hall of Fame.

My collaboration with the AIS and Australian swim team coaches headed up by Bill Sweetenham was a highly influential prelude to my work with runners and the way I design training sessions. But I don't think I could have understood my runners without having personally tried to become the very best runner I could be.

This I did, but not until I had hung up my cricket and football boots and I was well into my thirties. I may not have been in the same league as those I coached, but without experiencing those specific nuances of fatigue and the physical and psychological consequences of training at the knife-edge, my coaching could not have developed with the same sensitivity.

As to the style of this book, for the scientists among you, read no further if you want a published reference to support any position I hold on a particular issue. Quite deliberately, very few references are listed as I free-wheel into my writing in the same practical manner of day-to-day coaching, where judgments are made by feel as well as fact, and art holds its ground with science.

It's fair to say I write here as a coach with a science background rather than a scientist with a coaching background. And what a contrast that has been to the painstakingly rigorous processes underlying the submission of scientific manuscripts to international peer-reviewed journals.

On the other hand, many of my stories do relate to the science of running. After all, coaching requires creativity and systematic thought and theories need to be tested and inferences drawn from trials. That's also not a bad description of the role of a scientist. At the AIS we were always trying to find ways to give our coaches and athletes an edge, and we set up many studies. Some were eventually published, but publications weren't a high priority in my days at the AIS through the 80s and 90s. Medals and improved performances were what counted.

I'm hoping that this book of my coaching experiences might add to your own, and in some small way contribute to you getting the best out of yourself as an athlete or coach. Even if you don't run or coach, maybe you'll just enjoy a story or two about those who do.

Breathtakingly simple

I try to keep things as simple as possible, and I certainly received good early tuition on that aspect.

It was the summer of 1983, and a good pack of runners had assembled in Canberra under the experienced eye of Coach Pat Clohessy. The sensational form of Robert de Castella, 'Deek' as he is affectionately known, had put distance running back on the map; promising runners migrated to Canberra to train at the budding Australian Institute of Sport. The long runs in Stromlo Forest, a vast pine plantation punctuated with a eucalypt oasis right in the heart of the nation's capital was gaining the sort of legendary status of the famous Ferny Creek run in the Dandenong Ranges on the outskirts of Melbourne.

I wasn't a bad runner by ex-footballer and cricketer standards, and loved to run with that elite group whenever they set out on their so-called 'easy' runs, but even that pace often had me red-lining it. Deek's brother-in-law, Graham Clews was a talented young distance athlete who'd come across from Perth with a very realistic aim of representing Australia. A mist was lifting to gradually reveal one of those crisp clear cool mornings common to Canberra's high country climate, and we were cruising through an easy 10km when I noticed that Graham's breathing was disconcertingly arrhythmical. I listened intently. Every now and then his regular breathing was interrupted with one or two short sharp breaths, which appeared to be through the nose, resulting in a snorting sound.

Here was my chance. As the first ever full-time Australian sports scientist, wetness behind my ears was not simply the result of the morning Stromlo mist. Sensing an opportunity to demonstrate my trade I launched into a mini-lecture on control of respiration, that breathing smoothly and evenly will maximize the exchange of air in the alveoli of the lungs and the oxygen in the blood. I even cited some research that suggested a new technique of breathing for asthmatics might be useful to the runners. The pace must have been slower than usual, as my 10 minute sermon was relatively unimpeded by my own requirement for oxygen. Graham, a patient and polite young chap, was all ears, or so it seemed. I was Deek's boss in those days and he was always (read 'had to be') politely attentive. I was now looking for some words to the effect of 'Wow, Dick that was informative', but Graham's response was not quite as I had anticipated.

'Dick, that physiology stuff was fascinating, but the reason I've been making those irregular breathing sounds is because my new sunglasses keep slipping down my nose, and a good regular sniff and twitch of the nose was the best way to get them back up again.'

I didn't offer too much more advice on that run. Now, thirty years later, I often fondly refer back to it as a sobering reminder to keep things simple. Whether dealing with athletic performance problems or even designing a research project, it reminds me to stick to the basic principles, and not to jump headfirst into looking for complicated explanations and solutions before exploring the practical advice of those at the coal-face. For 35 years now I've listened very carefully indeed when athletes and coaches have something to say!

Discussing tactics with the then Prime Minister Paul Keating at the AIS.
Image: Australian Sports Commission

Chapter 2
Coaching kick-started

'Well now that we've seen each other' said the Unicorn,
'if you believe in me, I'll believe in you.'
Lewis Carroll

My first athlete

Coaches of distance runners will have different stories of how they first became involved. For some it has been a natural progression from a personal running career; for others it's as a parent of a child with early prospects, or as a teacher taking on the cross-country team. For me, it was a bit different.

Carolyn Schuwalow walked into my Physiology Department office at the Australian Institute of Sport, and fired a direct question. 'Dick, I've just lost my scholarship and the AIS coaches can't coach me any more ... will you coach me?' I really felt for this young girl who just hadn't been able to get her running together after committing to a shift to Canberra from Melbourne. But coaching was the last thing on my mind. AIS Sports Science was in its formative years and finding its place in the sun was challenge enough.

I enjoyed my role working with 'Clo' (AIS distance coach Pat Clohessy) and his running squad as the team physiologist, but coaching adds an entirely different dimension. Coaches can make or break an athlete. Relative to coaching, sports science is cushy. The buck stops with the coach, not the scientist. Through my football and cricket coaching I knew only too well the stress, but had also tasted the seductive nature to being at the helm of success or failure. I knew that the bigger the stress, the sweeter the success.

This young runner stood there in my office waiting for my reaction. But not for long and that was the start of my three decades so far of coaching runners.

It's interesting how a runner's personality can be perceived so differently. One of the AIS Track and Field staff whose judgments I've always respected advised me not to waste my time with the 20 year-old Schuwalow. 'She just doesn't have the temperament for distance running.'

Within a year Carolyn had asserted herself on the Australian distance running scene, culminating in a spot on the Australian Olympic Team in 1988. She set a new Australian 10,000m record of 32:10:05 in the first round in Seoul to make an Olympic final. That's when I came to realise that distance running coaches aren't in it for fortune or fame; it's the bond they develop with their athletes in breaking new ground.

It's a quarter of a century down the track and when I bump into Carolyn in Melbourne or somewhere else, I see the same lithe woman who walked into my office all those years ago, and that never-to-forget cheeky smile. If ever there was a perfect example of how running can keep a person biologically young as the chronological years creep by, it's Carolyn. A successful businesswoman, she presents a fine example of how training discipline and dealing with competitive stress provides the basis for success in life in general.

Mind you, we coaches need to be fully aware of the fierce desire our top athletes have to win. Darwin talked about 'survival of the fittest' and Richard Dawkins alerted us to the 'selfish gene'. They didn't know Carolyn but she exemplified their work pretty well ...

I'd been coaching Carolyn for a couple of years and we were running around a cattle trail through some paddocks behind the Canberra suburb of Chapman, the Brindabella Ranges cushioning a setting sun. We were enjoying the late afternoon warmth on our backs, and as I was soon to discover, so do brown snakes.

We had been chatting away about something or someone as runners usually do on easy runs, and my attention to the path ahead was not sharp. We were almost on top of the big 'brown' comfortably stretched across the trail, Carolyn a metre or so behind me. Its lazy repose doing nothing to diminish my utmost respect, I jammed on the brakes yelling, 'SNAKE!'. Carolyn responded by decelerating the best way she could. Placing her two hands squarely in the middle of my back, she neatly demonstrated Newton's 3rd Law of Motion. I now had all the momentum that Carolyn had lost and a stationary Carolyn had me accelerating forward. I had two choices. Fall flat on my face directly across the snake's glistening brown back or I somehow launch myself over the top. I opted for the latter. Well primed by Carolyn's manoeuvre, and a spike of adrenaline, I executed a Beamonish effort (with hitch-kick) to somehow clear the snake by inches. It slithered away undeterred, and luckily for me, it must have had late summer thoughts of a long nap rather than another bite to eat.

'Hey Carolyn, what the hell were you doing?' I looked behind and she gave me that smile.'Hey Dick, you tell me to think on my feet, so I did. And you said that we Australian athletes are few and far between and shouldn't take training risks. So I didn't. For the sake of Australian athletics if one of us was to get bitten it really shouldn't be me should it?' Point taken, Caz.

'Set it in a running angle please Doc', my second athlete

Andrew Lloyd was the 'Fun Run King'. In his early 20s, his solution to the usual cash-flow problem of young runners was to run races with prize money. He was harder to beat than Tom Cruise. The odd thousand-dollar purse wasn't in the league of professional athletes in other sports, but it paid bills. Athletic purists didn't approve; they reckoned Lloyd sometimes rated winning a fun run higher than a state championship. They were right. Track and Field was, and still is, very amateurish for most. You ran for your club, state and country, not for a dollar. After all, officials would remind them Landy, Clarke, Elliott, Lincoln, Doubell, Thomas, Stephens and Co. had run purely for the fame and country, not fortune. Not that they necessarily agreed, but they had no choice if they wanted to run the Olympics.

Andrew Lloyd was travelling down to the coast with his wife in the winter of 1985 when a truck appeared out of nowhere over the crest of a hill on the wrong side of the road. Tragically his wife did not survive that crash. Andrew was badly injured. In a semi-conscious state, his surgeon told him that his arm was shattered but they could reconstruct his elbow. The catch was that it would be locked.

'Andrew I need to fix your arm at a permanent angle.' The surgeon moved the limp arm into a couple of positions. 'Is it best like this...or this?',

'Set it at a running angle please Doc' was the reply. And so it was for life, at about a right angle, the right angle for running.

The 'Fun Run King' changed. He'd only just taken up a scholarship at the AIS and I'd seen him round the campus but hadn't met him. I'd heard all about him and the concerns about his ability to take instructions from a coach. Talking to a scientist wasn't high on his list of priorities. The lad's colourful mohawk did nothing to convince AIS administrators that he had what it takes to knuckle down into disciplined training. As for starting off a university course, which was part of the AIS deal, it was 'Are you kidding me?' Secondary school was challenge enough—for the teachers. Life around the northern beaches and rivers of Sydney left little time for textbooks but there was some early evidence of street smartness. One day walking to school across a bridge he spotted a good-sized fish. Not wanting to be late again, he made a quick calculation of how long it would take to race home, grab his rod, catch the fish, run back to the fridge and then get to school. It could work. It did. Quick running and quick thinking; a sign of things to come.

Lloyd became the second athlete to ask me to coach him. This time it wasn't as straightforward, because he was on scholarship and I wasn't an AIS coach. 'It's okay Dick, all under control. Tony (Rice, the Head Coach) has given it the go-ahead.' I came to realise that the AIS coaches had placed Andrew in the too-hard basket and gave it the 'Why not?' My squad doubled and the Telford-Lloyd partnership was set in motion.

The Lloyd book certainly couldn't be judged by its cover, and I now had two runners whose dedication to their task was second to none. The two runners' enthusiasm grew along with their friendship. Andrew and Carolyn married a year or so after they had met. Andrew Lloyd won national championships from 1500m to 10 km, and I describe his gold in the Auckland Commonwealth Games 5km later on. They had good fun when Mr Lloyd and Ms Schuwalow became the first (and to this date) only husband and wife to take out the male and female honours at the Sydney 'City to Surf' fun run in front of 80,000 others.

Twenty-five years after retiring from serious running that cheeky Aussie larrikinism has remained well intact with 'Lloydy'. So has that race-canniness and willingness to work hard. Like Carolyn he carved out a successful business career. Always a generous bloke when he had the means, he hasn't forgotten the young runner struggling to make ends meet. Now actively helping young runners through his company, he was recently honoured with the Medal of the Order of Australia (OAM) for his contributions to Australian sport.

Lloyd and Schuwalow set the scene of my coaching, and for advising runners who may have lost their way a little. As highly respected coach Chris Wardlaw once commented with his knowing smile 'Dick, you seem to attract runners who are different.'

A celebratory drink post Seoul Olympics 1988. Rob de Castella, Dick Telford, Lisa Martin (later Ondieki), Andrew Lloyd and Carolyn Schuwalow.
Image: Mirror Australian Telegraph Publications

Taking on a champion

Sue and I were staying at a friend's place in Melbourne in January 1987, when the phone rang. That call would shape a significant portion of my life over the next decade.

'Hello, Dick this is Lisa Martin. Do you remember me? I met you in Edinburgh at the Commonwealth Games a couple of years ago.'

'Of course I remember you, Lisa. Congratulations on your career so far, and that run in Edinburgh was terrific.'

'Thanks' she replied, 'I'm still based in US and ringing from Phoenix, but thinking of coming back to Australia. Is there any chance you might coach me?'

It's not every day a novice distance running coach (with a stable of two) gets a call like that from an already internationally accomplished athlete like Lisa Martin. My answer was a given. Anyway, I'd found coaching a refreshing change after a day in the lab. Not only that, the experience at the coal-face was helping me understand what coaches really need from sports science, and just as importantly, what was a waste of time. Lisa wasn't interested in an AIS scholarship as she had built up a solid base of support with Nike and wanted to continue this without conflict or responsibilities to the AIS sponsors. Like Lloyd, she valued her independence as an athlete, happy to share full responsibility for her performances with her personal coach, without debt to the AIS or government. In a few weeks Lisa Martin had set herself up with an apartment in the inner Canberra suburb of Kingston and we were on our way.

There's a natural tendency for a new coach to want to put his mark on the training program. I looked at Lisa's competition record. Seventh in the LA Olympics; 2nd in New York; 2nd in Chicago; 1st in Pittsburgh. She'd had an emphatic win in the Commonwealth Games in Edinburgh in 1986 and was ranked in the world top 10 marathoners by *Track and Field News* three times in 1984, 1985, and 1986. Not a lot wrong with the training of anyone with that record.

Lisa enjoyed her training routine with its discipline of week-in-week-out twice-a-day running. She also loved running on the track a couple of times each week in the middle of 200 km. Training had been set up by experienced coach/physiologist, Jack Daniels and more recently by husband Ken Martin, a competent and experienced marathoner himself. Now there was to be no Jack, no Ken, a new coach and a new environment. That's stress enough. No point in adding any more by changing training.

When cross-coaching came in handy

Coaching is a lot more than setting training. In what might be considered an unlikely analogy, I saw my role from the start of my coaching Lisa Martin as not dissimilar to my role with the Victorian Sheffield Shield Cricket Team in the late 70s. State Coach and former great England fast bowler Frank Tyson had asked me to help prepare the team, organise training and get the team physically fit. But Frank became unavailable to coach the state team when he took up a television contract with ABC TV to commentate on the Ashes Test Series.

I inherited the job of Team Manager, Fitness Consultant and Coach of some sort. There was no time for the Victorians to appoint a coach with international experience so I was 'it'. I'd coached the Preston Cricket Club right to the top of the tree, but this was a new ball game altogether. Now many of my charges had played international Test Cricket. I was to learn where I stood and how I might contribute very early in the piece.

Our first game of the season was up in Queensland. We were bowled out cheaply on a fast bouncy wicket, not an uncommon experience over the years for the Victorians up at the 'Gabba' oval. My instinct as a coach and sports scientist was to chat to the players about how they might better combat the Queensland attack. It seemed obvious to me, but I soon found out that coaching at club level did not transfer directly to coaching at State level. Although my words of intended advice did not attract any harsh retort or negative response from a polite and respectful bunch of players, I was taken aside quietly by former great Australian all-rounder Alan Davidson and acting captain Trevor Laughlin. They quietly pointed out that at this level, cricketers were well aware of their mistakes, and how to correct them. Revisiting the scene of the crime when the wounds were still healing was not the best tactic to adopt.

I took this squarely on the chin and the players knew it, and we developed a very close bond during that season and over the next couple. My focus was to create a culture that would bring out the best in each player. I loved chatting with individual players, doing my best to enhance their self-confidence and the team cohesiveness. We won a lot of closely fought games that 1978-79 season and after a drought of more than a decade Victoria captured the coveted Sheffield Shield. We won the one-day competition as well. The powers that be must have been puzzled. The Victorian cricket team had won without a proper manager or a proper coach. But we had a great cricket team, excellent captaincy, and I was fortunate to be assisted at training by two experts in their professions, fitness advisor Ron Rooney and motor learning analyst Neil Barras.

I suppose Victorian Secretary Ken Jacobs, Frank Tyson and the Selection Committee realized they couldn't top that season and I was appointed under the title of Coaching Coordinator for the next season. We won the Shield again. Looking back, it's clear that the team was a damn good one, and that's why they won of course, but I always felt that the team spirit and happiness of that group brought out the best in our players when it counted. Interestingly, I and my two assistants received a combined annual fee that barely paid our petrol bill to get to training, but we were very much richer for the experience.

But how's this related to coaching runners? Well, in two ways actually.

Firstly, just like any of the Victorian cricketers, I would coach Lisa for the honour of working with a champion. Despite Lisa's insistence that we set up a formal professional relationship we never did, but my charge was a very appreciative and generous person, always careful to make sure my expenses were well and truly covered.

Secondly, similar to my cricket experience, my first instinct with Lisa's training was to make a mark and revise her training program. But, again like the cricketers, here was an athlete with far more talent than I ever had, and with a successful history. So, profiting from the cricketing experience, I focused on creating a training atmosphere of confidence and happiness. I reckoned all else would fall into place.

I did have one card up my sleeve. If Lisa had a weakness at all it may have been in preparing physically and psychologically for a big international race. It was here my experience with coaches in a variety of sports over the years would come into play. As AIS swim squad physiologist, I had the opportunity to work with some master coaches, led in the early days by American Dennis Pursley and Australian Bill Sweetenham and I was in regular communication with legendary swim coach Forbes Carlile.

We explored the best way for swimmers to feel just right for competition after months of intense training. After much trial and certainly considerable error we began to better understand the nuances of the physical, mental wellbeing and nutrition interactions involved in the so-called taper period. The first runner to profit from the lessons learned from our swim squad was Rob de Castella. I've never been sure coach Clohessy and I got it completely right, but in running to a world championship title and a world best marathon time we probably weren't too far off track.

1988 was a great year for Lisa Martin. A PB (Personal Record for some) of 2:23:51 was recorded winning the Osaka Marathon. What followed was a silver medal and 2:25:53 in the summer temperature and humidity of the Seoul Olympics. Then in 1990 her gold medal in the Auckland Commonwealth Games, cruising in over the last 5km to win in 2:25:28 was another of her most impressive performances. Amongst many highlights, I really enjoyed Lisa's big road race wins, and these included the San Francisco Bay to Breakers and the Sydney City to Surf, and in our several trips to Japan she always ran exceptionally well both on the road or cross-country.

In 1992 leading up to the Barcelona Olympics and New York marathon Lisa was now Lisa Ondieki and with her world champion husband Yobes moved from Canberra to Flagstaff where Yobes became Lisa's coach. Leading into Barcelona Olympics she now had the benefit of a full-time day-to-day coach, a running partner at altitude and a coach with intimate Kenyan training confidence and experience with the objective of going one step further than her silver in Seoul.

Yobes was a quietly spoken champion, famous for his Ron Clarke-like courageous front running and in 1993 he became the first human to run 10,000m under 27 minutes with his 26:58.38 at the Bislett Games, Oslo, a stadium and athletic savvy city where the name Ron Clarke continues its legendary status. A wonderful example of the Ondieki courage and tactical skill was his win in the 1991 World Championships 5000m final in Tokyo. I watched in amazement that oppressively hot and humid day as he surged away from the world's best runners early in the race to open up what appeared to be a suicidal lead of 100m or more. It was nail-biting spine tingling stuff as Lisa and I saw his huge lead gradually diminish over the final 6 laps, the gnawing chase-pack led by Ethiopian Fita Bayisi and Moroccan Brahim Bouteyeb. History has it that Ondieki's plan to prevent the speedier runners 'sitting' on him and kicking away over the final lap worked, just. How those chasing runners must have regretted letting him get away so far so early. But on the other hand, had they gone with him, might they have regretted that too? We'll never know. The finish line came too late for the hungry pack and Ondieki's barrel chest crossed that line first by the relatively narrow margin of 2.19 seconds. He did what Ron Clarke did in many races, but just couldn't execute in championship races; he took the sitters and kickers out of the equation.

Unfortunately, Barcelona Olympics was disappointing, Lisa becoming exhausted midway through the race, forced to withdraw. From what Lisa and I could gather after that run, a great period of training had been undone by a mistimed taper. However, not to be denied she and Yobes went straight back to Flagstaff, then pulled off a triumphant win in New York. With a 2nd in the New York marathon in 1985 and 1986 and a 3rd in 1991, Lisa would rank her New York course record run of 2:24:40 as one of her best runs ever. Interestingly, for this race she arrived in New York only a day or so after coming down from several months of training at altitude in Flagstaff. Not what a lot of coaches would have recommended at the time, but it certainly did the trick.

Lisa and I did work together again to a degree leading into Atlanta in 1996, but injury upset the apple cart. Not a running injury, but a foot injury sustained from slipping on the polished floor of the family room in her Canberra residence. I have never been really concerned with non-running injuries, as they usually resolve quickly, and in many cases, running is not compromised too much. This turned out to be different. To our bitter disappointment that injury persisted, despite access to our best sports medical practitioners. Lisa, now with daughter Emma and separated from husband Yobes, soldiered on, but with recurring foot soreness, training never returned to the kind of quality or quantity we knew was necessary to mix it with the world's best. After her 7th in Los Angeles and 2nd in Seoul, Lisa could not complete the Atlanta Olympic course. She certainly exhausted all avenues in that preparation, even relocating to Townsville for heat acclimatisation, and when her time on those hot Atlanta roads was finally over she knew that her running career was as well.

Lisa O'Dea the young hurdler from Gawler, South Australia, retired as Lisa Ondieki; Australia's only marathon Olympic medallist and the only distance or middle-distance Olympic medallist since Ralph Doubell's 800m gold medal in 1968. You are probably wondering what she is doing now? Well, she's married to a delightful American doctor and they are happily settled in Arizona. Having completed a Master of Education Lisa teaches children with learning difficulties in Scottsdale. A teaching day does contrast dramatically with a routine 32km running day but her conscientious and meticulous approach is now well and truly applied to her students.

'Excuse me, Ms. Ondieki ... '

Lisa has never been one to seek out the limelight, a characteristic that some interpreted as aloofness or even reclusiveness. This completely missed the mark. If anything, shyness and lack of self-confidence had more to do with her resistance to seek publicity. She'd been teaching at the school in Arizona for more than a year when a staff member remarked offhandedly, 'Hey Lisa, did you realise that you have the same name as a marathon runner I'm reading about in this magazine?' Quietness in the staff room; heads look up; then excitement when it became obvious that the champion marathon runner and the quiet teacher of kids with learning difficulties were one and the same person. A bit like Lois Lane uncovering Clark Kent.

And coaching Lisa was always a lot of fun. It was the Auckland Commonwealth Games, and Lisa and I were strolling round the Village when we noticed a gathering of people and walked over. The Queen of England was resplendent in a pale blue frock and matching hat, chatting with the athletes who were taking photos. Lisa wanted to catch up with the great Scottish runner Liz McColgan (née Lynch). She suddenly spotted McColgan just over the other side of the gathering. Spontaneously Lisa called to her 'Hey, Liz, I'm over here!' With that Her Majesty, clearly unaccustomed to first name correspondence, turned to us to discover who indeed was over there! My photos just before and just after Lisa's call capture the moments. Lisa then realised there were indeed two Liz's within earshot, and by the smile on Prince Phillip's face and those just behind the Queen, others were in full realisation of situation. I could feel the heat radiating off my runner's face, but soon came to appreciate the lighter side of the incident.

Queen Elizabeth strolls through the Auckland Commonwealth Games village.

Lisa Ondieki inadvertently captures the attention of the Queen to the amusement of surrounding crowds.

Lisa Martin (later to become Ondieki) on a warm-up run prior to a track session at the AIS in Canberra.

Chapter 3
Why Coaches Coach

'It's not real work you are doing, unless you'd rather be doing something else.'

Lewis Carroll

I was once asked if motivation was an important part of my coaching role. 'Yes' I replied, 'my athletes continue to motivate me'.

Maybe this wasn't the expected answer but it was mine.

Being a motivator is a not high up on my daily 'to do' list as a coach. For mine, any runner requiring the threat of a big stick to train hard is not likely to succeed in the long run, and the kind of motivation that comes from within the belly is not something that coaches should have to teach, if indeed it's teachable.

Legendary coach Percy Cerutty guided his protégé Herb Elliott through a period where he may well have not continued, so we have plenty to thank Percy for. He was considered a great, albeit eccentric motivator, but I'm not convinced this was his major asset. Any champions he coached or advised, including Elliott were highly motivated. Percy was the breeze that kept the embers glowing rather than igniting the fire in the first place. He never lost the fire in his own belly or that breeze in his sails, and this rubbed off on his charges.

There are many athletes who keep my embers glowing and they include those chasing a moderate PB as well as those chasing an international medal.

The Canberra girls

During a period where my Canberra group consisted almost entirely of the fairer sex, we had just finished one of our favourite sessions. It's somewhat oxymoronically described as a 'surprise' fartlek session where runners never really know what their next effort involves. We were only a few kilometres away from Parliament House but on bush trails winding through ghost gums.

The session had been a good one, and I gathered the group together before the warm-down. Someone mentioned that she'd heard a mountain runner overseas had been hurt racing down a hill. 'It was very serious; I didn't hear whether he died or suffered the kind of serious injury that would end his running career'.

Budding marathoner Hannah Walmsley (then Flannery), nearly 20 at the time, asked, 'What's the difference?'

That comment typified the attitude of runners I coach. Running's not just a random something they just tack on to each day like a step class in the gym or a walk in the park. It's like eating and sleeping, psychologically habitual, even addictive. These girls have come to realise what many people never do these days; that physical activity is an inherited aspect of human being that enhances them physically and emotionally. They love running and love to run better each year, so they love to train hard. Some represent their club, some their state, some their country. Some just represent themselves; but they all share the common bond of a determined commitment to train to run faster.

Just to think, it wasn't all that long ago that men believed women might suffer irreparable damage if they ran for more than a few minutes! How ignorant. Or was it more than that; with sport a fiercely protected masculine domain? And how sad is it that this kind of mindless, testosterone-mediated repression of women expressing themselves through physical activity still exists within the superstitions of some societies?

There is a post-script to this story, brought about by my on and off writing schedule over many years. Several of the women in the group have made small contributions to Australia's population. During their pregnancies training attendance continued, slow jogging being the session of choice. They tell me they feel much better continuing to be active and getting out in the fresh air and bush trails with the group. I'm pleased too because it presents me with a good chance to keep up during the warm-ups, but I have learnt to wait about 5 months before throwing out a challenge of racing up a hill.

The Canberra squad in 2010 on Doyle's Hill in the bushland behind the AIS.

Image: Andrew Sheargold/Fairfax Syndication

One keen mum

An email arrives from one of my marathoners, Kim Wilmshurst, 37 years old, mother of 3, keen to run the Melbourne marathon in 5 weeks.

'Dick, with my husband away I'm going to have to mind the kids on Sunday so I'm not going to get time to myself for the long run. Would you mind if I did my long run on Saturday? I'd have to do it at 4 am while the kids are asleep and as I won't be able to leave the house it'll have to be all on the treadmill. Is that ok?'

Kim got that 40km run done on that treadmill in just over 3 hours without stopping. There was no way she was going to miss her long run.

'Running isn't just anything, it's everything'

I first met Nickey Carroll in Athens at the World Championships of 1997, watching the heats of the women's 5 km. She was very proud of her green and gold tracksuit suit, and as she had the the lean and keen appearance of an elite marathon runner I assumed it was Nickey Carroll. This was the girl nobody knew who had surprised everyone with a great 2hr 33 min run in the Las Vegas Marathon. I'd heard that she was shy, and this was more than obvious over the next few days as we watched my two athletes Kate Anderson and Darren Wilson make their finals in the 5km and 10km respectively. History has it now that in a few days time, Nickey was not able to complete the marathon course in Athens, but it was not until a year later that I understood why.

Some months after World Champs, I was in Auckland following the excellent track meets passionately championed and organised by the (sadly) late John Davies (Tokyo 1964 Olympic bronze medalist) and his good mate Dick Quax (Montreal 1976 Olympic silver medalist). One of the pleasures of coaching has been meeting athletic greats like these two New Zealanders. I'd seen Quax run at his prime and admired the graceful flowing movement of this runner in his all black gear. An athletic Cisco Kid.

My phone rang. 'Hello, this is Nickey. I was wondering if you had the time to help me with my training'. As I knew a few Nickeys it was not until she continued on that I realised this was Nickey Carroll. There was a sense of déjà vu about this call. Lisa Ondieki had contacted me on an international call while I was away, and with the same question some 10 years earlier. And like Nickey, Lisa wasn't able to finish a World Championships marathon. Again like Lisa, Nickey had proven she could run. The thought went through my mind that coaching this girl may not be straightforward. I was right.

Nickey Carroll had been a promising junior tennis player, having been chosen in an elite Queensland training squad that included a young fellow named Pat Rafter, who, in the off-chance my reader doesn't know, was to become one of the greats of Australian and world tennis. Nickey drifted out of tennis. The one-on-one highly competitive rectangular sport of tennis was in direct contrast to the bush trails she had come to love. Going for a run was where she found contentment, running effortlessly over distances other tennis players would not believe.

The teenage Carroll heard about a running group organised by Brisbane runner, coach and running shop owner Phil Hungerford and decided that training with a group might be fun. She rang Phil who was happy to have her join in, and he invited her to join them at Redcliff beach on Tuesday afternoon. Nickey got excited about her first formal training session but unfortunately at the last moment found that she wasn't able to borrow her mother's car. There was only one option for Nickey, and that certainly wasn't making a phone call to apologise for not turning up. She would run there, but would have to hurry. On went the running gear and off she went. Commendable, but a normal 18 year-old would have considered more seriously the fact that Redcliff was 25km away, and that's a hell of a warm-up for a training session.

She got there 15 minutes into the session, ran up apologetically to coach Phil who said she could join in with the last 3 of the 6 repetitions of about a kilometre. That she did, completing them quite well, keeping up with the group without too much fuss. At the end of the session Phil asked why Nickey was late. He was stunned to hear she had run down to Redcliff as quickly as she could. Staring in amazement at this wisp of a tennis player who had run 25km and completed half his group's training without any trouble, his response this time stunned Nickey.

'If you're silly enough to run down here before my training session then you can run right back home again.'

So Nickey did.

She was tired, very tired, but had done something rather special. I think that day signalled the beginning of serious running and the end of serious tennis.

Over the next few years Carroll ran whenever and wherever she could; in all sorts of challenging environments and distances with partner Don Wallace, a highly motivated and accomplished ultra-marathoner. Don distinguished himself by running top 10 in the famous South African Comrades ultra-marathon event, placing 8th twice, in 2000 and 2002. For Don and Nickey at that time, 50km events were the shorter ones! It was not until 1997, at the age of 25 that Carroll decided that it was time to have a serious go at running one of those shorter road races they call the marathon.

Nickey arrived a couple of days before race-day in Las Vegas (jet-lag wasn't a consideration), and grabbed a motel near the start. Well nearly at the start as getting to the start was a little confusing so she got there just a few minutes to spare. She finished second on that Las Vegas desert road in 2:33:24.

Nickey Carroll competing in the Las Vegas Marathon, 1997.

In a stellar 12-month period in 1999 Carroll stamped herself as the second fastest ever-Australian marathoner, behind Lisa Martin (Ondieki) and one of only a handful of Australian males and females who have won international marathon races. (Benita Johnson (nee Willis), the highly talented former World Cross Champion now holds the Australian record). Nickey's greatest triumph was her win in the 1998 Paris Marathon in course record time 2:27:06 and this is described in a different context later in this book. Carroll went on to run 5th in the International Osaka Ladies' Marathon in 2:26:52, 4th in the London Marathon in 2:25:52 and she won the California International Marathon in a course record of 2:29:21.

However, following Paris, and probably even before Paris, I came to realise that Nickey was unlikely to be able to train in the consistent manner required of an internationally competitive marathoner. It's hard to believe, given her performances, but an unpredictably intermittent lack of energy dogged her career. Her critics would claim that her unfinished races were purely 'psychological' and that she couldn't handle the stress of competition, but that wasn't true. Her unusual fatigue often came about during periods of training, sometimes resulting in an inability to train for weeks at a time. When it did coincide with big races, it caused havoc. Athens World Champs, Rotterdam, Chicago and the Sydney Olympics coincided with periods where her training energy was sapped. Medical specialists were unable to pinpoint the problem, until she was diagnosed with general auto-immune dysfunction including, but not confined to a thyroid disorder. While treatment resulted in some improvements in general health, it became obvious that the kind of stresses involved in training as an elite marathon runner could not be tolerated for any substantial period.

Bitterly disappointed with the brevity of her marathon running career Nickey Carroll continued her love affair with running in the Australian bush, but never regained the capability of training at a high level. Nevertheless, she has the memories of the three-deep crowd along the Champs-Élysées to the Arc de Triomphe, 25,000 runners in her wake and not one woman in front! The majority of Nickey's success I put down to partner Don Wallace, who has provided that kind of rock-solid common-sense support invaluable to any runner when times get tough, and for Nickey, that was most of the time.

'I want to run for England'

Bill Foster wrote to me from England and asked if he could be part of the 1991 AIS altitude training study. He told me he was 33 years old, was a keen runner, but admitted he wasn't up to the standards required for our study of elite runners.

'If I pay my own way, could I participate?' I couldn't say no.

At the commencement of the study I interviewed each runner, asking about their usual training, aspirations and food preferences, and took a few basic measures, height, weight, skinfold thickness. An important prerequisite was that the runners were in good condition, and that training would continue on without too much change. Bill walked in. His more than ample body shape clearly contrasted with the elite runners. I was somewhat annoyed that he was joining this landmark study at the Australian Institute of Sport, yet hadn't got himself sufficiently fit do it justice. I asked Bill about his ambitions.

'Dick, I'd like to represent England.' This took me by surprise, and coupled with his less than optimal running shape, my football coaching days must have got the better of me, as I was rather direct in my assessment to the polite and quietly spoken Englishman.

'Bill, are you having me on? Sorry mate, but to put it simply, you're too fat to run fast!'

It's no use me denying these words, as it got around quickly and even in recent years I've had an athlete or two remind me.

My rather rude comment must have really cut into Bill. After all he'd run a 2:19 marathon. I was to find out later that he had attended Worksop College, not far from Sherwood Forest in Nottinghamshire, where Bill had won the coveted but perhaps infamous Dorm Run, his name adjoining Olympians Jack and Tom Buckner (Tom also participated in our altitude study) on the perpetual trophy.

As it turned out my congenial guest became a great asset to our altitude study. He trained hard and was a happy man amongst athletes; his presence brought a smile even to the most serious of runners. His initial condition ruled him out as a providing valid data for the study, but his fitness and body composition improved remarkably. I offered to keep in touch and write him a training program if he wanted one, but as for representing England, that might be stretching things.

On arrival back in the Motherland, Bill continued on as he had in the study. We communicated regularly and I made plenty of training suggestions. His weight continued to decline and over the next few months training quality improved and mileage increased. Bill was 34 or 35 now and some of his road races suggested that a good marathon was on the cards, but how good? I had come to realize that Bill's objective of representing England was not completely out of the question, a notable change on my first reaction to Bill's aspiration.

In time I suggested he try to reduce his working hours to allow sufficient time for recovery; after all he was now training like an elite athlete. Within a couple of months Bill had switched to part-time work, a man on a mission. I was very pleased to hear that he had linked in with highly respected coach George Gandy. The Gandy-Foster combination produced the goods and I was delighted to receive an email from Bill letting me know that had been selected to represent England at the 1994 European Championships in Helsinki! I literally ran out of my office at the AIS to tell my physiology colleagues the good news. And he represented England very well indeed; 31st in 2:17:12 in Helsinki. The following year he ran his lifetime PB of 2:15:49 in Berlin, placing 11th. At 37 he'd done what he set out to do. He didn't set out to prove me wrong, but he did anyway.

The Bill Foster story doesn't end there. Bill went on to win many national masters titles on the track and road over the following 10 years. Furthermore he has become an accomplished coach in Loughborough, and I've got that first hand from young marathoner Hannah Walmsley, whom I now coach in Canberra, after being welcomed into Bill's sizeable group while visiting the UK. Well done Bill, on all counts.

Chasing that dream

Life, what is it but a dream?

(Lewis Carroll)

Joey had plenty of skill as an Australian Rules footballer at Epping Football club, a team I coached in the 70s. I was surprised to get a call from him some 20 years later.

'Dick, I'm coming up to train in Canberra. I can make the Olympic team as a 10km runner.'

'Wow, Joey, I didn't know you were into running ... particularly at that level.'

'Well Coach' (Joey always referred to me as 'Coach', and still does to this day) 'the truth is that I haven't run any races as yet, nor trained with any program, and that's why I want to come to Canberra.'

'But Joey, there's a huge gap between training to run well for a club and winning places on Australian teams. You've got to be in your late thirties now, so making an Olympic team at age 40 is just not on, mate. Let's be realistic, I've got top runners here in Canberra who are running close to 28 minutes for 10km and they're going to be struggling to make the team. Sorry Joey, but I have to tell you if you want to go to the Olympics, it'll be as a spectator. We can watch the 10,000m together.'

'Coach', Joey went on, 'is it completely impossible that I qualify for the Olympic 10 km? What if I train, without missing a day, for two years ... is it completely impossible?'

I made the mistake of adhering to the truths of statistical probability. 'I can't tell you it is completely impossible but it's got to be so close that it's not funny.'

Joey jumped at this.

'So ... you agree that there is a faint glimmer of hope ... I'm coming up.'

I got another call some months later.

'Dick, I'm here. I'm staying at the caravan park five kilometres up the main road that heads toward Sydney. It's cheap and I won't bother you. Just give me a training program and I'll do it.'

How was he going to survive? I couldn't give him due attention for fear that he'd get the idea that I can coach him into the Australian team. But I'd give him a program at least.

'Joey, what training have you done so far?'

'I've run the 5km every day you told me would be a good starting point. I haven't missed a day for three months. Now I'm ready to increase it.'

There was no way that I was going to change his plans, so I talked to him about gradually increasing his running, and moving toward 10km a day, or 70km a week.

Joey was, and remains, a very special individual as you may gather, and I didn't feel good knowing that he couldn't succeed, but it was a matter of fact that nothing was going to stop him trying to fulfil his dream. He had little money and no car. It didn't matter, all that mattered was the training, and he had planned to survive on what he had. I introduced a long Sunday run and medium long Wednesday run and moved the volume up to 120km per week. Joey got up at 5 am and went to bed at 6 pm. Like a monk in Tibet, he dedicated himself to the task. He ate, slept, and trained religiously through 365 days of that year in Canberra. Money almost completely ran out but he was not going to let working to make some money interfere with his training and recovery.

What he did during the day still mystifies me. He was a loner in the true sense of the word, powered by living his dream.

'Anything is possible coach, if you want it bad enough, and I want this bad'. The year passed and Joey was ready to test his fitness. He went back to Melbourne and entered a 10km road race, and ran about 36 minutes. Not a bad start, thought Joey, but better will come as he knew that races are required to gain specific race fitness. Deciding to test himself on the track, Joey joined a club. He ran 5km in 16 minutes and was encouraged. A series of track races later he had improved to run around the mid 15-minute mark for the 5 km. He began to realise that his plateau had been reached. That he was a very fit 40 year-old, and that there is a lot of difference between being very fit and a champion distance runner.

A few months passed.

I spoke with Joey by phone. He had resumed his work down in Melbourne. 'Well coach, I didn't make it. But I tried. I gave it my best shot, isn't that what you were after?' I was hit with a pang of guilt—I should have spent more time with him in Canberra. But I had made it clear from the start that I couldn't. Joey didn't expect it or ask for it and completed the process; for a year he had dedicated himself to becoming an Olympian. It was not to be and he had found this out the only way he could, and he would never die wondering.

Joey still lives in Melbourne. We often talk sport on Sundays. 'Coach, I ran into your old team-mate Barry Leslie the other day, and he said to say hello; and so did Peter McKenna, the straightest kick in AFL ... did you know that ... ' and Joey would relate stories about this person or that. He remembers more about what I did on the footy field 50 years ago than I do. Now working as a deliveryman, his sporting ambitions and experiences leave him a happy man. I said he is special, unique. After all anyone who dreams for years about meeting his idol Muhammad Ali, gets on a plane, chases him all around the USA for weeks and ends up staying in the hotel suite of the great man as part of his training camp in Hawaii before a title fight—has to have something special going for him. But that's another story for another time.

We live and learn. Joey reminds me that life's about setting out a clear picture of what you want to do, planning a clear pathway towards its achievement and then doing your ultimate best to get the job done. Some say it's about having a dream. That's part of it, but in the real world the guts of it is the planning and concentrated effort. Joey taught me that when things don't work out exactly as you planned despite doing everything in your power, then that's the way it is meant to be. It becomes history; no point dwelling on it, but learn from it and attack the next task with the benefit of that experience.

Joey had two major projects; becoming a friend of Ali and becoming an Olympic distance runner. A 50 percent success rate is not too bad.

'Sorry, what was your last name?'

It was around late 1990 or early 1991 when when Australian Institute of Sport Physiology Department administrator Robyn Power asked me if I could take a call from a chap named John, who was asking about training for a marathon. Calls from the public weren't an unusual occurrence, and despite our limited time, I always felt that anyone prepared to make the effort to contact the AIS deserved a polite and informative response.

'Dick, I'm in my mid forties now and I reckon I need to be a lot fitter than I am at the moment and want to begin training with the aim of running a good solid marathon.'

I asked what his background was—wondering where to start and at what level to comment.

'Well Dick, I've played sport at a fair level, and was pretty fit in my day ... did a bit of running but not anywhere near marathon level.'

He was calling from the Melbourne area I assumed his sport was Australian Rules football.

'If you could give me a program that starts basically from scratch I reckon I'll be able to work out how to put it into action. I wouldn't worry you too often with phone calls, just very occasionally if that was ok.'

I had some pressing work to do, but I talked a little about training, and as we spoke, although he was mindful of not taking up too much of my time, one or two of John's comments caught my attention as unusually insightful. We finished the conversation.

'I'd be very interested to see how your training progresses, John, what was your last name?'

With a little hesitation he replied. 'It's Famechon.'

Johnny Famechon was, and is, a hero of mine. He captured my youthful imagination, as he did with fans worldwide with the beauty of his boxing movement. 'Fammo' was the elusive pimpernel of boxing, any boxer getting a glove into his face was a rarity. Boxing is clearly a dangerous game to play. Interestingly I was knocked out momentarily at the start an Australian Rules Grand Final in 1968; one more time than Fammo was in his 67 fights.

That marathon-training program was ill-fated. During a training run in Sydney in 1991, Famechon was hit by a motorcar, leaving him partially paralysed, unable to walk let alone run. Engaged to be married he told his fiancé that he could only marry her when able to walk down the aisle.

By 1997 he did just that, and my wife and I have exchanged Christmas cards ever since with John and his wife Glenys. It was an honour when I finally met him at the annual Australian Sporting Hall of Fame Gala Dinner in 2014. He certainly fitted in well there.

Chapter 4
Can anyone be a good runner?

'I think I could, if I only knew how to begin.' For, you see, so many out-of-the-way things had happened lately that Alice had begun to think that very few things indeed were really impossible.

Lewis Carroll

Anyone can be a good endurance athlete. But to be a champion—well that's a bit different.

Human athletic capability is set by our genes and our environment. Our genes direct the construction of proteins, which determine the size, and efficiency of our power plants. Our main environmental influence is training, with altitude, temperature and nutrition all chipping in. DNA and environmental influences don't just act independently, they work together. For example training at moderate altitude influences the 'expression' (activation) of genes which direct synthesis of EPO (erythropoietin, a hormone that directs the production of new red blood cells), this process in turn requiring nutritional support in the form of iron intake.

Such interaction goes further. Right from our very first steps, Mum and Dad influence our body type and exercise pattern, not just through the genes they pass on, but coaxing our own individual combination of genes to operate in a fashion even more like theirs. And this coaxing is gender specific.

In a neat study in Plymouth, England, called the EarlyBird Study, the research group headed by Professor Terrence Wilkin showed that, quite apart from the inherited characteristics, the body shape and weight of a young boy tends to be like his fathers' and a daughter like her mothers'. And because body shape and weight are related to physical activity and fitness, and that these characteristics tend to track positively with age, a parent's behaviour during the first few years of a their child's life is likely to influence their offspring's distance running performance right into adulthood. So we have a double-whammy of parental influence on the distance running potential of their offspring, through their own current habits of physical activity as well as their DNA.

Our parental influence can go further still, even prior to birth. Apart from obvious deleterious effects of smoking and alcohol and other drugs that may be consumed during pregnancy, an expectant mum's nutrition, stress levels and physical activity are likely to impact upon the way foetal genes go about their early work. This is called an 'epigenetic effect' and can influence physiology throughout a lifetime. We know that babies nutritionally deprived in utero and born small are likely to up-regulate the action of a set of genes to defend blood glucose levels, for example by reducing the effectiveness of insulin to lower blood glucose. These children are then likely to experience a 'rebound effect' during the pre-teenage years, with a tendency to put on more fat than normal and even enter puberty at an earlier age. And any epigenetic impact on metabolism, body composition and growth will affect endurance and running ability, and possibly even the motivation to be physically active throughout life. Following on from this line of thinking, we can expect our grandmother's behaviour during the time she was pregnant with our mother to have influenced our running ability as well.

It is very clear that our parents have a huge influence on the way we are—and our ability to run is no exception. Some of us inherit an ability to generate high speed but only over short distances while others don't have the same top speed but can sustain moderate speeds over long distances. Talented sprinters possess a greater proportion of high contractile power muscle fibres that like to get our chassis moving fast, but not for long periods (the 'fast-twitch' Type 2 fibres). The opposite is true for our best marathon runners whose muscle fibres happily contract with relatively low force but for hours at a time (slow-twitch Type 1 fibres). Fortunately, we humans are reasonably malleable, adapting appropriately to meet challenges. We can actually modify the performance of our fibre types and so our speed and endurance with specific training, but the ease and extent we can do this certainly varies between individuals with their variable proportions of fibre types.

Coaches like to spot 'natural ability' and to identify runners with varied levels of 'potential'. In recent decades it's become obvious that running ability varies not only at the individual level, but also at the racial level. These days it's unusual to find a white runner in the final of the Olympic 100m sprint, most are of West African descent, and we're most unlikely to find an East African or descendent of this region in that race. Similarly, it's unusual to find a white runner in the top 8 of the Olympic marathon, but in this race a runner of West African heritage would also be a rarity. Champion distance runners are predominantly of East African heritage. Genotypes of the west and east determine sprint and endurance characteristics respectively, and the variation in appearance (phenotype) is clear to see. The lithe slim builds of the Ethiopians and Kenyans contrast with the more heavily muscled, bigger framed Nigerians.

However, runners have to get it right on the day, and a better pedigree or PB certainly doesn't guarantee a better placing. Australia's Michael Shelley (whose stock is of the Irish variety) proved that point in the Glasgow Commonwealth Games marathon when he ran away from the pack of better-credentialed Africans. I liked the caption of a photograph in the Melbourne Herald Sun showing Shelley just in front of eight Africans threatening to pounce and kick away from Shelley's conspicuously contrasting white frame. The caption 'Shelley, you can't be serious!' depicted our general disbelief that anyone of the Australian's heritage would have the temerity or the ability to challenge the Africans.

Can anyone be a good runner?

'I can make any man with a sound heart and no physical disabilities a sub-four-minute miler.' Franz Stampfl (circa 1961)

Having highlighted some individual differences within the *Homo Sapiens* species, they are in effect really relatively minor because we share a remarkably similar, almost identical set of genes. If that is so, then can anyone in good health of mind and body be a good distance runner? Legendary coach Franz Stampfl certainly thought they could. Stampfl was well aware of the inherited impact on athletic performance, but he also believed that training had more to do with running success than genetics.

It's just over half a century ago since Stampfl made the above promise, and even though the four-minute mile is now commonplace among the best middle-distance runners, Stampfl's four-minute mile for any man was a very big call indeed. In fact I'd have to think very carefully before I promised any man sound of body and mind that I could coach him to a five-minute mile!

However, it's not unreasonable to take Stampfl's 'any man' and turn him into what we might classify as a 'good' distance runner, although I imagine many of us would still shake their heads in disbelief at this prospect.

But let's see. Firstly let's define what we mean by a 'good' distance runner. I reckon any man who can run 10km in less than 40 minutes or any woman who can do it in 45 minutes is fairly described as a 'good' runner. Only a small proportion of the population would ever aspire to this level of athleticism.

My thesis is that given the time and effort, everyone can, and I'll prove it—well virtually anyway.

Our endurance capabilities fall somewhere within that bell-shaped normal distribution curve. Even for those of us way down the left-hand tail of the curve, those with the least distance running talent can still be good; it just might take a bit more effort. Interestingly, the greatest individual challenges to the premise that anyone can be a good distance runner are likely to be those who have the potential to become top sprinters and throwers. More explosive individuals start with the disadvantage of a set of muscles which are happy to contract powerfully for a short time, but not happy to contract at lower power too many times in succession.

And for those of you who feel being a good distance runner is beyond you simply because of your size, recall Dean Lukin, our huge Olympic heavyweight lifter who got 240 kg above his head in the 1984 Atlanta Olympics to win gold. He was hardly recognisable a few years later as a slim chap who had lost half of his body weight. That sort of metamorphosis would impress an Emperor Gum moth caterpillar. The length of tape that measured the circumference of one of his huge thighs in 1984 fitted neatly around his waist a few years later. We are indeed exceptionally adaptable animals.

One way to explore our premise that anyone can become a good distance runner, is to determine whether any child can become a good distance runner in adulthood. Now the term 'any' renders this assignment a difficult one, but with some creativity and a little background knowledge we can set about finding an answer.

A thought experiment

Thought experiments are the tools of trade of theoretical physicists, but although we won't resort to a blackboard of E, M and C-squares, we can use a bit of imagination to design a thought experiment to test our hypothesis that anyone can be a good distance runner, given an appropriate environment and upbringing.

Actually, I've borrowed the design of our virtual experiment from a very real research project I've been working on through the Clinical Trials Unit at the Canberra Hospital, Australian National University, and the University of Canberra Research Institute for Sport and Exercise. In this project we're investigating the effect of physical activity on the physical and psychological health of 800 primary school children. It's called the Lifestyle of our Kids (LOOK) project and we intend to monitor the health and quality of life of our cohort right through to age 80. (The kids are now teenagers in year 12 at secondary school and we've published some exciting evidence that well-designed physical education conducted by the Melbourne based Bluearth Foundation and better fitness benefits not only the health of these participants but also their academic progress).

So here is our 'thought experiment', and although this is virtual reality, several of the hypothetical outcomes are based on our current scientific understanding arising from the LOOK study, with some aspects inspired by the remarkable East Africans runners.

Title

The impact of regular physical activity through childhood and adolescence on distance running performance and well-being in adulthood: a randomised controlled *virtual* trial.

The full manuscript has been submitted to the Journal of Virtual Exercise Science (JVES), an open access journal for virtual researchers. Here we provide a summary, virtually an elongated abstract.

Abstract

Objective:

We aim to determine whether anyone can be a good distance runner with appropriate early attention. We hypothesize that any child of sound body and mind can develop into a good distance runner, providing he or she enjoys a physically active childhood and adolescence.

Methods

Our cohort was 1000 six year-old Australian children, 500 boys and 500 girls in 20 schools. Half of the children, in 10 randomly selected schools, were provided with special physical education (PE) and sport programs that contributed to at least 1 hour of moderate and vigorous physical activity per day during primary and secondary school. This was the Intervention (Physically Active, PA group). The other 500 children continued on with their normal Australian lifestyle and this was our Control group (C group).

Measurements:

Along with height and weight, percent body fat was assessed by DEXA scan. A resting fasting blood sample was taken to measure insulin and glucose to provide an index of insulin resistance (high levels in adults being symptomatic of Type 2 diabetes) and low density and high-density lipoprotein cholesterol (low and high levels respectively being indicative of good cardiovascular health).

Physical activity and heart rate were assessed every day for 2 weeks using a satellite navigation-accelerometer device worn to provide detail of the volume and intensity of physical activity. A standard 20 m shuttle run assessed running fitness. In addition a questionnaire was provided to assess each child's perception of their physical attributes (body image) and how they felt about themselves in general (self-esteem). The measurements were taken at age 8, and repeated at ages 12, 16, and 21 years. At age 21 years everyone participated in a road race on a flat surface and took part in a laboratory treadmill test for maximal aerobic power.

Procedures:

The Physical Activity Intervention Group (PA)

A team of PE specialists (university trained teachers with supplementary training from the Bluearth Foundation and ACHPER (the professional body of Australian PE teachers) developed a plan with parents and teachers, whereby the children participated in one hour of moderate and vigorous exercise (activity of equal or greater intensity than brisk walking) every day. We called this PE specialist a Physical Literacy Facilitator, as his or her main role was to help classroom teachers teach PE more effectively and to organise sport in a way that all children could become satisfactorily engaged (even if each primary school had a specialist PE teacher they would only be able to teach each class once per week). PE was taught every day without fail, for about 30 minutes, and focused on balance, coordination, and games to develop teamwork and introduce plenty of running around. Yoga-like activities were also employed and so was the eye-hand coordination skills of catching and throwing, as these are important prerequisites for many sports. All activities were designed to develop a long lasting enjoyment of physical activity. The Physical Literacy Facilitator also liaised with parents and the sporting clubs so that the PA intervention group children were able to safely walk or cycle to school and 95 percent of them joined sports clubs that suited their talents and personal interests. These were usually ball sports requiring running, jumping and catching but everyone learnt to swim and many children chose gymnastics. The PE teachers generally participated in the class activities, and the children responded accordingly with increased motivation.

In grades 5 and 6 when the children were 10 and 11 years old, some formal running was introduced into the school programs of the intervention PA group where the children would complete a course of 2 km, increasing to 3km a couple of days of the week. This was sometimes before or after school and sometimes shorter runs were organised between literacy and numeracy classes. This running was non-competitive, usually in small groups, chatting along the way. The PA group children enjoyed this as they were used to running, throwing and jumping activities did not find it taxing. Furthermore, because they had learnt how to compete well during the PE classes, competition was not stressful and they realised that the main thing was to improve their own personal performance rather than compare their performance with other children growing at different rates. Opportunities continued to be created for children to walk or even jog part of the way to and from school and parents made arrangements to escort walking groups therefore, ensuring safety. The visiting Physical Literacy Facilitators organised information sessions for the parents to encourage them to develop their own physically active lifestyles because of the great influence parental behaviour and attitudes have on their child's level of physical activity.

When the children entered secondary school, the program continued, the physical education activities gradually increased in complexity, volume and intensity, but always maintained a challenge and were always fun. The team of Physical Literacy Facilitators (there was now one allocated to a group of 5 schools) collaborated with the secondary school PE teachers to ensure the PA intervention group maintained 1 hour of moderate and vigorous physical activity every day. PE classes were provided daily for 30 minutes actual class time, these usually including 20 minutes of quality physical activity in modified games, the remaining time being spent continuing to develop gross and fine motor skills. Special attention was given to the girls, as it was well known that the physical activity level of girls drops off markedly through adolescence. The group runs continued, mainly as easy runs of 3-5km on 4 or 5 days of the week, at least. Some children opted to run with athletic or orienteering clubs they'd joined, usually over trails and hills. PE and the training runs remained highlights of the day for the children, and that the teachers joined in during many activities certainly enhanced the quality of the physical activity. The volume of the organised running carried out by the PA group increased to around 20-30km a week by age 17 in year 12. For those who had joined athletic clubs, running had become their main sport and they averaged 50-60km per week with some quality sessions supervised by their club coaches.

The Control group (C group)

Things were quite different with this C group. These children in 10 primary schools without access to the specialized PE continued with their normal home and school lifestyles. The primary school curriculum did include PE but the general classroom teachers conducted this. However, with their increasingly demanding teaching schedule across all areas of the curriculum and in particular the pressures applied to do well in the national numeracy and literacy evaluation schemes, PE was not a strong priority. More often than not, teachers weren't able to fit PE into a busy day. Most of the generalist classroom teachers were not trained or particularly interested in PE, and lacked confidence in teaching skills, so they rarely participated in any activities, and children who were lacking in certain skills often found it difficult to become involved.

Only 30 percent of children in the C group decided to join sporting clubs. Of these 7 percent joined Little Athletics. Some of the classroom teachers sent the children on a run in place of a PE class but by age 11 in grade 6 most children, especially the girls, simply walked around the school oval. The C group girls and a lot of the boys lacked interest in sport, probably because of a lack of self-confidence and absence of fundamental motor skills, which may have embarrassed them. The questionnaires suggested they already found much greater satisfaction and security in playing their computer games and participation in social media operations.

In secondary school PE was geared more toward playing traditional sports, basketball, football, cricket and many children with poor coordination opted out. In the first two years, the majority of children didn't bring a change of clothes for PE. Teachers paid even less attention to ensuring that these teenagers were satisfactorily engaged in physical activity, preferring to work with those who were sufficiently motivated. Participation in PE and sport dropped off considerably, especially in the girls, who now in adolescence even found a new excuse to miss PE that was not available to the boys.

Results

Baseline: There were no significant differences between the PA group and the C group in any of the baseline measures in the six year-old boys. Nor were there any differences between the six year-old girls in the PA group and C group. However, the percentage of body fat of the girls overall was already 2 percentage units higher than the boys (BMI was the same in boys and girls showing how BMI misreads percent body fat in children). The physical activity tests show that the girls are 15 percent less active than the boys already across both groups.

Physical Activity: From the age of 8 years, the PA group boys and girls achieved their average of 60 minutes of moderate and vigorous physical activity per day, and this was sustained through early adolescence. Physical activity actually increased at the age of 15 in the PA group as children began to train more seriously for their sporting clubs.

In the C group the primary school boys and girls achieved only 10 minutes and 6 minutes of physical activity of greater intensity than brisk walking all day, typical of Australian children. The physical activity of the C group boys and girls declined as the children approached their teens and was at its lowest level ever at age 14 in the girls. The boys maintained a steady but still unsatisfactorily lower level of physical activity.

Blood tests: Of most interest was that in the PA group at age 12 there were only 2 percent of children who had elevated insulin resistance and 3 percent with elevated cholesterol levels, but in the C group the corresponding figures were 23 percent and 25 percent (again this was found to be typical of a recent report in the LOOK study of Australian children).

Psychological Assessments: Group differences emerged in the psychological test of self-esteem and body image. With no differences at baseline, the Intervention PA group boys and girls averaged 18 percent higher self-esteem/body image scores than the C group. Most surprising to some teachers, but not to others, even though the PA group children spent more time in organised sport as well as other forms of physical activity they still achieved greater improvements in the national standardized literacy and numeracy (NAPLAN) tests, which corresponded with another report in Australian boys and girls in the LOOK study. Interestingly the improved results in the PA group academic tests were slightly greater in the boys.

Fitness: Although the children in each group achieved similar results in the 20m shuttle run at age 8, a slight difference appeared at age 10 and from age 12 to 16 to 21 there was a 7 percent and 15 percent and 22 percent superiority in the intervention group. At age 21 we introduced the treadmill test of the maximal aerobic capacity ($\dot{V}O2max$) in each runner. The average $\dot{V}O2max$ of the PA group was 56 ml/kg/min (males) and 46 ml/kg/min (females) and for the C group these figures were 46 and 36.

Body Composition: With no differences at baseline, by the age of 21, the PA group of men had 17 percent body fat and the women 25 percent compared with the C group of 26 percent and 32 percent respectively.

The Road Race

Approximately 5000 competitors from the city and surrounding areas participated in a 10km Road Race specially set up for this project, but open to the community in general as a fun run. 460 children (220 boys and 240 girls) of the A group and 430 children (210 boys and 220 girls) of the C group participated. Absentees were traced and accounted for. Most had left the district permanently or temporarily and a few in each group were ill or had a sporting injury. Pre-Race interviews revealed that the PA participants were keen to run, but the C group less keen, and not sure if they will be able to run the distance. They were advised that they could walk if jogging or running became too difficult.

Overall, 10,428 runners from the surrounding districts participated in the 10km race. The PA group participants filled 7 of the top 10 places in the males and 8 of the top 10 places in the females. From the C group, one boy made the top 10 and the best girl was a creditable 11th, these two individuals having been keen sports participants all through their school days.

Of the PA group every one of the participating males completed the 10km under 40 minutes; and every female ran under 45 minutes. The fastest male in the group stands out as a runner and he won the 10km in 29:50 (He made the Australian World U20 cross-country team last year and ran an excellent 9th in the World Junior Championships). The slowest was 38:45, a big lad who has been offered a Rugby Union football contract. The fastest PA group female also won the Women's section in 32:25. She was ranked No 1 Australian junior in the 1500m last year and was a member of the national World Cross-country U20 team (she finished 11th in the in the World Junior cross-country championships). The slowest PA group female ran 44:10. She is 1.91 metres tall and has a promising basketball career ahead of her. Of the C group, 16 percent of the males ran under 40 minutes and 7 percent of the girls achieved the 45 minute standard.

Conclusions:

Our data provide virtually solid evidence that everyone can be a 'good' distance runner provided they participate in sufficient physical activity during childhood and adolescence.

Furthermore the PA group was a healthier group than the C group. From as early as age 9, three years into the project, physically active children were considerably fitter and leaner. By age 12 the PA group blood tests revealed that they were at much lower risk of developing a metabolic disorder such as Type 2 diabetes or cardiovascular disease. By age 12 and also in their mid-teens both males and females in the A group also felt better about the physical appearance and physical capabilities than the C group adolescents.

Following better results in literacy and numeracy tests in grades 5, this continued on into adolescence. At age 21, 83 percent of the A group were attending university compared with 66 percent of the C group.

Our data also suggest that in a randomly selected group of 500 children who have access to high quality physical education in primary and secondary school, and who are encouraged to be physically active by parents, teachers and coaches, there is a strong likelihood of producing an internationally competitive distance runner.

So, the answer is a virtually resounding 'yes.' Anyone can be a good distance runner. But in relation to the Franz Stampfl claim, that any man of sound body can be trained to run a mile in 4 minutes, our thought experiment does not lend itself to comment. However, our data do suggest that in any group of 250 boys given sufficient opportunity and encouragement to be physically active through their school years, one or two may well become 4-minute milers.

Can anyone be a champion? That's a different question

To join that illustrious group we loosely define as 'elite' runners, conditions apply. You will not only require a set of genes which allow you to develop the necessary power and efficiency for a particular event, but you will need to apply an appropriate training stimulus to fully exploit your inherited potential.

Physiology or psychology ... what really maketh the runner?

Distance runners have been studied from all angles, physiologically, anatomically, psychologically, and biomechanically and measures from each of these areas explain much of the variation in running performance. Bearing in mind that most of these characteristics are not independent (that changing one will affect another), it's the physical capability of the athlete, their engine power and economy that have the overwhelmingly significant impact on a distance runner's performance. Motivation, competitive spirit, dedication, confidence, pre-race stress control and race tactics are all important but they are really only ways to optimise use of the power we generate physiologically and biomechanically.

Chapter 5
The Power of One

My hand moves because certain forces – electric, magnetic, or whatever 'nerve-force' may prove to be – are impressed on it by my brain. This nerve-force, stored in the brain, would probably be traceable, if Science were complete, to chemical forces supplied to the brain by the blood, and ultimately derived from the food I eat and the air I breathe.

Lewis Carroll circa 1870

Our power plant has one distinct advantage over a car motor—ours has the capacity for self-improvement. But where the car has us covered is that if we don't use our power we lose it.

The stress of training

Stress can be thought of as our response to any threat to disrupt our normal state, our so-called homeostasis. Cold, hunger, illness, competition, and interpersonal conflict are all stressors. So is physical activity. Most living things have evolved with mechanisms to cope with stress, and to adapt in such a way as to offset the effects of that stressor the next time round. This is why distance runners train. Running is the stressor and we respond by improving our ability to dampen the disruption to our homeostasis. But there is a trap for young players.

We've got to get the level of stress right. Too much will inhibit adaptation and too little won't produce any.

But why would exposure to the stress of running improve running ability? Dr Darwin's premise of survival of the fittest can be taken literally. If our predecessors of eons past were forced to move to avoid danger or capture food, then those who adapted better to the challenge were most likely to survive and pass on their genes. The 'fittest' and so the 'survivors' in this case were those with a genotype most conducive to moving better and improving more with repeated challenges.

Times have changed. Rather than avoiding physical stress at all costs, we now seek to impose physical stress on ourselves purely to improve our physical capacity for sport and to offset disease processes caused by the absence of physical activity.

Nowadays coaches and athletes seek specificity of adaptation to meet the requirements of the sport. For runners, running is obviously the most specific form of stress coaches need to apply to improve running ability, and there is another level of specificity required in meeting the needs of the distance and speed of the race. And then, most races involve tactical changes in speeds, so coaches seek that optimal combination of training to equip their charges with the ability to cope with those changes. But there is another reason to apply stress at different speeds and durations. Training at levels higher, as well as lower than race-pace can induce better adaptations than constantly training at anticipated race-pace.

Finding that balance of faster and slower work is not straightforward because it varies for each individual as well as event. Even in the well-informed coach there is both trial and error, but the well-informed coach is certainly likely to select the more appropriate trial and make less error.

Our dual power plant

We have inherited a fully automatic centrally controlled dual power plant with a silky smooth automatic gearing transmission and a sophisticated feedback-controlled graduated power supply. One of our power plants requires oxygen and the other doesn't, so we call them aerobic and anaerobic respectively.

We running machines simply decide how fast we want to go and the proportionate use of each engine is set automatically. We don't have to think about it. At any given speed the proportion of aerobic and anaerobic power will vary with our individual physiology and fitness. Both engines are in constant use to a certain degree no matter what the speed, but as the more efficient and less disruptive of our two power plants, the aerobic engine does most of the work both at rest and during prolonged steady running. However, a bit like in a hybrid car programmed for petrol to take over from electricity when we put our foot down, our more powerful anaerobic engine kicks in when we decide to run very fast.

Luckily, the software of our autonomic nervous system adjusts the power of these engines without us having to think about it, as the mental stress of constantly calculating the proportional use of each power plant would certainly add a challenging cerebral dimension to distance running! No doubt evolutionary forces sorted this out early on. Thinking about which energy supply to turn on in the face of sabre-tooth tiger would certainly reduce the odds of that set of genes being passed down the line.

Aerobic power

Where does it come from?

We release energy systematically from that secured within the molecules of our food, which the plants had captured in the first place from the sun through the process of photosynthesis. A series of chain reaction exchanges take place in tiny envelopes of enzyme-rich soup called mitochondria situated in intimate juxtaposition with the contractile machinery of our muscle fibers. We harness this food energy by converting it to our own energy currency in the form of a 'high energy phosphate bond' of adenosine triphosphate (ATP). ATP powers up the muscle contractile directly, energy released as one of its phosphate bonds is severed and lost in the process. The resulting diphosphate (ADP) then awaits the next unit of food-derived energy to regenerate ATP, a process that occurs rapidly over and over again.

You may be wondering where oxygen comes into the picture.

The gradual extraction of energy from food, mainly from the sugar and fat molecules, involves a series of chemical reactions where the molecules lose electrons. As this occurs the electrons are, in effect, passed along an 'electron transport chain' which, to stretch it a bit, might be likened to a relay runner passing on a baton. But just like a relay runner needs a final receiver of the baton to finish off the race, a final receiver is required for every electron to keep the energy extraction process on a roll. That final receiver is oxygen and so we call this whole process of losing electrons 'oxidation'.

Our aerobic power plant has the label 'aerobic' because it only functions if the oxygen from the air is around to accept those electrons. Without oxygen the chain of electron transfers comes to a screaming halt, forcing us to seek energy from other (anaerobic) sources that do not rely on oxygen as the final receiver. As we all too well realise, if that oxygen molecule is in scarce supply, even at rest, and our main power supply comes to a grinding halt, then so do we. It's a pity that oxygen is the only plentiful electron acceptor we have access to on Earth but— that's life.

How much aerobic power can we generate?

To get an idea of the capability of a top-end human aerobic motor, let's consider a world class male runner who can run 10,000m in 27 minutes, that's an average of close to 65 seconds per 400m lap run 25 times without stopping. Our runner would be in control and reasonably comfortable running in cool still conditions at 28 min 25 sec 10km pace or 68 seconds per lap, which is 17 seconds per 100m. Being relatively comfortable tells us he is able to produce most of his power aerobically without having to resort to using too much of the more disruptive anaerobic energy supply which would soon make him feel uncomfortable. This speed coincides with a half-marathon of just under 60 minutes, which is now achievable by the best runners in the world. So while the aerobic system may be our long-term reliable 'go-to' power supply, it can generate a surprising amount of power in an elite runner. Similarly a world class female can run 31 minutes for the 10,000m. That's 74.4 seconds per 400m lap, so 77 seconds per lap and a 67:22 half-marathon is going to be very much within the capabilities of her aerobic system, illustrating again the kind of aerobic power possible in an elite runner.

We can measure power output much better on a cycle ergometer than on a treadmill. An elite level cyclist is capable of sustaining a power output of around 300 watts for an hour and because we are about 25 percent efficient (most of our energy being dissipated as heat), producing that sort of power actually means we have to produce about 4 times the energy. Our cyclist can power up three 100W light bulbs for the hour, but if we were to capture all the energy he generated he'd keep 12 of those globes glowing.

Why do human aerobic motors differ so much?

Possessing a large aerobic power to weight ratio is a distinct advantage to a distance runner and we all use the same sort of system to generate the power. But why can some runners develop more aerobic power than others even if on a similar training program? To answer this question we might address the general question of what limits our aerobic power supply.

In a nutshell, the two most obvious limiting factors to churning out aerobic power are: (a) the mass of the power generators (the mitochondria) in our muscles cells (b) the speed at which we can deliver oxygen to the mitochondria.

Then there is a third and less obvious possibility; that it's all in our head. Perhaps our aerobic power is limited by our brain and nervous system imposing its own 'red-line' limit of work and its associated heat production, which may be perceived subconsciously as a threat to our health.

Let's assume that oxygen transport to the muscle is 'the' or at least 'a' limiting factor to an athlete's aerobic power production. What actually limits oxygen delivery?

Oxygen transport

'It's our blood'

Ask most elite distance runners and their coaches about limiting factors and they are likely to tell you it's in the blood, that it's their ability to deliver oxygen that stops them running faster. They have little doubt that one of our hormones, erythropoietin (EPO) will improve performance. And its main effect is to stimulate the production of new red blood cells and increased circulating haemoglobin, so improving our ability to deliver oxygen to the muscles.

EPO is now synthetically produced, a lifesaver for patients with erythropoietic dysfunction. But as soon as physiologists pointed out that increasing oxygen transport increased aerobic power and endurance running performance, and that growing more red blood cells was a good way to increase oxygen transport; and that injecting more blood and/or EPO into a runner's veins had an ergogenic effect, unscrupulous athletes, coaches and managers hopped into it. Now with better methods of detection, the would-be cheats are far more reluctant to try to beat the system. But recent positive urine samples and suspiciously high red cell counts show that there are still some athletes and their medical teams willing to risk their reputation for a bag of gold. A very welcome added deterrent these days is that blood from athletes is stored for potential re-analysis in ensuing years, at which time new procedures will be available to detect subtle abnormalities unable to be currently detected.

In any case, the legitimate alternative is to train in rarefied air with reduced oxygen pressures (at moderate altitude venues) or reduced oxygen concentrations (in altitude simulating rooms or tents) where EPO secretion is naturally stimulated and red cell production increased. (It's noteworthy that some athletic federations consider these artificially induced hypoxic conditions as unethical and have banned their use.)

But what if a well-trained athlete going to altitude already possesses more than sufficient haemoglobin in his or her blood to more than accommodate the needs of his or her muscular capacity to produce ATP? That oxygen transport is not the limiting factor to this athlete's aerobic power? Might this be one of the explanations as to why some runners do not seem to find any particular advantage in going to altitude venues to train? Some researchers do suggest particular athletes may be 'responders' or 'non-responders' to altitude training, and as discussed in a later section, one or two of my athletes may well be in the latter category.

'It's our heart that counts'

We often equate endurance with a big heart. The size of champion Australian racehorse Phar Lap's heart is legendary. But how important is a big heart in an endurance athlete? Cardiac output is a product of the stroke volume (the amount of blood pumped per beat), and the heart rate (the number of beats per minute). A larger left ventricle is likely to produce a larger stroke volume, assuming a similar ejection fraction (the proportion of blood squeezed out per beat). But maximal heart rate may be just as important as stroke volume in determining maximal cardiac output. A smaller left ventricle and higher maximal heart rate might circulate the same amount of blood as a larger left ventricle with a lower maximal heart rate. And a smaller heart might also pump out a greater proportion of the blood in the left ventricle, i.e. a greater ejection fraction.

So it seems that bigger in this case may not necessarily be better, but one of the adaptations to endurance training in an increased heart chamber volume, and so a bigger stroke volume and lower heart rate at rest or at any particular running speed. Permitting me to indulge in a heartfelt personal example, an illustration of how our left ventricle responds to endurance training volume is shown in Figure 5-1.

As my training volume increased from an average of just over 20 miles a week in 1978 (we always used miles not kilometres in those days) to about 60 miles per week in 1982, my maximal aerobic power ($\dot{V}O2max$) increased 21 percent from 57 to 69 ml/kg/min. My body weight dropped 2 kg in this period, the absolute value of my $\dot{V}O2$ max increasing about 18 percent from 3.8 L/min to 4.5 L/min. Coinciding and perhaps contributing to my increased aerobic power during those four years was the increase in my resting left ventricular volume at end-diastole (the non-contractile part of the heart cycle where the ventricle has just filled up) which increased about 67 percent from 96 to 160 ml. My resting heart rate dropped along the way in a reciprocal manner, from 60 to 46 beats/min, as I was pumping out more blood per beat with the enlarged heart volume. Now with all this happening it would have been disappointing if I hadn't improved my marathon time, and as it turned out, I did. In 1982 it was 3 hours 11 minutes and over these four years it got down to 2 hours 27 minutes, forget the seconds—I have anyway.

A final point of relevance in our discussion of what limits oxygen transport and so aerobic power, is that we can better predict an athlete's maximal aerobic power by measuring total haemoglobin mass rather than haemoglobin concentration or haematocrit. Concentrations are easily measured by taking a blood sample, and that's what we get when we visit our GP for a blood check. Total haemoglobin is measured in an exercise physiology laboratory and involves a 10 minute test outlined in Chapter 22.

Well-accomplished endurance athletes often have only average or even lower than average haemoglobin concentrations, but usually possess large blood volumes relative to their body size. This is relevant because it suggests that to maximize oxygen transport we need to maintain a free flowing bloodstream, one of low blood viscosity. Too high a haemoglobin concentration will compromise blood flow, and so increase the work of the heart, as well as compromising infiltration of the capillary beds around the muscle cells. Lowered blood viscosity therefore, is likely to be one reason that some middle and long-distance runners are better than others. To get an idea of how we might lower blood viscosity refer to the discussion on the perfect training environment later in this book.

Anaerobic power

The second power plant of our dual engine system is turbo-charged and kicks in when our old faithful aerobic system isn't powerful enough to do the job on its own. Its advantage is that extracting those electrons from our food molecules doesn't rely on the oxygen in the air we breathe (so we call it anaerobic) as we employ a final electron receiver to replace oxygen. It might be considered something of an emergency system to be called upon when we need that extra bit of speed and power to get us out of trouble in a hurry.

Indeed our anaerobic power may well have come in handy in the days of sabre-tooths, mammoths, or hostile fellow beings, the latter threat likely to be

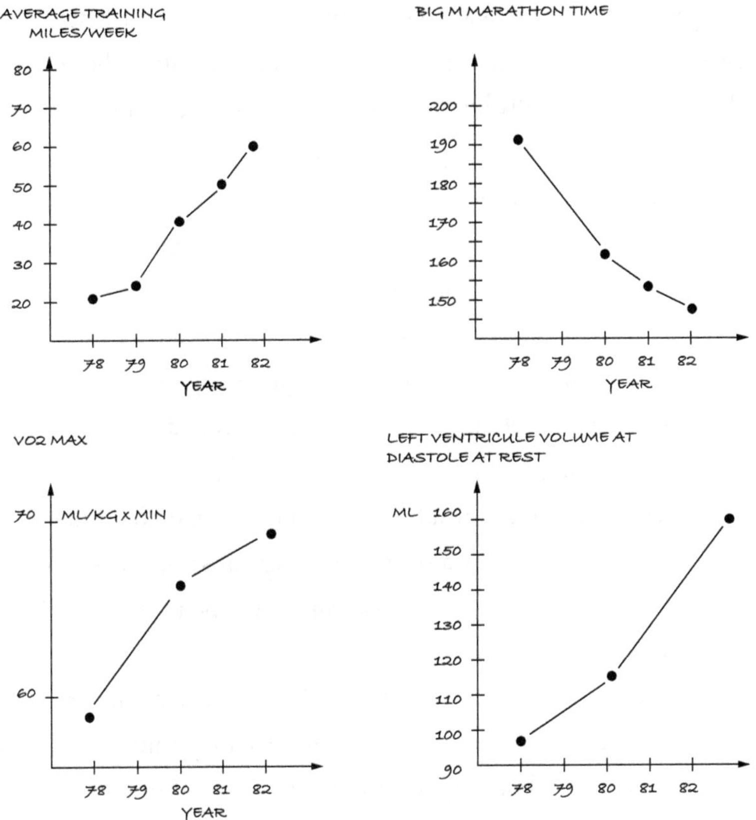

Figure 5-1: Progressions in the author's training for the marathon, marathon time, maximal oxygen uptake, and volume of the heart left ventricle.

more common today. I can't resist the opportunity here to put our personal running ambitions in a clearer perspective. Here we human beings are in the 21st century, with all the benefits of 'civilisation'; but multiplying out of control, polluting the planet at a corresponding rate and destroying other life forms in the process. And we continue to fight and kill each other. We fight for power, land and food. We fight and kill to preserve self-promoting medieval superstitions. The threat to our continued presence on this planet is now infinitely greater than anything a bull mammoth or sabre-tooth tiger could ever have mustered up.

Back to anaerobic energy, it seems too good to be true, much more powerful than aerobic energy production and doesn't even need the air to generate ATP.

But as you might guess, there's a catch, because in calling on our anaerobic power plant we commit a 'sacrificial' act. Athletes talk about 'dying' at the end of a race. Not a bad description really because the anaerobic system is inherently toxic. A few seconds of all-out anaerobic power production and our muscle homeostasis is threatened and then disrupted. Our muscles, then our bloodstream become more acidic (and hotter) which if unabated threatens to unravel our whole body chemistry. Ceasing to run is the only way to abate this internal pollution, and our brain certainly gives us a clear message to do just that. It's called pain. That pain in the backside of a runner may well save his life (providing that pesky sabre-tooth is not around), because prolonged exposure to toxicity and heat production will ultimately cause vital organs to shut down shop as well.

In the final stage of a race an all-out sprint finish is desirable, but in a state of anaerobic intoxication it can be a struggle getting our knees up and feet off the ground. Even our old reliable aerobic system can't cope in this situation and it struggles to provide ATP as well.

Middle and long-distance runners have to be very wary about controlling this anaerobic system. They have to be canny about when they want to really put their foot on the power pedal, knowing that this requires the anaerobic system to kick in and that it's going to initiate the 'dying' process. The middle-distance runner has to judge when and how much he or she can power up with the anaerobic system but at the same time prevent muscles and brain from going on strike completely before the finish line. This applies to the longer distance runner as well, as utilising too much anaerobic energy at any stage of the race requires a speed reassessment and appropriate adjustment. Slowing down permits the aerobic system to come into play and clean up the toxic substances, and to restore, at least in part, the disrupted homeostasis, but it's a delicate balance. Inexperienced runners tend not to read the warning signs too well and we all know how a poorly paced race can throw a spanner in the works.

Understanding a bit more about anaerobic power might help you design your training, and perhaps your diet as well. For example, unlike our aerobic motor, the anaerobic system is fussy about its food, and demands glucose, rejecting offerings of fatty acids or amino acids from our fat and protein intake.

Each molecule of glucose ends up as lactate (lactic acid is hydrogen lactate), in effect replacing oxygen as the final electron receiver, the energy released along the way producing a couple of energy laden ATP molecules. We only extract two ATP molecules initially from each glucose molecule through this process called anaerobic glycolysis, compared with 38 if we are running slower and in a position to use oxygen as our final electron receiver. That's a big difference of energy production from a molecule of glucose, but we can get those two ATP very quickly indeed.

Don't get the idea though that we can work exclusively aerobically, and then kick in anaerobically when the speed is required. Middle and long-distance runners always produce some anaerobic energy, even if we feel we are running at a comfortable 'aerobic' speed. Even in the middle stages of a 10,000m event at so-called 'threshold speed', a good proportion of the ATP is being derived through anaerobic means, and a distance runner pacing his or her race intelligently will generate anaerobic energy at a sufficiently low rate so as to maintain biochemical control. American muscle physiologist George Brooks informed us that one important adaptation to training for any middle and long-distance runner is improving the reconversion of lactate back into pyruvate and shuttling it back into the aerobic system process. This is why we can run at a steady state while producing a certain amount of anaerobic power. The metabolically disruptive end-products are kept under control courtesy of the aerobic system.

As discussed in Chapter 8 the direct cause of fatigue is still controversial, but one aspect that makes muscle cell acidity a prime suspect is that training for middle-distance develops within-muscle adaptations to buffer or neutralize the acid part of lactic acid. Evidence of the ergogenic effect of buffering comes from ingestion of alkalis (antacids) such as sodium bicarbonate (baking soda), which can change the pH of the blood, a pre-competition strategy which has shown to be of benefit to performance. The bicarbonate molecule of the sodium bicarbonate combines with the hydrogen ion (proton) of lactic acid to produce water. However, as suggested in Chapter 8, what is not clear is whether the proton itself causes fatigue or a factor produced alongside it.

The 'other' anaerobic energy source

There is one other way we can extract some power without involving oxygen, but it doesn't involve lactic acid, so we call it our 'alactic' anaerobic power. It's an 'in-between' power supply, a little reservoir of ready-to-go energy when we need to take off in an extra hurry, even before we have time to turn on the lactic anaerobic system. When we decide we want to run, and run fast, it takes some time before the aerobic and anaerobic systems are primed up to produce new ATP. So we have evolved with another little 'survival of the fittest' pool of 'high energy' phosphate in the form of creatine phosphate, sitting in the muscle cell ready to produce ATP at the blink of an eye-lid. Most athletes would have heard of 'creatine loading' which aims at maximizing the concentration of creatine phosphate, and there is evidence that supplementing a normal diet with creatine can assist repeated sprint performances. Couple this with the small supply of oxygen molecules trapped within myoglobin, the muscle's equivalent of blood haemoglobin, and we can race 50 m flat out before the major energy pathways even realise we are moving.

Relative power of the aerobic and anaerobic systems

Recall our champion 10,000m runner with an aerobic power allowing him to run 100m after 100m in 17 seconds without stopping. That's 5.9 m/sec. A champion 200m runner, using almost exclusively anaerobic energy is able to run each 100m in close to 10 seconds, which is 10 m/sec, and 1.7 times or 70 percent more than the speed of the distance runner's aerobic effort.

That provides one sort of estimate of the relative power of the two systems, but to get another idea, we need to measure work and power more directly. While measuring work and energy output during running on a treadmill is problematical, it is much easier with a cycle ergometer. Some years back at the AIS we developed (and published) a routine test used for talent identification called the Tri-level test. As the name implies, we designed three separate tests using an air-braked cycle ergometer, to estimate in each of aerobic power, lactic anaerobic power and alactic anaerobic power.

To estimate Aerobic Power we measure the power output of subjects at 75 percent of predicted maximal heart rate (220 - age). The higher the submaximal power output at this heart rate the greater the maximal aerobic power through V̇O2max. This procedure was popularized more than 50 years ago by the Swedish physiologists Per-Olof Åstrand and Kaare Rodahl, using their famous nomogram.

For the Alactic Anaerobic Power we measure the maximal energy output in kilojoules during a maximal effort over 10 seconds, the athlete in a standing position on the pedals; and for the Lactic Anaerobic Power we employ a 30 second standing maximal effort.

Despite being able to accurately measure the power output with the air-braked cycle ergometer, our estimates of anaerobic power are of course just that, rough estimates that aren't intended to measure precise capacities, and the submaximal aerobic test is limited mainly by variation in individual maximal heart rate which may vary considerably from the assumed 220-age average.

Nevertheless, the Tri-level test has been useful for general talent identification and for investigations of changes in general fitness within an individual.

Consider the vast differences in the Tri-level profiles of the three athletes listed in Table 5-1 and we can get a rough idea of the differences in power production of the three systems.

The long-distance runner develops twice the aerobic power of the sprinter but the sprinter turns the table in the alactic department, developing more than twice the average alactic power of the long-distance runner.

Table 5-1 shows results from three very good male athletes, a 100m sprinter (DW), with a personal best of 10.4", a 1500m runner (GR) with a PB of 3'38" and a 10,000m runner (AS) with a PB of 29'10".

	Aerobic Power @ 75 percent max Heart Rate (watts/kg)	Alactic Power Peak (watts/ kg)	Alactic Work Index (average watts over 10"*)	Anaerobic Index (average watts over 30"*)
Male Sprinter DW	2.8	25.1	19.1	13.4
Male Middle-distance GR	4.2	16.1	13.2	11.0
Male Long-distance AS	5.6	10.3	8.4	8.3

(* We usually measure this in total kilojoules but for consistency of the units of measurement and comparisons within this table we list the average of the power output over the duration of the test.)

Table 5-1: Tri-level power profile of three runners

If we compare average watts over the 30 second test to the watts at 75 percent of heart rate, we get a ratio of 13.4/2.8 or nearly 5 in the sprinter. However, the equivalent ratio in the long-distance runner is 8.3/5.6 or about 1.5.

So to answer our question as to the relative power generated by the lactic anaerobic system and the aerobic system, our best 'guestimate' using these data is that the lactic anaerobic power is between 1.5 and 5 times as powerful as the aerobic system, depending on the type of athlete.

Also of interest is that the absolute peak power in the sprinter reached 2050 watts, nearly three times the absolute value of the long-distance runner of 700 watts. The distance runner of course turns the table in the aerobic department as he generates twice the aerobic power of the sprinter at 75 percent of his maximal heart rate.

The Tri-level test might also be considered a surrogate test for fibre typing; the sprinters alactic power is developed by a predominance of the Type 2 fast fibres while the distance runner's type 1 fibres provide his aerobic superiority. Hence, its applicability to talent identification.

Supervising Olympian Carolyn Schuwalow, in the Tri-level power test on the air-braked cycle ergometer.

Image: Australian Sports Commission

An air-braked ergometer is born

Ever wondered where the air-braked ergometers, the bikes and rowing 'ergos' were born? Take a guess. In the USA where the Schwinn company distributed them around the world? Wrong. How about in the workshops of the Concept air-braked rowing ergometer in Vermont, USA? Wrong again. It was conceived in the office of my late friend and colleague, mechanical engineer Lindsay Hooper, himself a fine middle-distance runner. The prototype air-braked ergometer was born a couple of months later in the laboratories of Repco Research in Dandenong, Victoria, Australia.

It was 1972 and I was exploring new ways to measure work output of rowers and kayak canoeists. At that stage highly respected exercise physiologist and Dr

Frank Pyke (who, sadly, died in November 2011) had cleverly rigged up a kayak ergometer movement around a Monark friction-braked cycle ergometer imported from Sweden. I thought we could improve on this set-up, and maybe even create the feeling of fluidity that rowers and canoeists experience out on the water.

I set up a series of discussions with engineer Lindsay Hooper out at Repco Research Laboratories in Dandenong, the far eastern outskirts of suburban Melbourne. It happened to be a hot day as we sat in his office and in those days the Repco plant workers weren't afforded the luxury of air-conditioning. Lindsay lent down to a power point and switched on a fan on his desk. As I explained why I'd like to be able to measure work and power accurately the fan began blowing air across our table. He looked at the fan and looked back at me. I knew what he was thinking. He asked me if I thought whether the fluid of the air would be a suitable form of fluid resistance for the kayak ergometer I was after. From the smile on my face he knew he had a job to do. I met Lindsay again a few days later. He'd already prepared some designs for cycle, kayak and rowing ergometers. Over the next few months, and asking advice of cyclists, paddlers and rowers we discussed modifications that led to the series of ergometers that closely replicated the actions and the 'feel' of the elite athletes.

Repco produced the cycle, rowing and kayak ergometers for several years. They were well used, the initial studies being carried out on prototype ergometers at the then Phillip Institute of Technology, now RMIT in Bundoora, a northern suburb of Melbourne, Victoria. Eventually, Repco Research sold the air-braked system patent to Schwinn, the USA company which I believe still manufactures and distributes their branded air-braked ergometers world-wide, or has sold the patent to others such as the manufacturers of the Concept air-braked rowing ergometer, popular all around the world as a training and testing 'ergo'.

Chapter 6
Dissecting Running Performance

'My dear, here we must run as fast as we can, just to stay in place. And if you wish to go anywhere you must run twice as fast as that.'

Lewis Carroll

Lab testing can be useful ... sometimes

Some physiologists have argued that the best way to predict a distance runner's performance is to measure the highest velocity achieved ($\dot{V}max$) or test duration using a standard treadmill protocol that gradually increases the speed and/or gradient to exhaustion. And they'd be right, an all-out run on the treadmill to exhaustion is certainly going to predict performance of an all-out run to exhaustion on the road or track because they are virtually measuring the same thing.

But really, what's the point? If we want to measure performance, all we have to do is arrange a time trial or a race. Sure there may be some variation according to how the runner paces him or herself, but given advantages of running freely on the track a time trial or race is certainly my preferred option of a performance measure.

On the other hand, laboratory treadmill testing to find out what contributes to individual performance can be useful. In so doing we can monitor how training impacts upon a particular characteristic, and study how variation in that characteristic influences race performance.

Aerobic power production, i.e. the number of watts generated through aerobic metabolism, is not routinely measured directly in the laboratory because it is too difficult. However, all is not lost. All we need to do is measure the maximal oxygen consumption (V̇O2max) on a treadmill, which is proportional to the maximal amount of aerobic power we can generate during running.

A higher V̇O2max tells us that the runner has a more powerful aerobic engine. The tricky part is making sure the runner gets to his V̇O2max. To attain this we usually gradually increase the speed then the gradient of the treadmill until the runner is at, or very close to exhaustion, at which time the runner would signal to the technician to stop the test. Distance runners are usually highly motivated and push themselves right to the limit. We can actually get a pretty good idea whether they have reached their V̇O2max by checking three of the runner's responses. Firstly we can check the runner's heart rate to see if he or she has reached maximal or predicted maximal levels; secondly we can check whether the runner is breathing out more CO2 than the O2 they have consumed which occurs when the runner is close to maximum. When the expired CO2 is in the order of 10 percent more than the O2 consumed (a respiratory exchange of 1.1) then that is a solid sign V̇O2max has been achieved. The third response technicians will check is the blood lactate level. V̇O2max coincides with excessive use of the anaerobic system, so a high blood lactate concentration is expected at V̇O2max. The long-distance runners don't have as high blood lactate concentrations as middle-distance runners but we expect something greater than 10 mmol/L. Middle-distance runners, whose anaerobic power is better developed are likely to be measured at around 15 or more and sprinters, the most anaerobic (and less aerobic) of all will achieve values in excess of 20 mmol/L (and more acidity, more pain, making it most unlikely a sprinter will be coerced into performing a V̇O2max test on a treadmill in the first place).

To measure the mechanical efficiency we need to measure the ratio of work performed and the energy the runner generates to do this work. But measuring a runner's work and energy are problematical. So to get a good handle on this ratio we measure the amount of aerobic power required to sustain a given running speed. Measuring the speed of running is easy on the treadmill, and we estimate the aerobic power by measuring the oxygen consumption ($\dot{V}O2$) at that speed. In contrast to the $\dot{V}O2$ max, this time a lower $\dot{V}O2$ is better, indicating less power is required to sustain the speed. We generally refer to lower oxygen consumption at a given running speed as better 'running economy'.

Like the 'max' test measuring running economy is also tricky, but for a different reason. Because we can only measure power generated aerobically from oxygen consumption, we miss out on measuring any anaerobic contribution. The more anaerobic contribution by the athlete the greater is our underestimation of the total amount of energy required by the runner which leads to the runner being determined as more economical than he or she really is. We can minimize this error by measuring running economy at much slower speeds than race-pace, so minimizing the anaerobic contribution. We can also check that the anaerobic contribution has been minimal by measuring the blood lactate which should not have risen from its resting value of around 0.5 mmol/L to more than 2 mmol/L.

Nonetheless, this still leaves us with a specificity problem because we really want to know how economical a runner is at their race-pace. We generally make the assumption that if a runner is economical at slow speeds then they are likely to be economical at faster speeds. While this assumption appears to be the case in most long-distance runners, it may not hold true for middle-distance runners who do much of their training, as well as racing, at faster speeds than we are able to validly employ to measure economy in the lab. There are ways of estimating the anaerobic energy contribution during treadmill running but these are cumbersome and time consuming and only used in specific experimentation.

The good news, as discussed below, is that despite the limitations of laboratory forensic work, $\dot{V}O2$max and $\dot{V}O2$ at a given running speed when considered together provide very good predictions of distance running performance, indicating the importance of these characteristics.

A good coach is an inquisitive coach

The scientific study of sport has been around a long time, but for many decades it was confined to academic work at universities as scientists used athletes to gain a better understanding of human performance. It is understandable that coaches were often sceptical and reluctant to offer their athletes for scientific research. Such research was interesting but did little to improve performance. Then with the emergence of sports institutes around the world coaches and scientists began to work much more closely in the quest to improve athletic performance.

In productive coach-scientist relationships, athlete testing is utilized to answer a question of importance to the coach. This is applied research, and while scientists like to test groups to be able to make inference with more confidence, some valuable work can be done even with a subject number N=1. After all, if we have a uniquely gifted athlete, he or she is likely to possess a unique physiology which may respond to training in an individually unique way.

What sorts of questions do coaches ask?

There is so much we have to learn about preparing athletes that the array of questions is almost unlimited. Here are a few examples.

On altitude training:

- Does training at moderate altitude improve the haemoglobin mass in one athlete but not another?
- Might altitude training still be of benefit without an increase in haemoglobin mass?
- What altitude is the best level to train for a middle-distance runner? Long-distance runner?
- What is the optimal duration for altitude training? Does duration vary with altitude, or with individual athlete, or with event?
- When is the best time to race after return to sea-level? Does this depend on the altitude, the athlete or event? Why?

And on general training:

- Does increasing only the training volume improve V̇O2max? Economy? Performance? If so, for which events, and are there individual differences?
- What's the effect of increasing the average speed of interval training on V̇O2max, economy and performance?
- What is the effect of increasing the number of repetitions without increasing speed?,
- Can V̇O2max and economy be improved at the same time?
- Should middle-distance coaches include high quality aerobic and anaerobic training in the one session or concentrate on just one of these for each session?
- Should coaches phase their training to improve one particular characteristic over a period of weeks or months or work on each of the characteristics right through a build-up? Does this depend on the event?
- How much threshold training and 10,000m pace work should a marathoner do when they never run at 10,000m speed during a race?
- How important is it for a 1500m runner to improve his or her 100m or 200m or 400m speed?
- Does getting stronger with resistance work help a marathoner run faster?
- How lean does a distance runner need to be to run at his or her best?

I could go on and on with a stream of questions, and I haven't touched on the questions surrounding psychology, nutrition and the biomechanics. I'm hoping that some of the things I write will assist coaches to develop well-informed opinions on the answers to these sorts of questions.

Sub-maximal testing

Not many runners like to do all-out treadmill tests; they require a huge physical and psychological commitment, and the elite runners in particular prefer to keep this for races. It stands to reason that motivation in a laboratory test will vary, and as such, so will the reliability of serial measures. So if a coach wants to monitor the improvement of an athlete and take regular measurements a submaximal test may be a better proposition because motivation no longer plays a part, and testing doesn't interfere with training.

In the early 1950s, as touched on above when referring to the Australian Institute of Sport Tri-level testing regime, Swedish physiologist Per-Olaf Åstrand and his colleagues popularised submaximal testing. Prof Åstrand's group exploited their observation that the lower the heart rate at any given submaximal power output on a cycle ergometer the higher was the V̇O2max. So they devised a nomogram to predict V̇O2max from the steady heart rate achieved at a given power output on the cycle ergometer. This provided a reasonable estimate, but didn't have the sort of accuracy required for work with elite runners.

In any case, and in the interests of specificity of testing of runners, a treadmill is obviously preferred to a cycle ergometer. Applying the nomogram principle, if the steady heart rate is reduced at any given treadmill running speed, then it's reasonable to assume the aerobic power has been improved. Alternatively, it may still be that running economy has been improved although this is less likely to occur. In any case, if either aerobic power and/or economy has been improved we can reasonably assume that running performance has improved, as we see a little later in this book.

Measurement of the blood lactic acid concentration is a useful adjunct measure to heart rate in a steady state heart rate test on the treadmill, because it reflects the extent to which the runner had to resort to his or her anaerobic power to supplement the aerobic power during the test. Should lactic acid be reduced at any given speed and duration of treadmill running this is another indication that aerobic power or economy has improved, a mode of assessment we now consider in more detail.

Eastern Bloc influence

The East Germans of the 1970s popularised blood lactic acid tests. With the remarkable success of the psychologically powerful secretive regime of Communist Bloc athletes, the Western World began to believe that monitoring of blood lactic acid levels and heart rates was a key component of Eastern Bloc sporting success. It certainly had a profound psychological impact. Even the successful and methodologically independent New Zealand coach Arthur Lydiard became a firm advocate of the East German blood lactate/velocity curve methodology for prescribing training doses.

A feature of these graphical plots was the point of inflexion of the curve which indicated the running speed (or swim, cycling, rowing or canoe speed etc.) at which blood lactate began to accumulate. This point signified the speed at which some sort of threshold of aerobic control had been exceeded. Interestingly it was called the 'anaerobic threshold' speed, but this tag is a bit of a misnomer as it suggests incorrectly that it is at this point that anaerobic energy starts to kick in. In reality anaerobic energy is always involved to a certain extent at lesser speeds. Anyway, the lactate/velocity curve became very much the norm in Australia, particularly in sports such as cycling, rowing, swimming, and to a certain extent running for a new wave of professional coaches with access to sports scientists.

In the absence of direct evidence from running coaches in the 80s, most of whom had never heard of lactic acid (although this wasn't necessarily a liability), let's momentarily turn to the sport of swimming where blood testing at the poolside was, and remains common practice. Not without its limitations, it did make one definite contribution to an Olympic gold medal.

A test worth its weight in gold

One of my fond memories of Olympic preparation with Australian swimming teams was in the weeks leading to the 1984 Los Angeles Olympics. We were training at Stanford University and with less than 4 weeks to the Olympics the team was beginning a taper period of reduced volume. This was the point at which the coaches would anxiously observe the results of a high volume build-up over many months, even years.

One particular swimmer, a 17 year-old named Jon Seiben was struggling. He couldn't complete the general group sessions and his personal and Olympic team coach Laurie Lawrence was concerned, wondering whether the swimmer was either ill, unfit, de-motivated, or all of the above. I knew Laurie pretty well, and while I didn't know the swimmer as well, I couldn't believe that any of these explanations held true. There was talk by team management of sending the swimmer back to Australia. I asked Coach Lawrence whether I could use some poolside blood lactate and heart rate testing to check a couple of things. He had nothing to lose.

The session I observed and measured was a short rest interval set 100m efforts and sure enough Seiben, after doing well in the first 2 reps, was just holding on after 5 reps, and fell away dramatically on the 6th, and clearly under intense physical and psychological pressure.

Pictured with Lance Leech from QLD who was at the AIS in the early to mid 1980's and swam for Australia at the Commonwealth Games in 1986.

Image: Australian Sports Commission

His blood lactates after that 6th repetition were around 16 mmol/L; much higher than those of his training group, which included one of his teammates, champion 400m swimmer Justin Lemberg, who completed the training set with lactates all below 8 mmol/L. Seiben was producing far more anaerobic energy than his training partner and building up to a point of severe disruption to his homeostasis, resulting in his inability to hang on to complete the set with the short recoveries. However, and most importantly, he had no trouble generating the extra speed in the first couple of 100s.

Coach Lawrence and I discussed those lactates, and I suggested that while the training group's strengths were mainly related to aerobic endurance, Seiben's emerging strength may be his anaerobic power and capacity. And that meant that he couldn't match it with the others in the latter repetitions of a short rest set of quality 100s. But, we discussed, Seiben's race was firstly a 200m butterfly preliminary and a period of at least 24 hours before his next race, and that's a 'hellova' lot longer than the minute or so between those 100m reps. There are no medals for winning short rest interval sessions.

Coach Lawrence took the discussion and the lactate evidence on board and modified his swimmer's program individually. He gave him longer recoveries, allowing him to get his muscle and blood lactate and pH under control through the entire training session. This produced immediate results. From a fish out of water the struggler became the king dolphin of his training lane, physically and psychologically.

Three weeks later, while working as part of Rob de Castella's team, I watched the swimming on TV from our Santa Monica home base. I saw John Seiben's beaming face on TV with an Olympic gold medal around his neck, living the dream, as they say of knowing his name was in the record books as the new world record holder in the 200 fly of 1:57:04, a 3 second PB. He had raced just the one 200m in that final and beaten the world. And no-one challenged him to a repeat race a minute later. I caught a glimpse of Coach Lawrence at poolside, an exuberant coach, to say the least. I was not to know I would again work alongside Lawrence 8 years later where another remarkable unanticipated gold medal in world record time eventuated, that of Duncan Armstrong. And I'm compelled to deviate from running again to relate that story later.

Back to running ... Now, some 30 years after the swimming physiology work—and having been fortunate to have worked with some remarkable runners, do I feel that maximal aerobic power, economy, lactate and heart rate testing are worthwhile in my running group? Yes and no.

Yes, I'm interested in knowing my runners' aerobic capacity and economy because individual physiology provides clues as to which event an athlete may ultimately be best suited.

But no, I don't need to monitor the athlete's 'anaerobic threshold' by lactate and heart rate curves, as I can determine this running speed on the track or road.

And no, I don't need regular treadmill tests to understand whether progress is being made. I can see improvement easily from the quality of standard training sessions.

Yes, I certainly like to see the heart rate and running speeds along with the splits of sessions, particularly when I don't get a chance to be with the athlete for the session. Measurement of heart rate is one way to gain some understanding of what training is actually doing.

Chapter 10 provides examples of how heart rate can be used to determine whether a training session has achieved its goal.

Can lab results predict race performance?

There's little sense in using testing to predict performance when a race or time trial can do it better. But what if we could predict race performance from just a couple of basic characteristics? That could be useful as we might target these characteristics with the knowledge that any improvement could lead to faster running. In fact there are two characteristics which in combination predict distance running performance pretty well—maximal aerobic power (V̇O2max) and running economy.

Previous reports in the scientific literature suggested that knowledge of just those two variables was enough to make a good fist of it, but I wasn't too sure whether it would apply to our best runners. In the late 80s we had a good opportunity to find out. A road race was coming up in Canberra and most of the top runners, including some of our scholarship holders at the Australian Institute of Sport were keen for a hit-out. We had already measured their V̇O2max and running economy in the previous few weeks. Here's what we found.

Figure 6-1 gives shows the range of the V̇O2max/kg of the runners (aerobic power per body weight, the higher the better) and Figure 6-2, shows their V̇O2/kg at 16 km/h (our running economy measure, the lower the better).

Note how much even very good runners vary. Their V̇O2max ranges from 62 to 78ml/kg/min, which is a 25 percent difference in aerobic power. Running economy varies even more. While one runner required only 47ml/kg/min to run at 16km/h (about 6 minute per mile pace) another required 64. That's a remarkable 37 percent difference in energy utilisation in relation to body weight. And all of these runners were very good, making the differences in engine power and efficiency even more remarkable.

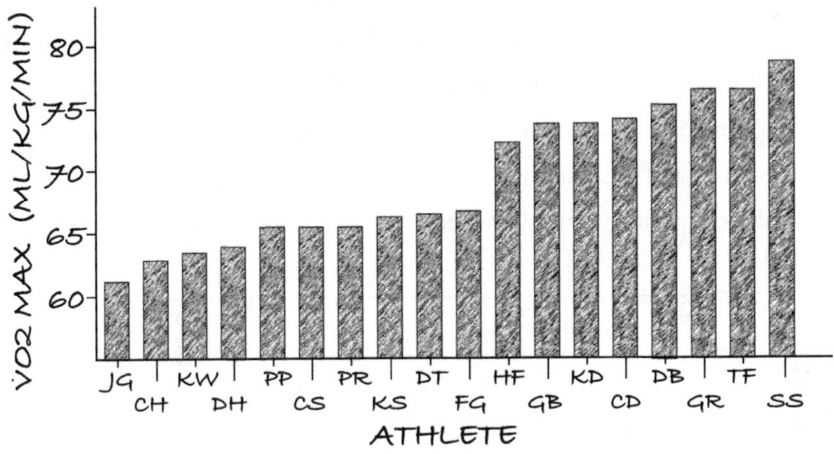

Figure 6-1: V̇O2 max of the runners in the 10k race.

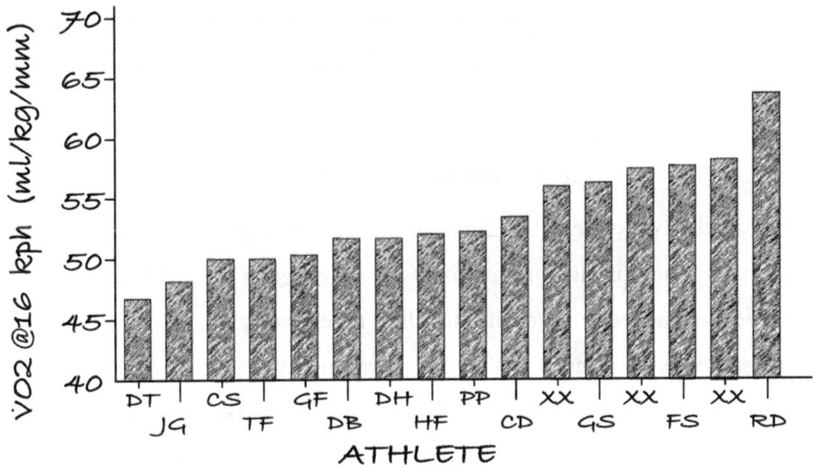

Figure 6-2: Running economy or the runners in the 10k race as indicated by V̇O2 @ 16 kph. (lower the better).

One way to see how well aerobic power and economy predict performance is to calculate a simple correlation between these variables and the runners' average race speed which represents their race placing as well. A correlation of 1.0 is indicative of a perfect relationship and predictive value and a correlation of zero indicates no relationship at all.

The correlation between running economy ($\dot{V}O2$ @ 16km/h) and average race speed in the 10k race was negative at -0.31. In other words, the lower the $\dot{V}$ O2 @ 16 km/h (i.e. the better the economy), the better the race speed. However, this relationship is not particularly strong. To get a rough idea of how strong, we can square -0.31 and the resulting 0.09 tells us that economy explained around 9 percent of the variation in the 10km performances.

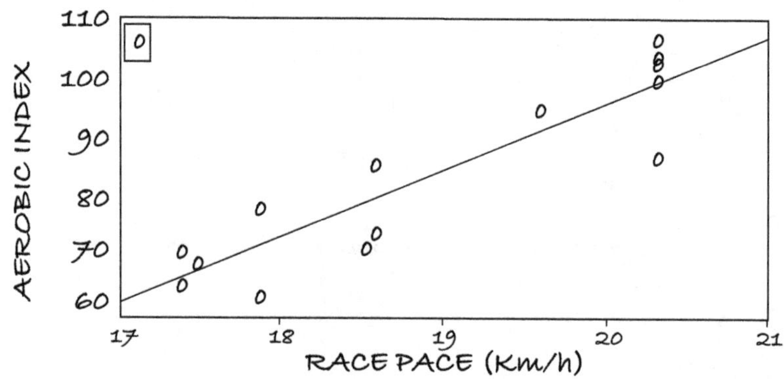

Figure 6-3: The Aerobic Index (as represented by the ratio $\dot{V}O2$@lactic threshold / $\dot{V}$ O2 @ 16 kph) for the runners in the 10k race.

The correlation between $\dot{V}O2$max and average race speed was much stronger, at 0.7, and using the squaring procedure as above, suggests that $\dot{V}O2$max explains about 49 percent of the variation in the 10km race speed.

But we can explain the 10km race performance and predict the outcome of the race even better by combining aerobic power and the economy into a ratio of $\dot{V}O2$max/$\dot{V}O2$@16 km/h because greater $\dot{V}O2$max represents an improvement, as does a smaller $\dot{V}O2$max@16km/h. Improvement in either one of these variables will increase the size of this ratio which we can call the Aerobic Index. Now the correlation between the Aerobic Index and 10km race performance is improved to 0.8, explaining about 64 percent of the variation.

That's a pretty good explanation of the differences in performance of the runners, especially considering the many other unmeasured factors likely to have played a part in determining the outcome of the race, for example anaerobic capacity, race tactics, taper, and motivation.

We can make one other small improvement on our prediction of the 10km race performance. It's possible to measure a close relative of V̇O2max, the so-called 'lactic' or 'anaerobic' threshold. This is the V̇O2 at where homeostasis becomes disrupted, where blood acidity increases, CO2 begins to accumulate and breathing becomes heavier in order to expire excess CO2. In practical terms it's that point where we feel if we don't slow down a bit we'll 'blow up.'

Anyway, if we replace V̇O2max with the oxygen consumption (V̇O2) at lactic threshold the correlation, our ratio becomes V̇O2/kg@ lactic threshold / V̇O2/kg@16 km/h and the correlation improves to 0.9, suggesting the new ratio explains an impressive 81 percent of the variation in the performance of these athletes. This relationship is shown in Figure 6-3 .

All in all, the importance of maximal power and efficiency to a distance runner is pretty clear. When we ranked a runner by his Aerobic Index any other runner with an Aerobic Index of 0.1 or more higher than another runner finished ahead of him in that 10km race. When we ranked the runners in that race according to their Aerobic Index 1–10, their placings in the race were 1,2,3,5,6,4,7,8,10,9. We picked the trifecta without having any knowledge of how the runners felt on the day or how their training had been, or whether they had any niggling injury. I wonder if we could get that sort of information on the horses before they run the Melbourne Cup.

Now while the particular results in that Australian Institute of Sport exercise haven't been published, I certainly don't want to suggest this knowledge is novel. It's just that this type of first hand observation over the years did much to influence my coaching methodology. Physiologists have noted these relationships in distance runners for a long time. Just to name a couple, noted coach and exercise physiologist Jack Daniels and French exercise physiologist Veronique Billat have been putting these types of measures to practical use to individualize training programs for decades. You can check their publications through entering their names into the usual search engines such as PubMed or Google. They also liked to use vV̇O2max (the treadmill running velocity at which V̇O2max is attained) to design of training but as I mentioned above this velocity parallels a time trial on the track so lacks the interesting explanatory power of the physiological characteristics.

Big motor or better economy: who wins?

Michael Patterson was a post-graduate placement at the AIS from Swinburne Institute of Technology in Melbourne (where my former lab technician, Robert de Castella, did his biophysics training). I was in my late 30s and Patto in his early 20s but we shared a lot of sporting interests as products of Melbourne town and running was certainly no exception.

We trained together most days through the eucalypt tree trails surrounding the AIS. We did our long Sunday runs through the pine tree trails of Stromlo Forest, some fifteen years before all but a few stray eucalypts were demolished in the great fires of Canberra in 2003. Needless to say, we developed a keen interest in our relative fitness with the usual healthy animated banter about who would win and at what distance. In training we seemed to be pretty well matched on the flatter faster parts of any run, although Michael had me well sorted out on the hills.

The Canberra Times 10km was a race most of the keen distance runners around the ACT like to have a crack at. Past winners include many Australian champions and Olympians including Rob de Castella, Pat Carroll, Shaun Creighton, Krishna Wood and Susan Hobson, and in recent times by Marty Dent. It's not a particularly fast course due to a slight incline for much of the first 7 km, being relatively flat for the last 3 km. Patto and I both decided to run.

Now what made it really interesting is that out of curiosity we had just measured our running economy and V̇O2max. As listed in the Table 6-1, Patto's V̇O2max was 8.5 percent higher than mine, but I was more economical, using about 21 percent less energy running to run at 16 km/h. As described above with those 16 runners, if the distance running index of V̇O2max/V̇O2@16 km/h represented our relative capabilities at the individual level then I seemed to have an edge, with an index of 1.42 compared with Patto's 1.27. But we both knew that even though this was a reasonably good predictor it wasn't perfect and there were likely to be exceptions in predicting the relative capabilities of any two individuals. If it only explained about 70 percent of a 10km race performance, the other 30 percent might make a lot of difference. One thing we both knew was that motivation wasn't going to explain any difference, both being well motivated to say the least. But the youthful Patto was definitely stronger than me and very likely to have better anaerobic capacity as well. And at his age he was certainly on the improvement curve, a feature not usually present in my vintage.

The gun went and we ran along together as we did in training on numerous occasions, but this time we were both on that red line of maximal pace while just maintaining control. We had both done our long runs and were running in the order of 130-140km a week with a three solid sessions included. We knew we could hang on to our red line, for 10 km, but whose red line was the highest? We got to about 7km and I was pushing it as hard, on what I perceived to be that red line, the fastest I could run without losing control. Patto certainly wasn't doing it easy either but I thought up the very slight incline through the first part of the race he did it a little easier than me. However, at 8 km, within a few strides, Patto dropped back just a fraction, a couple of metres, and that was enough to give me that little boost of confidence. It seemed he had slightly exceeded his threshold pace and at that stage it was beginning to take its toll.

I ended finishing 16 seconds in front my good mate. Not a lot really, about 80 m in 10,000m, less than 1 percent difference on the day. We had a great laugh about it. 'At least', he conceded, 'our Running Aerobic Index difference proved pretty sensitive!' In this relatively flat race, my more efficient motor seemed to trump Patto's bigger motor. I wondered whether prior knowledge of my slightly superior ratio had any psychological bearing on our race. Did Patto expect me to be slightly better in this flat race and ran accordingly? Did I expect to be slightly better than Patto and run accordingly? I suspect there may have been something in this. Just as I expected Patto to always be better up the big hills, and he was.

Michael Patterson went on to complete an excellent PhD in muscle physiology in the prestigious John Curtin School at the ANU, and is now well settled with his family in Seville, Spain. He is working as an administrator in a scientific research organisation as well as running a company assisting non-English-speaking scientists to prepare manuscripts for English language journals. Needless to say, whenever I've had the pleasure of meeting up with Michael over the years I feel the need to remind Michael of our *Canberra Times* 10 km. Funny that he seems to forget the details!

As I have indicated elsewhere, writing this book has been a drawn out affair and it's now 2015. Last year I received an email from Patto, about to turn 50 and keen to get fit to run the Australian and World Masters championships. That's about 30 years after our 10 km. This time he will have no challenge from me. I'm a very keen jogger, but no longer a racer!

	$\dot{V}O_2$max (ml/kg/min)	$\dot{V}O_2$@ 16 km/h (ml/kg/min)	Aerobic Index ($\dot{V}$O2max/ $\dot{V}$O2@16km/h)	10km Race Time (min:sec)
Dick	66.8	47.0	1.42	31'42"
Patto	72.5	57.0	1.27	31'58"

Table 6-1: The aerobic power, running economy and Aerobic Index of the two 10km runners

I mentioned previously that the nature of the maximal treadmill test and running economy test take do not measure anaerobic fitness, a large component of middle-distance running. Here is how we investigated our middle-distance runners at the Australian Institute of Sport during my time.

The MD test: a test of middle-distance performance

Whilst $\dot{V}$O2max contributes well to the prediction of distance running performance, as does running economy, the anaerobic source of energy and in particular its capacity must also play a part. It stands to reason that its influence will increase in the shorter events. I recall that of Australia's best 200m and 400m swimmers, representing similar event durations to 800m and 1500m running were those who produced the highest blood lactate values, indicative of greater anaerobic capacity. This was found to be true in a recent Italian study of highly credentialed middle-distance runners where the best runners were better equipped to generate both aerobic and anaerobic power, muscles being able to make use of more oxygen as well as generate more lactic acid.

In the early 90s, during the AIS international altitude training study described elsewhere in this book, we wanted to get a measurement of middle-distance running fitness, but without subjecting the athletes to another time trial. The test needed to employ faster running speeds and a time to exhaustion of around 2 to 4 minutes, similar to the track 800m and 1500m events. This is in contrast with the aerobic power treadmill tests which gradually brought the athletes to exhaustion in 10 minutes or more.

Given that athletes generally don't like to perform maximal tests to exhaustion on a moving platform in a laboratory, I was keen to develop a submaximal test. A submaximal test would also remove the confounding effects of varying motivation to which all maximal tests are subject.

The two middle-distance tests are described in detail in the Australian Sports Commission publication, Physiological Tests for Elite Athletes. Here are my considerations in developing the tests.

The submaximal MD middle-distance Running test

The test involves one minute of running at 18 km/h for males and 16km/h for females at an inclination of 10 percent gradient after which the heart rate, lactate and pH are recorded. $\dot{V}O2$ could be measured for detailed analysis but this is optional. It's 'submaximal' in the sense that although it requires a strong effort, it doesn't require an all-out effort.

It was set up to provide an idea of how well an athlete can control his or her biochemistry after the standardized strong effort of one minute, replicating, to a certain degree at least, the first lap of a middle-distance race. The rationale is that the lower the change in lactic acid, respiration rate, and heart rate at the end of this test (as in the bell of an 800m event), the better an athlete can negotiate the second lap.

Well-performed male and female middle-distance runners have no trouble getting through it, although it's not meant to be easy. Interestingly though, in a 2hr 20min male marathon runner we measured in a subsequent study, this protocol turned out to be maximal, as he only made it to 50 seconds, illustrating the very low anaerobic capacity of this very good marathoner, whose $\dot{V}O2max$ was a respectable 74 ml/kg/min.

The maximal MD middle-distance running test

The maximal, all-out test involved the males and females running as long as possible at the same speeds and gradient as the submaximal test, 18km/h or 16km/h and 10 percent grade. The times to exhaustion in our group of high level Australian and internationally successful middle and long-distance runners ranged from 1 min 30sec to 4 min. Care must be taken in administering this test as running to exhaustion on a treadmill always poses the risk of falling, especially in highly motivated athletes.

The runners who perform best in the maximal test also show least homeostatic disturbance in the submaximal test. This relates to Arthur Lydiard's comment that although Peter Snell was the slowest 200m runner in the 800m final at the Rome Olympics, he was the fastest over the last 200m of that 800m, indicating his superior control of homeostasis at the 600m mark. Lydiard was renowned for developing a very strong aerobic 'base' in his athletes, and it's likely that a very responsive aerobic power would have contributed to Snell's finishing ability. Had that Rome 800m field performed our submaximal test we might predict Snell to have shown a much lower increase in lactic acid, respiration rate and heart rate than his competitors.

Chapter 7
Running Economy

'... no coach should change the natural style of an athlete for no other reason than it is unorthodox. Nine times out of ten, free and natural movement is more relaxed than a style artificially imposed...'

Franz Stampfl 1955

In the previous chapter we demonstrated the importance of running economy to a distance runners' performance. But is it possible to train for better economy as we can for better aerobic power?

Mechanical efficiency and running economy

Mechanical efficiency is the ratio of work done and the energy required to do that work. Unlike rowing, cycling, or kayak paddling where specific ergometers permit a direct measure of work done, measurement of work done running on a treadmill is problematical. So instead of measuring work done, we use a direct proxy of work, the runner's speed. And as usual we make use of oxygen consumption as a proxy for the energy requirement.

Consequently 'running economy', the $\dot{V}O2$ at a given running speed, is really a proxy for mechanical efficiency; lower $\dot{V}O2$ indicating better economy. We usually measure the $\dot{V}O2$ in proportion to body weight to account for our expectation that a heavier runner of equivalent running economy will consume more energy at any given running speed. This assumption of direct proportionality between oxygen cost and body weight is actually not quite true, and without going into the rather complex area of allometrics and the study of human function relative to body size in any detail, it suffices to say that comparing the economy (or comparing $\dot{V}O2max/kg$) of runners of different heights and weights is not straightforward.

Smaller and lighter runners tend to be measured with a high Submaximal $\dot{V}O2$ per kg body weight than taller heavier runners and therefore, incorrectly inferred as having superior aerobic power but inferior economy.

It stands to reason that exercise physiologists would provide better information to coaches and athletes if they referred mainly to what I called the Aerobic Index, the ratio of $\dot{V}O2max$ ($\dot{V}O2$ at a given running speed), which removes the confounding effect of body weight, so offsetting the potential bias due to body size. This is an especially good idea when runners are being compared, although we all should remember that exercise physiologists are always working with estimations and should not to be too cute about their results, especially in terms of comparing the performance of runners. A race will do this very nicely, and even that result may change from time to time.

Nevertheless, serial measures of physiological characteristics can be very useful in informing the coach how an individual runner is responding to training.

Food and running economy

What we eat affects our running economy but, seemingly paradoxically, it doesn't affect the true measure of mechanical efficiency. This is because we estimate running economy using oxygen uptake as a proxy for energy utilisation, and the amount of energy (i.e. ATP) we generate alongside any given oxygen consumption varies with the proportion of glucose or fatty acids we metabolize. From any given amount of oxygen, glucose will produce up to 10 percent more ATP than fat. In other words, by manipulating a runner's pre-test diet, we can alter the amount of oxygen required to run at that speed (so changing running economy) while amount of ATP required has not changed (i.e. an unchanged mechanical efficiency).

This glucose effect may have relevance for pre-competition nutritional regimes. Irrespective of running economy, if oxygen is a limiting factor to race performance, the more ATP we can generate per litre of oxygen the better it is for a track runner, preferential use of glucose may not, suit a marathoner. We consider this premise in Chapter 19 in our discussions on pre-competition nutrition.

It follows that when we measure running economy during laboratory treadmill running, the athlete's diet prior to the assessment has to be taken into consideration. If a runner has a pre-test diet of predominantly carbohydrate he or she is likely to be measured with better running economy than when a high fat and/or protein diet has been consumed.

But typical of our physiology, it is not that simple. Pre-test or pre-race diet is not the only determinant of fuel utilisation, so not the only thing to affect measurement of running economy. Well-trained distance runners have an in-built glycogen sparing system and tend to use more fat even when supplies of glycogen are high. In addition, distance runners on high training volumes often present for laboratory assessment with partially depleted glycogen stores which will also create a tendency toward fat utilisation. It follows that assessment of running economy in an elite distance runner is likely to be somewhat underestimated compared with a middle-distance runner or a distance runner who has trained lightly for a day or two and presents to the lab with running muscles well-stocked with glycogen.

When high precision is required in measuring economy, for example in an experimental situation to determine the effect of a special training program or dietary regime, we can 'correct' the measured submaximal oxygen consumption (i.e. the running economy) according to the mix of fuel used during the assessment.

Fuel mix is gauged from the respiratory exchange ratio (RER), the ratio of carbon dioxide produced divided by the oxygen consumed. When we metabolize fat exclusively this ratio is about 0.7 and when glucose is used exclusively it is 1.0 and somewhere in between in a usual mixed diet.

So to make a point with an extreme example, let's take the case of a runner taking part in two tests of running economy, say a couple of months apart.

The coach wants to see if the training has affected running economy. The lab staff doesn't check his pre-test diet. As it turns out, prior to the first test he consumed a high fat diet, but on the second he happened to consume a high carb diet. His coach gets the report and is elated when she sees that running economy has improved nearly 10 percent. However, unbeknown to the coach all of this change could be explained by the different pre-test diets. Now this is an extreme example, but clearly if your exercise physiologist doesn't monitor pre-test diet, and take account of the RER during the running economy test, then to help make realistic inferences, it'd be a good idea to ask him to do so.

Technique and running economy

Distance and middle-distance coaches love to give athletes advice on running technique. 'Stay tall.' 'Tuck in those elbows.' 'Lift the knees a bit more.' 'Relax the shoulders.' 'Run on your toes.' These are all familiar calls from the coach, but on what basis? If the coach is seeking to improve running economy, where is the evidence that he can?,

Improving running economy by technique modification is a feasible proposition. After all, our 'running economy' measurement evolved from 'mechanical efficiency', and changing technique or a runner's 'mechanics' makes sense. This may well be possible in a runner with an obvious impediment such as extremes of upper body rotation, lateral sway, or other violations of symmetrical motion. However, in my experience with well-trained runners, even in those with unorthodox movements of the arms and shoulders, I have no solid evidence that technical modifications can lead to improved running economy.

For example, during the first 20 years of the Australian Institute of Sport when distance runners were part of the Track and Field program under coach Clohessy, there were several accomplished runners whose techniques suggested compromised economy. We explored the effect of technique modification on their economy by measuring their oxygen consumption during treadmill running at various speeds. Changes were made so that the runners appeared more symmetrical and better balanced, or reduced what we perceived as an excessive shoulder or torso rotation. The result was consistent. Coaching instructions to adopt a 'better' technique produced no detectable improvements in running economy.

Now it may be that our measures were not sufficiently sensitive to detect small changes, or that months of practice may be required to obtain a benefit to the changes in technique. Nonetheless we were dealing with the best runners in Australia, and our initial observations did little to encourage us to tinker with individual actions that had brought about their success. It seemed that running actions appearing uneconomical to the experienced naked coaching eye or even to sophisticated biomechanical analysis may be appropriately matched to the anatomical and physiological characteristics of the individual runner.

So I think you were on the money, Franz Stampfl. An evolved natural action is likely to be better than any new trained action.

John Landy's arms

Changing a runner's technique may not work in general, but nothing's set in stone. Ever tried running with the arm and leg on the same side of your body moving together in the same direction? Now that sort of radical change in technique really does change running economy! It may be that minor changes in arm carriage are beneficial sometimes. And it may be that changes in technique have benefits other than to economy, perhaps to speed.

The world's second sub 4-minute miler and former world record holder, John Landy was a self-coached and scholarly runner. During one of our several discussions on training methods, he mentioned that during a trip to Europe he noticed that European runners ran with a higher arm action than his own. He also noticed that the spikes the Europeans used were different from his own sprinting type spikes, the only ones available in Australia. Landy, the young athlete wondered whether these two observations might be related. He was delighted to find that they were, at least in his case. On acquiring a pair of running spikes in Europe, which featured a heel and shorter spikes, he naturally developed a higher arm action, and this coincided with a more relaxed stride, which he felt contributed to his improved performances during the following year. The more relaxed stride may well have contributed to Landy's better performance, and in part been due to a higher arm action. On the other hand, his improved times may have been due to a myriad of other factors, such as improved aerobic or anaerobic power, or a more direct benefit of the better racing spikes.

I've often wondered whether a runner with an unorthodox or asymmetrical arm action may have developed this over the years to specifically counterbalance asymmetric lower body torques. If this is so, it follows that copying a champion's arm action may not be a particularly productive exercise. Rob de Castella for example, was one of the most economical runners we have tested in the AIS lab, yet he had a distinctively asymmetrical arm action, one hand flicking out to the side. This was the way he ran, the way he felt most comfortable and relaxed. In my marathon training days, I often found myself running behind (I can't remember ever being in front) of Rob in the pack as he ran comfortably along the Stromlo Forest trails. Along with his distinctive arm action, I observed his distinctively asymmetrical leg action, the sole of his left foot flicking out laterally as well. These actions may have been reciprocally related. Whether any attempt to correct this asymmetry of motion would have improved his performances or increased his resistance to injury we'll never know. However, one thing is a surety. It would have taken a braver scientist than me to suggest any changes to the then current world champion's technique either directly or to his coach!

Minimalism

I have heard coaches pick up on a distance or middle-distance athlete whose arm action is minimal, assuming this to be a flaw in technique; a sign of inefficiency or lack of balance or power; and I've wondered whether they were right.

If a runner's arm action is naturally minimal, then this infers one or both of two things; either minimal generation of lower body torque so requiring minimal upper body counterbalance, or increased trunk rotation to replace the counterbalancing action of arm. The latter is usually the case. But does increased upper body rotation mean reduced efficiency? Many would automatically say yes, but I haven't seen the evidence.

The mass of the shoulders and the region of the trunk, being relatively large compared with the arms, requires only a relatively small amount of movement to produce the required compensatory torque. It may be that for some runners, shoulder and trunk movement is just as efficient, or even more efficient, than accentuating arm action. In some support of this premise, some of our most economical runners at the AIS had minimal arm action and slightly more shoulder rotation.

Ron Clarke's arms

Ron Clarke, in his book *The Unforgiving Minute*, actually delayed his early running career as he felt his 'clumsy and inefficient arm action' would only become ingrained if he trained on without a good coach to correct his flawed technique. But the Australian multiple world record breaking runner pointed out his arm action didn't change all that much over the years. He recalled with amusement in his later days that some coaches even used his arm action as a model for their young runners to emulate. Clarke was also concerned in his early days that his running style was too erect and his stride-length too short in relation to his height. I wonder who or what triggered this self-assessment and concern, which seemed to persist even to the time he held world records in 5 km, 10 km, 20 km, 1 hour, and in corresponding imperially measured distances! Could it have been possible that the running style of the fastest distance runner in the world needed revision? Well, possible I suppose—but most unlikely.

From what I have seen of Ron Clarke's action, he could certainly be described as an arm action 'minimalist', having probably developed an optimal combination of upper body rotation and arm swing to maximize economy through many miles and years of running adaptation. I recall watching him run in my football and cricket days, well before any thoughts of running races or coaching Olympians had entered my mind. He was impressively fluent. Ron's brother Jack also captured my imagination at the time. Jack was a champion Australian Rules footballer and captain of the Essendon (Bombers) Football Club in the dominant Aussie Rules state of Victoria. As a kid I was a Collingwood supporter through and through. When I put Jack Clarke in the same category as former Collingwood champions Bob Rose or Bill Twomey in terms of skill, balance, grace, and courage many an old-timer will understand the magnitude of this compliment. It came as no real surprise to read that Jack was able to take a clear-headed view of Ron's concern about his technique, and advise his brother to get on with his running and forget worrying about his arms. Brotherly advice at its best.

As has been the case with uncanny and delightful regularity over the years, I met up with both Ron and Jack through my work at the AIS. Jack visited the AIS well after his stellar football playing and coaching career had come to an end. As a masters 40 plus athlete, he was now very interested in improving his own distance running. It's an interesting experience meeting one of your boyhood idols. I felt humbled when Jack approached me for some advice on his own running at the time.

Percy Cerutty and economy

As much as I admired the Percy Cerutty drive and zest for life, it came as no surprise to read that Ron Clarke was less than impressed with Percy's advice on his running technique. The wily old coach's advice was always animated, literally; urging his followers to emulate the actions of horses, dogs, deer and cheetahs. Percy told his audiences that:

> ... all the power that actuates the legs in running is, or should be, first initiated by the forelegs, now called our arms.
>
> When the forearms are powerful, and the movements from them strong, the running movement is more powerful and can be maintained longer.
>
> Percy Wells Cerutty, *Schoolboy Athletics*

Percy may have had a point when it came to developing running speed, but his analogies with our four-footed friends seem to be at odds with long-distance running, where the main function of the arms and shoulders is one of maintaining good running posture through counterbalance of our single legged driving forces.

Minimalism in arm action is not uncommon in middle-distance runners either and former world champion and world record holding middle-distance runners Hicham El Guerrouj and Said Aouita come immediately to mind. In more recent times, there is Mo Farah. Their arms were 'quiet' and 'understated' during most of the race, only to increase their activity in response to increased leg drive in a surge or kick home, when power assumes greater importance than economy.

Australian athlete Steve Moneghetti is a marathoner who ran with quiet arms, a former champion with a flowing action and more elastic energy and correspondingly greater stride length than many marathoners. For those of us in the Australian scene, we still marvel as Mona's running form, in his 6th decade of life as I write this paragraph, still keeping our young guns very honest indeed. Sarah Jamieson (Australian 1500m record holder astutely developed by coach Bruce Scriven) and Lisa Corrigan (Australian mile record holder) are two other 'locals' I've always admired for their comfortable and flowing actions, and fitting the mould of the natural minimalist, and uncontrived arm action category at their mid-race cruising speed.

Flexibility and running economy

Many a coach of distance runners would relate flexibility to economy of movement. I would agree, but perhaps the way I see it might surprise some. Distance and middle-distance runners with low flexibility seem to be the most economical.

With decades of coaching experience, Pat Clohessy (former AIS distance coach) always liked his runners to do a little bit of stretching, with emphasis on 'little'. 'Clo' obviously didn't believe rigorous stretching played much too much of a role in a distance runner's training program, and his gut feeling was probably on the money.

I don't recall ever discussing Clo's approach to flexibility in relation to running economy but as it turned out two of his best ever runners first alerted me to the potential relationship between these two variables. Versatile Olympian and former Australian 10,000m and steeplechase record holder Shaun Creighton stood out in our lab testing regimes in several ways, one being for his remarkable lack of lower back and hamstring flexibility; and another in that he was the AIS 'lab record holder' as the most economical runner we had ever measured. At 45 ml/kg/min $\dot{V}O2$ whilst running at 16 km/h on the treadmill at zero degrees gradient he had the lowest oxygen uptake (best economy) we ever recorded over my twenty-year period of working at the AIS. A close second in the 'AIS lab economy stakes' was former world record marathon holder, Rob de Castella, with an oxygen consumption of 46 ml/kg/min at 16 km/h, and it was touch and go as to who was the least flexible.

The evidence doesn't stop there. Two other runners whose running economy was up with the best, but whose flexibility was down with the worst, were two of my own runners at the time. For Darren Wilson, whose Australian half-marathon record is still intact at 60:02 and Martin Dent, former Australian steeplechase champion and now self-coached Olympic marathoner, touching their shins with straight legs was a challenge, let alone their toes. Both these runners were among the most economical we've ever measured at 48 ml/kg/min V̇02 at 16 km/h. And for readers interested in the sub-elite category of runner, I was surprised to discover that my own running economy was close to the best we had measured in the AIS physiology lab, 46 ml/kg/min at 16 km/h. And you've guessed it...my flexibility, despite working at it the best I could, was always extremely poor as a footballer and even worse as a veteran (masters) runner!

Continuing my case, at the other end of the scale, the two most flexible runners I measured in the lab were Australian cross-country representative Graham Clews and (the sadly late) Ethiopian and Australian Olympian Mizan Mehari. Both had the flexibility of ballet dancers, and Mizan's put this to good use on the dance floor where his performances around the Canberra clubs became as legendary as his running. Both loved to stretch, (probably because it didn't hurt) and both had low, even poor running economy! Graham used around 55 ml/kg/min of oxygen and Mizan 60 ml/kg/min at the standard 16 km/h treadmill running speed. For Mizan that's about 30 percent more energy per kg body weight than Shaun Creighton at 16 km/h. To match him he'd need to have a big advantage in V̇O2max. Mizan just about did this, at about 86 ml/kg/min, and his best time for 5000m on the track in his brief career as a senior athlete (13:20.85) was not far behind Shaun's (13:17.22).

Recall that smaller athletes will tend to have higher V̇O2max and lower economy than bigger athletes when expressed relative to body weight, and with Shaun at 70 kg and Mizan at less than 50 kg the aerobic disparity in their body weight partly but by no means totally explained the differences in the aerobic characteristics of these two athletes. Graham Clews was a very big runner, by distance running standards, at about 188 cm height and close to 80 kg, which tends to produce a lower $\dot{V}O2$/kg and a better economy, yet Graham's economy was 15 percent worse than Shaun Creighton's, supporting the premise (but certainly not proving) that increased flexibility leads to poorer running economy.

Now if there is a causal relationship between running economy and hamstring, hip flexor, and hip joint flexibility, might there a feasible explanation? Yes, there is. A less flexible or stiffer system of tendons, muscles and ligaments around the hip, knee and ankle joints, indicates better elasticity (i.e. a quicker return to original length following distention) which in turn means better conservation of energy. A runner with a 'stiffer' system, particularly around the hip and ankle joints will have a greater 'spring in each step' and better economy. The more economical runner maximizes the recoil effect at the end of the eccentric (muscle lengthening) contraction phases of the knee extensors, plantar flexors (toe down action) and hip flexors. The same may apply to the postural muscles as they contract with every footstrike to maintain control of the erect running position. A stiffer and tighter postural stability system will further reduce energy costs and improve running economy.

But the tendons seem to be the most significant unit in all of this. Tendons, despite their stiffness, can be stretched. Longer tendons (with their greater stiffness and elasticity) and shorter muscle bellies (with their lesser stiffness and lesser elastic qualities) will tend to do this energy conserving recoil job better. Another contribution to this 'recoil' effect may be the muscle's stretch-reflex contraction which occurs when a muscle-tendon unit approaches maximal length. Very flexible runners may not approach maximal length as readily, so reducing a stretch-reflex recoil effect. Should this be the case, we might anticipate that the optimal flexibility and range of motion of faster runners to be greater than distance runners. It is reasonable to assume that middle-distance runners, with their greater stride length will still be able to 'catch' that elastic recoil energy at the end of their correspondingly greater range of hip movement. Coaches intuitively develop greater flexibility in sprinters and 800m runners to permit freedom of stride length. They seem to intuitively optimize flexibility and elastic energy.

The data from international level male athletes I described and my 'gut feeling' as a coach are consistent with the biomechanical evidence. The scientific literature shows clearly that stiffer, longer tendons are more conducive to repeated muscle contraction with lower energy cost. So, long-distance runners and coaches, gentle stretching to sustain sufficient flexibility for optimal stride length proportional to mid-race speed would seem an appropriate training objective.

Plyometrics, running drills and running economy

Running itself is actually a series of plyometric actions; a series of stretch-eccentric contractions followed by a concentric contraction as each running muscle group is sequentially engaged. Plyometric exercises are specifically designed to overload this natural running action, to amplify firstly the initial eccentrically applied force, and therefore the resulting stretch and concentric muscle contraction.

So plyometric exercises specific to running are really exaggerated or overloaded running steps, the initial amplified stretch sometimes being developed by single leg landings from increased height (from a bench) or in advanced levels by carrying increased weight. In overloading the normal running plyometric action, the aim is to improve power specific to running.

Middle and distance running coaches hope for three possible benefits from plyometric training. Firstly an increase in maximal power at runner's top speed which might improve the 'kick' over the final stages of a race. I say 'might' because speed in the last 200m of a middle or long-distance race is also dependent on how well the runner has maintained homeostasis in that final stage; the fastest sprinters in the field are not necessarily the fastest finishers.

Secondly, with an improvement in maximal contractile power, power requirement at any given race-pace will be a lower percentage of maximal power. This might, but again, cannot be assumed to improve the runner's specific muscular endurance, the ability to sustain the pattern of repeated submaximal muscular activity during the course of a race.

Thirdly, and most relevant to our current discussion, plyometric training might improve running economy by improving the elastic properties of the muscle fascicles (bundles of muscle fibers surrounded by their connective tissue), in turn capturing more of the energy lost to the ground and reducing the energy cost of running at any given speed.

The preceding uncertainties concerning these outcomes are because effects are so difficult to pin down in elite runners, who aren't all that keen, understandably, to engage in any controlled experiments which may require modifications to their training programs. However, one study conducted at the AIS on good club runners, but not international standard runners did provide some evidence for a plyometric training effect on running economy. In a trial involving an 'experimental' group who had plyometrics added to their training, and a 'control' group who continued without the plyometrics. AIS physiologist, middle-distance runner and coach Philo Saunders (a PhD student and athlete of mine at the time), found that three plyometric sessions per week over 8 weeks resulted in a small, but statistically significant (i.e. results were unlikely to have occurred by chance) improvement in running economy. How this occurred we couldn't tell, but overloading tendons and increasing strength of the lower limbs may have increased stiffness and elasticity and contributed to improved economy.

A reasonable position to take on specific plyometric training for middle and long-distance running, is that yes, it is worthy of inclusion and, with a greater emphasis in middle-distance programs. After all, overloading the running action couldn't be more specific. Simple bounding drills, jump squats, tuck jumps with and without rebound for both middle and long-distance runners are worthwhile additions to the weekly running schedule. While there are many variations to these exercises, the principle of specificity would indicate the value of working toward techniques which minimize ground reaction times and so more closely replicate the stretch-contractile actions experienced during running.

Irrespective of whether plyometrics improve economy, here's as good a place as any to discuss the issue of plyometrics in general as a training tool for middle-distance and distance runners.

Plyometric sessions can fit comfortably into a middle-distance and distance running training program between the high-quality running sessions.

One way that has proven sustainable is to introduce it into speed and technique sessions on the days between those more stressful sessions devoted to developing aerobic or anaerobic power. Plyometric drills can be integrated into speed and technique work, even merging these forms of training in the one exercise. For example, bounding might merge into a high knee drill with progressively greater forward speed, finishing the drill by merging into a 50m stride performed with the pattern of high knees set into the runner's mind.

Plyometric overload can be introduced by transferring from grass to the synthetic track surface. For middle-distance runners who are well-trained and competent with body weight resisted plyometrics, further overload can be introduced by adding weight. Weight belts or sand filled tyre tubing might be used as overload in jump squats or high knees drills. These exercises and any gymnasium weights or machine resistance work needs to be carefully supervised to ensure correct posture is maintained throughout the exercise. The potentially damaging effect of poor posture is evident in any form of training of course, but is accentuated further when gravitational forces are increased through added weight. As alluded to in Chapter 21, any inclusion of split leg drills such as lunges or one legged squat jumps with additional resistance have to be introduced in an especially cautious manner, if at all.

That some of the very best distance runners in the world have not practised any formal plyometric work is not all that surprising, but it's not as though they are lacking plyometric work. With the greater volume of training undertaken by world leading distance and middle-distance runners, they are effectively executing 150,000 or more plyometric running steps every week, including up and down hills. With the residual fatigue and difficulty in recovering from training in excess of daily 30km each day, it's not hard to understand why distance runners may be reluctant to introduce further training stress.

The potential benefit of plyometrics for marathoners is certainly debatable. For a start, marathoners are typically very economical runners anyway and if it's the extra speed that might attract a marathon to a plyometric training regime, it's also debatable whether top running speed is the major deciding factor when two fatigued, glycogen depleted athletes battle it out in the last 400m of a 42km race.

However, we've all witnessed those sorts of finishes and we can't discount the possibility that an introduction of a plyometric program to a marathoner's program might provide the competitive edge at this point of the race.

The opinion of internationally successful triathlon coach Darren Smith should never be taken lightly. Darren, a member of my physiology team at the AIS in the early nineties with a PhD in Exercise Physiology places a lot of importance in optimizing running technique with a variety of drills to improve stride length and symmetry of movement, a practice he believes improves the running economy in his athletes. Without a controlled experiment we'll never know whether it is improved economy or other running related characteristics which have contributed to Darren's coaching success. It's possible that his plyometric drills might be especially important in his triathletes, who can't fit in as much running training as pure runners. Special attention to running technique through plyometric drills might offset a tendency for deterioration in technique following the cycling and swimming legs.

A final comment

Although adjustments to obvious technique abnormalities in young and novice runners may lead to improved economy, the jury is still out on whether we can improve running economy through changing the action of well-accomplished runners. Scientific evidence to this effect is non-existent and doubts have been expressed by a great technician in Franz Stampfl. But we live and learn, and the experiences of coaches and athletes who believe otherwise are worth listening to.

Chapter 8
What makes us slow down?

'Sometimes it seems to fill my head with ideas – only I don't exactly know what they are! "Curiouser and Curiouser"'

Lewis Carroll

We can offset fatigue by training, but why we fatigue is still mysterious.

Why do our muscles refuse to do what we desperately require of them at the end of a race? Not an easy one to answer—physiologists around the world continue to debate why distance runners tire. Interestingly, and sadly our lack of understanding of fatigue is not just confined to slowing down in a running race. Medical scientists are equally nonplussed as to what causes the so-called 'chronic fatigue syndrome' or 'post viral fatigue' that afflicts athletes and non-athletes alike, let alone how to prevent or cure it. It is likely that the causes of such different modes of fatigue share some common factors.

It seems that the reasons runners fatigue vary with the length of the race and the fitness of the runner. Tim Noakes, eminent physiologist and keen runner, discusses various 'models' of fatigue in his publication The Lore of Running.

There's a Cardiovascular/Anaerobic Model which proposes we tire when our aerobic system fails to provide sufficient power, and over-reliance on our anaerobic system results in an 'internal milieu' toxic to muscle contraction.

A Central Governor Model has the brain applying the brakes unconsciously when we approach an intensity or volume of energy output capable of inflicting bodily damage. Then we have a Muscle Power Model which blames the muscle machination, the sliding filaments within our muscle fibres losing their grip of the situation, with failing contraction. The Energy Depletion Model has fatigue occurring when muscle fuel (glucose, fatty acids mainly) runs critically low and the Biomechanical Model explains the onset of fatigue in terms of a loss of elasticity of muscle and its connective tissues, with the reduction in efficiency increasing energy costs and upsetting homeostasis. Finally we have the Psychological/Motivational model explaining fatigue at the conscious level through failure to tolerate the pain and discomfort associated with fatigue.

Noakes among others thinks the Central Governor is likely to play a dominant role. According to this model, runners may do everything in their conscious power to maintain race-pace, but conscious intent is over-ridden by phylogenetically primitive autonomic nerve centres in the base of our brain refusing to authorize the required power supply. In one way, we can liken this to a modern computerized car that automatically restricts power when the red-line rev counter is exceeded no matter how hard the driver plants his foot. But unlike the runner, the car does at least maintain that red-line speed.

This model remains controversial because of the experimental difficulty in proving its existence, but it does seem feasible at least from a Darwinian point of view. Genes tend to be passed on by the fittest, sure, but only when the fittest don't kamikaze with strenuous exercise. Imagine a Fred Flintstone without a brain wired up with this kind of safety valve. He'd run himself into the ground literally, hunting or being hunted. And a set of genes stopped in their tracks.

But as is often the case with we humans, characteristics are expressed in degrees. It's often not just a case of have or have not, and there's likely to be a normal distribution of that ability to physically drive oneself into the ground. At one end of that normal curve we have some runners who can push themselves into dangerous physical states whereas at the other, the redline is reached well before any physical distress eventuates. Former world marathon record holder Derek Clayton immediately comes to mind as a runner who often trained with the single-minded intent of enduring extremes of discomfort and pain. Doing his best to re-set an already high red line higher still.

Athletes of the Clayton mould are known to train with such excessive volume and intensity that they break down physically and sometimes mentally. Bones fracture, muscles tear, tendons and ligaments rupture, immunity fails, heat stress and stroke are well known, and psychological disorders seem to be related to the kind of physical stress they endure.

Middle-distance fatigue

Going 'lactic'

Ask an athlete why he couldn't finish any faster in a 1500m or 5km race and he or she might reply 'I tied up with 50m to go...I was just so lactic!'.

Coaches, athletes, scientists over many decades have assumed that muscles fail us when our aerobic system just can't supply the demand we make on it, forcing us to resort to high levels of anaerobic power, and muscles flooded with lactic acid. Then we learned that the lactate part of, hydrogen lactate (lactic acid) shouldn't be blamed as the cause of pain and fatigue. In fact lactate was indeed a valuable fuel that could be 'shuttled' away from the site of production and put to use as fuel elsewhere. After all, there's a lot of chemical energy left in a lactate molecule. Almost as much as in the glucose molecule it started out as. Transfer it off somewhere else where oxygen is in better supply, even to a less stressed muscle, and, it can be aerobically processed to generate 36/38th of the amount of energy able to be generated from a glucose molecule. So lactate itself is most unlikely to cause fatigue.

The culprit, the cause of fatigue was then thought to be the hydrogen part of lactic acid (i.e. hydrogen lactate), the accumulation of protons or hydrogen ions, H^+, the we refer to as acidity. We humans normally operate at a certain acidity level or pH, a lower pH designating higher acidity. The pH of our blood is 7.4, which is slightly alkaline, and if this gets too low, or indeed too high, enzymes don't work as well as they should and chemical processes vital to our survival slow down, threatening life. So exercise physiologists have usually attributed fatigue to the decrease in pH at the site of the sliding filament process of muscle contraction. It made sense. Muscles stop working properly as protons build up.

However, as is often the case in science, what seemed to be the end of the story of fatigue was not. The next chapter of the saga questions whether this acidity is really the cause of the muscle dysfunction. Researchers are now suggesting that, like the lactate part of lactic acid, the acidity part just happens to be there when we tie up in a race.

If it's not lactate and not pH, what is it?

According to investigators working with isolated animal muscle preparations, the culprit is the accumulation of potassium ions (K^+) inside the muscle cell. They reckoned it was potassium which directly inhibited the process of ionic exchange across the muscle cell membrane and so sabotaged the contractile process. And doing their best to sabotage the exercise physiology textbooks, a research team based in Switzerland went further. They showed that creating an acidic medium around an isolated skeletal muscle cell which corresponded to 20 mmol/L lactate, (a level associated with an extremely intense and prolonged anaerobic effort) actually improved, not impeded the contractile process!

It's reasonable to assume well-prepared isolated muscle to behave similarly in vivo (real life), but we can't be sure until this is demonstrated. For example, what if blood acidity or even the lactate ion itself triggered a chain of events with an indirect effect on fatigue through our nervous system, possible through the autonomic nervous system in line with the Central Governor model of fatigue?

And if lactic acid is not directly involved in the fatigue process, how do we explain the beneficial effect of alkalizing the blood (raising the pH) prior to middle-distance events can improve performance. Could it be that the introduction of a so-called 'strong' ion like Na^+ in the ingested alkalizing salt, usually sodium bicarbonate, was the active ingredient, dampening the destabilizing effect of accumulating K^+ within the muscle cell?

We haven't heard the end of this story as yet. In fact it's far from complete. We can still refer to 'lactic' fatigue too, as there is no doubt accumulating lactic acid coincides with fatigue, but as to whether it actually causes it—that's the ongoing story.

Physiologist Rob Robergs, who worked at the University of New Mexico, Albuquerque, USA, for a couple of decades, before coming back to Australia to take up a position at Charles Sturt University, Bathurst didn't hold back on his opinion concerning whether lactic acid itself is the cause of fatigue. He reckons, 'the most important reason to discard the lactic acidosis [of fatigue] concept is that it is invalid. It has no biochemical justification and, to no surprise, no research support.' But physiologist Bruce Gladden of Auburn University in Alabama, and a former Editor in Chief of the prestigious Medicine and Science in Sports and Exercise journal, adopts a more moderate position in writing 'surprisingly, there is little direct mechanistic evidence regarding cause and effect [of fatigue] in acid-base balance. However, there is insufficient evidence to discard the term "lactic acidosis."'

What did Lydiard think?

Arthur Lydiard may not have viewed fatigue in quite the same terms as provided by the models we have outlined. However, as a pioneering coach of world champion middle and long-distance athletes he clearly had a good understanding of how to train to resist fatigue. For example, he spoke about Peter Snell being one of the slowest runners over 200m when compared with his competitors in an Olympic 800m final. But Lydiard also proudly pointed out that when his protégé won 800m gold in Rome and Tokyo, he was clearly the fastest 200m runner in the field when it was preceded by a very solid 600m.

Looking at this from another angle, Snell's homeostasis was less disturbed than his competitors as he passed the 600m mark, placing his muscles in a physiologically advantageous position to continue to contract powerfully. Lydiard spent time in East Germany, and listening to him speak of his experience four decades ago it was clear that he was a strong supporter of the lactic acid theory of fatigue. To Lydiard and Snell, whether the acidity was the cause or merely the correlate of fatigue mattered little. What did matter was a reduced accumulation of lactic acid at that 600m mark which coincided with a greater ability to kick home.

Marathon fatigue

Fatigue is event specific. For example the fatigue of a marathon is very different to the fatigue of an 800m.

The Energy Depletion Model is the obvious model of choice when it comes to marathon running. Running speed declines when muscle glycogen stores run low and fat assumes a greater proportion of the fuel mix. We might even point the finger at the liver glycogen stores. As I discuss elsewhere, a liver unused to topping up blood glucose concentration under the extreme demands from a marathoner's heart and respiratory muscles, not to mention brain, can falter. Dizziness and distress are not unusual in the latter stages of a marathon, a sign that the normal blood glucose level hasn't been maintained.

The Muscle Power model also makes a strong claim as a cause of marathon fatigue. When a muscle is asked to contract strongly every second or so for 2 or 3 hours, extremes of mechanical, biochemical or neural demands might reasonably be expected to contribute to the reduced contractile power.

The Biomechanical model has to be considered as well. Fatigued marathon runners usually shorten their stride length. It's a fair bet that 20,000 vigorous muscular contractions and a bitumen surface in light racing shoes pulling 20,000 times on tendons, and in particular the Achilles tendon, have a compromising effect on elasticity and therefore, stride length and running economy.

The Psychological/Motivation Model has it that the athlete who wants to win most will have a decided advantage. Fair enough, but it's been my experience over the past few decades that at the true elite level, variation in will to win is not likely to be a significant factor. Observation of an elite runner struggling to make the finish line at the end of a major marathon makes it painfully obvious that moving any faster is simply impossible.

I'm sure any mere mortal marathoner reading this will have experienced this same frustratingly helpless feeling.

Endurance in general depends on the environmental conditions and the marathon is a conspicuous example. Marathon fatigue certainly depends on the weather.

In what was touted as a showdown between the world's best marathon runners, in the cool conditions of Rotterdam in 1983 Robert de Castella edged out Carlos Lopes to win by 2 seconds in 2:08:37. Although there was a miniscule time difference, it seemed that de Castella may have maintained his physical and psychological homeostasis slightly but significantly better than Lopes on that day. A year later in the Los Angeles Olympic marathon in 1984, these two again went head to head. This time it was hot and humid, and core temperature became a critical factor. Lopes turned the tables on de Castella taking the gold, de Castella running in 5th. In contrast to Rotterdam, a foremost homeostatic threat was to maintain body temperature. De Castella, the larger runner, was at a disadvantage and it showed. He was forced to drink even between drink stations. But which model of fatigue fits best here?

I'm certain it wasn't the Psychological/Motivation model. No-one wanted to win more than 'Deek' and he gave that race everything he had. We can't rule out The Central Governor Model though; the involuntary protective mode of the de Castella brain in that heat may have over-rode his conscious will to win. The Cardiovascular Model comes into strong consideration too, as overheating will compromise oxygen transport as blood is re-routed away from the working muscles to the skin to promote cooling. The Energy Depletion Model certainly holds here as well, because glycogen is metabolized at a greater rate in hot conditions. We discuss running in hot conditions and the de Castella-Lopes comparison in more detail in Chapter 18.

Too tired to run faster? Are you sure?

It was the Wednesday. Rob de Castella had just returned from his triumphant Rotterdam marathon last Sunday, that field including Alberto Salazar as well as Lopes. We were enjoying an easy post-race run and Rob was tired and sore.

While certainly not a classical runner's manual style runner, Rob was especially asymmetrical that day, hobbling along at a pace even I was able to negotiate quite comfortably. I was wondering how far Rob would go before he decided to turn around and call it a day. He chatted about the surging efforts that ultimately paid dividends for him in that race. I pondered over the reasons he was able to do this, at periods of the race where fatigue was clearly setting in. And at the end why had Rob withstood the stress of the previous 40km better than his rivals?

And why, right now as we jogged, was he so spent? No doubt trauma to his running muscles was the main culprit, but general post-race central nervous system exhaustion was probably playing a part as well. Throw in jet-lag and even the effects of post-race celebrations and our champion runner had every reason to be very tired. I jogged and Rob hobbled past one of the bigger houses in our suburb of Chapman in the ACT with its well-manicured nature strip of green grass.

As we ran across this lawn, an automatic water sprinkler system suddenly burst in action. That was surprising in itself; but most surprising was what happened a split-second later.

The always beautifully chilled Canberra water supply could not have been better directed, Rob copped in straight in neck and down his right side. Our marathoner took off with Usainian speed! I couldn't believe that this muscle damaged, fatigued, jet-lagged and sorely crippled slow-twitch marathon man had been able sprint like that! 'How did you manage that?' I asked incredulously. 'Hell, mate, I don't know. Must have some energy hidden away somewhere I guess.'

Maybe that tells us something about fatigue. No matter what the state of mind and body, when the motivation is high enough, there is always something somewhere left to be found in the tank. Might this be the very same reserve that some elite athletes exploit where others can't? Or was this simply an example of the 'fight or flight' stress reactivity we've all inherited? That mammoth or sabre-toothed tiger in the form of a sprinkler had been 'fought and Deek had 'flown'. Maybe our sprinkler case might provide a clue as to how our great Central Governor above the shoulders might, under some circumstances, be trumped by a spinal cord reflex!

Fatigue and running economy

Fatigue is likely to compromise running economy through its effect on the elasticity and stride length, but possibly through other avenues as well. When we are fresh, we run with a particular posture employing a particular set of muscles in a particular sequential pattern in a particular direction. In a fatigued state this will change. When the muscle fascicles (clusters of fibers) run out of steam, we recruit new fascicles to derive the resultant force.

Modifications to technique are likely to occur at a conscious level as well. For example 'I'll take the pressure off my twitchy calf by running more flat-footed'. Coincidentally, as I review this chapter and that last sentence I'm sitting on a train from Rotterdam to Brussels. Yesterday one of my runners, Dutch champion Miranda Boonstra cramped in the latter stages of the 2015 Rotterdam Marathon and we were disappointed that a 2 h 28 min turned into a 2 h 32 min. At the 35km mark an obviously dismayed Miranda was desperately trying to recruit muscles that would behave the way she needed them to, shuffling to spread the work away from those refusing to take orders, transferring the work away from her calves and thighs to her hips.

Technique and running economy are also likely to be modified at an automatic level, less fatigued parts of the muscle being 'turned on' as the fatigued areas are turned off. In other words the motor units within the muscle (the tiny nerve branch and the muscle fascicles it innovates) are deployed in different proportions. A reduction in running economy will occur if the newly resorted to combination of motor units necessitates a greater number of motor units to produce the same resultant force. The net changes we see in fatigued runners may initially be quite subtle, but become obvious as fatigue sets in and might contribute to the upward drift in heart rate we observe even when running just under anticipated 'steady state' or 'threshold' speed.

Lisa and the Japanese biomechanists

Some 27 years previous to that Rotterdam race, I was made aware of another example of an automatic change in technique accompanying fatigue. Lisa Ondieki (then Martin) and I were asked by a panel of Japanese sports scientists in Nagoya to answer some questions related to her performance in the Osaka marathon earlier that year where she'd run 2:23:51, a course record and lifetime PB.

> Our biomechanics team has analysed the race and found that Lisa's stride length was significantly decreased over the final 8km or so of the Osaka marathon. How did you conceive of this plan in the first place, why was it introduced at such a late stage? Why do you think it was so successful?

I remember the look of disappointment on the faces of the panel when I told them that any reduction on stride length was of not part of any ingenious plan of ours. Lisa explained that she had not made any conscious effort to reduce stride length and wasn't aware that she had done so until the research team posed the question.

Following some discussion we agreed that Lisa had executed a natural, seemingly unconscious response to a gradual build-up of fatigue. With muscular force per stride diminishing in line with her fatigue Lisa was subconsciously compensating for a reduced stride length with an increase in stride frequency. Economy may have been reduced in doing so, but on nearing the end of the race our runner still had enough fuel in the tank to sustain the pace to the finish.

Alberto's dilemma

Alberto Salazar came over to visit us at the AIS in the early 90s. He was extremely fit by normal athletic standards but frustrated and confused by his inability to regain the form that had taken him to the top of the world marathon tree during the 80s. The general consensus was that a combination of some very fast marathons, years of high quality training at around 200km per week, and several instances of heat stress during races may have all added up to take their toll.

Despite thorough medical investigations, his physicians weren't able to pinpoint why he had lost his world-class form. The first thought that came to my mind was an immune system related inflammatory disorder in the same family as post-viral syndrome or mononucleosis that produced chronic fatigue. Given that medical specialists remained puzzled as to the genesis of chronic fatigue, and Alberto was only visiting for a few days, I didn't like my chances of making any useful contribution to his dilemma.

As discussed above, marathon running performance is reasonably well predicted by a runner's $\dot{V}$02max and economy and I'd seen some of his previous test results. I thought we might get some sort of a clue as to Alberto's loss of form by measuring these characteristics.

He ran impressively on the treadmill. He was certainly still very fit, but being very fit is one thing, and reproducing his 2:08 marathon form was another. The first thing we noticed was that Alberto's engine capacity, his $\dot{V}$O2max, had not changed from earlier values reported in the US, at around 77 ml/kg/min. Maximal aerobic power is generally a more stable variable than racing performance itself, but it was good to know that his aerobic engine hadn't lost anything at the top end. On the other hand, this was not the case for his running economy. At 16 km/h and 18 km/h, he appeared to have deteriorated about 8 percent from the values reported when he was running at his best. That is he was using about 8 percent more energy to run at these speeds.

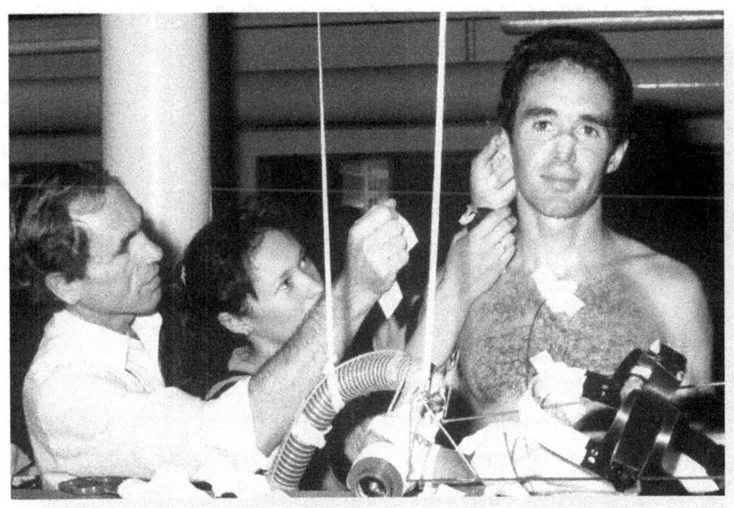

Supervising Alberto Salazar, in the physiology lab at the AIS.
Image: Australian Sports Commission

I told Alberto about the finding, but didn't make a big deal of it given it was a once-off test. For me to be confident about the finding we would have needed to confirm it with repeated tests, and check the exact protocols of the comparative data. Running economy can vary according to type of shoes worn, type of treadmill mat, pre-test diet, pre-test training. In any case, should the reduced economy be real, improving it would have been problematical.

But it did get me thinking. What if this reduction in economy had been real? We've seen how important running economy is to race performance, particularly to a marathoner, where reduced economy runs down the glycogen tank more rapidly. But let's assume for the purpose of this discussion, that Alberto's economy was compromised—what could have possibly caused this?

Running technique? It didn't look to me as though much had changed here. Alberto's easily recognized minimalist knee action had always given me the impression that elastic energy around the lower leg wasn't the key to Alberto's outstanding performances. Moreover, in our best runners at the AIS, I'd always found it difficult to predict running economy from variations in running style.

One other possibility is worthy of consideration. Alberto was a running warrior who gave me the impression that he just loved the combat of racing, and more often than not, the thrill of being chased. I recall a conversation with Rob de Castella in the mid-eighties before Alberto's visit where we wondered how Alberto was going to keep churning out races and training at such a high level. If the decline in form was related to a change in economy, might it be possible that the repeated stresses evoked by fast marathons, hot weather races and relentless 200km weeks of training had compromised Alberto's ability to convert energy within the muscle fibre at the mitochondrial level?

We'll never know, but it leads into some interesting general discussion and speculation as to how running economy might be compromised in this way.

Leaky mitochondria and running economy

Our dodgy design and free radicals

In Chapter 5 we discussed the mitochondria, the little satchels of enzymes that go to work teasing out the energy contained within the molecules of our ingested sugars, fatty acids (and amino acids when the former two are in short supply). Their energy is released during a systematic extraction of electrons and we've already used the analogy of a baton flowing through a relay team, with oxygen as the final receiver or anchor runner. The vital nature of oxygen's role is acknowledged with naming rights and we refer to any chemical process of electron extraction from a molecule as 'oxidation' whether oxygen is involved or not.

Now it's fair to say that we human beings remain a work in progress, still of dodgy design in many respects, and the way we extract our energy from our food is no exception. There are some shaky baton changes along that electron transfer chain in the cell's mitochondria; shakier than a US men's 100m relay team. That causes us some concern because electrons can play merry hell as they look for lodging elsewhere. They do this with haste, forming highly unstable highly reactive molecules called reactive oxygen species, and in particular cases 'free radicals.' These unstable particles crave stability, only to be found by seeking a partner for their newly acquired electron. And partner electron they quickly find, usually by stealth, extracting it from any unsuspecting molecule hanging around with an insecurely guarded electron. So these free radicals are themselves powerful oxidizers (electron extractors) and while satisfying their voracious appetite they leave their 'victim molecules' in a similar state of instability they once possessed. The hunted then becomes the hunter, setting off a chain reaction similar to a lined up set of dominoes toppling in turn all because the first one lost its balance.

These rampaging free radicals have splendid names like 'superoxide' and 'hydroxyl radical'; and hydrogen peroxide (once well-utilized by bottle blondes) is not a free radical itself but is a compound which can produce free radicals and so extract electrons (which it can even take from a strand of hair, removing its colour). When this chain of reactions occurs in our tissues, such as in the arteries of our brain, pancreas, or even our big toes, oxidative damage is likely to occur.

Now having alerted you to the dangers of rampant free radicals and you are fired up about making sure you do everything you can to remove their influence, think again. When these reactive species are kept under control they are very useful, perhaps even critical for our survival. For example nitric oxide is a free radical used in the control of blood vessel diameter and blood flow, so has a big influence in regulating our blood pressure. Other free radicals such as the one called the superoxide radical are deployed in our white blood cell immune defence system to 'zap' and kill invading pathogens. So free radicals do deserve a bit of respect.

Our bodyguards

However, given the darker aspects of uncontrolled free radical effects, following millions of years of evolution, Homo sapiens (environment scientist Paul Ehrlich has a point when he re-labelled us as 'homo stupidus') has developed a system to prevent the chain reaction of tissue oxidation getting completely out of hand. We make use of special 'bodyguard' molecules which take the hit from the free radical. We call them 'anti-oxidants' and they provide the electrons for the rapacious free radicals, sparing our tissues. We can make these anti-oxidants ourselves, homegrown molecules with impressive tags like 'superoxide dismutase and hydroxyl radical. We can also eat anti-oxidants (electron donor) molecules made by plants to supply our tissues, and these include the vitamins such as E, C and A to quench the appetite of the free radicals.

Without these bodyguards we wouldn't survive too long, but unlike Kevin Costner our bodyguards are not infallible. Over time, we can't offset all of the oxidative damage and they probably do slowly perform their lethal act, a process we might refer to as 'ageing' but that's another story.

Leaky mitochondria

Getting back to the running economy issue, tissues close to the oxidative action right in the muscle cells' mitochondria are especially vulnerable to oxidative damage. At the best of times we lose a lot of those electrons passed along the respiratory chain of ATP production on the way to their finally rendezvous with oxygen. These electrons are in a way, wasted, as they don't lead to production of ATP for the production of muscular power.

The term 'leaky mitochondria' has been coined by physiologists and biochemists to describe mitochondrial loss, and especially to describe mitochondria which lose more electrons during the metabolic processes that might be expected.

So these stray electrons can have two detrimental consequences. Firstly, they can increase free radical production and oxidative damage at the mitochondrial level. Secondly, they signify a reduction in the efficiency of glycogen and oxygen usage, two limiting factors in a marathon runner's performance. And if the damage is done to mitochondrial DNA with subsequent mutation then the potential dysfunction and electron wastage is likely to be even more serious. This process has been linked with ageing, but it might also be linked with an increase in the energy cost of running.

Mitochondrial leakiness varies in different species. For example the mitochondria in the pectoral muscles of migrating birds have very 'tight' mitochondria, with a very low leakage of electrons, rendering these birds extremely efficient converters of their food into muscular work, and capable of flying for extraordinary distances without refuelling.

Mitochondrial damage

Emphasising the hypothetical nature of my comments, it's not difficult to imagine the excessive metabolic demands and heat stress of an intensely training 200km a week marathon runner overwhelming his anti-oxidant system and leading to mitochondrial damage, mutation and permanent metabolic dysfunction.

And Alberto's was a high profile case, but not on his own when it comes to unresolved marathoner 'burnout.' Take Australian marathon runner Dave Chettle. Dave had come to train in Canberra with Pat Clohessy's AIS squad following a prolonged decline in form. Just a couple of years after he had run 2:10:20 in 1975 in a rainy Fukuoka marathon he found himself incapable of reproducing anything like that sort of performance. Sadly, in 1982 he was barely capable of running 2:25. Like Salazar, sports physicians could pinpoint no abnormalities. Also like Salazar, he engaged in a particularly demanding training program involving very high mileage. I remember his former coach in Tasmania, Max Cherry, telling me that high volume training even up to 250km was essential for world-class marathon performance. And yet again, like Alberto, Dave had a great work ethic, and his coach's intensive and high volume training was a challenge he did not shy away from. A final similarity to the Salazar situation was that Dave's $\dot{V}O2max$ was high and his running economy low when we checked these following his decline in world rankings, but we lacked prior records of Dave's economy, so cannot determine whether any decline occurred.

Derek Clayton is another wonderful marathoner who may have been in the same boat. He had world bests of 2:09:36 in Fukuoka in 1967 and 2:08:33 in Antwerp in 1969 and was another who seemed to find a peak but whose world class marathon, performance was confined to a relatively short period. He was also a prolific trainer, believing that suffering in training was necessary to achieve greatness in his chosen event. He may have been right to some extent, but judging the degree of that 'extent' seems to be a key issue. In their intense desire to do whatever it takes to achieve their 'ultimate' performance, elite level marathoners appear most susceptible in their judgment of how much their body can endure, an insidious psyche of 'more is better' often converting a golden patch of performance into a training kamikaze. Some, perhaps many, or even most marathon runners may consider this a risk worth taking to achieve their perfect race. Having met and physiologically assessed Clayton I strongly suspect that typified his philosophy.

In the absence of any other leads, mitochondrial dysfunction seems a feasible mechanism to explain, at least in part, the decline of marathon running performance in elite runners training and racing with high intensity and volume, and in some cases in torrid environmental conditions. I commend this area to our exercise and metabolic physiologists as one well worthy of investigation.

A former PhD student under my supervision at the AIS, and now a sort-after nutritional advisor to professional sporting clubs and athletes, Melbourne based Dr Ian Gillam, is a firm believer that supplementation of anti-oxidants to those training at with high power requirements and high levels of oxygen flux through their muscles require protection from free radical damage. Gillam proposes that failure to adequately protect against reactive oxygen species in athletes with high levels of oxygen flux will cause muscle damage, delayed recoveries and sub-optimal training adaptation. He may be correct, but perhaps the greatest threat is to the mitochondrial DNA.

Don't lose any sleep about your metabolic inefficiency. You're a lot better off than a mouse. The excessive mitochondrial respiratory chain electron leakiness and metabolic inefficiency of this unfortunate rodent means he has a much more difficult time in warding off self-destruction right from his very first sniff of oxygen. On the other hand he's smart enough not to attempt to run for 42km as fast as he can without stopping!

Chapter 9
Training Fundamentals

Variety is the spice of life; and it's the spice of training too.
Avery Weissman (2015)

Now I realize that some coaches set the same session in the same way in the same place on the same day of the week, month after month. I don't, firstly because I'm looking for variety in the type of running stimulus and secondly because doing the same thing week in week out is boring. I like to set training in the bush, on the track, through the streets, in the mountains, and sometimes in the water (with apologies to Winston) and vary the arrangements of the stimulus (i.e. vary the repetitions and recoveries) every couple of weeks.

In one way, runners are lucky, not unlucky, in that they tend to break down when subjected to more than a couple of hours a day of running training stress. They're lucky because they have to restrict their running training to around a couple of hours a day. So top runners can indulge in a normal life (well almost), and still train with uncompromised volume and intensity, with time to think about matters other than refuelling and recovery. Granted, our elite level runners will squeeze that extra one or two percent out of themselves with increased intensity and/or volume. Others by adding resistance work and cross training, although many champion distance runners have demonstrated that non-running training is not an essential component to reach the top. So we runners should spare a thought for elite swimmers who focus their attention on a black line at the bottom of the pool for 4 or 5 hours a day. And what about the cyclists who train for 6-8 hours every day, and how our top triathletes keep a grip on the realities of life on Earth beats me.

Specificity of training

Successful distance running coaches know that it's not just matter of getting hold of a program that happened to work for someone else and taking the stopwatch to the track. Coaching requires specificity of design according to the event, individual runner and the training phase.

Specificity of training: the event

A hypothetical: which five events?

Despite sharing common characteristics, every running event is different, requiring its own training program. There are very large differences between some events but only subtle variation between others. To see what I mean, let's set up a 'hypothetical' challenge.

Swimmers are known to win multiple medals in World Championships and Olympics. Let's suppose the IAAF decides that it is not in the best interests of international competition for any small set of individuals to dominate the track as swimmers have done in the pool.

Our hypothetical challenge is to narrow the current range of events, the 100m, 200m, 400m, 800m, 1500m, 3000m steeplechase, 5000m, 10,000m, half-marathon, and marathon to five events so as to minimize the chance of any one runner winning more than one event.

Which five would you choose? In other words which five events do you think are best characterized by their unique specific fitness?

Making the cut

To my mind, there are five core events that stand out most in their specific fitness requirements; the 100m, 400m, 1500m, 10,000m, and the marathon. But don't throw this book at the wall, you 200m, 800m, steeplechase, 5000m and half-marathon enthusiasts because they are all great races and I'm certainly not promoting their extinction. This exercise is purely to illustrate the concept of event specific fitness.

Here is my reasoning for the five that made the cut

The 100m is the purest running test of raw speed and maximal (alactic) power. Energy system-wise it's almost all alactic anaerobic power. Elite 100m runners are not limited by acid-base or other disturbance at the muscle fibre level. Neither are they limited by maximal capacity of lactic anaerobic energy and certainly not by aerobic power. Their energy is already sitting in the muscles, waiting to be unleashed at the gun.

The 400m is the purest running test of anaerobic (lactic) capacity. Granted, anaerobic energy is not exclusively utilized, and alactic anaerobic power and aerobic power come into play, but elite 400m runners are the anaerobic capacity kings and queens.

The 1500m event gets my nod because it is the ultimate hybrid event. Referred by some (mainly the 1500m runners) as the 'blue-riband' event, elite 1500m specialists are the ultimate all-rounders of the track, requiring a highly developed combination alactic power, lactic capacity and aerobic power.

The 10,000m race is the truest test of running aerobic power. The 'threshold', 'red-line' or 'maximum steady state' pace that can be held over this roughly 30 minute period is the main determinant of 10,000m performance, and aerobic power and running economy are key determinants of performance. Anaerobic power and capacity and alactic sprinting speed do play their roles in winning championship 10,000m events, so it is a 'hybrid' event, but the 1500m event requires a more even use of each power source.

The marathon is the ultimate test of endurance, unique in its dependence on a runner's capacity to store readily available fuel; together with the anatomical and physiological challenges of maintaining homeostasis while running as fast as possible for more than 2 hours.

Missing the cut

The 200m specific characteristics are a hybrid of the 100m and 400m events. Depending on the athlete's strengths, the world's best 100m runner will have a reasonable chance of being the world's best at 200m; alternatively the best 400m runner could be a champion 200m runner, although it is conceded that in the 21st century competition arena, the latter combination is less likely.

The 800m is unlucky to be excluded, but the 1500m gets my nod as the hybrid race of choice; the race that involves the most even spread of aerobic, lactic and alactic anaerobic power requirements. Furthermore, a champion 800m runner has a better chance of winning the 400m than a 1500m runner doubling up in the 400m or 10,000m.

The 3000m steeplechase is certainly a unique event, but it combines the fitness required of 1500m and 5000m runners, opening up a possibility for a winner in one of these events winning the steeple as well, given an appropriate race schedule.

The 5000m lost out to the 10km because of the former's predisposition toward hybrid classification. The 5km seriously challenges the 1500m as 'the ultimate hybrid event', but I feel it falls a little short because its specific fitness is skewed more towards aerobic power and away from anaerobic capacity and alactic sprinting power. Moreover, the specificity of training for the 5km is close to the 3km steeple and not all that far removed from 10km, so we might expect a 5km trained athlete to have a chance of doubling up to win any two of these events, again race scheduling permitting.

The half-marathon is not as reliant on the muscle energy stores as is the marathon; and the aerobic power requirement is similar to that of the 10,000m event. A runner might win both the 10km and half-marathon, made much more realistic given the half-marathon championship is conducted months away from the 10,000m.

From the above hypothetical we can see why a certain specificity of training applies to every event; but also that some events belong to the same family whereas others are just distant cousins.

Just as an aside, try the above exercise in differentiating Olympic swimming events. It's not easy, which is why multiple medal winners in swimming are not uncommon, even in tightly scheduled championships. Swimming event distances (and strokes) share more fitness characteristics than running events. From 50m through to 1500m events swimmers train with relatively high volumes to develop aerobic fitness and 'feel' of the water. In contrast, prolonged phases of high volume concentrating on aerobic power aren't characteristic of the programs of elite 100m, 200m, and 400m runners. To the contrary, development of aerobic power might well be considered detrimental.

The other consideration is that swimmers can more easily back up from one race effort to another. A good part of the reason for this is the absence of weight-bearing footstrike. Footstrike is characterized by short and sharp eccentric contractions, damaging to the muscle fibers and connective tissues, while the swimming stroke is much less anatomically disruptive, involving predominantly concentric muscle contractions spread over a longer duration.

Specificity of training: the individual

Given the individuality of the physiology, biomechanics and psychology of a runner, it follows that the very best training programs of any two individuals will vary, even if it's for the same event. In some cases training programs will vary widely. The 800m event presents as a very good example.

Consider two 800m runners with the same personal best performance. 800m runner 'A' is from a sprint/400m background with naturally good top speed and anaerobic capacity and 800m runner 'B' comes from a 1500m background, naturally well-endowed with aerobic power. Their most profitable training programs for the 800m will vary considerably. But the question is how? It's not straightforward. Do we work on their strengths or the weaknesses of these athletes, or both, and if so, to what extent?

If we focus on the athlete's weakness, the aerobic power of athlete A, we might de-train his 'strength', the anaerobic capacity. And this might be a net negative adaptation. If we focus on further improvement of the 'strength', the anaerobic power and capacity, we might again run the risk of moving further away from that optimal combination for best 800m performance.

Consequently the middle-distance coach might be considered to have the most challenging task of all running coaches. The most common and obvious approach is to focus on the athlete's weaker characteristic, on the assumption that this is the lesser developed aspect and so offers the best chance of improvement. For athlete A this might entail introducing a more extensive aerobic preparatory phase build-up (punctuated with some speed and anaerobic revision each week in order to help offset any detraining in this area). For athlete B we might shorten the aerobic build-up phase and introduce a longer pre-competition period in which to develop speed and anaerobic power and capacity (with a program aimed at sustaining aerobic power).

In this situation trial and error is inevitable, as we can't predict how much an individual will respond to working on a weakness or strength. But with long term coach-athlete relationships, errors tend to be minimized. With repeated preparations over successive seasons, long-term coaches learn the 'lines of least resistance' to training adaptation. Resistance to improvement in 300m speed if emphasising anaerobic work, or to 1,200m time-trial if emphasising aerobic work, might signal caution in pursuing this plan. The longer term coach can also gain a better understanding of the proportions of training these characteristics which produce the best performance in a coming season.

But even for the experienced coach this is not an easy task.

I recall a conversation in Sydney with Beijing Olympian 800m runner Lachlan Renshaw. He was coached for many years by highly respected Australian middle-distance coach John Atterton. Always considered a 400/800m runner, the focus of training was on his anaerobic power and speed. Lachlan's strength was considered to be his 400m speed, and this needed to be preserved and improved; but his 1500m fitness was totally unexplored. Later in his career, following discussions with coaches and athletes in Europe and a period of training in the US at Oregon influenced by Mark Rowland, former British Olympic bronze medallist in the steeple-chase, there was a distinct change of focus. Lachlan, with agreement from Coach Atterton explored the impact of greater aerobic fitness through cross-country work, longer repetitions, less speed work, and more volume. Predictably, his 400m time blew out a second or so and his 1500m time improved markedly. The upshot was that off this late career acknowledgment that aerobic fitness had a role to play, Lachlan ran his fastest ever 800m, 1:45.66 in 2011 improving marginally on his previous best in 2008 of 1:45.79. I asked Lachlan whether he would change anything if he had the opportunity to turn back the clock over all those years of low volume high anaerobic power training. Without hesitation he replied that he regretted not having worked more on the aerobic power aspect, i.e. on his 1500m fitness.

We can't draw any general inference from this example. But it does raise the question of whether even so-called 400m/800m runners might benefit from more aerobic power work? Traditionally the answer has been an emphatic 'No!' But Renshaw's carefully considered opinion was an emphatic 'Yes!' What would have been the outcome had Lachlan Renshaw developed his aerobic power over the major part of his running career in Australia? Maybe we got a clue from that late career personal best time, but we'll never know.

Specificity of training: the session

Can we develop anaerobic power or capacity in the same session as aerobic power, or vice versa? This would appear to be entirely feasible if we include respective training elements into the one session. For example beginning the session with a solid aerobic power developing 2km or 3km run, then introducing some anaerobic power work like a set of 300s. But would it be better for the overall adaptation of the runner to concentrate on one characteristic per session? To plan one session focusing on aerobic power, for example the 3km run plus some strong aerobic short-rest 400s, and focusing the next training session exclusively on anaerobic work like an extended set of 300m efforts with long passive recovery?

There is no solid evidence to support one approach or the other in highly-trained athletes, but we might consider that adaptation of skeletal muscle cells require specific instructions from genes, the expression of which can be 'directed' toward achieving a particular goal. One might hypothesise or even expect, then that mixed messages for adaptation to the stresses of high contractile speed and power as well as low contractile speed and power might produce a dampened response in both areas. But so what? Dampened, more gradual responses might produce a better response in the long term. After all mixing up the power supply is exactly what happens in middle-distance running so this form of training might be considered more race-specific.

Another consideration is that the relative merit of these approaches depends on the training phase. As we approach the competition, we might increase the emphasis on more complex (mixed energy system) training sessions on the premise that these are more specific to racing requirements. Even if we accept this, nothing should be set in stone in coaching, and there may be times when a complex session might suit an early phase and a more concentrated session in a later stage. This is the art of coaching, no sessions or even general principles should be set in stone; they serve to guide a coach's thoughts for the specificity of the occasion, but that's all.

Specificity of training: the phase

The common practice in middle-distance running is to plan a winter aerobic phase followed by pre-competition phase of race-pace and anaerobic work. But is this the best way to arrange training or are we better off to include each of these forms of training in one extended training phase, constantly working toward improvements in every aspect of middle and distance running fitness?

Working on specific phases of predominantly aerobic, followed by anaerobic training is generally favoured by successful coaches of elite level athletes, whose improvements are smaller and more difficult to achieve than in developing athletes. A more intense focus on an energy system within a phase of training provides a better opportunity to overload elite athletes and that's probably why the phasic approach to training has earned its proven track record in international athletics. Distinct phasic training was popularized by the Eastern Bloc sports institute research as well as coaches such as Arthur Lydiard and Franz Stampfl in the Western World. It lends itself more to the middle-distance rather than to marathon runners, most marathon coaches favouring aerobic power and endurance training all year round, punctuated only by recovery periods from races.

What about the order of these aerobic and anaerobic phases? It makes sense to build an 'aerobic base' cake before dealing with putting the icing on with the introduction of faster work. Runners will explain that they feel the need to regenerate their aerobic base following a period of competition, during which reduced training volume accompanies increased average speed of sessions. A period of lower intensity training following a stressful period of competition makes eminent sense. Human bodies and minds are very resilient, but it is a fact of high performance running that injuries are common, and not just to the body. A series of racing stresses over 800m or a build-up to an all-out effort over 42.195km needs to be respected to allow body and mind to recover even if the occasional highly motivated athlete (usually the long-distance runner!) may suggest otherwise.

How long should an aerobic phase build-up be? Coaches generally favour the seasonal approach. Obviously more practical, 6 months of winter seems to provide a reasonable period of time to recover and then achieve the intended adaptations. There are always exceptions. Some athletes thrive on competition programs others simply can't contemplate. Mistakes are common though, where the lure of financial reward dulls common sense, but sometimes managers, coaches and athletes are prepared to take the risk, not being too concerned about the potential brevity of an athletic career. Another consideration is that optimal length of a phase of training may depend on the athletic experience. Athletes seem to have an inbuilt 'fitness memory', meaning that those who have trained for many years and achieved high levels of fitness a number of times are more likely to respond to training more rapidly. Such an occurrence might be explained by epigenetic modifications. A set of genes whose role is to stimulate production of proteins and so improve fitness (e.g. by making more mitochondrial enzymes) might become more efficient following repeated training experiences. Interestingly, a similar process might also apply to an 'altitude memory'; athletes who have regularly trained at moderate altitudes seem to respond more rapidly to their next hypoxic stimulus than the uninitiated.

Specificity of training: speed

Race-pace training is likely to be an important inclusion into the training program. It's a fair bet that regular training at race-pace will improve running economy at race-pace, although I must admit to a lack of solid evidence.

However, it seems to me that running at race-pace provides an opportunity to optimize the balance of physiology and biomechanics at this most important speed. For example, the more obvious aspects of our physiology such as respiration rate and heart rate, as well as less obvious ones such as cellular ATP production may all be dependent to some degree on the speed-related pattern of muscle contraction and relaxation. Most runners will tell us that getting a race or two under the belt makes a big difference to performance, even after a lengthy and intensive training build-up. This may have something to do with a physiology-biomechanics matching effect that comes about from true race-pace experience.

That leads on to another question, 'Do distance and middle-distance runners benefit from training at faster than their race speed?'.

Experience suggests that they might. We could link this to the generally vague principle of training variety, as it certainly would increase variety. But runners not only enjoy the opportunity to run faster than race-pace at times in training, but they've often reported that they feel better when 'speed' work is introduced into of the program. For example, Olympic medallist marathoner Lisa Martin (Ondieki) always enjoyed a set of 200s on most Mondays after her long run on Sunday and marathoner Michael Shelley welcomes a set of 400s every now and then to allow him to 'turn the legs over'. Faster running means increased speed and force of contraction, and an accelerated oxygen uptake as well as increased anaerobic contribution. Then there is the pure enjoyment of running freely and fluently over shorter distances that even a hard-nosed distance runner will appreciate. But whether benefits of faster than race-pace running are physiological, biomechanical, or psychological is not of great importance. A wise coach listens to his or her athletes and learns.

When faster than race-pace produced the goods

Departing temporarily from the world of elite athletes, I was preparing for a 1500m race as a 40 year-old 'masters' runner looking for my first sub-2 minute, 800m, and sub-4 minute 1500m, working hard to regain some speed I could vaguely recall I possessed from my football days. I wondered whether that speed was simply history following nearly a decade of high volume marathon training. Professor Terry Dwyer, soon to become President of Athletics Australia (and later Director of the hugely productive Murdoch Children's Research Institute) was watching me on the track at the AIS.

'Dick, I reckon a good session for you would be four all-out 400s with five minutes recovery'. Terry had a keen eye for middle-distance running, having been a well-performed middle-distance runner himself in his younger days. I took this advice and made it one of my stock sessions. What he was telling me, was that I needed to work specifically on the anaerobic capacity side of my fitness to fast-track my pathway to best 1500m performance.

He was right, and in coming weeks as this session improved, so did my 1500m and 800m.

Modes of training

Training can be classified many ways. The classification that suits my way of thinking is aerobic interval training, anaerobic interval training, sustained running, hill work, resistance training, cross-training, altitude training, and heat training. Let's expand on these now but we'll consider the more complex and controversial role of altitude training in distance running in a separate chapter.

Following in the footsteps of Emil Zatopek and Franz Stampfl, most if not all runners and coaches of the modern eras recognize the value of interval training. Interval training makes use of controlled peaks and troughs of speed and power, characteristics of training not exploited by sustained running over an equivalent duration or distance. That's not to say it's better than a sustained effort, it's just different.

Interval training can produce a variety of training stresses, depending on the speed and duration of the repetition and the recovery.

Aerobic interval training

The terms 'threshold', 'maximum steady state' or 10km race-pace are basically all the same thing. In the middle of a solid training week the normal maximal distance we expect to sustain 10km race-pace is about four laps at the track or 1600m, and if done correctly, 1 min 30 sec to 2 minutes is sufficient recovery. Longer repetitions are usually performed at something a little less than 10km race-pace.

Moving up from threshold to maximal aerobic power work provides a more intense stimulus to the aerobic power supply. But any effort approaching V̇O2max is accompanied by a high anaerobic complement. Consequently it demands a longer recovery time, not just between repetitions, but also between these types of sessions. In the middle of a training week, near-maximal efforts of 600m to 1km will produce a maximal aerobic power peak in an experienced runner. A recovery of 3-5 minutes is sufficient, middle-distance runners needing a longer recovery than distance runners given their superior speed and lactic anaerobic power.

Anaerobic Interval training

Anaerobic capacity is the total amount of anaerobic work that can be done at near top speed before exhaustion cuts the engines. Anaerobic power is the rate at which anaerobic work can be done; the power developed at full throttle.

Although direct assault on the anaerobic capacity via interval training efforts of say 400m repetitions are effective, there are other ways to increase anaerobic capacity. Running 500s, 600s, or even 800s and 1km will also challenge and so improve anaerobic capacity. These longer repetitions are not as fast as a set of 300s or 400s so the anaerobic power is lower and may not be as specific to the 400m event. However, the anaerobically initiated disruption of homeostasis occurs over a longer period of time in the longer repetitions, and may even produce a greater amount of anaerobic energy than the shorter repetitions. In any case, longer repetition anaerobic efforts are more specific to middle-distance racing and are well-suited to the pre-competition phase.

Hill training

Most of the important races are on fairly horizontal surfaces and this applies to all outdoor track races and the fast big city marathons. Exceptions are cross-country races where hills add to the experience, some of the famous big city Fun Runs, and of course mountain racing and orienteering events. Athletic tracks are generally fairly flat, although I've heard many an athlete swear the last 100m of an 800m is uphill. Road race directors usually provide flattish routes as runners and race organizers love fast times. A reputation for a fast course is a strong lure for any runner.

The principle of specificity would suggest that track and road runners might be best served by training mainly on flat surfaces. Likewise the mountain race specialists and orienteer competitors might benefit most by training mainly on hills and rough surfaces. This does make sense, but the principle of training variety needs to be considered along with that of specificity. Best race performance is not achieved with purely race specific training. If that were the case, and taking specificity to its extreme, training might consist of just running time-trials and races. But after an intense period of racing, form begins to fade away, only to be recovered by a period of training focusing at the basic components of fitness.

Hill work can contribute to flat race performance. One advantage of hill work is that in lifting the body against gravity we are able to generate high power without high speed, so reducing, or at least changing the usual anatomic stress and reducing risk of injury. We can also profit from hill work in the downhill component, where faster speeds can be attained, but a word of caution: gravity-assisted running of this type may have advantages in improving fluency of movement and running speed, but it also adds to the risk of injury, with its increasing emphasis on shorter and sharper eccentric muscle activity. Learning to flow downhill to minimize breaking is a skill worth developing. It's not a natural exercise to 'free-wheel' down a hill and clearly we need to ease into this sort of training, which initially requires a solid, relatively smooth and gentler gradient.

Hill running in both the up and down directions at good speed is clearly the most specific form of training for mountain running and orienteering competition. For these events, runners might even seek, rather than avoid rough hilly training surfaces. Such training will assist what we might call 'proprioception training', to develop the 'brains' in the joints as they negotiate unexpected nooks and crannies in the running surface. The ankle is the joint often under the greatest challenge and the nerve endings can be trained to do its own 'thinking' to rock and roll with the bumps of usual competition terrain.

Exceptions to the rule

As is often the case in science, art and coaching, there are exceptions to the rule. For some runners, hill work is not an option. Olympian Lisa Weightman and rookie marathoner Melanie Panayiotou (who coincidentally rings me excitedly just as I write this paragraph to tell me she has been selected for the 2014 Commonwealth Games in Glasgow) were introduced to hills through my training programs. Lisa, despite taking things reasonably quietly at first, developed hamstring soreness. Mel also took care not to overdo things, but developed soreness around the sacrum area. I certainly wasn't prepared to take any further risk once the soreness subsided and removed hill work from both programs.

It wasn't as though I was too worried about an absence of hill training affecting these running careers. Marathoner Lisa Ondieki won an Olympic silver medal and a couple of Commonwealth Games gold medals without doing any hill work, even in her long runs; except for negotiating the minor undulations around Lake Burley Griffin in Canberra. I was very pleasantly surprised when Lisa ran strongly through the challenging San Francisco Bay to Breakers with its notorious 'Heartbreak Hill' and the even more challenging Sydney City to Surf with its seemingly never ending uphill climbs and its long downhill run into Bondi beach to finish. Lisa won both of these races and certainly proved hill running sessions weren't necessary to win hilly big city road races. It's possible of course that she could have run even better in those hilly races had we introduced hill work into her training program, but I must admit it's hard to imagine she could have done too much better.

One of my favourite sessions with my Canberra-based middle and long-distance running group is one we call the AIS double hills. This session, in the bushy surrounds of the Australian Institute of Sport involves a varied inclination but finally steep hill section on one side and another of lesser inclination on the other. Doing the 'double-hill' session involves running up one side and down the other, turning around and doing it in reverse. Each 'double hill' takes about 6 minutes, 1:30 min up and down each way, depending on how it is negotiated. We vary this hill session according to the response we want to generate. Maximal power hills involve repeated all-out efforts and slow jog downs. Threshold hills are performed by holding back up the hill to ensure continued strong running over the top and sustained running down the other side. In the latter session the aim is to keep the heart rate as steady as possible, on the down as well as the up. Fast running down is a skill that is worth developing even for flat race runners, but lesser gradients are better suited for this type of work.

Fast downhill running may have other advantages. Firstly, it might translate into better running economy. After all, running downhill is really a specific and repeated plyometric activity so has a good chance of increasing tendon elasticity and promoting better conservation of energy. Secondly training with increased eccentric loading by running downhill has the potential to 'toughen up' running musculature, rendering muscle more resilient, more resistant to damage.

Some runners have an uncanny ability to recover between heats and finals or after races. The champion Ethiopians and Kenyans in particular demonstrate this remarkably well. One obvious reason is that they negotiate their preliminary races at lower speeds relative to their maximum than less gifted runners, minimizing metabolic stress. Another reason might be their relatively slender body types and lightness on the feet minimise the mechanical stress on muscles and joints. Africans are well known for their high quality group runs through the bush trails, and their downhill running may play a significant part in their ability to 'back up' after races.

However, as with any form of training, too much can be damaging. One of the Ethiopian athletes I looked after in Australia loved to run very fast in his hill session. Extraordinarily talented Australian Olympian Mizan Mehari (he ran a 13:34 5km at the age of 16) loved to train with great intensity at all times. Unfortunately Mizan's motor was too powerful for his chassis, and he failed to take advice on the impending danger of this mismatch. Mizan's reluctance to accept that recovery days were a vital aspect of any athlete's running program led to a series of recurring injuries that ultimately ended his brilliant but all too short career in his early 20s.

Long slow running

Long runs, even long slow runs are considered important by most coaches and athletes, and many would consider that they contribute to aerobic power. Arthur Lydiard proselytized the long run, and was one of the first, if not the first to introduce long running to middle-distance runners. Maybe volume, not just the rate of aerobic energy production makes an independent contribution to aerobic power, especially in the early phases of aerobic development, after which higher levels of aerobic power training may be required for further adaptation. In any case, long runs fit in well during the build-up phase, for other reasons, physical and psychological. We know for sure that repeated challenge to a muscle's energy stores is the primary method of increasing the capacity of those stores.

The 'long slow' title can be misleading, especially as it applies to elite runners. More often than not, long slow runs are a series of harder and easier efforts, perhaps better viewed as a prolonged interval training up and down short and long hills, and striding out along flat stretches. Throw in the added stress of a reduced number of oxygen molecules in each breath at moderate altitude and we have another dimension to long running. Then there's the group effect. Running in a pack of motivated distance runners is often far from a long pedestrian-like affair. Just ask those who participate in the legendary Sunday morning runs over the hills of the Dandenong Ranges on the outskirts of Melbourne or the Stromlo Forest in the in-skirts of Canberra. Or simply ask any top east-African runner.

We wouldn't ever train that hard!

A group of female Japanese runners were training at the Gold Coast one year, and one of the Australian helpers to the Japanese group commented to me and my new marathoner Nickey Carroll that he'd just watched them do a track session of forty 400s. The session lasted nearly two hours. Nickey was amazed.

'Wow' she said 'that's a massive session. How do those girls do it? With that sort of discipline it's no wonder they do so well.'

'Yes that is a big session Nickey' I commented, 'but you're going along pretty well so let's not worry about trying to replicate that sort of robotic behaviour, let's stick to our plan. You've got your long run tomorrow. Remember what it was?'

'I sure do,' she smiled, 'it's our (meaning 'her') 32km run we normally do, and we (meaning 'I') really work solidly on all of those hills, then for the last 5km I run in as strongly as I can.'

'Correct' I smiled.

In the Australian bush forest trails Nickey had at least 30 hills to be negotiated with good quality, some shorter, only 200m, some longer up to 600m, some interspersed with longer straighter stretches others without much recovery on the flat. The temperature was in the high 20s, it took a good 2 ½ hours and Nickey spent the rest of the day recovering.

'Thank your lucky stars you haven't got that Japanese coach, Nickey, I wouldn't ever set you anything as hard as the sort of interval sessions those girls did!'

Nickey was probably wondering why I was smiling.

A long run in a small world

I have fond running memories of Alice Springs and surrounds. This trip was no exception. It was a Sports Medicine Australia convention, and I was enjoying a run out the back of our hotel into the scrub with Dr Tim Noakes, author of *The Lore of Running*. (By the way whoever borrowed my hard copy 14 years ago, have you finished? I'd like it back).

I wanted to get my weekly long run in that afternoon so I was keen to do a few extra miles more than Tim, and decided to keep going out a bit longer as he turned back. It had been a hot day, and everything was red as the sun settled down on the MacDonnell Ranges. I figured that as long as I ran directly away from the sunset, and then ran directly back into it I wouldn't get lost. There wasn't really any trail, but the slightly loose surface on a hard dirt base made for pleasant running, where watching the ground was more to make sure I didn't step on any local wildlife.

Then out of nowhere there he was, running alongside me. The young man of obvious indigenous heritage had an engaging smile with white teeth flashing from a handsome brown face. His shorts were a bit on the tattered side and his feet were bare. This chap certainly wasn't here for the training and must live somewhere nearby in the bush. That's doing it pretty tough I thought as I was now about 12km from my idea of civilization.

He made an enquiry 'What the hell you doing out here mate?'

'I'm training for a marathon' I replied. 'I live in Canberra and there's a conference I'm attending in Alice. What about you? Do you live out here?',

I conjured up thoughts of a typical nomad on his way to Alice to get some supplies.

'Hell no mate, I'm just out here visiting my girlfriend. Her house is only a couple of kilometres away and I thought I'd try to find a bit of bush tucker. Not that I usually eat out here.'

We both had a good laugh when he added 'I live in Canberra as well ... studying at the ANU!'

It was time to turn around and head back west as the glimmer of sunset was fast disappearing.

'Thanks for the run mate' he said. I asked him to give me a call at the AIS when he got back to Canberra, and I added 'We could go for a run around Black Mountain.'

It's a small world.

On middle-distance and mileage

Is running 120km to 150km a week during the build-up phase the best way to prepare that 'base' most coaches feel is so important even for a race that lasts less than 4 minutes? Or would the winter months be better spent working on more specific fitness requirements of the race? We've discussed Lydiard views, and his long running base has produced some great results. Encouraging as this is, when it comes to the crunch it proves nothing. Who is to say that instead of the ninety minute or two-hour runs over winter each week that a faster 1 hour run might not have produced equal or even better results?

We've suggested that long slow training builds resilience but we could just as easily have argued that running high volumes increases the risk of overuse injury and that the weight of evidence would suggest that it is the faster higher aerobic power running rather than the slow training that is more likely have the better effect on aerobic power.

Then there's the school of thought that the addition of 8-10km runs as second runs each day aid recovery between the quality training sessions. But how can more running, albeit slow, lead to recovery from faster running? It doesn't help glycogen replenishment; if anything it's doing the opposite. Perhaps these between-session runs help recovery by stimulating blood flow to fatigued muscles, but if this is the objective, then why not some non-weight bearing physical activity such as swimming walking, and a good massage, along with some easy stretching?

All in all, there really doesn't seem to be any compelling argument for 1500m runners, let alone 800m runners to undertake high mileage phases of training. Evidence is lacking to support the premise that 1500m runners benefit from a period of slow relaxed 25-30km runs, especially in comparison with faster 8-15km runs. A more compelling argument to set long runs for a middle-distance runner would be when they take the form of a long fartlek session; it's easy to see value in that but that's not a long slow run.

Now that I've put my case, what do I recommend for the middle-distance running off-season build-up over winter? Well, I happen to like that Sunday medium or long run but not as a regular long slow run. Adhering to the principle of training variety, I like to vary the pace, sometimes moving along at a good pace with as steady 'puff' as I like to describe it to my troops; or as a series of hills introducing the fartlek element. Occasionally though there's place for a 'body-mind recovery' run, a leisurely enjoyable run with the group on a Sunday morning followed by the group coffee!

Reducing footstrike force

This usually takes the form of water running or cycling; often referred to as cross-training. These modes of exercise remove the sharp eccentrically developed forces we deal with during footstrike which appear to play a major part in overuse injuries. Cross-training can sustain certain aspects of endurance fitness in a runner during periods where soreness prevents or hinders usual running training.

However, there seems to be little point in adding cycling or swimming to a running training program in an elite runner who is already training twice a day on several if not all days of the week. There is a fair point made in substituting a 'recovery' run with another, mode of exercise, especially when that extra recovery run is suspected to be the straw (or extra stress) that breaks the camel's back (or runner's navicular).

Water running sessions are best confined to short repetitions of 10 seconds through to 2 minutes. In this way high knees and strong arm actions can be performed at contraction speeds more closely resembling running, the assumption being that this would transfer more readily to running fitness. Variation in form can be achieved by wearing a float vest; but experienced water runners happily (perhaps grudgingly is a better adverb) proceed without a vest which increases the metabolic cost.

The principle of specificity would also suggest that in the water an upright posture should be maintained and a range of hip and shoulder movement similar to that of running. The same is true for cycling work for a runner. It doesn't make a lot of sense just sitting on a bike and rolling along using the usual hip extensors with the mid-foot on the pedal. A runner can profit more from cycling by getting out of the saddle at times (assuming this doesn't aggravate the injury) to permit a more upright body position and full extension of the knee. Toe-clips increase the benefit of the cross-training too. The 'ankling' action with the toe on the pedals brings anterior lower leg muscles into play along with the calf muscles and pulling up on the pedals using the toe-clips activates the hip flexors.

However, a gentle word of warning for keen cross-trainers. Don't assume that you are injury risk free with water running or cycling, just because ground impact and eccentric muscle activity has been removed. Introducing any new activity is best done with caution, and a novel muscular activity of any type can cause problems in a highly motivated athlete. Pat Carroll, a former excellent runner and scholarship holder at the AIS and now a popular coach and running enthusiast, was as conscientious and dedicated as any athlete I've come across. At one stage he was diagnosed with a stress fracture and advised to substitute his usual running sessions with water running. He took this to the letter and instead of his usual track session of 8 x 400m, with a 200m float, he replicated this in the pool; instead of his hour runs in the bush he water ran for an hour; his 1hr 45 min Wednesday and 2hr 30 min Sunday run in the forest were replicated by time in the pool. Pat was undertaking his usual program but in removing impact he assumed this was risk free training. So he did a bit more, a two-hour session in the pool being the norm for the day.

Now stress fractures are often thought to be caused by repetitive forces applied by contracting muscles to the surface of the bone to which they are attached. It's this repeated tugging at the bony surface that can lead to damage and we all learned a lesson when Pat developed a new stress fracture in the pelvis area at the insertion site of his hip flexor muscles. The hip flexors are employed during land based running of course but in water running the contraction phase is longer and applied against a constant resistance throughout the duration of the contraction. Pat's newly introduced extreme water running had exceeded the athlete's adaptive capacity and a new weak link emerged despite the absence of footstrike. Plan B had to be put into action; to rest completely, then introduce any cross training with more caution. Pat recovered and his career highlight was his terrific 2:09:39 to win the 1995 Beppu marathon.

There are a couple of more recent methods of reducing the footstrike reaction forces. Elliptical training devices were based on the principles of cycle ergometers but designed to more closely replicate the action and increased energy output of running while removing the sharp forces involved in footstrike. They combine a dampened heel-toe movement of running in a smooth continual action with some upper body work through hand held levers. In effect the technique falls somewhere between cycling and uphill treadmill running. In removing impact with the ground and using the propulsive muscles of running, albeit with different contractile patterns, it is a useful form of cross training for rehabilitating runners or simply as an occasional replacement for running in the regular training program.

Even more recently on the market is a treadmill integrated device called the AlterG where air is pumped into a plastic airtight sleeve around the lower body, applying a vertical force and so lifting the body off the treadmill. This effectively reduces body weight and the force of footstrike impact. Runners can dial up the body weight equivalent to as low as 20 percent body weight, and wearing tight neoprene shorts they generally feel reasonably comfortable, reporting that their normal technique is closely replicated.

This form of light treadmill running might also be put to good use in general training as well as rehabilitation, although in reducing ground reaction forces runners do less work and heart rate is correspondingly lower at any given running speed. Consequently the training load is not as great as normal running. But because a runner can run faster, the preparatory or non-running propulsive muscles such as the hip flexors are unaffected. In fact, marathoner Lisa Weightman tells me that after using the AlterG she tends to run faster when she returns to train in a normal environment. The reduced-weight training might be considered a kind of neuromuscular training, resetting the perception of contractile speed of muscles involved in the knee lift and so increasing stride frequency. To fully exploit this effect, the propulsive muscles of the hip knee and ankle would need to adapt in the same way to avoid any mismatch. During rehabilitation this might be achieved through cycling or resistance training through squats and calf raises, assuming of course that they were compatible with the rehabilitation process.

Use of this AlterG is more costly that water running, and just as I write this section, Ben Ashkettle, a New Zealander aiming to quality for the Rio Olympics in the marathon, calls and informs me that a half-hour session will cost him $30. This precludes its regular use to most runners but elite athletes in Australia do have free access through support through their state sports institute. All in all, the AlterG technology offers another form of training to reduce the impact of footstrike, and does so with greater specificity than cycling, elliptical training and water running. A combination of each of these modes of exercise would seem to be ideal for a rehabilitating runner, where variety may not just release the load on the body, but release the load on the mind as well!

Resistance training

Systematic increments in the resistance to muscle contraction using body weight, added weights or machines increases the force with which the muscle can contract. When contractile speeds are slow and resistance is high we say we are training muscular strength. Proponents of this high resistance training for middle and long-distance runners assume that developing strength at slower speeds of contraction will transfer over to improved power at the faster speeds associated with running. It is also assumed that the increased power developed at slower muscle contractile speeds increases the ability to repeat the faster low power running muscle contractions more times before fatigue sets in. In other words that increased muscle strength leads to increased muscle endurance.

But is this the case?

It certainly makes sense for sprinters to participate in high resistance training because they have a high resistance power exercise to perform every time they start a race. Minimizing the time to get to top speed from a stationary position in the blocks is an important factor in sprinting over the 100m, 200m and 400m events. And given that sprinting consists of a sequence of powerful eccentric and concentric muscle contractions together with extensive exploitation of the elastic properties of musculature and tendon around the hip, knee and ankle, the value of high resistance training should not be questioned in sprinters.

But is resistance training an important adjunct to middle and long-distance training? Yes, it is, but it becomes a consideration of the balance in the sense that the middle-distance runner must train to develop the optimal combination of explosive (alactic) anaerobic power, lactic anaerobic power and capacity and aerobic power. A point of concern is fatigue and potential injury. In considering training balance, residual fatigue and muscle fibre damage induced by non-running activities can affect the quality of specific running sessions, and even lead to injury if recovery time between high quality running sessions is compromised. So the relative importance of resistance training is dependent on the event. The shorter the event the greater the requirements for speed and power so greater is the potential benefit of resistance training.

We have all heard of successful middle and long-distance runners who have used extensive resistance training and others who haven't. But a point in favour of resistance training for any runner is that middle and long-distance runners alike need good finishing speed to excel. Championships races can become 'cat and mouse' events with sudden kick-downs into high speed 200 or 300m sprints home being common in any distance event.

As to how and when to introduce resistance training into the program, machine and free-weight resistance work in the gym is one way, but circuits using body weight is a form of resistance training that may suit your group better than gym work. Plyometric work is a variation of resistance training. Bounding, jumping from a box and re-bounding, tuck jumps or one-legged hopping and jumping squats are plyometric forms of resistance training. Hill training is a form of resistance training; which because of its specificity may even be the best form of resistance training for long-distance runners. There are many permutations and combinations for coaches to consider; the extent and mode of resistance training requiring consideration of age, event, access to facilities, and injury history.

In further support of resistance training for middle and long-distance runners, is the role it can play in strengthening postural muscles. The muscles that maintain our optimal posture during running are also subject to fatigue. So resistance work, in helping prevent those inevitable changes in fatigue-induced running form, may indirectly contribute to better running performance.

And I've left a word of warning until last. It's asking for trouble if you or your runners engage in high speed running or even high volume running with residual soreness from resistance training. Soreness signifies minor or major trauma to musculature and surrounding tissues, and associated inflammatory processes are probably the culprits upsetting the way a muscle contracts and relaxes. If the timing of the contraction and relaxation phase of running is disrupted and the muscle is partly contracted when it should be relaxing, then an injury is likely as the muscle tends to tear itself apart. Over the years, I've seen instances of hamstring or calf fatigue from resistance squats or calf raises preceding injuries to these muscle groups during subsequent running sessions. I sometimes wonder whether this kind of neuromuscular dysfunction is behind the commonly reported hamstring injuries in professional footballers, where weight-training is emphasized, and training in is often twice day.

Consistency of training

We usually think of adaptation to running training, i.e. getting fitter, as occurring in response to a gradual increase in the volume or intensity of training or both. Chris Wardlaw, an Olympic marathoner himself and former astute coach of champion marathoners including Steve Moneghetti and Kerryn McCann, has always stressed the importance of consistency of training. He places great value in training at an intensity that permits uninterrupted training. It is not really building 'strength' in the true sense of the word, as resistance training was not a great part of the Wardlaw program, but 'strength' is a word that the distance running fraternity identifies with general endurance and resilience. Former coach of Rob de Castella, Pat Clohessy was another who valued consistency of training highly, often de-emphasising any need to make continual improvements to standard training sessions, but rather treating the weeks and months of training as the main stimulus for improvement.

It's not surprising that many athletes, especially the marathon breed, take great pride and care in recording training mileage in their training diaries, sometimes to the point of obsession, to ensure weekly training volume was maintained at all costs.

I remember cautioning de Castella against training at a time where he was clearly unwell. His training diary proved a stronger influence than my words of caution and out he went for his 32km run, painfully slow, but it got done; and just as importantly, recorded. It certainly hindered the quality of his training in the remainder of that week, but the training diary showed no impediment in relation to volume as another 200km de Castella week was chalked up.

'We can't afford to get soft' Rob told me.

Taking a check on Rob de Castella's blood lactic acid level.
Image: Australian Sports Commission

Fair enough, I thought to myself, as I came to realize that this was the hallmark of a world champion. He epitomised the old adage that what didn't kill him made him stronger. I conceded. He didn't die soldiering through that 32 km, and he probably did get stronger; at least between the ears.

Consistency of training, coupled with gradual progressions in running intensity or volume or both will produce the best response to training. The greatest threat to consistency in a motivated runner is injury so this is where close coach-athlete communication is so important. In my book, at risk of being deemed a bit soft by the de Castella standards, consistency does not mean continuity at all costs. Sometimes the human body requires a little extra time other than the 8 or 24 hours between training sessions to organize its recovery and adaptation. A running free day is far from being 'soft'; in many cases it is eminently sensible, permitting more consistency of training in the long run.

Having been witness to so much illness and injury in marathon runners over the years, I have come to suspect some sort of epigenetic modification in these runners. Could it be that a group of genes responsible for "eminent sense' have been down-regulated by their high mileage?

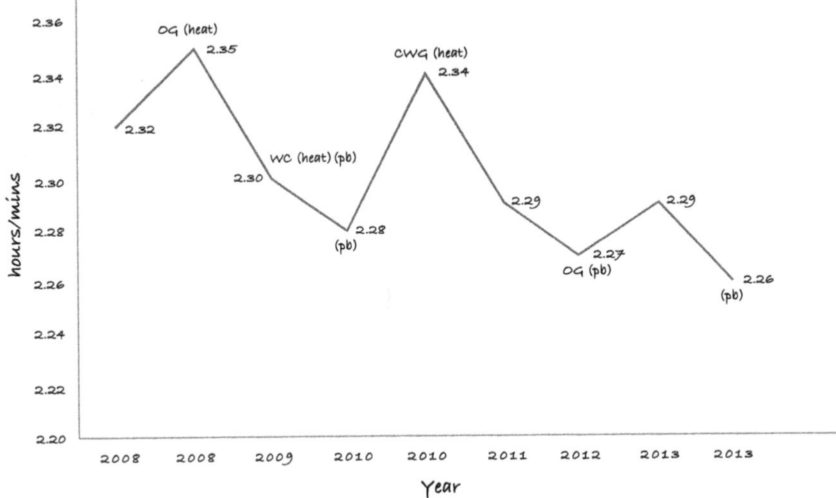

Figure 9-1: Marathon time progression for Lisa Weightman, who has been rewarded for her consistent training after a number of years of persistent injury. In 2014 Lisa gave birth to her first child Peter Richard.

Chapter 10 Classifying training

'If you don't know where you are going, any road will take you there.'

Lewis Carroll

Setting training is one thing; understanding individual responses is another.

No need to be concerned if you don't have access to laboratory assessments of $\dot{V}O2max$ and economy or anaerobic capacity. These tests are useful for gaining a general understanding of running performance, and certainly for researching new ideas about training, but they're not essential by any means in designing training to bring out the best in a runner.

Nevertheless there is one characteristic that coaches can put to very good use in preparing training programs, and that is the so-called anaerobic threshold speed which we've referred to simply as 'threshold' or 'maximal steady state' speed. This is the fastest speed at which a runner's biochemical control or homeostasis can be maintained during sustained running over a period of around 30 minutes.

And to determine this speed all we need is a stop watch.

Measuring threshold speed

In the exercise physiology lab 'anaerobic threshold' is measured during a progressively faster treadmill protocol as the speed/gradient combinationat which blood lactate or our respiration starts to get out of control. Heart rate, oxygen uptake, blood lactate, treadmill speed and inclination are noted.

But the only equipment coaches need to measure this characteristic is a track or flat road to conduct a time trial, a stop watch, a wrist watch heart rate monitor and reasonable weather.

In an un-tapered training condition, the middle portion of an 8km trial, i.e. the average speed from 2km to 6km on a flat hard surface is a pretty good indication of threshold speed. Alternatively, we can use the middle 6km of a 10km race following a suitable preparation. The steady heart rate (we say steady but it always tends to drift up a bit) is useful, because when we train on hills, or in hot weather, or in windy conditions an athlete may be producing a threshold effort physiologically but at lower than threshold speed. Heart rate then becomes a better indicator of training intensity and stress than speed.

Exploiting the threshold speed

We can make good use of threshold speed (or heart rate) in training, designing sessions spot-on threshold, or above or below threshold. Each has its place in a well-balanced program.

Figures 10-1 to 10-14 show sessions undertaken by runners in my group. Following each session, these runners provide me with a report of speed, duration of efforts, elevation changes if off the track, heart rates, weather conditions and a comment as to how they feel. With this knowledge I can determine the success or otherwise of the session. These reports are particularly useful for athletes situated interstate or internationally where I haven't been present at the session.

Training reports sometimes lead to modification of ensuing sessions. For example, if speed has not reached the expected level in a session targeted as threshold, and heart rates are correspondingly low, then that might suggest residual muscular fatigue is a limiting factor; perhaps through insufficient muscle glycogen replenishment following the previous days' training. If discussion with the athlete is consistent with this conclusion, an extra easier day (or days) may be introduced before challenging the runner with any similarly high quality session.

Without this feedback I run the risk of being misled as to the precise training that has taken place. For example, an intended threshold session may have turned out to be a sub-threshold endurance session. This needs to be understood, and appropriate steps taken to accomplish the true objective next time.

Characterising training sessions

Reproducibility

Reproducibility or reliability is an important characteristic of any measurement, especially one upon which training judgments are based. We have to have confidence, for example, that a lower heart rate during a particular session in not likely to be just a chance variation or methodological error of the watch. On the other hand, we have to expect some sort of variation from session to session. Athletes aren't Swiss watches. Diet, sleep, and training immediately prior to these sessions can change an athlete's response to training as can mood and motivation.

As it turns out, observations of repeated sessions in various athletes over the year do indicate pretty good reproducibility of heart rate response. Here is a typical example of a repeated session in a male distance runner.

Two identical sessions were run 4 days apart. Session 1 was run on a bush trail one week after a 10km track race. Session 2 conducted at the same venue 4 days later.

Set piece (in minutes): 1',2',3',4',5',4',3',2',1' (all with 1' recovery jog).

The distances covered were (in kilometres):

Session 1 – 0.36, 0.68, 1.02, 1.36, 1.65, 1.33, 1.02, 0.7, 0.37.

Session 2 – 0.35, 0. 68, 1.04, 1.37, 1.68, 1.33, 1.01, 0. 69, 0. 37.

After Session 1 the athlete commented he felt quite good but not fully recovered from the race. After Session 2 the athlete commented he felt a little better than last week.

Given the variation in circumstances prior to each session we might expect some variation in the performance and the heart rate response. As you see, for the distances covered and the heart rate as shown in Figures 10-1 and 10-2 below, the variation was relatively minor. We have good reproducibility of the responses in an elite level athlete.

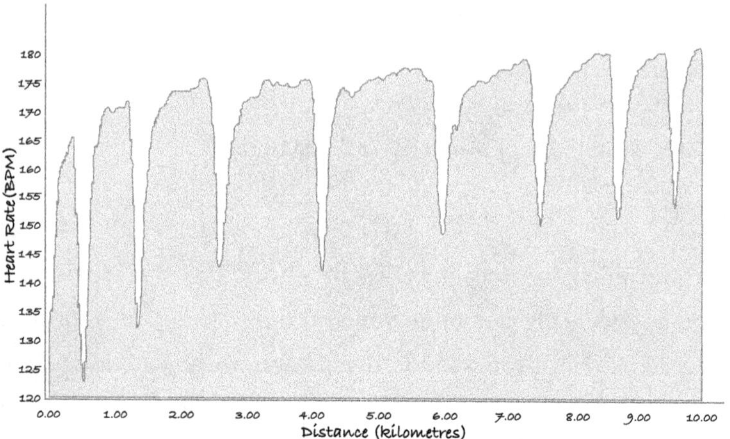

Figure 10-1: Session 1 to check reliability.
A ladder of 1', 2', 3', 4', 5', 4', 3', 2', 1', (minutes with 1 minute recovery).

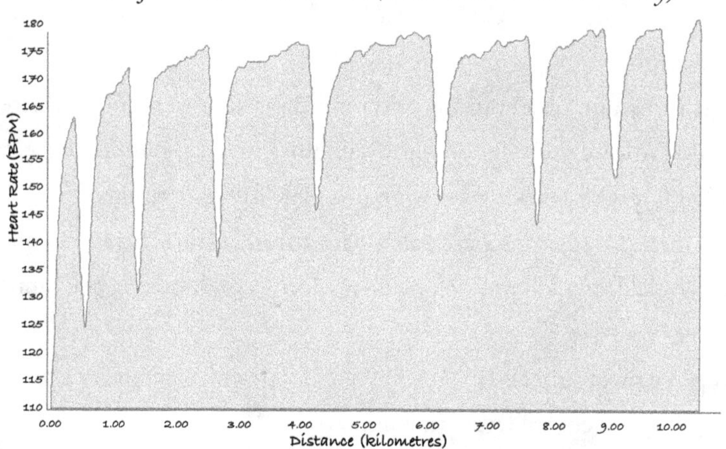

Figure 10-2: Session 2 to check reliability.
A ladder of 1', 2', 3', 4', 5', 4', 3', 2', 1', (minutes with 1 minute recovery).

The following graphs and comments on some training sessions help us understand what the training is achieving and so help with ongoing program design. Athletes providing the examples were good athletes running between 28 and 29 minutes for 10,000m around the time of the sessions.

Our working definition of threshold speed is as the average speed attained over the middle 8km of a 10km best effort, the maximal cruising speed. We refer to any faster running as supra-threshold speed and anything slower as sub-threshold.

Typically a well-conditioned distance runner has to run with a good deal of motivation to reach threshold speed (10km speed) during the course of a solid training week in the untapered state. An appropriate duration for a threshold speed repetition is 5 or 6 minutes. Longer efforts make it very difficult to hold threshold speed. More often than not the session becomes a sub-threshold speed session. That is not to say that longer efforts are less effective. For example, in a marathoner an excellent session might be a sub-threshold speed but longer effort, which is more like marathon pace. The specific matching of physiology and biomechanics that occurs when a 10km runner trains at his or her 10km speed is less relevant for the marathoner. In the middle of a solid training week, if the marathoner runs as well as possible in a 10-20 minute piece then it is likely that all the physiological characteristics of a threshold session will be achieved, i.e. the required heart rate and aerobic power, despite the fact that 10km speed is not attained. Indeed it is more event-specific than the 10km speed work because it is closer to marathon pace and may have some added benefit of improving economy at that pace, while tired or low in glycogen.

But to clarify, I'm not suggesting that if a 10km runner doesn't achieve 10km pace during a threshold effort then this is not going to be useful. If the physiological responses are achieved, then it doesn't matter if 10km speed is not achieved. My point though is that for the 10km runner it's desirable to run at 10km speed in some sessions, just as it's desirable for a 5km runner or a 1500m runner to run at their race-pace for some sessions.

Specific sessions for a distance runner

The magnitude of the heart rate response depends on individual maximal heart rate (which decreases with training status and also with age). Fitter individuals have lower heart rates at any given speed, but often have lower maximal heart rates as well. The shape of the heart rate curve will also depend on fitness. The heart rate of aerobically fitter individuals such will decline more rapidly following an effort than less aerobically fit runners. In general longer distance runners will recover more rapidly than middle-distance runners because of the their reduced reliance on anaerobic power at any given speed.

Sustained running

In the following section minutes are represented by the ' sign, and seconds by the " sign; e.g. 30 minutes 20 seconds is 30'20".

a. Continuous sustained running.

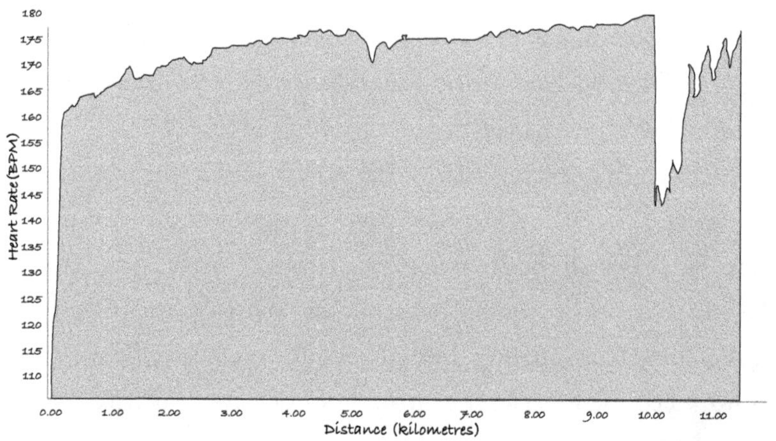

Figure 10-3: Continuous sustained running: 30 minutes close to threshold.

Objective and Session: Continuous 30', at sub-threshold (between half-marathon and marathon effort) out and back, followed 4 x 3" (30" jog recovery) speed technique running.

Venue: Bush dirt trail.

Outcome: Distances: 5.05km out, 4.89km back / 190m, 200m, 190m, 190m

Athlete Comment: It was quite warm but finished feeling strong. Snake interrupted the middle of the longer effort!

Coach comment: This is a sub-threshold speed (sub 10km speed) effort. An important feature of this session is the sustained heart rate. While speed was not at threshold, the heart rate response certainly was, particularly in the latter half of the effort. Note the small blip reduction in the heart rate. This was not an artifact, nor the turnaround, the decline illustrating the coolness of our athlete as he politely declined an invitation to join his potential training partner of reptilian specification.

b. Broken sustained running.

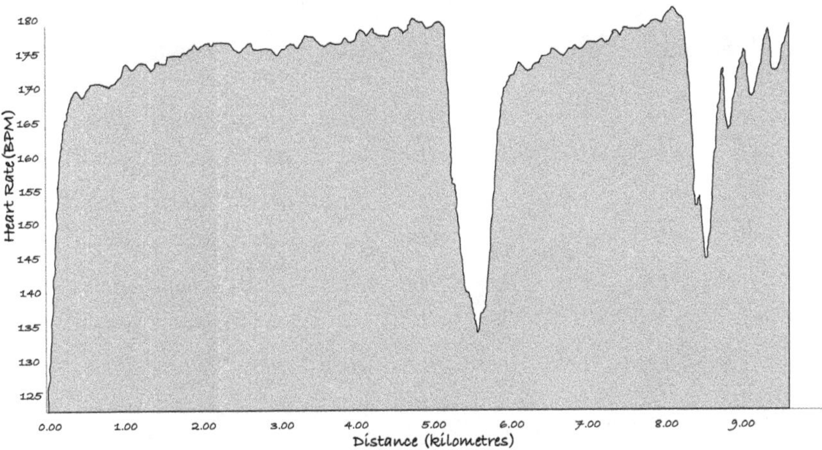

Figure 10-4: Broken sustained running: 15' (3' jogging), followed by 7'30" then 4 x 30" (30" slow jog recovery).

Objective and session detail: 22'30" effort. This is not a magical duration but one derived from a section of his bush trail which took approximately 7'30"; this could easily be 7' or 8'. Alternatively, we could have programmed 2.5km efforts in this runner. In any case this session is a high sub-threshold speed (close to half-marathon pace) tempo run on this dirt trail surface of 22'30". To achieve the average running speed desired in the middle of a demanding training week, rather than running 22'30" continuously, the session is broken into two segments, a 15' best training effort (3' recovery) then 7'30" effort. There followed 4 x 30" (30" recovery) set to focus on some greater than race-pace speed at the end of training.

Venue: Bush trail.

Outcome: distances (km) 5.12; 2.51, then (m) 190,200,200,200.

Athlete comment: I struggled toward the end of the 15' but the break helped me maintain pace in the last 7'30' effort.

Coach comment: Breaking up the continuous run into two sections with the recovery helped maintain the 175 plus heart rate and higher average speed for the 22'30" even in the middle of a high volume week of 210 km.

Long running (marathon specific)

(a.) With sustained effort.

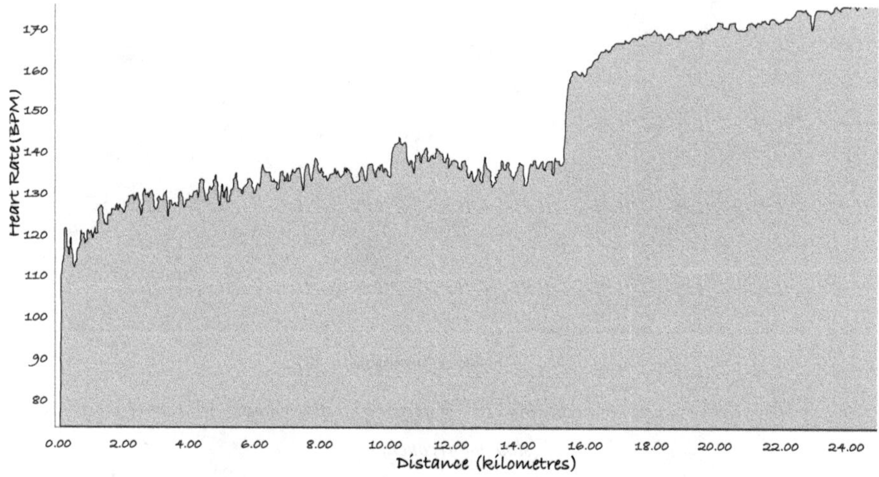

Fig 10-5: Long run with sustained effort: 15k easy to steady followed by 10k solid, close to threshold.

Main objective: To induce fatigue (and lower glycogen levels) and run with good pace in semi-fatigued condition. The set training was 15km easy 10km solid.

Venue: Road.

Result: The distances and times were: easy 15.4km in 1hr 4'05", and the solid 10.18km took 32'02". The total run was 25.6km in 1hr 36'08"

Athlete comment: This was a very hot and humid morning even at 7am and so more testing during our initial 15km, knowing the hard part was to come.

Coach comment: A good effort, and the heart rate drift up during the 'easy' 15km was the result of the heat and humidity. The 10km effort may not have been at threshold speed but would have aproached physiological threshold.

(b.) Medium long run with short repetitions

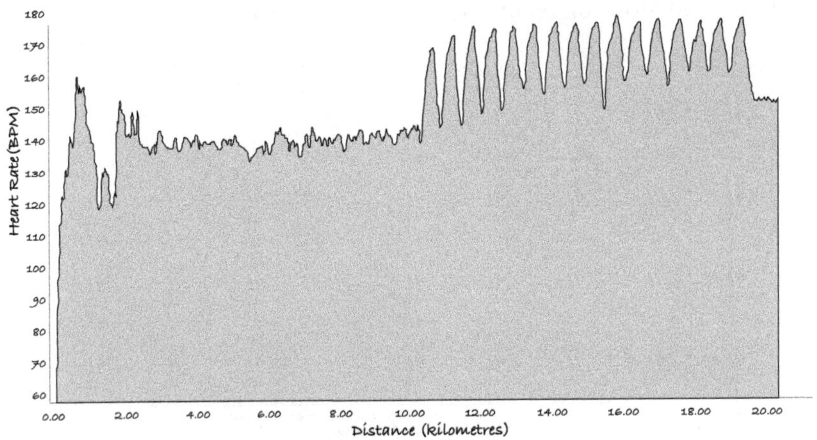

Fig 10-6: Medium long run with short repetitions: 20k run with 16 x 1' (1' recoveries).

Objective and session detail: This session involved running 10km steadily then 16 x 1' with 1' jog recovery. The aim of this session was to introduce faster than race-pace running, induce repeated sharp increases in $\dot{V}O2$, and to practise change of pace and maintain technique whilst in a semi-fatigued state.

Venue: Forest trails all relatively flat.

Result: Total distance was 20.7km in 1hr 20'04".

Athlete comment: Being so wet made it a particularly tough session but got the job done; ran 330-350m on the dirt trails in each one minute effort.

Coach comment: This session provided an opportunity for some faster running and made strong aerobic demands on lowered glycogen levels in the middle of a 180km week, a level lowered further by the first 15km of this long run. A profitable session, both psychologically and physiologically.

Medium repetition running

Medium length repetitions of 1km to 3km form an important part of a distance training program. In accordance with the principle of variety as part of best-practice training, we can modify medium repetitions all sorts of ways; and we can run them on the trail, or the track or the road or the hills. Here are some examples (a.) Objective and session: Close to threshold pace (10km pace). 4 x 7'30" effort (1'30' slow jog recovery) session on bush trail

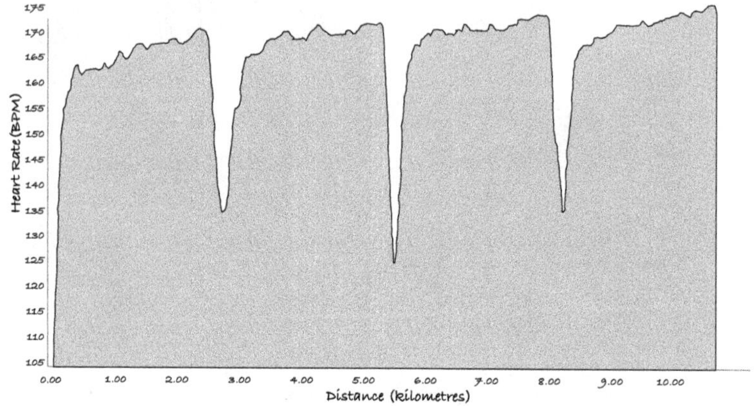

Fig 10-7: Medium repetitions, 4 x 7'30" (1'30" jog recoveries).

Venue: Bush trail

Result: Distances 2.47km, 2.52km, 2.46km, 2.47km.

Athlete comment: Another warm one so was a bit cautious with speed.

Coach comment: We normally expect 7'30" efforts to be close to threshold speed. That's why we break a 30' running session up into repetitions. In this case the runner decided sensibly on a relatively conservative approach to the session, given the heat and humidity.

(b.) Objective and session: Close to threshold pace, but with less physical and psychological stress than synthetic track; 5 x 5' (1' recovery)

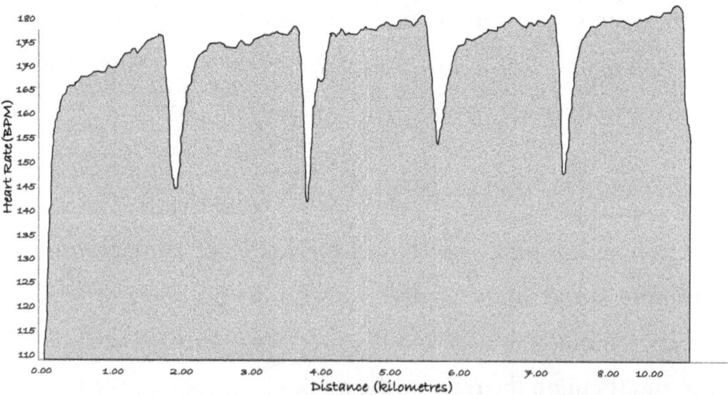

Fig 10-8: Medium repetitions: 5 x 5' (1' jog recovery).

Venue: Bush trail

Result: 1.7 km, 1.68km, 1.66km, 1.66km, 1.66km.

Athlete comment: Effort was there but hampered by the heavy shoes and some rain made the trails through Stromlo a little slippery in parts.

The speed is generally slower than an equivalent track session (see Fig10-11 below) due to trail and footwear, so below 10km speed, but the heart rate indicated a physiological response that approximated physiological threshold. The repetitions were repeated well, considering the one minute recovery, indicating that anaerobic contribution was minimal and well controlled.

(c) Objective and session: To run at close to threshold (10 km) pace, even on dirt trail. This session of 8 x 3' (1' recovery) is a common session among distance runners

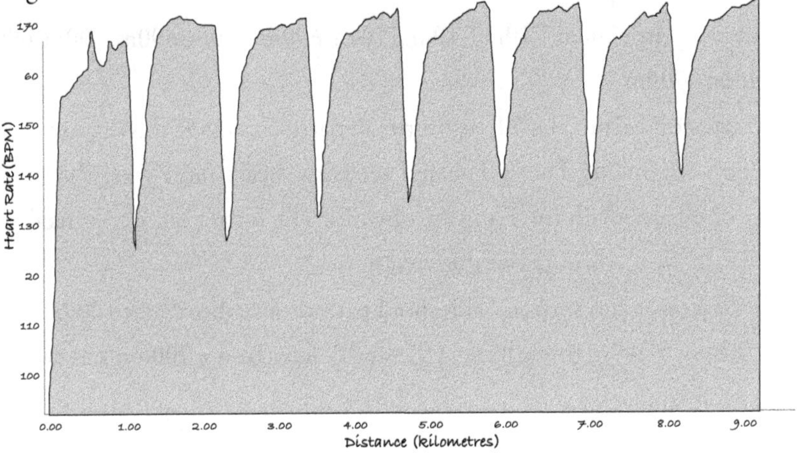

Fig 10-9: Medium repetitions: 8 x 3' (1' jog recoveries).

Venue: Dirt trails.

Result: Distances .99km, 1.03km, .99km, 1.01km, .99km, 1.01km, .98km, 1.01km

Athlete comment: An average session. May not be completely recovered from dental surgery.

Coach comment: This session did not quite achieve threshold pace but under the circumstances it needed to be taken carefully, and it was good to get this session completed as well as this.

(d) Objective and session: Supra-threshold speed (approximating 3km pace) with change of pace practice. 12 x 2 min (1 min, 30 sec jog alternating jog recoveries)

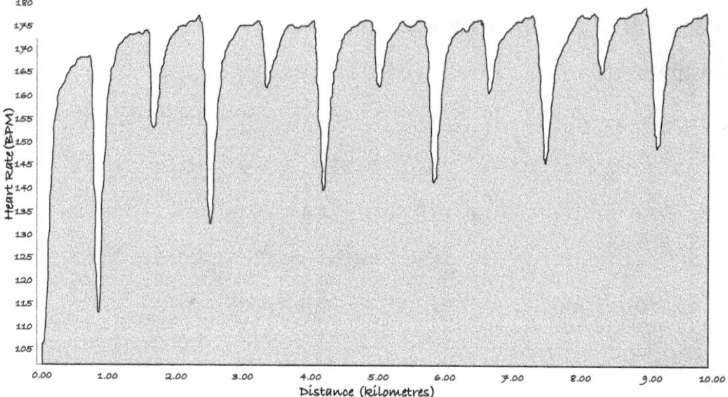

Fig 10-10: Medium repetitions: 12 x 2' (alternating with 1' and 30" jog recoveries).

Venue: dirt trail

Distances (m): 700m, 710m, 710m, 710,m, 690m, 700m, 690m, 700m, 690m, 690m, 680m, 700m.

Athlete comment: The 30" recoveries in particular made this session tough.

Coach comment: The attenuated recovery heart rates with the 30" jog recovery compared with the 1' jog are obvious. The longer recoveries facilitated repeated fast efforts throughout this session.

(e) Objective and session: Threshold pace or just above; 4 x 1600m with a 6' cycle (about 1'30" in this athlete) followed 3' later by 4 x 200 on a 1' cycle (i.e. starting each minute).

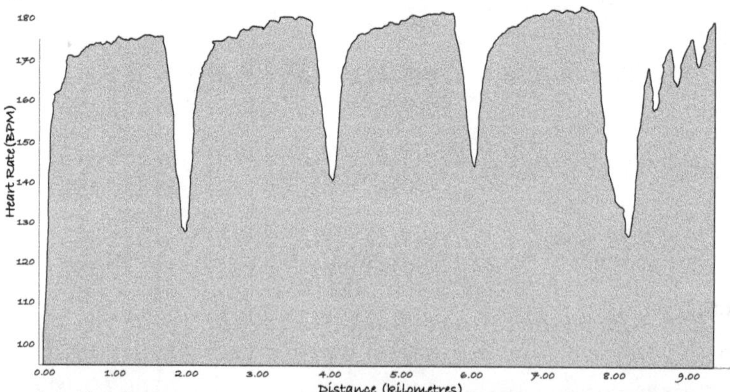

Fig 10-11: Medium repetitions: 4 x1,600m (6' cycles) followed by 4 x 200m (1' cycles).

Venue: Mondo track.

Result: The times were 4'27", 4'26", 4'24", 4'21"; then 30", 29", 29", 28.

Athlete comment: Training with our group helped the speed as did wearing spikes on the track.

Coach comment: This duration and intensity of this session allowed our athlete to achieve a heart rate higher than in the longer repetitions and threshold pace (about 28' 10km pace for this athlete) was exceeded. A highly specific session for 10km runners; and a good 10km threshold speed session for any distance runner.

(f) Objective and session: A high quality aerobic/anaerobic power session. 10 x 1'30" hills solid efforts up but maintaining good running speed down followed by 4 x 30" hills.

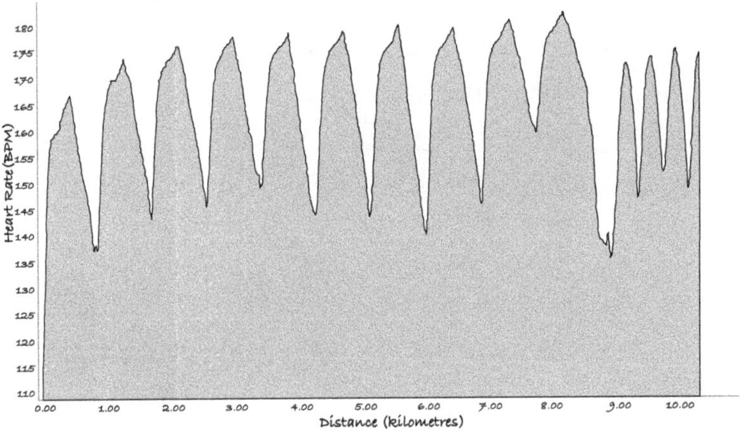

Fig 10-12: Medium repetitions: 10 x 1' hills followed by 4 x 30" hills.

Venue: Dirt trail on hills.

Result: The times (up/down): 1'33"/1'30", 1'29"/1'27", 1'28"/1'29", 1'28"/1'29", 1'30"/1'35", 1'30"/1'34", 1'29"/1'39", 1'31"/1'36", 1'30"/1'27", 1'30"/1'20", Total = 30'14". The distances: 420m, 430m, 420m, 420m, 430m, 430m, 430m, 430m, 430m, 430m; 30" hill: 160m, 170m, 160m, 170m.

Athlete comment: This was a very hard session especially with running down at a solid pace.

Coach comment: This session involves sharp accelerations in heart rate and both aerobic and anaerobic power. Here the heart rate approaches the runner's maximal training heart rate of 185, in turn suggesting maximal aerobic power was reached, especially in the later 1'30" efforts. Minimum recovery heart rate (at end of downhill section) begins to rise in the first 4 hills and the athlete adjusts this intuitively in the 5th, 6th, 7th and 8th hills by reducing his downhill speed.

Short repetition running

Short repetitions include anything less or equal to 500m. They provide faster than race-pace work and repeated sharp increases in aerobic power. Here are two examples with different structure, objectives and responses.

(a) Objective and session: High quality aerobic work, repeatedly running faster than threshold pace. Broken 4.8km effort consisting of 8 x 400m with 200m float recovery, i.e. faster than jogging; 3' recovery, followed by 200m with 100m float, (starting with the 100m float).

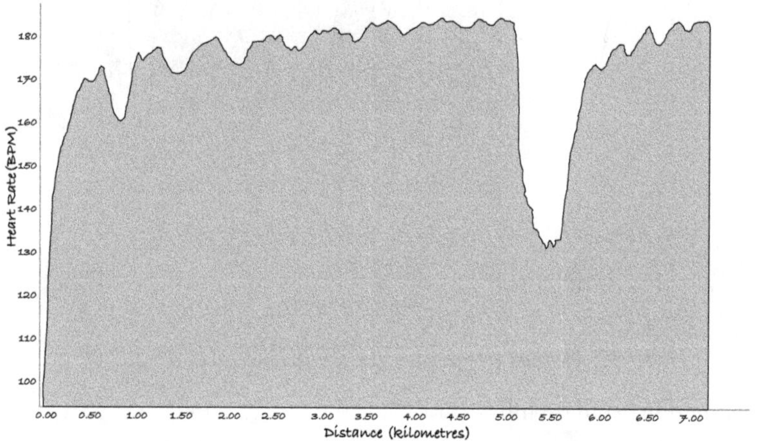

Fig 10-13: Short repetitions track: 8 x 400 (200 float) then 5 x 200 (100 jog).

Venue: AIS synthetic track

Result: The times, beginning with 200m were: 38", 64", 41", 62", 39", 64", 39", 65", 38", 65", 38", 66", 37", 66", 37", 64", totalling 13'51" for the 4,800m; then 5 x 200m (100m jog recovery) starting with the 100m: 19", 31", 22", 31", 21", 30", 21", 31", 19", 31".

Athlete comment: This was really starting to hurt in the 200s at the end.

Coach comment: The float recoveries of 37"–39" 200m do not allow more than a minor recovery as indicated by only small reductions in heart rate. This session has a strong history in Australian running, having been practised in Melbourne for many years, popularized across Australia through the Pat Clohessy and Chris Wardlaw coaching regime, which included this session in most training weeks. These coaches achieved excellent results from their distance runners, including champions de Castella and Moneghetti and the heart rate curve above shows why. High sustained heart rates, race-like acceleration and decelerations provide a session of good intensity and specificity.

(b) Objective and session: To run faster than threshold pace; to practise matching pace of each effort with pace of recovery and so understand more about control during races; 20 x 1' (30" jog recovery),

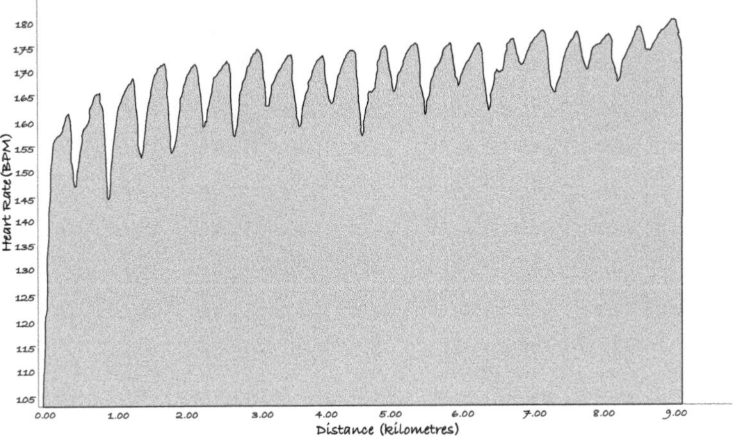

Fig 10-14: Short repetitions: 20 x 1' (30" varied pace recovery).

Venue: dirt trail, flat.

Result: Distances 340m, 340m, 350m, 350m, 40m, 340m, 350m, 350m, 350m, 350m, 340m, 340m, 350m, 340m, 340m, 350m, 340m, 350m, 330m, 350m.

Athlete comment: Maintaining speed and form became progressively difficult; a tough session.

Coach comment: This session is based on profiting from the biomechanical as well as physiological and psychological benefits of running considerably faster than race-pace. The athlete's struggle over the last half of the session corresponds with the gradually increasing maximal and minimal heart rates, indicating difficulty in maintaining homeostasis, control of biochemistry and core temperature. Continual acceleration and deceleration of aerobic power provides variety of challenge to aerobic and anaerobic power.

Chapter 11
Training for Fun Runs

Read the directions and directly you will be directed in the right direction.

Lewis Carroll

A fun run can be fun; but when we run as fast as we can for 10km the fun comes after we finish.

There's a buzz of anticipation and a sea of jiggling bodies keeping warm waiting for the gun. A few look to win, some to run a personal best, some just to finish. Fun runs are exciting and can be really satisfying, and, more satisfying for those who stuck to and completed a good training program. For a runner who trains to improve and does, it's a win, no matter what placing. A win for the mind and body.

Here's some help for you to become a winner.

Too busy to train... really?

The Australian Institute of Sport in Canberra is picking up steam. It's 1986 and we've been going 5 years and there never seems to be enough hours in the day. I don't like missing training but it's impossible to get out for a run today. Winter is approaching and it's getting dark, and it's chilly.

My laboratory staff has headed home. Today I was supposed to do an interval session of 400s; it's not going to happen outside. The treadmill is looking good. It's wide and solid and the lab temperature of 21°C beats the 4°C outside. But there's a problem doing faster reps on that treadmill because it's manually controlled and the controls are designed to be operated by the technician, not the runner. There's one button for elevation, another for the speed and a big red one for start and stop. None are within comfortable reach of the runner, and leaning across might be a bit of a risk when running pretty fast at the end of a solid repetition.

I was just about to settle for an easier paced tempo run when the solution walked into the lab. Here began our cleaner's career as my personal trainer. We did a deal. 'How about I clean up my office if you supervise my interval training session?' The deal was done. I did 10 times a minute at 66 second 400m pace with a one minute slow jog in between. It worked well, and this Thursday night session helped get me pretty fit over the next few weeks. As it turned out our treadmill was automated a few months later which allowed me to set the program without any problems and my personal trainer resumed her normally contracted job.

Anyway, I reckon even the busiest of people can find time to train. I'd go further and suggest that in spending some quality training time away from the office, productivity might increase rather than decrease.

Preparation for a fun run

The following do-it-yourself training program is for fun runners who want to commit to the challenge of running really well, not just finishing. But a set-in-stone, week-by-week training program makes little sense. How can it, when we vary so much in fitness, rate of improvement, the training environment, work commitments, family commitments, susceptibility to injury, and motivation? Here you are the coach; and you are the athlete. After all, who better than you to understand how you feel during sessions and how you recover after them?

A discussion on injury prevention is included in chapter 21, but it's worth pointing out here that running is actually a 'contact sport.'

We collide with terra firma every step of the way, shocks waving their way up from the soles of our feet to the nape of our neck. The stress is proportional to the product of the magnitude of each shock and the number of shocks and this product directly related to risk of injury. In the last training session I conducted before revising this section, one of my runners who hadn't been injured for a long time told me he was 'bullet proof'. I'd heard this sort of confident statement before, but I've never seen it borne out. While some athletes are certainly less injury-prone than others, no one is bullet-proof. Many elite level athletes would train all day if they could. But they can't. Sooner or later their individual 'threshold of resilience' is exceeded and the weakest link gives way, whether it is bone, cartilage, ligament, muscle or tendon. It's the same for fun runners, where the threshold of resilience is generally much less than that of experienced and well-trained elite runners, so increments in training stress have to be conservative.

All distance runners need a certain amount of time between training sessions; time to allow mind and body time to adapt to the training stress, and so become 'fitter'. Walking to survive in a desert might provide plenty of endurance work, but without sufficient recovery time and good nutrition to facilitate adaptation to the physical activity, there'll be a downward spiral to ill-health.

Here are preliminary steps to guide you along the way to your successful fun run.

The service

See your GP for a general engine check, especially if you are unaccustomed to jogging. Sounds a bit over the top just to start some easy jogging, especially as the health risk of doing no physical activity is likely to be greater than introducing some light exercise, but a routine check for any underlying faults in your engine makes sense.

The equipment

Invest in a couple of good pairs of training shoes. Find a specialist running store and have one of the staff fit you out. If prior experience suggests that you are likely to get soreness in knees or hips even with slow jogging, consult a podiatrist early in the piece. It's often said that prevention is better than the cure. A conservative and thoughtful approach consistent with injury prevention inevitably works out to be a far more sensible and successful approach over the course of a training program. Looking for quick short term gains in fitness with risky increases in training load often means wasted training time while the cure is sought. And sometimes that cure is very elusive.

The diary

Keeping a training diary is important. You'll be able to look back as the months go by to see exactly how you've progressed. Not only is this great motivation, but it may hold the key to modifying any features of the training that led to overtiredness or soreness. Setting down your goals in writing is also a very useful exercise. As an example, a short term goal might be implementing an uninterrupted training program for the next 8 weeks. A longer term goal might be to complete a targeted fun run in a certain time.

General training tips and nomenclature

Start your jog conservatively. Never get to the stage where you are gasping for breath. If you feel you need to stop to regain your breath then do so without hesitation. This may happen at times if you are new to running but far less frequently as fitness and pace judgment improve. A steady 'puff' (i.e. a respiration rate that is well under control) is consistent with an optimal training load for the aerobic system. If you do start to breathe too heavily but haven't completed the training objective don't worry; just accept that you were a little too ambitious and stop. Recommence the jogging or walk to complete the session when sufficiently recovered. Your objective, in time, will be to complete the session without stopping.

The term 'building' throughout your program means adding the next component in your own time. You might build the program daily or every second day or take several days. You progress when you feel you can comfortably achieve the additional unit at that level. Whatever your basic level of introduction, build it up so that each week you have made some progress. If any unusual 'niggle' or soreness develops, make the next day an adaptation running-free day; swim or cycle or go to the gym as long as it doesn't cause any pain or irritation. Note that you can also make a progression by increasing training speed slightly, even without a change in quantity of training.

The term 'introduce' means 'gradual introduction'. It is important to feel comfortable before moving to the next level. Never force the training and think about your posture as you run; stay tall, head up, shoulders square, and elbows tucked in to your side but not stiffly; enjoyable running is relaxed running. Arm movement should be minimal and relaxed, elbows staying well flexed at all times.

Vary the surface and terrain of your training. Mix in grass, dirt trails, bitumen, and undulations. It's best to avoid steeper hills as you develop your early fitness, but for previously experienced runners this should present no problems, as long as respiratory control is maintained.

Before and after the session, introduce some gentle stretching of the hamstrings, Achilles tendons, calves, hip flexors, and ilio-tibial band; you only need to do about 5 to 10 minutes of gentle stretching a day with this program, holding an end position for approximately 10 to 15 seconds. Stretching does not need to hurt.

Keep that diary up to date and take pride in filling it in on a daily basis. Measurement of progress is a great motivator. In Chapters 10-13 we see how top athletes report back on their session responses with measured times, distances, and heart rates. You don't have to go to that length at this stage, just some simple times or distances are good to add into your diary. And watch them change as your fitness increases.

As a final reminder, be sure to introduce that full recovery day. In fact as you are your own coach, you have the right to introduce a full running recovery day into your program at any time you feel it is needed. You are the best judge of when you need a full day to fully absorb the previous few days' training.

Phase 1 developing a base

Duration of this Phase: Dependent on starting fitness, 10-15 weeks.

End of Phase Objective: To jog for 30 minutes, 3 times per week

Your starting point: Level (1) as set out below, is a 20 minutes daily walk, but this depends on what you have done in the past; and particularly in your immediate past. You may decide to skip Level (1) and go straight to Level (2) or (3).

Progression Guidelines: You can proceed from one level to the next once you have comfortably achieved the weekly goal. In general take a week at each level, but some levels may require more time before you are able to achieve them. On the other hand, if you feel really comfortable as you negotiate a new level, you could consider an accelerated program, taking only a day or two before moving on. Alternatively, you may opt into this program at any point down the list of progressions. You're the coach; you call the tune, but sensibly bearing in mind that 'prevention is better than the cure.'

Training Note: Take one running-free day every week. Keep active on this day with a walk, bike ride, swim, or non-running physical recreation of some kind. Playing with the kids is perfect.

The 10 levels of base training:

(In general, a week at each of the first 9 levels but you are the coach and in control. Progress safely and surely when you feel the time is right.)

(1.) A daily brisk 20' walk.

(2.) 20'/day: Introduce 30" of jogging into the walk every second day building to 5 x 30" jog (2' walk recovery) every day.

(3.) 20'/day: Introduce a 1' jog, and build gradually to a daily session of 5 x 1' jogs every day with 2' walk recoveries.

(4.) 20'/day: Introduce a 3' jog, building to 3 x 3' jogs with a 2' walk recovery.

(5.) 30'/day: Introduce a 5' jog (2' walk recovery), building to 3 x 5' (2' walk recovery).

(6.) 30' /day: Introduce a 10' jog; then 2 x 10' (5' walk recovery).

(7.) 30'/day: Introduce a 20' jog; 10' walking (start and finish with 5' brisk walk).

(8.) 30'/day: Jog 20' every second day with 10' brisk walking. Choose a previous walk/jog combination as a recovery day for the remaining training days in the week.

(9.) 30'/day: Jog 30' every second day. Choose a previous walk/jog combination for the remaining training days in the week.

(10.) Consolidation period: Complete 4 weeks of phase (9), modifying the easy intervening day as you feel.

Injury prevention tactic: take one completely runnng-free day each week (even if feeling good).

To give you some idea of a program, let's take some typical weeks for a fictitious fun-runner who we'll call Alex (sex: not required, I mean it's irrelevant).

Note that Alex introduces some variation into her or his program. While there are systematic increments throughout the two weeks, sometimes an increment is a little less or a little more according to how Alex's recovery goes from day to day.

Here's a 2 week block from Alex's diary at Level 3 (Note 1' is one minute; 30" is 30 seconds).

Monday: Easy 20' walk with 1 x 1' jog (2' walk recovery) and 4 x 30' jog (2' walk recovery)

Tuesday : Easy 20' walk with 2 x 30" (2' walk recovery) and 2 x 1', jog (1' walk recovery)

Wednesday: Easy 20' walk with 3 x 30" (2' walk recovery) then 2 x 1' jog (2' walk recovery)

Thursday: Easy 20' walk with 3 x 1' (2' walk between jogs)

Friday: Running free day; a swim or bike ride would be a bonus

Saturday: Easy 20' jog with 2 x 30" (2' walk) and 3 x 1' (2' walk)

Sunday: Easy 30' walk

Monday: 20' walk with 3 x 1' jog (2' walk) and 2 x 30" (1' walk)

Tuesday : Easy 20' walk 3 x 1' (2' walk recovery) and 3 x 30" (2' walk)

Wednesday: Easy 20' walk with 3 x 1' jog (2' walk)

Thursday: Easy 20' walk with 4 x 1' (2' walk between jogs) and 2 x 30" (2' walk)

Friday: A 30' bike ride

Saturday: Easy 20' walk with 5 x 1' jog (2' walk)

Sunday: Easy 30' walk

Here's a week's extract from Alex's diary at Level 8.

Monday: Walk 5', easy 20' jog, walk 5'.

Tuesday: 30' brisk walk.

Wednesday: 10' brisk walk and easy 20' jog.

Thursday: 10' brisk walk, 5 x 2' jog (1' walk recovery), 5' walk

Friday: Running rest day. A 30' bike ride.

Saturday: 4 x 5' jog (1' walk) then easy 10' walk

Sunday: 20' jog, 10' brisk walk

Phase 2: transition to interval training

Duration of Phase: 5-10 weeks (depending on rate of adaptation)

Entry qualification: Phase 1, base training Level (10)

End of Objective: Comfortably accomplishing two interval sessions per week

Guidelines for Progression:

Always start these interval sessions with a light stretch of the hamstrings/lower back, Achilles tendon, and hip flexors. Begin with jogging, not the faster work.

As a general rule, each of the following phases spans 2 weeks.

(1.) Into two of your continuous 30' jogs, introduce 3 x 1' of slightly faster jogging than usual with 2' very slow jogging between. Not so fast that it makes you want to stop, but a bit faster than your usual jogging pace, so you can continue on jogging. Your other 30' session(s) in the week remain constant pace.

(2.) Into two of the 30' sessions introduce 3 x 2' of faster jogging with 2' of slower jogging in between

(3.) Into two of the 30' sessions introduce 3 x 3' of faster jogging with 2' of slower jogging in between

(4.) Into two of the 30' sessions introduce 3 x 4' of faster jogging with 2' of slower jogging in between

(5.) Into two of the 30' sessions introduce 3 x 5' of faster jogging with 2' of slower jogging in between

An example week in this Interval Transition phase

Monday: Easy 30' jog or 20' jog and 10' brisk walking.

Tuesday: Easy 30' jog with 3 x 2' faster jogging (2' slow jog recovery)

Wednesday: Easy 20'-30'jog or 20' jog and 10' brisk walking

Thursday: Easy 30' jog with 3 x 2' (2')

Friday: Running free day; a swim or bike ride is encouraged.

Saturday: Easy 30' jog with 3 x 2' (2') slightly faster efforts

Sunday: Easy 30' jog

A Progression: If your venues have been flat surfaces, then during one of the quality sessions on Tuesday or Thursday, introduce a slightly hilly terrain. It is beneficial to run at least once on varying gradients during each week.

An example of one of the training weeks

Monday: Easy 30' jog

Tuesday: 30' jog with 3 x 4' slightly faster running, (2' slow jog recoveries)

Wednesday: Easy 30' jog. Don't hesitate to break any of these runs up with a stretch along the way if you are feeling tight or tired

Thursday: 10' warm-up; 3 x 4' (2' jog)

Friday: Running rest day. A swim or easy cycle if coping well with the running. Otherwise take a full rest day.

Saturday: 30' run (in a slightly hilly area) with 3 x 4' (2' jog)

Sunday: 30' constant pace run well under control

Training notes:

Depending on the time frame of your goals and previous running experience, you can move from one phase to the other after just one week; alternatively you can extend the usual 2 week block into 3 weeks if you feel this suits you best. It is usually best practice to repeat new weekly programs at least once, as you have a better idea of what is to be expected in the second week and can set about trying to make small improvements.

Note also that the quality sessions are usually interspaced by a relative recovery session of a very easy jog or a jog and brisk walking. However, the quality sessions Tuesday, Thursday and Saturday should be enjoyably intensive, i.e. always performed under control, puffing steadily but not uncomfortably. If you are starting to 'lose your breath' then slow down in early anticipation to avoid losing control and having to stop.

When you do push yourself a little harder than you intended, you can introduce a walk as part of the recovery. However, there is advantage in jogging the recovery, so try not to push too hard in each effort to avoid having to walk. The recovery periods must allow you to repeat each effort at the same intensity. If you can't do this, then you have gone too hard; slow down and allow the body to adapt gradually.

As a progression, try to do one of the quality sessions in an area with some small hills.

Phase 3; Interval training

In order to design the interval training we need to determine the target speeds.

Duration: 2 weeks

Entry qualification: completion of Phase 2 Transition Phase.

Objective: determination of your threshold speed (roughly your best 10km average speed) and your supra-threshold speed (your best 1.6km speed).

On an athletic track or on a bike path, measure out a flat 5–10km course (5km for less experienced runners and 10km for more experienced runners) and warm-up with an easy jog and five 200m strides at around the pace you think you can sustain over the measured distance.

Run the course as well as you can as a time-trial. This average speed will approximate your 'threshold' speed (also called anaerobic threshold pace or maximal steady state pace). We construct your training program around this speed.

To be sure that you have done this properly, repeat the effort after three to five days where you have rested or jogged easily to recover. You will have a better idea of the pace you can sustain now, so the second one may be run at a more constant pace and maybe a bit quicker. Use the faster average speed as your threshold training speed.

Repeat this best effort time trial over 1600m on a marked 400m track or on a bike path you have measured out yourself. An effort over this distance is more taxing as there is a greater contribution by your anaerobic system. But be careful to hold back that little bit from the start. If you run it well, you will be breathing very strongly at the end, but you won't be on your hands and knees gasping for breath. You should be able to continue on walking then be able to break into an easy jog warm down after a couple of minutes.

Calculate your average pace per 400m. This is your 'supra-threshold' pace and it too will be used in your personal program design. As for the threshold pace time trial, repeat this time trial a week later as per the following schedule, given you will have a better idea of how to run it the second time.

Here are the first couple of weeks of our assessment phase

Monday: Easy 20'–30' jog

Tuesday: Warm-up jog and strides, 5km time trial

Wednesday: Easy 30' jog

Thursday: Easy 30', jog

Friday: Running rest day

Saturday: Warm-up jog and strides. Repeat 5km or 10km time trial.

Sunday: Easy 30' jog

Then:

Monday: Easy 20'-30' jog

Tuesday: Warm-up and strides, 1.6km time trial

Wednesday: Easy 30' jog. Don't hesitate to break this up and stretch along the way if you are feeling tight.

Thursday: Easy 30' jog

Friday: Running rest day.

Saturday: Warm-up and strides. Repeat 1.6km time trial

Sunday: Easy 30' jog.

Now we are ready to design your interval training program.

Your interval training program

Duration of phase: 10 weeks

Entry qualification: Completion of the introductory interval training phase and speed assessments

End of Phase Objective: To train consistently using three specific interval sessions per week

Duration: 10-16 weeks leading into a race

Here we progress to a more sophisticated level of training, the kind employed by elite level athletes. Naturally, accomplished and experienced athletes will be running faster, and they will include more repetitions in their sessions. They have to do this to ensure ongoing adaptation and improved fitness. The excitement for novice runners is that improvements are achieved with new additions to training, something that becomes harder to come by as you get fitter.

Here is your guide to your new level of training. When we talk about threshold speed or your 1.6km supra-threshold speed, we mean a speed close to that speed. Every training session is a bit different. You are not a machine, and sometimes you feel better than other times, and speeds vary accordingly. Be flexible with your training and use these two measured speeds as rough guides only, because that's all they are—but useful rough guides at that.

Week 1

Monday: easy 30' jog

Tuesday: 15' warm-up jog including 4 x 50m strides at 1.6km pace;
2 x 400m @ 1.6km (supra-threshold) pace (1' walk recovery);
10' warm-down jog

Wednesday: Easy 30' jog. Don't hesitate to break this up and stretch along the way if you are feeling any tightness.

Thursday: 10' warm-up including 4 x 100m strides at threshold pace; 2 x 1km @ threshold pace (2' walk); 10' warm-down.

Friday: Running rest day. Some cross training optional.

Saturday: 10' warm-up; 1 x 2km solid pace run, well under control, not a maximal effort, (3' walk); 10' warm-down

Sunday: Long Run. 40' easy pace and again well under control. Try to judge pace so that you don't have to stop and slow down if you begin to breathe too heavily. Don't hesitate to walk if you misjudge the pace and begin to lose control

Over this training phase of 10 to 12 weeks the objective is to progress as follows:

build Tuesday interval session gradually to 10 x 400m;

build Thursday session to 5 x 1km; and

build Saturday session to 3 x 2km.

The volume of these sessions at 4km, 5km, and 6km, so be careful not to overdo the speed.

Week 2, repeat week 1 (it's always good repeating a week, trying to improve on at least one aspect).

Week 3

Monday: Easy 30' jog

Tuesday: 15' warm-up jog including 4 x 50m strides at 1.6km pace; 3 x 400m @ 1.6km (supra-threshold) pace (1' walk recovery); 10' warm-down jog

Wednesday: Easy 30' jog.

Thursday: 10' warm-up including 4 x 100m strides at threshold pace; 3 x1km @ threshold pace (2' walk); 10' warm-down.

Friday: Running rest day.

Saturday: 10' warm-up; 1 x 2km solid pace run, well under control, not a maximal effort (3' walk); 10' warm-down

Sunday: Long Run. 45' easy pace and again well under control.

Week 4, repeat week 3

Week 5

Monday: Easy 30' jog

Tuesday: 15' warm-up jog including 4 x 50m strides at 1.6km pace; 4 x 400m @ 1.6km (supra-threshold) pace (1' walk recovery); 10' warm-down jog

Wednesday: Easy 30' jog. Don't hesitate to break this up and stretch along the way if you are feeling tight.

Thursday: 10' warm-up including 4 x 100m strides at threshold pace; 4 x 1km @ threshold pace (2' walk); 10' warm-down.

Friday: Running rest day. A swim or easy cycle is recommended if coping well with the running. Otherwise take a full rest day.

Saturday: 10' warm-up; 2 x 2km solid pace run, well under control, not a maximal effort (3' walk); 10' warm-down

Sunday: Long Run. 50' easy pace and again well under control.

Week 6, repeat Week 5

Finally, here is an example of an advanced training program in Week 10 if things have gone to plan (but may take 16 weeks or so); let your progressions happen gradually.

Monday: Easy 30'–40' jog

Tuesday: 15' warm-up jog; 10 x 400m @ 2km pace efforts (1' walk recovery); 10' warm-down

Wednesday: Easy 30'–40' jog.

Thursday: 15' warm-up; 5 x 1km @ threshold pace (2' walk recovery); 15' warm-down.

Friday: Running rest day.

Saturday: 15 warm-up; 3 x 2km @ approximately 90 percent of threshold pace (2' walk recovery); 15' warm-down.

Sunday: Long Run. 1 hour steady pace pace, well under control, over hills.

Your 400m, 1km, and 2km reps will increase in speed as training proceeds. They will be considerable quicker than was indicated by your short and long time-trials. That's to be expected, as the time-trials were there to provide an initial guide to training speeds.

Aim to do that one session or even part of a session every week on a hilly course. Where a session, for example a 2km effort on Saturday includes hills, we cannot expect to hold the designated threshold speed we devised from running on a flat hard surface. Here is where heart rate is a handy additional guide to training intensity. The steady heart rate which accompanied our threshold speed remains relevant on a hilly (or sandy or grassy) trail. In the absence of heart rate information you will learn to judge what sort of pace you are able to maintain by monitoring your breathing and muscle fatigue. As you gain experience you'll learn more about pacing yourself, to read your early respiration and muscle 'feel' to avoid an over-ambitiously fast start to a repetition.

Re-evaluation of your training speeds

You will gradually find you are running your interval training sessions faster than you first assessed them. This will happen naturally, so make sure you record all your training in your diary. You'll also find you're recovering quicker.

This signifies that it's time to repeat the threshold and the 1.6km supra-threshold tests. It's good for motivation and to get a good handle on your improvement.

In preparing for a race it's always good to get one or two sustained 'hit-outs' in the lead-up weeks. This 8-10km solid effort to re-evaluate your threshold speed, together with your very solid 1.6km can serve that purpose. There is another strong sustained effort the week before the race, as shown below in the two week taper phase to follow. After re-evaluation of your two training guide speeds you can implement those speeds into the interval sessions; the 1.6km speed for your 400s; your 5km or 10km (threshold) speed for your 1km; and a bit under your threshold speed for your 2km.

You'll be pleased with the increase in those speeds.

Notes on your progressions

You have the idea; gradually working up to the 10 x 400m; the 5 x 1km and the 3 x 2 km. The Sunday long run can build up to 1 hour, run easily but moving it along a bit better each week according to how you feel.

You are now becoming the kind of accomplished runner I've sometimes referred to previously.

The sessions on Tuesday, Thursday and Saturday remain well under control. Never exhaust yourself in training as you continue to develop your fitness. Remind yourself that you will adapt best by holding back that little bit and that prevention (of injury) is better than cure.

Once you have got into the swing of things, select a hilly area for either the Saturday or Sunday run. Running up the hill at a slower pace should elicit the same breathing response as running on the flat, and adds valuable variety.

Make an adjustment every week so that your training diary records a modest but positive progression every second week (where the previous week is repeated). A positive progression is

(a.) A small (5 percent) increase in the weekly volume, or

(b.) An improved average time in one of your quality sessions, or

(c.) An increase in the number of repetitions in one of your quality sessions.

Never get too ambitious with the progressions. Remember that adding extra repetitions is a progression, so you may wish to moderate your speed. In every second week where there is no progression in training volume try to nudge up the speed slightly in one or two of the sessions. Don't get too ambitious in trying to improve speed as well as volume. One at a time is fine and will get you fitter either way.

Bear in mind that soreness can be thought of as a minor injury and this may lead to a major injury that may seriously impede training. Injuries can pop up when you least expect, so be conservative. Again as a general rule, if you feel any unusual soreness, such as a minor muscle strain, or a slightly sore back or Achilles tendon, then take two days off running. There is no rush. Taking time off is not shying away from training or being 'soft.' In contrast, it's being sensible, and will improve rather than hinder your training consistency and race performances in the long term.

Phase 4: the taper

Duration: 2 weeks.

Tapering for a race refers to the freshening up process, removing any residual soreness and tiredness. Whether you are a fun runner or an Olympic athlete, the basics remain the same, a reduction in training volume with some revision of race specific quality (see Chapters 14 and 15 for more detail on tapering).

Let's assume you progressed well through the interval training phase and your most recent week of training looked like the following:

Monday: Easy 40' jog

Tuesday: 15' warm-up jog; 10 x 400m @ 2km pace (1' walk recovery); 10' warm-down

Wednesday: Easy 45' jog. Don't hesitate to break this up and stretch along the way if you are feeling tight

Thursday: 10' warm-up; 5 x 1km @ threshold pace (2' walk); 10' warm-down

Friday: Running rest day

Saturday: 10' warm-up; 3 x 2km (3' walk); 10' warm-down

Sunday: Long Run. 1 hour steady pace well under control

Now it's two weeks out from the target Fun Run (which might now be viewed more as a 'road race' as you have developed the fitness to 'race.'

The penultimate week

Monday: Easy 30' jog

Tuesday: 10' warm-up jog; 6 x 400m @ 2km pace efforts (1' walk recovery); 10' warm-down

Wednesday: Easy 30' jog

Thursday: 10' warm-up; 4 x 1km @ threshold pace (2' walk); 10' warm-down.

Friday: Running rest day

Saturday: 10' warm-up;, 5km as well as you can run; 10' warm-down

Sunday: Easy 45' run

And the final week

Monday: 20' easy jog

Tuesday:10' warm-up jog; 3 x 1km at threshold pace (3' walk); 3 x 400m @ 1.6km pace (1' walk recovery); 10' warm-down

Wednesday: Easy 30' jog and stretch. Don't hesitate to break this up and stretch along the way

Thursday: 10' warm-up; 6 x 1' (1' walk recovery) easy session on grass @ intended race-pace, i.e. threshold pace (2' walk recovery); 10' warm-down. This is an easy session for you, with no stress at all

Friday: Easy 15' jog and stretch

Saturday: Easy 15' jog and stretch and 6 x 100m strides at race-pace with 1' walk recovery

Sunday: 8–12km Road Race or Fun Run. Have a good one. There is no need to wish you good luck as luck is not an issue!

Missing from the above program are the circuit exercises and gentle stretching sessions known to complement the stresses of running. You only need 10 minutes 2 or 3 times a week, but it will be 20 or 30 minutes very well spent.

A tale of two cities

Sydney City to Surf and the San Francisco Bay to Breakers

Cities all around the world love to host a big city Fun Run. It's no wonder, as there are winners all round; good publicity for sponsors; showcase for the city, a healthy pursuit for the runners; fun for the families, funds for charities, prize money for the top athletes, and profits for the organizers.

There are many great city fun runs, and two ranking up there with the most popular, are the 12.4km San Francisco 'Bay to Breakers' and the 14.2km Sydney 'City to Surf'. The 'Bay to Breakers' has more than a century of history, and attracts about 35,000 registered runners, although it's been estimated that the numbers of non-registered runners may well near that mark as well! It certainly was the largest fun run in the world in 1986 where 110,000 runners registered. The 'City to Surf' has actually upstaged the 'Bay to Breakers' in recent years, with books being closed at around 80,000 registered runners.

Both 'Bay to Breakers' and 'City to Surf' are tough runs because distance and hills present a real challenge, and runners without the consistency of training such as the program set out above might best be advised to walk up the steep parts. A skill displayed by an experienced hill runner is to run just on or under that 'red-line' evenly throughout the race, both up-hill and down-dale; running up slower than on the flat, but running down faster. It's not too difficult though, you just have to hold back slightly up the hill, conserving energy to run strongly over the top and to stride down the hill, rather than having to use the downhill section as a recovery from an exhausting run up.

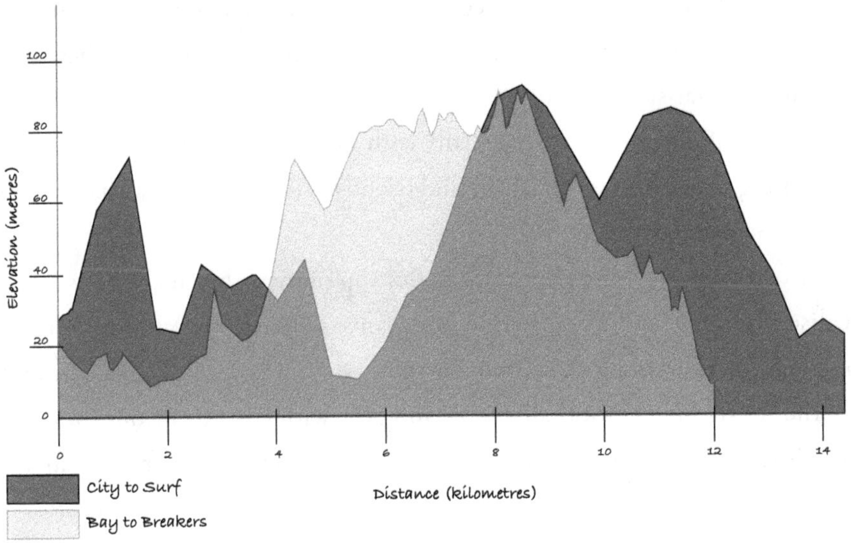

Profile comparisons– City to Surf and Bay to Breakers.

Note the profiles of the 'Bay to Breakers' and the 'City to Surf'. It's not hard to see which run presents itself as the greater challenge in terms of gradient. The 'City to Surf' wins hands down, and has the dubious honour of winning my vote as the most taxing big city 'fun-run' in the world. Compare the profiles of 'Bay to Breakers' and 'City to Surf' in the accompanying diagram.

Both 'Bay to Breakers' and 'City to Surf' have their 'Heartbreak Hill' but 'City to Surf' has the bigger heart-breaker. In the 'Bay to Breakers', there is basically one really good climb to negotiate, with some testing sharper inclines and declines on the way; the overall climb being 70m over 4km, beginning at around the 2km mark. By comparison the biggest hill in 'City to Surf' has an altitude change of about 80m over 3km and includes three other mini heart-breakers, perhaps we might call these 'lung-busters'; each with accompanying, 'quad-breakers'. In case you're wondering, a 'quad-breaker' is a steep downhill section, deceptively damaging to the thighs due to the obligatory breaking 'eccentric' muscle action we discuss in Chapter 9.

If you are not really well prepared for either of these runs, it can be a most stressful task, a stress which is multiplied when the temperature climbs into the mid to late 20s or even to30 degrees C. Cool hills become hot mountains. So for most participants 'City to Surf' and 'Bay to Breakers' might better be described as 'satisfaction' runs rather than 'fun' runs. But the satisfaction in their successful negotiation, especially with a personal best time or placing is something to celebrate with family and friends at the finish. Now that's where the fun begins.

Road races are more important to our top runners than many of us might realise. Training and competition programs required of our top runners preclude them holding down regular jobs, and unlike professionals in high profile sports such as football, tennis and golf, with few exceptions they earn very little money. Consequently any income runners derive from road and track races is very important, and in many cases has led to opportunities to travel overseas, with a big impact on international careers.

Many years ago I accompanied Lisa Martin (Ondieki) over to San Francisco where she comfortably won the 'Bay to Breakers' and took home a new Mercedes Benz! The winner's prize is not the same nowadays unfortunately, but at least the 2015 'Bay to Breakers' still makes an effort to support the top runners, with added prize listings for masters and local runners and a good cash prize for the fastest to the top of Heartbreak (real name Hayes) Hill.

Ray Charles meets Yobes and Lisa Ondieki after the 1992 San Francisco, Bay to Breakers. Yobes was second in the men and Lisa won the women's event.

In Australia it's hats off to the 'Burnie 10 km' in Tasmania for being one of the first races to recognize that people loved to see our best runners racing on the road. They decided to share the event profits with the elite runners by providing some decent prize money. Others have followed suit over the years with well-organized races which respect the top performers. Launceston does this with its 10 km, Sydney with the 'Sydney Harbour 10 km', 'Sutherland to Surf', and 'Sydney Half' and Marathon. Melbourne has its 'Melbourne Marathon Festival', Adelaide the 'City to Bay' 10 km, Brisbane the 'Bridge to Brisbane', Perth has its own 'City to Surf,' Gold Coast has the 10km and 'Gold Coast Marathon' weekend, and Noosa has its 10k Bolt. These events, in allocating some prize money, have contributed well to many runners' careers.

The 'Leonora Mile' in the West Australian outback is another case in point. In a most unlikely but exotic and historic venue, this event is directed solely at our best middle-distance runners. It's a winner all round and with good prize money (including a gold nugget!) has certainly kicked along the careers of many aspiring young runners. Australian mile record holder Lisa Corrigan is one such runner. The 'Mitchell St Mile' in Darwin also sees fit to support elite athletes and is attracting some of Australia's best track runners to the the north end.

'Life wasn't meant to be easy'

Former Prime Minister Malcolm Fraser famously informed Australians that life wasn't meant to be easy. This certainly applies for some of our best athletes who want to run for their country.

Australian middle-distance runner Lisa Corrigan had been struggling at training for some weeks. It was the middle of summer, hot and dry. Lisa suffered from asthma especially on windy days and I was worried that this period of training had really drained her. I'd reviewed the training, discussed her diet, had her iron status checked and she appeared infection free.

'How has your sleep been, Lisa?' I asked. 'Not so good, Dick, it's just been pretty hot at night for Canberra'. It had been unusually warm at night and most apartments didn't have air-conditioning and could stay uncomfortably hot all night.

'How's your room in your apartment Lisa ... can we do anything about cooling it down a bit for you?'

I was taken aback at her reply.

'Oh, actually Dick, there wasn't enough room for all of us in the apartment, and I couldn't really afford to rent a room anyway, so I sleep in the garage and park the car outside now.'

Amazing, here we had a 23 year-old who has represented Australia in the last Olympics, World Champs and Commonwealth Games and who is the current Australian mile record holder (still is as I revise this in 2015) ranked in the top 30 in the world, and she can't afford a room in a flat with her friends.

On a lighter note, I have to tell this road race story. Well I don't really have to, but I will.

The 'City to Surf', Lisa and me

Lisa Martin (later Ondieki) had been training well leading to the Seoul Olympics and we'd decided that Sydney 'City to Surf', some seven weeks before the marathon would be a good hard, home country hit-out. Lisa usually recovered from hard runs on the road very quickly, probably because she did almost every training run on bitumen surfaces, regularly negotiating the 16km bike path around Lake Burley Griffin in Canberra.

I had been doing a bit of training with Lisa, although I couldn't handle the regular training on hard surfaces myself, old football injuries having something to do with that. Anyway, Lisa trained far too fast for me and unlike my champion marathoner, I loved training in the hills at Stromlo Forest.

I was pretty fit at the time, and those hills in Stromlo got me specifically fit for the exceptionally demanding hills of 'City to Surf'. If 'City to Surf' had been the Olympics, I would have pressed Lisa to do more hill work, but we had bigger fish to fry. The Seoul Olympics was flat and Lisa's preference for flat fast training made a lot of sense.

The coach-athlete banter at training was about who was going to get to Bondi first. Not whether or not Lisa was going to win the women's race; I simply couldn't see her being beaten, although Lisa herself was never over-confident in her prospects for any race. The banter was about who was going to come in first between the two of us! Leading up to race day though, at the race hotel in Sydney, our little personal duel wasn't mentioned, as the focus was on Lisa getting a confidence boosting fast race hit-out.

On the other hand, I'm pretty sure that even amidst the 'hype' of race day the Lisa Martin-Dick Telford contest was in the back of the mind of our country's champion marathoner. It was certainly in the front of her coach's mind!

As we lined up, and looked back at the 60,000 strong sea of runners, Lisa had her job to do and I was out to run a good time, at least for a 40+ year-old (but in addition, what fun I would have if I did get in ahead of her!).

I reckoned my best bet, and possibly only chance, was to be invisible to Lisa right from the start, so she would never know where I was. Wishing her all the best, and with the cameras focused on her and the other elite runners, I drifted off to the other side of the road, right up the front. I could see her, but she couldn't see me, and when the gun went, I took off as hard as I could, hoping I wasn't committing hari-kari.

Runners illegally darted in out of the side streets and I had to be careful to avoid collisions, many of whom were unseeded I guess, hoping to feature on the TV coverage. As it turned out these runners were quite useful, as they formed a shield between Lisa and me, ensuring my 'invisibility'. At the 1km mark I knew that I was ahead, but she would have had no idea. All I needed to do was to stay far enough in front on that winding, hilly course, about 100-200m would be plenty, but that would not be easy with Lisa setting out to run fast.

That race had to be one of the hardest I can remember. It's nearly three decades ago now, but I well remember red-lining those hills, getting to what I thought was the summit, only to find another hill around the corner. I tried to put my hill racing theory into practice, holding back slightly up the hills and then racing down them as hard as possible, flowing all the way without breaking. It didn't work as well as I'd hoped, mainly because I didn't hold back enough on the climbs, and coming to the final descent into Bondi, I was well and truly spent.

I tried to let myself roll down the hills, but easier said than done. 'Rolling' down was a misnomer. I had to push hard even with gravity assisting me. Finally as every 'City to Surfer' knows, we get to the bottom of that descent with the feeling that the race is almost over. But it's not, and that last section, flat as it is, seems to go on along the Bondi stretch forever before the turn back down along the service road to the big friendly sign that said 'Finish'. Like everyone else, I mustered up my last legs, to run through in 45:03. I was happy to have run the race out completely.

I knew that Lisa hadn't passed me of course, and as her coach I was pleased to see Lisa come in about 44 seconds later, looking extremely strong and remarkably fresh, in contrast with the way her coach had finished. But she always did look composed and fresh.

The press grabbed her for interviews, and in between she was signing autographs. Lisa had run extremely well, set a new race record, and probably held back a bit too. Great news, considering she really wasn't prepared for that extremely hilly sort of run and in the middle of hard training for Seoul. It was about ten minutes after she had finished when I went over to congratulate her.

We talked for a while, and as she was asked by a reporter to do another interview, she asked, 'Oh Dick, how did you go?' 'Not bad, thanks Lisa, I ran 45.03'. I pretended not to notice her change of expression and I thought to myself, 'I'm out-a here'. Luckily another interviewer approached Lisa, and I disappeared for a while. When Lisa had cooled down, both physically and mentally, I re-appeared. We had a good laugh about the times (well I think Lisa laughed). It occurred to me that had my charge spotted me during that race, her new women's race record would have been even quicker ... about 45:02 I reckon!

Chapter 12
Training for track

Alice: 'How long is forever?
White rabbit: 'Sometimes, just one second.'

Lewis Carroll

We can always consult the training manuals, but our best coaches have the knowledge and confidence to work from first principles.

Setting a training program – off the shelf or bespoke?

Let's say a good young middle-distance runner asks us to write a training program. There are few ways to proceed. We could copy a successful runner's program; we could take a general textbook approach; or we could have a go at writing a new program.

The problem with copying a champion's program is that it's geared to someone else's physiology, anatomy and psychology and that might be very different to the athlete in question. The problem with a general textbook event program is also that one size doesn't fit all.

On the other hand, the problem of the bespoke program is that we probably don't know enough about the athlete to tailor it with sufficient precision.

So while the answer that gets 10 out of 10 in the Coaching Course final examination is that we set programs which take individual characteristics into account this is easier said than done. In reality even the best coaches recognize their limitations in this respect and will combine their knowledge of how a champion trains with a model based on a general middle-distance training template, and then fine tune it along the way as individual characteristics come to light.

In other words, let's not get too cute about individualizing training. It's not that easy and only through repeated trial and error will we get near to optimizing a program at an individual level; and herein lies the value in long term coach-athlete relationships. There is no question that setting training based, at least in part, on individual athlete requirements is the most rewarding approach, both mentally and physically for both coach and athlete. It reinforces the special athlete-coach relationship that exists in nearly every successful athletic career.

The good news is that a program developed mainly from first principles at an individual level is well within the grasp of even the novice coach. The nuts and bolts of the physiology are set out in Chapter 5 and the frame of reference for session design is set out in Chapter 10. A coach with the basic understanding of the science of the event who understands how specific training produces specific adaptation in the short and medium term is well-equipped. But then, imagination, initiative and observation contribute to the art of coaching, and the degree of success related to these characteristics in a coach should not be underrated.

Race-pace sessions

In the previous chapter we constructed interval training from two race-paces, best 10km pace and best 1,600m pace. For track race training we do something similar but perhaps in a somewhat more refined manner.

Race-pace is a sensible and convenient way to set target times for repetitions on the track. Race-paces from 800m through to marathon represent a gradual increase in the proportion of aerobic power contribution and decrease in the proportion of anaerobic power. So by setting training at 800m to marathon race-pace we can systematically influence the proportionate use of energy systems. It certainly made sense for accomplished British coach Frank Horwill way back in 1970.

He based his program design around best 400m, 800m, 1500m, and 5000m pace, adjusting length of repetition and recovery accordingly. His methods certainly lived on within the programs of long term British coaching guru Alan Storey, whose methods were in turn passed on and put to excellent use by Australian coach Nic Bideau, who has guided many distance track runners to international success, two outstanding examples being Craig Mottram and Benita Johnson (Willis).

This system of session planning involves matching a certain length of repetition with the race-pace. For example, a set of 400s might be run at a runner's 1500m race-pace; a set of 800s at 3km race-pace; and a set of 1,000s at 5km pace and 1,600s at 10km race-pace. These particular match-ups are the ones I use as I feel they are suited to (untapered state) training in the middle of solid weeks. Nothing is set in stone in training, and variation of these match-ups will (and should) vary with specific objective of the session. For example, by changing the recovery time and speed we can alter the relative contributions of aerobic and anaerobic power supply.

Table 11-1 provides some examples of sessions that may be used as a basis for this type of session design. Remember that no sessions target any particular energy source exclusively; the power source nominated simply indicates the predominant power supply. The pace guides refer to the runner's current estimated race-pace which will change through the course of training. In other words, the repetition times will improve through the training phase. If they don't, it's back to the drawing board!

Be patient

Many of us have made the mistake of being too hasty and impatient; looking for success prematurely. As indicated in the section on stress fractures in Chapter 21, too much volume, intensity, or change in training can lead to trouble. In terms of injury prevention as well as the ultimate quality of performance, 'slowly and surely' is better than 'rapidly and riskily'. Bearing this in mind, consider a period of training that is going exceptionally well with an athlete who is increasing in confidence and motivation. There is a temptation to make every training session a personal best, but the astute coach will subtly hold back for a session or two.

One way to do this is remove the 'track and stop-watch' effect, and to conduct a session that can't be measured with any precision.

Benita Willis at the Athens Olympic Games.
Image: Australian Sports Commission

Most coaches can look back and see the year by year improvement in age-groupers and young men and women moving into senior ranks. The 'slowly and surely' principle is is especially important in developing athletes. Benita Johnson (Willis) is one athlete whom I had the privilege of coaching during her transition from hockey/running to concentrate on running from age 17 through to 22 at the Australian Institute of Sport. Clearly a girl with great potential I tried to keep a lid on the progression, only increasing her workload enough to ensure a reasonable progression each year, and playing down expectations. During those five years Benita's best 5km time improved about 20 seconds each year without exception; not an insignificant improvement although we did realise we could have accelerated this progression. I must admit to being tempted, but decided against it, holding back on her training, injury prevention being the foremost objective.

Her only disappointing performance was a result of my disappointing coaching before the Commonwealth Games in Glasgow. I was oblivious to the extent of psychological stress Benita was undergoing during a training camp at Aix les Bains, France, which naturally affected her physically. Blood tests taken after her lacklustre performance in the 1500m and 5km revealed a rather severe iron deficiency. Her health soon improved and moving over to experienced coach/ manager Nic Bideau and residing in London and Melbourne, she became the fastest 3km, 5km, 10km and marathon runner Australia has ever produced. I like to think the outstanding Johnson (Willis)-Bideau coach-athlete partnership may have been facilitated, to some degree at least, by that early conservative approach to Benita's development during her years at the AIS.

Sessions for middle-distance runners

Here are some examples of track sessions classified by power supply, but there are an infinite number of variations, created by changing the number, lengths and durations of repetitions and recoveries.

Threshold, (10km pace)	Aerobic Power (3km pace)	Aerobic/ Anaerobic Mix (1500m pace)	Anaerobic Capacity (800m pace)	Anaerobic Power (400m pace)
4 x 1600m (1'30"–2') @ current best 10km pace or 8–12 x 400 (200 float)*	6 x 800m (2'–4') @ best 3km pace or slightly faster	8 x 400m (1'–2') @1500m pace	5 x 400m (4'–7') @ 800m pace or slightly faster	10 x 200m (3'–5') @ 800m pace or slightly faster

*A float refers to a running recovery rather than a slow jog. This can be varied, but as a rule of thumb it is around 40'–45' for accomplished male runners and 45'–50' for females in this set of 400s. There are two ways to organize this session; the float can be fixed in time with the 400s run as well as possible; alternatively 400m times can be fixed with the float time adjusted accordingly. The recoveries are shown in brackets.

Table 11-1: Matching energy systems and sessions: track

Grass, trail, or hill variations

Track runners can't always train on a synthetic track. The pace of repetitions on the grass or trail will tend to be slower than on the track and the biomechanical stress tend to be lower. Physiological responses tend to be lower as well, probably because a synthetic track brings out the best in runners who race on that same surface. Consequently slightly longer or more repetitions can be set on softer surfaces.

Threshold pace	Aerobic Power	Aerobic/ Anaerobic Mix	Anaerobic Capacity	Anaerobic Power
6x5'(1') 8x3'(1')	8x2'(2') 5x3'(2')	10x1'(1') 8x1'30" (1'30")	6x1'(3') 4x1'30"(4')	10x30"(2'–3') 6x40"(2')
1',2',3',4',5',4', 3',2',1' (all with 1' jog recovery)	1'30",2',3',2', 1'30" (recovery equal to rep duration)	2x(30",45",1', 1'15",1'45", recovery equal to rep duration).	45",1',1'15", 1'45" (recovery is 3x rep duration).	15",20",25", 30",25",20",15" (recovery is 2x rep duration).

*recoveries can be walk or jog, distance runners more suited to the latter

Table 11-2: Matching energy systems and sessions: trails, grass, road

Composite sessions

Composite sessions permit a more thorough combination of training components within the one session. They suit the pre-competition phase, because energy requirements for middle-distance races demand simultaneous deployment of each of our power supply systems. Numbers of repetitions will vary with the training status of the runner, and we usually work toward more anaerobic efforts toward the end of the session consistent with the demands of a race. Here are two examples of composite sessions on the track, with a comment on predominant areas of effect.

Example A

2 x 1,200m (3') @ 5km pace: threshold, aerobic power
Lap jog recovery
3 x 600m (3') @ >3km pace: aerobic power, anaerobic capacity, lactic tolerance
Lap jog recovery
4 x 200m (1') @ close to 800m pace: anaerobic power

Example B

2 x 800m (3') @ 3km pace: aerobic power and lactic tolerance
Lap jog
3 x 400m (200m jog) @ 1500m pace: aerobic power, anaerobic capacity and lactic tolerance
Lap jog
4 x 150m (30") @ 800m pace: anaerobic power

Another composite session that may fit into your plans is to preface a track session with a sustained threshold or sub-threshold run. Australian coach Norm Osborne used this to great advantage with his 1500m runner Margaret Crowley. Margaret often ran a 10–15 minute solid aerobic effort prior to many of her track sessions during the winter build-up. She attributed these sessions, together with a good winter which included 6–8km cross-country racing (physiologically threshold pace runs on hills and grass) to her stellar performances leading up to and including the Atlanta Olympics where she placed 5th in the 1500m final.

Time-trial and maximal effort sessions

From time to time my athletes discuss some terrific training sessions reported by other runners on social media, only to wonder why corresponding race performances never materialize. Of course, some coaches and athletes are a bit slow to start their watches and a bit quick to stop them; but on the other hand we're all aware of athletes 'leaving their best performances on the training track.'

We have to be careful to avoid turning routine training sessions into all-out race-like efforts or time-trials. An effective training session, one that produces a positive adaptation, involves the application of a specific stress of optimal magnitude, not maximal magnitude. Repeated all-out training sessions where body and mind are maximally stressed are not the best way to achieve adaptation over the long term.

As most athletes come to learn, racing week after week ultimately results in a loss of best performance.

Nevertheless, strategically placed time-trials performed in a pre-competition phase can be very useful for tuning an athlete's racing mind-set and linking recently developed components of fitness into the one concerted effort. For those who have played football, a good analogy is pre-season training preparation before the first practice match. You can be really fit for the sprinting and the endurance work in pre-season training, but it doesn't prepare you well for an actual match. Playing that first match or two is required to achieve specific competition or 'match fitness', just as races or time-trials are required for any runner to achieve best race fitness.

400s: the 'bread-and-butter' track repetitions

400m repetitions are basic tools of the trade for a track coach; perhaps like a 5-iron for a golf teaching 'pro'. They are extremely versatile. We can modify the speed and the recovery to target all aspects of a runner's profile; endurance, threshold work, aerobic power and anaerobic power and capacity. Here's how:

Consider this very good male runner with the following PBs: 400m, 52"; 800m, 1'52"(i.e. average of 56" laps); 1500m, 3'45" (60" per lap); 3000m, 8'00" (64" lap); 5000m of 13'45" (66" laps); 10km in 28'20" (68" laps).

Here are some sessions involving 400m repetitions for this runner, and the areas they tend to target most

(a.) 16–20 x 400m (slow 200m jog) in 66"–70"; mainly aerobic power and muscular endurance

(b.) 10–12 x 400m in 68" (200m float in 45"); around threshold

(c.) 2 sets of 3 x 400m in 64" (200m jog in 55") with a lap jog recovery between sets; mainly aerobic power complemented with anaerobic power

(d.) 5 x 400m (5' recovery) in 56"; mainly anaerobic power and capacity

1600s: a 'bread-and-butter' track session for 10km

One of my 'bread-and-butter' training sessions for 10km is 4 or 5 x 1,600m (1'30" recovery). This short recovery session of close to a mile allows an athlete to achieve threshold pace in the middle of a solid training week. The specificity of this session is supported by it being a good predictor of performance.

For example, in the six sub-28 minute 10,000m runners I've had the pleasure to coach, their average 1,600m repetition speed in a set of 5 x 1,600 min (on a 6' cycle, i.e. starting each new rep at the 6 minute mark) predicted their 10,000m performance quite well. As a case in point, recalling the training of Michael Shelley, when he was training for 10,000m some years ago, he averaged 4'27" for the 5x1,600m in the middle of his normal training week running by himself, i.e. just less than 67" per lap, then went on to run just under 28' for the 10km. Another, Darren Wilson did the same session averaging 66" and ran 27'37" a couple of weeks later. Similarly, if a top female can run 76" for this session, then a 31'40" 10km might be anticipated in a race following a good taper.

It is recognized that with the world record for the 10,000m standing at 26'17.53" as I write this section, a sub 28' run is no longer considered a great accomplishment but it's still a good run by current Australian history standards. Champions tend to come out of good numbers of talented runners working together and competing against each other. That only 18 Australians ever belong to the sub-28 min club is something that would need to be rectified should we have any thoughts of producing a 21st century equivalent of Ron Clarke. By rights we should have 18 current sub 28 min runners working towards sub 27. After all, the Kenyans have literally hundreds of runners in this category.

I suppose it's consolation for some Australians that we have better Australian Rules footballers and cricketers than the Kenyans. Producing Australian distance runners is not that easy given the attractions of our sparsely populated youngsters to major professional sports. Maybe our 10km runners need more recognition for the training they put in and the talent they possess. In Chapter 11 I acknowledged those road race directors who look after the professionalism of our top runners. Here's a small recognition to some of our best performers over the years. I'm hoping that by the time this book is published these lists are longer.

The Australian Men's Sub 28 minute 10km Club

27'24.95" Ben St Laurence–Palo Alto, USA 1 May 11
27'29.73" Collis Birmingham–Berkeley, USA 25 Apr 09
27'31.92" Shaun Creighton–Melbourne 25 Nov 96
27'34.48" Craig Mottram–Stanford,USA 4 May 08
27'37.00" Darren Wilson–Melbourne 25 Nov 96
27'39.89" Ron Clarke–Oslo, Norway 14 Jul 65
27'46.71" Bill Scott–Melbourne 6 Feb 80
27'47.69" Steve Moneghetti–Oslo, Norway 4 Jul 92
27'49.09" Sisay Bezabeh–Taraniki, NZL 21 Jan 02
27'50.70" Gerard Barrett–Moscow, Russia 21 Jul 79
27'50.73" Dean Cavuoto–Taraniki, NZL 21 Jan 02
27'51.27" Lee Troop–Inglewood, NZL 15 Feb 03
27'52.10" Shawn Forrest–Stanford,USA 2 May 09
27'53.30" Steve Austin–Stockholm, Sweden 9 Jul 81
27'54.93" Brett Cartwright–Taraniki,NZL 21 Jan 02
27'57.34" Andrew Lloyd–Melbourne 12 Dec 87
27'59.64" Paul Patrick–Melbourne 16 Dec 93
27'59.77" Michael Shelley–Berkeley, USA 25 Apr 09

The Australian Women's Sub 32 minute 10km Club

30'37.68" Benita Willis–Paris, France 23 Aug 03
31'11.72" Lisa Martin-Ondieki–Helsinki, Finland 30 Jun 92
31'26.34" Susie Power–Melbourne 6 Dec 01
31'43.14" Haley McGregor–Melbourne 4 Dec 03
31'43.31" Eloise Poppett-Wellings–Stanford, USA 1 May 11
31'51.71" Kylie Risk–Vancouver,Canada 1 Jun 96
31'54.57" Susan Hobson–Mito, Japan 6 May 96
31'54.95" Carolyn Schuwalow–Melbourne 10 Dec 91
31'55.65" Clair Fearnley–Sydney 24 Feb 00
31'55.94" Kerryn Hindmarsh-McCann–Melbourne 6 Dec 99
31'56.35" Jenny Green Lund–Melbourne 10 Dec 91

It's also worth noting the 28'02.73" Rob de Castella ran in Melbourne,15 Dec 1983, but the marathon was his passion, and he ran 28'50.40" as an Under 20 runner. Of note in the women was Natalie Harvey's 32'07" in Norway in 2000.

Every sub-28 minute run in Australia has been achieved at the famous Zatopek meeting in early December. The traditional Olympic Park venue near the famous 'Tan' Botanical Gardens on the Yarra has often provided the coolish and calm conditions required for a personal best over 25 laps. Three football codes (soccer, Australian rules, and rugby league) had the finances to make a claim to that precinct, so Australian sport's poor cousin Track and Field had to find another landlord. Let's hope that the new venue closer to Port Phillip Bay at South Melbourne can facilitate some more of our traditionally great 10km races.

It's been a few years now since I wrote that last sentence and I sadly add that the Zatopek 10km seems to have lost its 'mojo'. Did it lose it because it got kicked out of home? Probably, Zatopek's new home is a bit draughty and lacks the ambience. Runners are inclined to seek the fast races internationally these days.

Chapter 13, Training for the marathon

'Why', said the Dodo, 'the best way to explain it is to do it.'
Lewis Carroll

From football fitness to marathon fitness!

In 1978, at the age of 33, and having finished my football and cricket playing and coaching days, I decided to run a marathon. So did one of my keen young Human Movement students, Gavin Hopper, who later became an internationally successful tennis coach. We were both pretty fit from our ball sport training, and starting just 10 weeks out from the marathon we had in mind, we decided to throw the training manual away and increased our volume with gay abandon. We finished that 10 week stint with a couple of weeks at close to 100 miles (160 km) with 25–28km Sunday runs. The target was the Frankston to Melbourne marathon, called Big M in those days. It turned out to be a memorable one in many ways, one being my first encounter with ultra-marathoner Cliff Young, before he became a household name, as fondly described in Chapter 23.

All felt remarkably good for 30km and I reckoned I was on track for a 2hr50' debut as we passed 35km, and really looking forward to the last leg, when I hit that proverbial wall. A few minutes after feeling no worse than normally tired, I felt a few tell-tale muscle twitches in my calves, which in retrospect was a signal that the fuel tank reserve warning light had switched on. My reserve fuel tank must have been miniscule, as a minute or so later I was on empty, cramping in both calves. I couldn't even walk.

Then the Good Fairy appeared at the side of the road, and to her I will be eternally grateful. She held out a hand cupping eight jelly beans. I thanked her profusely and asked if I could have them all, and she gave me a Good Fairy smile 'Of course'. Within what seemed as little as 3 minutes, which I find fascinatingly fast, her magic worked. Those jelly beans kicked in and I resumed walking ... then jogging ... appreciating every successful step, to the Melbourne GPO, 3 hours and 11 minutes after I started. That first marathon is still fresh in my mind nearly 4 decades later and so is the satisfaction I got from finishing. I visualize marathoners reading this nodding your heads in agreement.

That happened to be the year I collaborated in some research with Drs Ian McDonald and Neil Blair, cardiologists at St Vincent's Hospital in Melbourne, together with my postgraduate research supervisor at Melbourne University, the late and dear Dr Mary Chennells. We were making use of the relatively new non-invasive technique of ultrasound to measure the size and shape of athletes' hearts. I was keen to see what happened to my ticker during the metamorphosis from footballer to marathoner. Over the next few years as I shaved more than 40 minutes off that debut marathon time I developed a heart of considerably greater volume which helped to power a bigger aerobic engine as described in Chapter 5. We human beings adapt to different types of training very well indeed.

And it's interesting that the adaptation took place in my 30s, a period of life where sportspeople used to be considered 'over the hill' and less responsive to training. That notion has certainly changed considerably in recent decades with professionalism doing much to prolong sporting careers. It's become apparent that world-class sporting performances are now possible well past the age of 30 in all sorts of sport. Carlos Lopes was 37 when he won Olympic marathon gold. No doubt I lost outright speed during this phase of marathon training, but as it turned out, it wasn't really lost, only hidden, because I got it back to a large degree in my early 40s as I switched to middle-distance competition, as described in Chapter 23.

Training for a marathon: get 10km fit and build the fuel tank

On the surface, setting out a training program for the marathon is relatively uncomplicated; a matter of working on threshold pace and muscle glycogen stores. Underneath though, it turns out to be quite a challenge, mainly because keeping runners injury and illness-free over a 4-6 month build-up is not easy.

Marathon training volumes can bring about gasps of disbelief from short distance speedsters, but in reality marathon training is no tougher than training for middle or even shorter distances. The vast proportion of time in a marathoner's training is long running, often a long relatively stress free run through a pristine forest or mountain trail. Even the quality runs are mainly aerobic and so less stressful than those of middle-distance runners.And consider too that the middle-distance runner has to race and repeat training sessions while blood acidity is increased to levels incompatible with life. On the other hand the well-conditioned marathoner can negotiate three quarters of the race in relative comfort and never has to endure extremes of acidity. Sure, it gets tough over the last 10km or so of the 26 miler, and sure, the legs have difficulty in following the brain's instructions, but it's usually not accompanied by intense pain, more a feeling of helplessness that comes when the power is turned off.

So, now that I've taken away some of the fear factor for marathon running—or have I increased it? Here are some guidelines for a successful preparation.

It's always good to know what we are supposed to train. Here are the four limiting factors to marathon performance.

(a) threshold (i.e. best 10 km) speed

(b) running economy

(c) glycogen storage

(d) anatomical resilience

Let's consider these one by one.

(a) Threshold training

Training to increase threshold speed, which approximates best 10km pace, has been addressed in Chapters 10,11 and 12. To 'tease' up the threshold we sometimes train above this pace (supra-threshold), sometimes right on it (threshold), and sometimes just below it (sub-threshold).

Examples of sessions:

Supra-threshold pace

10 x 600m (1' walk recovery)

16 x 400m (1' jog recovery)

16–20 x 1' (1' jog recovery) on a bush trail or grass.

On-threshold pace

4 x 1,600m (2' walk)

8 x 400m (200m float)

12 x 300m (100m float);

or bush trail of 5 x 5' (2' jog).

Sub-threshold pace sessions (on trails or grass or bitumen),

3 x 10' (3' jog)

2 x 15' (3' jog)

30' continuous

Note that during marathon training, physiological threshold, i.e. that level of exertion required to elicit maximal steady state heart rate and blood lactate concentration, is likely to be achieved at speeds lower than best 10km pace for three reasons. Firstly, running up hills or into a wind or on a softer surface doesn't allow 10km speed to be achieved, but the training stress is similar. Secondly it's common during months of high volume training that the marathoner's 10km speed may be reduced as other marathon characteristics are developed. Thirdly, marathoners often train in a semi-fatigued state in the build-up period, so 10km race-speed may not be attained even in reps as short as 1 km. This doesn't really present a problem for the marathoner (as distinct from the track runner), because learning to run fast in a lowered muscle glycogen state contributes to beneficial adaptations in fatty acid metabolism.

However, easing training back to allow marathon runners to run high quality threshold sessions makes sense too.

(b) Running economy

As discussed in Chapter 7, it remains debatable as to whether economy can be improved in a well-accomplished and experienced runner. But if the principle of specificity has anything to do with it, then marathon pace training would be most likely to elicit an improvement in economy. Runners tend to become more economical around these sub-threshold speeds as their age, career and volume of training accumulates, which is consistent with this premise.

(c) Glycogen storage and blood sugar control

Muscle glycogen storage capacity is improved by repeatedly challenging it. Long runs, long quality sessions and high weekly training volumes all challenge muscle glycogen stores, the adaptive process involving an increased concentration of glycogen synthesizing enzymes in the muscles that power running. In long runs of 25km to 40km it's normal for legs to begin to feel like lead as glycogen stores are lowered. It's one of the wonders of life that we are able to respond to a stress with an improved capacity to offset any future potential distress of a similar nature. In this case we respond by learning to store more fuel.

There are some scientists and coaches who suggest that marathon fitness might be enhanced if runners reduce their glycogen stores prior to their long runs by restricting carbohydrate ingestion. They argue that the runner doesn't have to run as fast or as far to deplete the stores which may offset the risk of overuse injury or even accelerate glycogen stores. The theory seems reasonable, starting off with a half-full tank will certainly get you to a fatigued state earlier. Something to think about, especially in a runner who finds sufficiently big training weeks are out of the question because of susceptibility to overuse injury or lack of time. In any case, this theory is probably inadvertently put to use without intentionally manipulating diet prior to running because marathoners running 150-220 km/week are likely to begin most training runs with compromised muscle glycogen stores.

While training up muscle glycogen stores is widely acknowledged, little consideration has been given to training the liver. Well, for mine, a 'fit' liver is an important part of marathon fitness as this organ assumes a great deal of the responsibility for maintaining blood glucose levels; and under the stress of running 42.195km as fast as possible this is not easy. Many a runner has suffered the dizziness and loss of coordination brought about by an inability to keep blood sugar levels within normal range. For those who experience hypoglycaemia as it's called, we can speculate that the liver fails to cope with a duel role of trying to maintain blood glucose while also being called upon to contribute glucose to the working muscles as their own supply runs low. The liver, on the other hand, gets no help in return from the muscles to maintain blood glucose, because once a glucose molecule enters a hungry muscle cell that muscle cell makes sure it can't get out again by cunningly attaching a phosphate unit.

We know how to train the muscle, but how do we train the liver? It's probably easier to explain how we inadvertently 'de-train' it. A detrained or 'lazy' liver in this marathon context might develop by a relative lack of use so that its response to hypoglycaemia is dulled. It's possible that even in runners a relatively lazy liver can be brought about by excessive and regular consumption of simple sugar; sweet-stuff regularly introduced directly into the bloodstream via the mouth and digestive tract, regularly offsetting the liver's responsibility to supply glucose to the bloodstream in its own measured and controlled manner. And the liver is like any other organ; if you don't use it you lose it. When a runner's blood glucose level is severely challenged toward the end of a marathon, even ingestion of glucose through drinks and gels during the run might not be sufficient to compensate for a liver that's not up to the task.

Digressing somewhat, it is interesting that many medical scientists feel that repeated excess consumption of sugar in the form of drinks, candy, cakes and biscuits may eventually lead to metabolic dysfunction in the form of insulin resistance (meaning that increased levels of insulin are required to reduce blood glucose levels). This may lead on to Type 2 diabetes, a life threatening disease in epidemic proportions all over the world. It's also interesting that physical inactivity does the same thing. So an inactive person who also bolsters up his or her blood glucose directly through their small intestine, rather than giving this task to the liver, would be at greatest risk to chronic disease.

Back to running, and we can speculate that marathoners might benefit from day-to-day nutritional strategies. One sensible strategy is to avoid repeated oral injections of glucose throughout the day and to confine most of the carbohydrate intake to the complex non-sweet variety; refraining from ingesting concentrated sugars such as candy snacks, sweet beverages and biscuits in between meals. And it's been proposed that runners (and indeed the rest of us) would do well to avoid 'hits' of sugar on an empty stomach. Of course runners, like anyone else need not completely remove sweet stuff from their diets, but to satisfy their sweet teeth mainly as after-dinner desserts and treats.

This makes good sense to me, and the term 'glycaemic index' has been coined, and subsequently researched and publicized to a large degree by respected nutritionist, Jenny Brand-Mllller from the University of Sydney. The GI is a measure of the speed at which sugar is taken up into the bloodstream, along with the corresponding obligatory secretion of insulin, the pancreatic hormone tasked with the extremely important responsibility of reducing the concentration of blood glucose. Now in recent times cold water has been poured onto the concept of GI by some nutritionists, in that it mainly measures the speed at of the glucose-insulin response, rather than the total response. However, I wouldn't discount the benefit of a relatively low GI intake, with its dampened increase in blood glucose and insulin; this appeals as potentially less threatening to the liver's control of the situation.

For its anecdotal worth, my coaching experience has found that athletes on lower GI diets seem less likely to suffer from hypoglycaemic-like symptoms during training and races. Moreover, a modification of the diet to a lower GI over a six-month period in one of my marathoners who had trouble with low blood sugar during racing did correspond with a better marathon performance. It could have been purely coincidental of course ...

(d) Anatomical resilience

Marathons are usually run on flat hard bitumen surfaces in light racing shoes. With each footstrike a shockwave has to be tolerated by an upright human frame of somewhat rickety construction. And with hard training and racing comes repeated metabolic stress. Resilience is the ability to maintain anatomical and physiological health during this stress. For runners this means not only resisting injury to bones, muscles, tendons, and ligaments but also maintaining healthy immune and metabolic systems.

As discussed in more depth in Chapter 21, it's important that this shock of footstrike is varied, to avoid the same pattern of shock on the same sites, thereby increasing the risk of overuse injury. Footstrike shock can be dampened by varying the running environment; choosing flat and undulating gradients, softer forest trails and grass surfaces, and by wearing heavier training shoes. And if you've got orthotics in your shoes, check with your podiatrist, but choosing not to wear them sometimes, perhaps for some easy runs, will vary the direction of the shockwave. So would the occasional run in bare feet if the surface permits.

On the other hand marathoners must learn to endure the stress of flat, hard-surface running, so a graduated inclusion of race-pace running on flat roads in racing shoes is an important aspect of marathon preparation. Leaving the specific speed and surface work simply to a pre-marathon 10km or half-marathon lead-in race may not be sufficient to develop the kind of resilience required to get through a marathon at tapered race-pace. It makes sense to gradually introduce some specific hard-surface running reasonably early in the training program.

How long is a long run?

Long runs are the 'bread-and-butter' training sessions for a marathoner. If a runner were to be restricted to just one kind of training run, then the long run is 'it.' Long runs repeatedly lower glycogen in the muscles that power running, stimulating an increase in their ability to store energy, glycogen and fat. Long runs also provide a challenge to the marathoner's homeostasis, developing better control of blood sugar, acid-base balance and body temperature. The requisite length of such a run to achieve this effect depends on the endurance fitness of the runner. Overload and adaptation will result from little as 5km for an untrained person, 15km for a moderately trained runner, to between 25km and 40km for accomplished marathoners.

A marathoner's training week

Some marathon coaches write a cycle into the program where sessions with similar characteristics are repeated every 10 days. More commonly, a weekly cycle is set out involving a long run on Sunday, a medium long run Wednesday, three faster sessions on Tuesday, Thursday and Saturday and easy-paced recovery running on Monday and Friday. Training is twice a day for the serious runners and mileage is around 150 to 220 km/wk, the lesser volumes planned when higher volumes can't be sustained without injury or illness. Some successful marathon coaches emphasize consistency and set a weekly program that does not vary all that much all through the year; others like to vary programs from week to week and in different phases of training.

The seven-day cycle suits my personal training philosophy, and my programs vary, usually every couple of weeks and from month to month. I like to include three quality sessions in each week, all around physiological threshold, a supra-threshold session on Tuesday with shorter repetitions, a threshold session on Thursday with medium-length repetitions, and a sub-threshold quality session on Saturday with longer repetitions or a sustained run. I often vary the actual session every couple of weeks, but keep certain sessions as test sessions to see how the athlete is progressing. Apart from making the training more interesting, variation of the repetition distance and the recovery periods might better prepare a runner psychologically as well as physiologically for the variety of race tactics encountered as athletes surge and slow to test their opposition.

Combining the long run and quality – the 12 week out program

Another feature of marathon training I favour, and one that increases its specificity, is incorporating specified faster running into a long run. Rather than setting a traditional track, trail or grass session that includes a discontinuous formal warm-up and warm-down, the quality session can form part of a continuous long run. This faster quality work can be placed either in the middle or toward the end of the run depending on the desired effect. So rather than a quality session Tuesday and Thursday, interspersed with a long run Wednesday, the quality could be done within a long or medium long run of around 25km on Tuesday or Thursday or indeed both these days, with a recovery day on Wednesday.

I often prefer to use the latter program as we approach the final 12 weeks of marathon preparation as it allows me to enhance the race specificity of the training week with less risk of runners becoming overtired. Faster running, in a 'fresher' state of mind and body can be introduced earlier into the medium or long run. If I want the athlete to provide a 'best effort' while in a semi-fatigued state, I program the faster work later in the long run.

Typical marathon training weeks

Let's assume our runner has built up gradually into the following work. We'll use 1500s as the threshold session; the 3 minute efforts as the supra-threshold session; the 10 minute efforts as the sub-threshold pace session. Here we incorporate quality in one of the midweek long runs. In order to describe how volume can change I haven't changed the nature of the quality sessions. Note the 'easy' recovery runs on Monday, Wednesday, and Friday in this program; and a back-to-back quality effort and long run on Saturday and Sunday. We also incorporate a 'session' on Thursday within the midweek long run. Bracketed numbers are recovery times.

A 120km week

Monday: Easy 10km

Tuesday: Track, 4km warm-up, 4 x 1500m (2'), 5km warm-down (15km)

Wednesday: Easy 10km

Thursday: Trails, 25km including 8 x 3'(1') @ 10km mark

Friday: Easy 10km

Saturday: Trails or Grass 5km warm-up, 3 x 10' (3' jog), 5km warm-down (20km)

Sunday: Trails including hills: Long Run 30km

Adding three second runs on the easy days, as indicated after the semi-colon, we have a 150km Week:

Monday: Easy 10km; Easy 10km

Tuesday: Track, 4km warm-up, 4 x 1500m (2'), 5km warm-down

Wednesday: Easy 10km; easy 10km

Thursday: Trails, 25km including 8 x 3'(1') @ 10km mark

Friday: Easy 10km; easy 10km

Saturday: Trails or Grass 5km warm-up, 3 x 10' (3' jog), 5km warm-down (20km)

Sunday: Trails including hills: Long Run 30km

Increasing one of the two easy day runs, and adding second runs on quality days, we have a 180km week:

Monday: Easy 15km; Easy 10km

Tuesday: Track, 4km warm-up, 4 x 1500m (2'), 5km warm-down; 8km

Wednesday: Easy 15km; easy 10km

Thursday: Trails, 25km including 8 x 3'(1') @ 10km mark; 8km

Friday: Easy 15km; easy 10km

Saturday: Trails or Grass 5km warm-up, 3 x 10' (3' jog), 5km warm-down (20km); 8km

Sunday: Trails including hills: Long Run 30km

A 200km week

Monday: Easy 15km; easy 10km

Tuesday: Track, 5km warm-up, 5 x 1,600m (2'), 5km warm-down ; easy 10km. (An alternative here in an advanced program is one run for the day of 25–28k long run including 5 x 5' (2' jog))

Wednesday: Easy 15km; easy 10km

Thursday: Trails, 25km including 8 x 3'(1') @ 10km mark; easy 8km,

Friday: Easy 15km; easy 10km

Saturday: Trails or Grass 5km warm-up, 3 x 10' (3' jog), 5km warm-down; 10km

Sunday: Trails including hills: Long run 32km

How much volume?

There have been some examples of internationally competitive marathoners running well off 150km training weeks, but most would run 160–220 km. There's a trade-off between speed and volume; an athlete may achieve similar stress on glycogen supplies in a long run by running less distance but running faster. Faster running over any distance demands not only more energy per kilometre but a greater proportion of glycogen to fat as the fuel source. Faster running in the long run is also likely to contribute more to aerobic fitness. The catch is that running faster in the long runs amidst weeks of high quality work may increase the risk of injury. That's why many coaches and runners feel that an easy long run is the way to go on that traditional Sunday morning. Nevertheless, if, and only if, faster long running can be negotiated without risk then it's likely to afford an advantage.

It's vital to test the water carefully in the shallows before adventuring out into the deep unknown. Any runner plunging into higher volume or speed in the long run or indeed in any of the weekly sessions runs the risk of drowning. Well not literally, but perhaps drowning in the sorrow of overuse injury. No-one is bullet-proof.

Characterising marathon training

To describe some sessions, I've selected sessions from some runners who had run around the 2hr25'–35' min mark around the time of this training. Training for marathons can be varied enormously depending on athlete characteristics and preferences but here are a few sessions I like to include in any of my programs.

Long run with finishing sustained effort (Figure 13-1)

Here we have the heart rate response and speeds (as minutes per km) in a 25km run, including 15km 'easy' i.e. at a comfortable well-controlled pace, then 8km solid (about 3'25" per km) with 2km warmdown to finish. Note the steady climb in heart rate even in the supposedly 'easier' part of the run but this coincided with a gradually increased pace. This places the runner in a semi-fatigued position at the time of putting in the solid finishing effort. Heart rate climbs steadily and approaches the 'threshold' or 'maximal steady state' heart rate. (This athlete's maximal heart rate was around 180 beats per minute at this stage of training.)

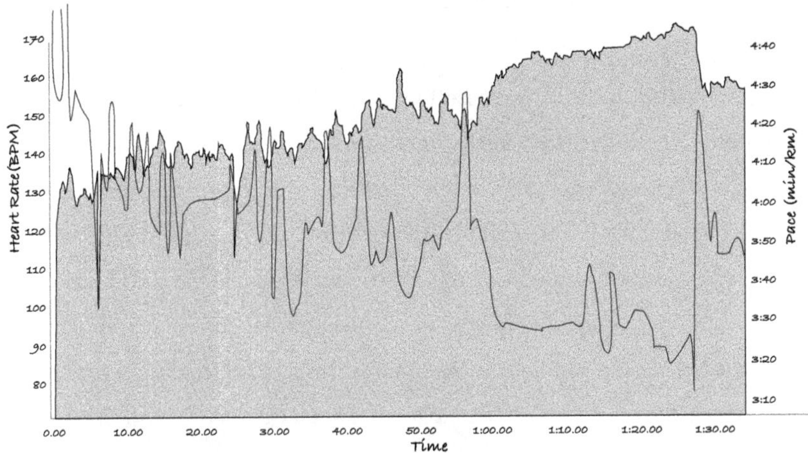

Fig 13-1: Long run with finishing sustained effort: 25km, 15km easy 8km solid, 2km easy.

Medium duration repetitions at close to threshold (Figure 13-2)

This session was 4 x 7'30" solid effort with a 1'30" walk recovery, performed on a firm dirt track. There was a gradual increase in average speed as the session proceeded, showing that our marathon runner began a little conservatively to maintain good control. Threshold heart rate for this runner was around 170 at the time, but it's difficult to achieve threshold (10 km) pace in the middle of a solid week of training and on a dirt track, so this session is better described as a physiological threshold effort but at sub-threshold pace.

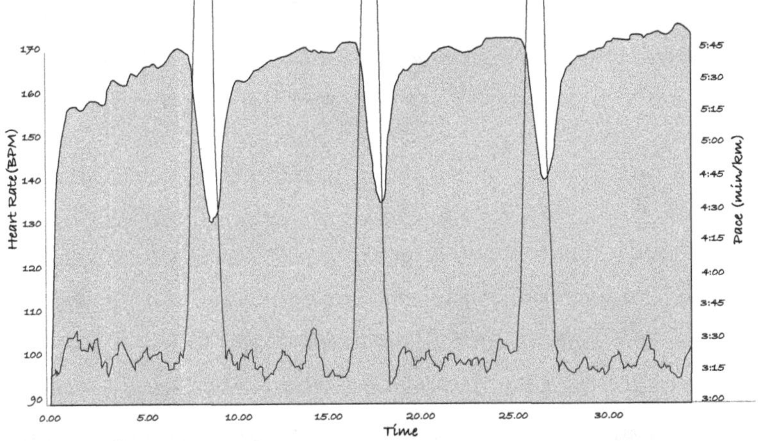

Fig 13-2: Medium duration repetitions at close to threshold: 4 x 7' 30" (1'30" walk recovery).

Short repetition float recovery or supra-threshold repetition (Figure 13-3)

This session on the track was 4 x 400m with a 200m 'float' recovery rather than jog, repeated three times with a lap jog recovery. This is a variation of the 8 x 400m (200m float) track session described in Chapter 10, adding some quantity while maintaining quality. Note that the recovery heart rates during the float remain high, this session resembling 3 sustained efforts with speed variation rather than a series of 400 repetitions. The lower curve shows that recovery speeds were a bit slower in the last set (i.e. higher min/km), but this served to maintain the speed of the 400m repetitions. Even with the lap jog between the second and third sets the heart rate remains relatively elevated in the mid to high 130s.

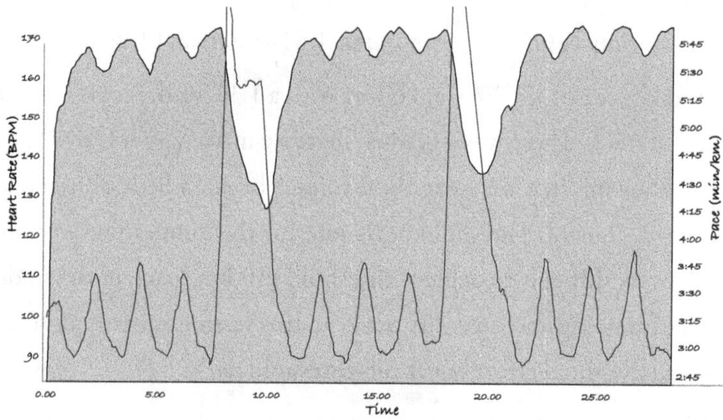

Fig 13-3: Short repetition, float recovery (supra-threshold running): 3 x 4x 400m (200m float)] with a lap jog recovery.

Maximal aerobic power (Figure 13-4)

Set piece: 8 x 800 (200m slow jog)

This session is run at supra-threshold i.e. faster than 10km pace, the objective to approach 3km pace. $\dot{V}02$ max would have been approached during the latter parts of each of the last 5 or 6 efforts. This session also includes obligatory demands on the anaerobic system, but this long-distance runner's anaerobic contribution would be less than in shorter distance track runners, facilitating quicker recovery between efforts.

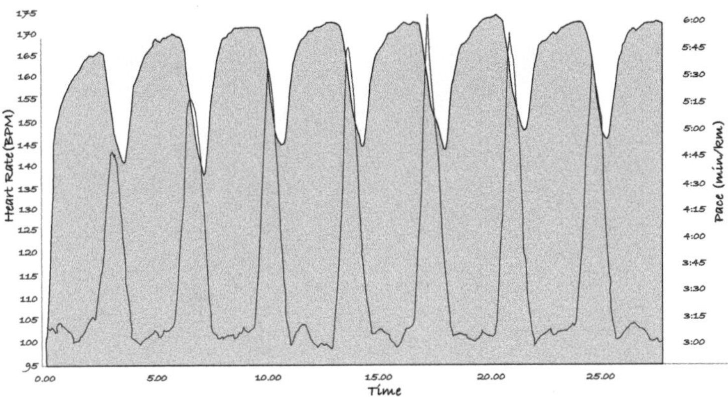

Fig 13-4: Maximal aeorbic power: 8x 800m (2' slow jog recovery).

Sustained strong running (Figure 13-5)

Set piece: 8km running at best training pace (as distinct from best tapered pace)

The average speed was around 3'30" per kilometre for this run. This is slower than threshold pace which was about 3'20" per kilometre at this stage of the runner's build-up, but was race specific and a very good training effort, holding heart rate at very close to the physiological threshold level. Average speed varied more than heart rate because of the undulating nature of the terrain and sensitivity of the scale of measurement.

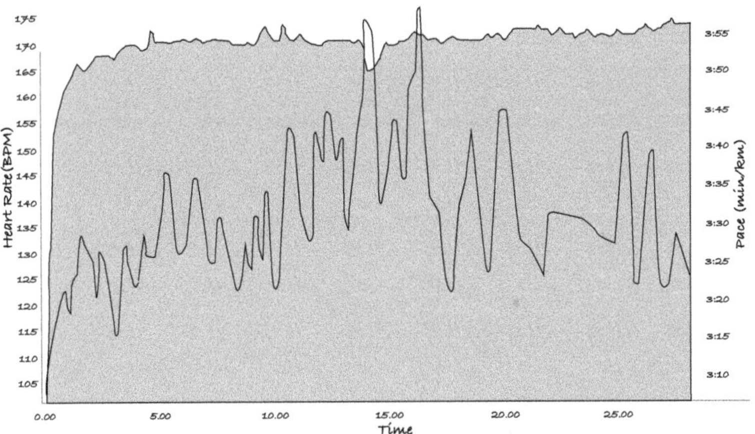

Fig 13-5: Sustained effort: 8k at best training pace.

Chapter 14
Pre-race tapering: the body

A taper removes the cloud of fatigue with reduced volume to let the fitness and performance shine through.

Tapering for a race epitomizes the science and art of coaching. The science is the application of principles of physiology; the art is developing that feeling of readiness to perform.

What exactly is a taper?

A taper is the process by which the coach and athlete work together to optimize the physical and psychological characteristics for the race. It is useful here to separate these characteristics to explain tapering, but we should always remember how body and mind constantly interact.

The way we think affects the way we move and the way we move affects the way we think.

Champion New Zealand middle-distance runner of the 1930s and Berlin Olympic 1500m gold medallist Jack Lovelock was one of the first to recognize the value of systematic tapering for a race, his initiative and methods no doubt influenced by his studies of physiology and psychology during his medical training. Lovelock was well ahead of the game when it came to race preparation, playing out likely occurrences based on his knowledge of the opposition, and setting up potential strategies.

Getting the body right

Mistakes occur in the week or so before a big race when 'race anxiety' coerces a runner into last minute attempts to get that little bit fitter. Olympic bronze medallist Alan Lawrence in his book *The Self-coached Runner* doesn't waste any time in relating what he believed to be a cardinal error made by the self-coached Ron Clarke. On the very first page of his first chapter Lawrence writes of the then current 10,000m world record holder Clarke's training session three days before the 10,000m final at the Tokyo Olympics.

'His first mile is fast; the second is faster; 5000m comes up in world-class time. At four miles the watches of bystanders record an unofficial world record.'

Lawrence continues, 'then at last responding to the pleas of several other Australian runners, he slows, jogs off the track and ends his workout. But the damage is done; three days later in the Olympic final, Clarke is third, an outstanding result but far below the expectations of the track world, and of Clarke himself.'

Compare and contrast Clarke's late stage workout with the immediate pre-Olympic training of 800m runner Doubell. I discuss the Doubell situation in detail in Chapter 21 but I like this story so much I couldn't resist introducing it here in context of tapering.

Training with Franz Stampfl leading up to the 1968 Mexico City Olympics, Doubell had done a lot of work, including, as he told me one day 'big track sessions of 50 x 100m one day, 20 x 400s the next followed by 10 x 1200m or if the track was flooded a very solid 10 miler'; around 20k per day.

He'd built into this program over the years, although it's quite remarkable that he really only started serious running at age 18 when he enrolled at the University of Melbourne where Stampfl was the professional Track and Field coach. His Australian record of 1:44.4 still stands (as I revise this section I'm happy to report that this Aussie record has now been equalled by Alex Rowe); and would be considered respectable in international circles nearly half a century later.

But it nearly wasn't to be. An Achilles tendon injury had Doubell doing absolutely no running at all in the 7 days leading to the first heat of the 800m in Mexico City.

It is natural for athletes to worry if they can't run, to feel sluggish and anxious without some sharp work to sharpen up. Physiologists might be concerned that the reduction in muscle enzymes seen in bed-rest experiments might accompany a week of no running. But not Ralph or Franz; the consensus was that the Achilles was the number one concern and it had to be rested; the training was done over the past four years and a few days of obligatory rest was of no concern at all.

Well history has it that Ralph Doubell ran a blinder, equalling the world record and out-kicking the world's best 800m runners to take the gold. Could that compulsory complete rest have been a vital factor in that wonderful performance? Would that stunning and once in his lifetime racing form have been realized without that full week off after his gruelling training build-up? It's hard to believe that he could have run any better, and easy to imagine he may not have performed as well if he had done a couple of sessions to 'sharpen up.' We'll never know the answer to those questions, and by the way, for all you altitude enthusiasts, Ralph's only pre-race altitude training was a couple of weeks of jogging and walking in Mexico City!

But just in case you are thinking of doing nothing for a week or so before your big race, think again. Unless of course you've trained like Ralph for the previous year and have a sore Achilles. It's a very personal thing, this tapering. It's also likely that a runner can do too little for too long before a race, just as he or she can do too much. And there have been many great runs remarkably soon after other big efforts. One that I recall hearing about was when Alby Thomas paced Herb Elliott's world record mile (3:54.5) in 1958. Alby finished off the race to run 3:58.6. But the next day Alby broke the 2 mile world record, running 8:32. Does that mean a flat-out mile the previous day was the perfect taper? Not what we'd recommend but it does provide food for thought as to what might suit you best, with your physiology and current level of fitness. We know that Ron Clarke broke 18 world records in a 40 day campaign of racing in Europe. It seems that when you're fit you're fit; and 'in the zone.' Physical and psychological recovery is rapid from day to day and running very fast happens 'any which way' you approach a race. But being in the zone can't last forever.

I know it's a different kettle fish, so to speak, but during my days of working with the Australian swim team, swimmers trained with much greater volumes and intensity than Doubell (as aquatic exercise permits). The coaches employed long taper periods of 2 to 3 weeks of very easy swimming, with very little race-pace work, to remove that 'cloud of fatigue' and to be at their best on race day. However, sometimes the swimmers seemed to lose their spark in the pool with a low-key extended taper.

In the early 1980s at the AIS I coined the phrase 'spiking' for our swim coaches in suggesting how we might treat the power plants of their charges during the period of reduced training prior to competition. This 'spike' session is a high quality but not exhausting session aimed at one or more of our energy systems as a timely reminder that the body and mind is going to be called upon for a huge task in a few days' time. The spike had to be sufficiently intense to keep the energy system tuned up, and to allow the swimmer to get the 'feel' of the water at close to race-pace. Most importantly a subsequent spike session could only be prescribed if the swimmer felt fully recovered from the previous spike session.

A problem with a training squad of swimmers or runners occurs when all athletes are set the same taper programs. Tapers are dependent on both the individual athlete and the event. The story in Chapter 6 about the swimmer who was nearly sent home prior to Atlanta Olympics but went on to win a gold medal is a great illustration of the individual specificity component of tapering.

Bearing this individuality in mind, here are some general guiding principles of taper for a distance runner. Let's assume training has been proceeding well and the athlete is not unusually tired and is illness free.

Generalities of a taper

Three weeks out: reduce overall training volume (distance) by around 15 percent but maintain the quality sessions. For example, weekly training of 150km per week is reduced to around 130 km.

Two weeks out: reduce the volume by another 15 percent. In our example training is reduced to about 110km per week. The athlete should be recovering almost fully between each quality session, held every second day. These sessions now operate as spikes, i.e. they are not designed to continue to induce improvements in the power of each energy system, but simply to maintain that power, and as the fatigue is removed performance is enhanced.

Final week: reduce the predicted weekly volume to around 50 percent of usual training volume. This is about 75km in our example of a 150km week. Reduce the volume of the Tuesday quality session by 25 percent and the Thursday quality session by 50 percent, so that these two 'spike' sessions are performed with good quality but carefully controlled to ensure that recovery is complete in the following 24 hours.

Last three days: Easy jogging and some strides at race-pace to maintain rhythm. Figure 14.1 and 14.2 provide schematic representations of the interactions between the volume, fatigue and performance leading into major competitions. Removing the cloud of fatigue that accompanies the build-up phase frees up the underlying fitness to be translated into performance.

Tapering for a marathon

Seriously competitive marathoners usually only race two, perhaps three times a year. Because personal best performances in this event mean so much, it's important to find a marathon offering cool conditions and on a flat course without too many twists and turns. This often means international travel.

So let's look at a couple of real life examples in the one athlete but in different circumstances and how the races turned out.

An international marathon with large time zone change: from Australia to Europe

Female athlete example A with around 2h30' as her personal best, averaging about 160 km/wk for the 8 week lead-up period.

I use the asterisked notation to designate the quality of the effort

* easy-paced; ** solid but well controlled; *** an intense or very long training session; **** race

3 weeks out

Monday: Arrive Europe

Tuesday: two easy runs with some changes of pace

Wednesday: am 20km*, pm 8km*

Thursday: am 16km including 16 x 1' (1')**; pm 8km*

Friday: am 12km*, pm 10km*

Saturday: am 18km including 4 x 1600 (2')***; pm 5km

Sunday: am 30km** as feel. One run today.

Penultimate Week

Monday: *Two very easy jogs am 8km; pm 8km,

Tuesday: am 16km including 4 x 2km**(*) (1') threshold then travel 5 hr by road to marathon city. On arrival stretch and walk or 3–5km jog

Wednesday: Two easy runs; am 10km*, pm 6km*

Thursday: am 25km* long run including 8 x 3'** around marathon race-pace (2'-3' easy recoveries). Never an intense effort but some race-pace work in a long run. One run for the day

Friday: Two easy runs; am 8km*, pm 5km*

Final Week

Saturday: am *** 6km threshold effort plus 4 x 30" (30") technique strides. This is a very solid 6km but well controlled.

Sunday: 25 km** @ 11am as feel, comfortable all the way ... don't worry about getting a bit tired in the legs toward the end.

Monday: am easy 10km; pm *easy 8km

Tuesday: **11 am 1 x 8' (2'), 3 x 3' (1'), 6 x 30" (30"); pm easy 30'

Wednesday: *am easy 50'; pm easy 30'

Thursday: *One run @ 11 am easy 30' including 4 x 1' (1' jog) and 2 x 30" (1')

Friday: *One run 11 am easy 8km including 10 x 150m strides

Saturday: *One run 11 am 8km including 6-8 race-pace strides of 100m

Sunday: 20' jog warm-up, include 6 relaxed 100m strides at race-pace then **** the marathon

Outcome: Our runner felt really good before the race and expressed that her legs felt ready to go. She raced well, reducing her personal best by 2 minutes and finishing 10 places higher than her pre-race ranking by personal best time.

International Marathon with little time zone change: Australia to Japan

Female athlete example B also with around 2h30' personal best

3 weeks out

Monday: *am 10km; * pm 15km

Tuesday: *am 10k; ***pm Track 15k including 8 x 800 (1') @ as close to 3km pace as possible

Wednesday: *am 15km; pm 10km both very easy

Thursday: am *** 25km including 20 x 1' at 10km at around race-pace; *pm 10km

Friday: Very easy *am15km; *pm 10km

Saturday: am ***Grass: 4 x 8' (2' jog) in 15km; pm jog 8km

Sunday: am **32km.

2 weeks out

Monday: am 10km; pm 15km

Tuesday: am 8km; pm 15km including, 8 x 3' (1') @10km pace on dirt trail).

Wednesday: am 10km; pm 10km both very easy

Thursday: am 25km including 4 x 5' (2' jog) solid but well controlled @ close to 10km pace

Friday: am 10km; pm 10km

Saturday: am 15km including a 6km at half-marathon pace and 4 x 30" (30") strides. No second run.

Sunday: 11 am 25km very comfortable all the way. No second run

The final week

Monday: am easy 10km; easy 8km

Tuesday: am 1 x 8' (3'), 3 x 3' (1'), 6 x 30" (30") a good solid session but never forcing it; pm easy 8km

Wednesday: am Travel. Easy 10km if practical and feeling well

Thursday: am easy 10km including 4x1' and 2 x 30"

Friday: am 8km with 6 x 150m strides at race-pace

Saturday: am 8km including 6 x 100m at race-pace

Sunday: am Marathon race

Race Outcome: Athlete B reported feeling good before the race. She ran accordingly, a one minute personal best.

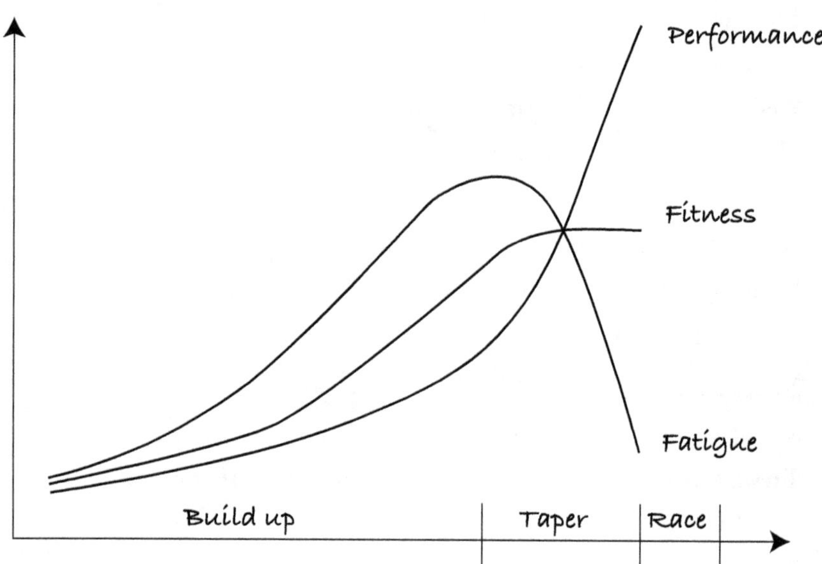

Fig 14-1: General relationships of Fitness, Fatigue and Performance. Removing the cloud of fatigue allows the fitness to be translated into performance.

Tapering for a 10,000m run on the track

Here our example of a taper session for a 10,000m runner who improved his personal best by almost half a minute to run close to 28 minutes.

2 ½ weeks out (the 10km is on a Thursday night).

Monday: *Two very easy runs to prepare for tomorrow

Tuesday: am *8km easy; pm ***Track 400 (1') 800 (1') 1,200 (1') 1,600 (1') 1,200 (1') 800 (1') 400, (rough guide to pacing: 1,200s and 1,600 about 66s; 800s at 64, 400 in 62 then sub 60

Wednesday: *am 8km, *pm 16km, strength work as usual

Thursday: **am trail 12 x 1' (1'jog), *pm easy 8km

2 weeks out

Friday: *One or two easy runs as feel

Saturday: *** am 30' continuous strong run on trail; * pm easy 8km

Sunday: am **25km as you feel

Monday: *Two very easy runs to prepare for tomorrow's quality

Tuesday: *am easy 8km; pm ***Track in spikes 4 x 1,600 (1'30") in around 4'30" (1'); then 4 x 200 (1'). Looking for a high quality effort, although make sure form is maintained

Wednesday: * 16km

Thursday: *am easy 8km, pm **Trail (8 x 1' (1' jog) 1' (30" jog)) Looking for some spring in your step. Good quality 1' efforts, with easy jog recoveries, allowing you to concentrate on technique

The penultimate week

Friday: *One or two easy runs as usual

Saturday: *** am 4 x 8' (2') and 6 x 30" (30" float). Solid session at as close to 10km pace as you can manage on the trail

Sunday: ** am 22km as feel; no second run

Monday: Two easy runs

Tuesday: * am easy 8km; pm*** 2 x [4 x 400 (200 float in 37"–38")], 3' between sets

Wednesday: * am easy 16km; *pm easy 8km

Thursday: *** 20' very solid effort and 4–6 x 30" (30")

The final week

Friday: * 2 x Easy 8km

Saturday: ***1 x 8' (2'); 3x 3' (1'); 6x 30"(30") all really solid efforts on a dirt trail or grass

Sunday: * am easy 10km, pm easy 8km

Monday: *am easy 8km; pm ** 8 x 1'(1') as feel good technique or 8 x 300 (1') on track

Tuesday: *Easy 8km including 4 x race-pace 150m relaxed strides

Wednesday: *Easy 6–8k including 4 x 150m race-pace strides

Thursday: **** ZATOPEK 10km

Outcome: Our runner reported that he felt 'good' during the race warm-up. He ran strongly, doing his share of front running and running his personal best.

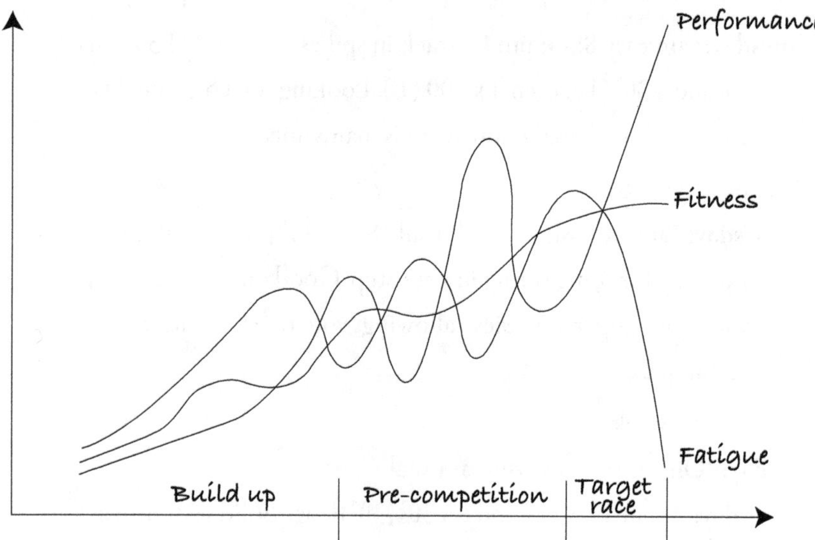

Fig 14-2: Relationships of Fitness, Fatigue and Performance including pre-competition races before a targeted race.

Characterising three of the taper spike sessions for the 10km race

Session one week out from race day.

Session: 20' solid (4' recovery), 6 x 30" (30")

Distances: 6.78 km, 190m, 180m, 200m, 190m, 200m, 200m

Comment: The sustained effort on dirt trail was 2'57" per km; a solid effort on slightly uneven and soft surface. The 30" efforts were well above race-pace of course, allowing the runner to finish with a good 'feel' about his speed during the taper.

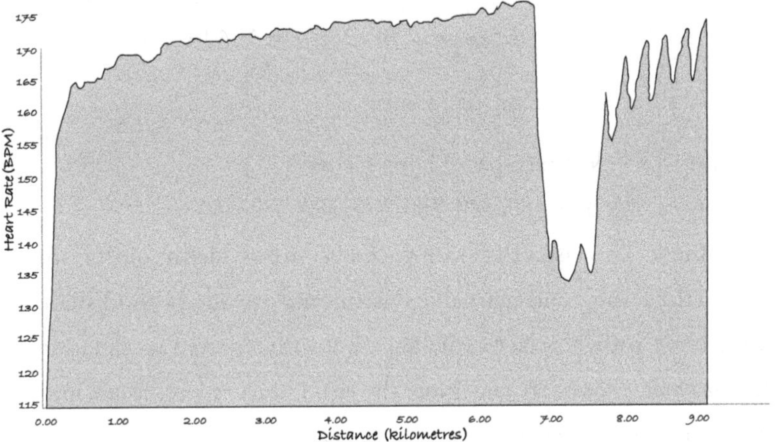

Fig 14-3: Taper spike session : 20' (4' recovery), 6 x 30" (30").

Session 6 days out from race day

Session : 7' 30" (1'30"), 3 x 3' (1'), 6 x 30" (30")

Distances (km, m) 2.53, 1.04, 1.03, 1.04, 200, 180, 200, 190, 200, 190

Athlete comment: felt pretty good throughout.

Comment: This session 'spiked' the aerobic system, as indicated by speed and heart rate up in his usual 'threshold' zone, and the finishing set provided some faster than race-pace work. That this felt comfortable was a good indication the taper was appropriate.

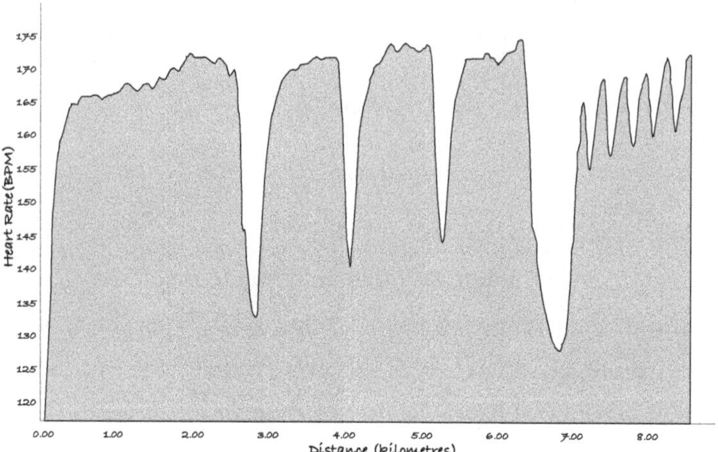

Fig 14-4: Taper spike session : 7'30" (2'30"); 3x 3' (1'); 6 x 30" (30").

Session 4 days out from race day

Session: 8 x 1' near race-pace (1' jog recovery)

Distances (m): 380, 380, 380, 380, 380, 380, 380, 380

Comment: This faster than race-pace session provided a comfortable session that spiked the aerobic and anaerobic systems, and provided a good 'sharpener' for mind and body, with little lactic tolerance, but with repeated acceleration of heart rate up into race-pace heart rate. Note the rapid heart rate recovery, indicative of an athlete in the taper period.

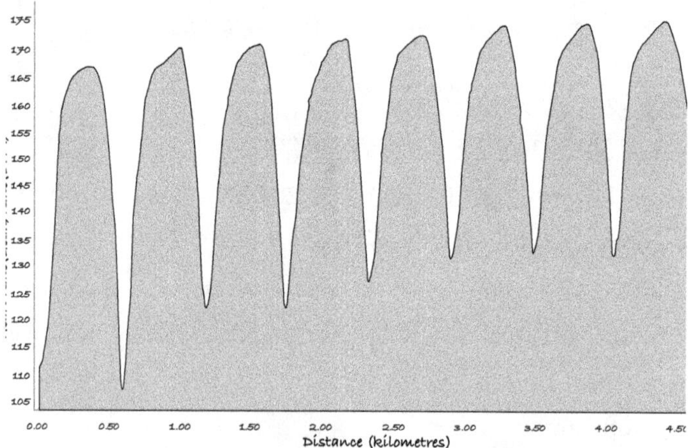

Fig 14-5:Taper spike session: 8x 1' (1' jog).

The post-race debrief

We learn a little bit more about pre-race preparation every race from the feedback athletes provide. As an example, I asked my two marathon runners, Lisa Weightman and Michael Shelley some questions following their New Delhi Commonwealth Games runs. I was particularly keen to hear how they rated their preparation for that race as they both did very well with medals in trying conditions; and it wouldn't be the last hot one we prepare for. Their preparation included training in warm conditions in the Gold Coast (Shelley) and in Melbourne (Weightman). Lisa ran a couple of sessions a week on a treadmill at the Victorian Institute of Sport at room temperature in the 20°s with no fan cooling effect. Then we all joined up for couple of weeks in the tropics near Cairns, Queensland, before they travelled to India 5 days before the marathon, a week after the rest of the team.

They told me that the abbreviated time in the Games Village in New Delhi was perfect. Enough time to recover, do the last routine taper sessions, and avoid feeling too hemmed in, given that no one was allowed out for sight-seeing.

I asked them the question 'What stopped you running faster? Breathing problems or fatigued legs? Too hot? Thirsty?' Lisa told me she felt really easy the first 13km but 'we weren't running fast'. She wasn't breathing hard except at the drink stations when trying to run and drink at the same time. Lisa recalled that the air became thicker as the race progressed and as the heat increased. 'Didn't feel thirsty but in the last lap I felt hot in the face, not extreme though. I think I felt hotter from the sun when I ran Berlin at World Championships.'

Michael commented that he was limited by a combination of leg fatigue and breathing hard near the end, but he'd actually forgotten most of the last couple of kilometres. He did add that on the replay he looked like he was hurting! 'But in saying that it felt just like a regular long run to be honest.' He didn't remember getting thirsty at all, sponging with cool water at every opportunity and picked up a drink every 5km without fail, with an opportunity to pick up a drink again in between.

It was good that the two runners were confident about doing the right thing before the race. It's important to think that way, and the job of the coach to ensure that kind of mindset. It's interesting that the runners didn't get over-hot or thirsty even as the temperature approached 30 ° with high humidity. Pace was slower than in a cool marathon, but it showed how experienced marathoners can keep things under control when running according to feel. Interesting too that Lisa recalled that she might have felt the heat more in Berlin where the temperature was about 10 degrees lower on average, but the sun was shining on the runners. This shows how potent the radiant heat can be irrespective of temperature and humidity.

Lisa Weightman and Michael Shelley after winning medals at the Commonwealth Games in New Delhi.

Warming up

It's always interesting talking to old-timers, they (nowadays I have to say 'we') are full of interesting memories. The other day I was at the Canberra Yacht Club enjoying a feed of fish and chips by the lake with a group of my wife Sue's colleagues from the National Gallery. Sue introduced me to the chap sitting next to me, whose name was Howard Styles and I mentioned that I couldn't stay long as I had some runners competing at the AIS track.

I could see Howard's mind tick back through the years 'I was a competitive swimmer in Sydney in my early teens, in the 1950s ... my one and only claim to fame is that I broke Murray Rose's Under 14 200m butterfly record.'

Now Murray Rose was one of the greatest ever Australian freestylers.

'You should have that record framed' I commented sincerely. 'Did you know Forbes Carlile?' I have always had great admiration for Forbes and Ursula Carlile not only as coaches but as pioneers of sports science in Australia.

'Oh yes' Howard's eyes lit up, 'I remember Forbes coming along to a few of our sessions to learn more about warming up.' And with a clarity of reflection that belied a 60-year recall.

'Forbes had six of us sitting in a bath at around 100 degrees (Fahrenheit of course). We'd then swim a standard training session and Forbes would check our times and take our heart rate with his fingers on our necks as he leaned over at the end of the pool.'

I love hearing about the early days of applied sports science. During my days as AIS swim team physiologist, Forbes sent me plenty of letters, each with the pearls of wisdom that only decades of experience can bring. Forbes was a Cerutty-Lydiard-Stampfl of the swim world, and with the likes of multiple world record holder Shane Gould under his wing, he was just as successful.

Immediately pre-race. The warm-up

An effective warm-up lets our bodies know that a big effort is imminent and has our lungs, heart, blood, muscles, tendons, ligaments and brain ready to perform. In an optimally warm environment, blood flows more freely, muscle enzymes function more effectively, connective tissue becomes more pliable and our brain benefits from the feeling we get when we engage in an agreeable forms of low stress exercise such as jogging, strides, drills and stretches.

It's fair to say that the shorter and faster the race, the more critical is the warm-up to race performance, because in the sprints and middle-distance events systems are called into immediate high intensity action. That is not to say the warm-up isn't important at the marathon end of the spectrum; indeed it is, especially in most big city marathons which typically occur in very cool winter conditions. Just as for the faster races, failure to warm-up adequately for a typically fast, sometimes even frenzied marathon start may find your aerobic system sluggish in kicking into action. Exacerbating this effect may be the inordinate duration many marathoners have to wait on the starting line, and shivering from the cold as well as from the nervous expectation of the 42km challenge ahead. The consequently greater proportion of anaerobic energy engaged in the first kilometre or so and obligatory increased glycogen utilization could cost dearly at the end when every single molecule of glycogen is precious.

The same principle applies to the track middle and long-distance runners. Running out of glycogen is not the problem, but having to switch on anaerobic power prematurely has a runner's early race control (homeostasis) under unnecessary stress. We know that if, at the bell, two runners differ in the proportion of aerobic and anaerobic energy they have utilized, the runner who has relied less on anaerobic power will be in better control and, all other things equal, will be able to run that last lap faster.

So don't skimp on the warm-up. It's certainly not a waste of energy, even for marathoners, although in the interests of ensuring that glycogen supply is not compromised, it makes no sense to warm-up for a marathon with the same intensity as a 10km runner. Here are a couple of examples of warm-ups but bear in mind it's very much an individual thing and there are plenty of permutations and combinations that would work equally well.

Discussing final race plans with Lisa Weightman before the Berlin World Championships marathon.

A warm-up for a well-conditioned middle-distance race

- Time required: 60'. Outside Temperature: 24°C.
- Race flats. 15' jog on grass outside the track or trails;
- 10' easy stretch all muscle group with usual stretch routine, held for approximately 10 seconds in each position. Concentrate on usually performed easy stretches including those for Achilles, calves, hamstrings, lower back, hip flexors
- Jog another 10' on the track introducing some change of pace work over 100m intervals
- 6 x 50m strides with walk back;
- 5' easy stretching; 5' of favourite drills, activating the hip, knee and ankle musculature (e.g. high knee skipping drills, bounding, lunges or easy double leg half-squat jumps you are used to in training).
- Change to spikes: 3' easy stretch then 4 x 100m race at race-pace with walk back; 3' easy stretch; 4 x 200m including the middle 100m at race-pace, with walk back;

- Easy stretch and to Call Room. From start line, immediately prior to race 2 x 30–40m strides at race-pace.

A warm-up for a well-conditioned marathoner,

- Time required 30'. Outside temperature: 12°.
- In training shoes: 15' jog;
- 10', easy stretching of all muscle groups;
- Racing shoes: 10', jog including 6 x 200m at 10km pace with 1' jog between; 5' stretching.
- On line prior to race: Easy jogging for 3', (elite runners usually get this opportunity) 4 x 50m at projected starting marathon pace (which is usually quick over the first 500m)

Now, one of the themes running through this book is that there are always more ways than one to skin a cat. While applying sensible physiology and psychology to training and race preparation is the best way to proceed, athletes are all different. Sometimes conventional wisdom has to be put aside; sometimes an unorthodoxy offers the best chance of success.

The next story is a story about a marathon runner, and it could easily have been included in Chapter 13 where marathon training was discussed. However, it also fits in here, as it provides one of the "extreme outliers of the normal curve" of marathon preparation and taper.

Athletes are all different; some more so than others

'When I used to read fairy-tales, I fancied that kind of thing never happened, and now here I am in the middle of one!'

Lewis Carroll

It's 1998 and I had been coaching Nickey Carroll (no known relationship to Lewis) for four or five months. I'd already learned a couple of things; firstly that she was an exceptional talent, and secondly that she wasn't your 'run-of-the-mill' marathon runner. Not that any marathon runner is I suppose. But any young girl venturing overseas for the first time, travelling alone and arriving a couple of days before a daunting new experience of an international marathon, and unknown to the race organizers or indeed anyone else across the USA let alone Las Vegas and runs 2:33:24 has to be unusual to say the least, and pretty damn good.

But that was the way Nickey liked to do things, under the radar and independently. With her combination of sensitivity, lack of confidence, and burning ambition, I soon came to realize how much stress this runner placed upon herself simply in meeting her own expectations. Her love of running for running's sake was her solace and pleasure and training in the bush was her way to combat life's stresses. It just so happened that the more she ran the easier it got. Some people are like that, with very responsive engines.

Nickey was in Brisbane and I was in Canberra so most of our communication was by phone. I had visited a couple of times and was very pleased to find that her partner Don Wallace, an exceptional ultra-marathon runner, was extremely supportive of her running. I was never a big fan of planning an individual training program by the book, but the marathon training manual was definitely not applicable to this girl. There was no way any orthodox training program was going to work. Interval work, track work, hill work or time-trials just weren't going to be part of Nickey's program. It wasn't as though Nickey didn't want to train using these methods; it was just that she couldn't. Pacing herself wasn't a training concept that Nickey had heard of. You either ran hard during a session or you didn't run at all, so interval training never worked out properly. And as for running round a track, that was completely out of the question. 'How can I enjoy running around in circles when there are bush trails to run on between the gum trees up in the hills?',

Fair enough, I thought, why should she run around in circles on the track? And we never did. The program I set focused on running in the bush but in different venues that promoted some shorter harder efforts, or longer efforts, or hills, but mainly solid sustained running for various periods between 30 minutes and 2 hours. She'd run 2:33 without any real structure in her training and I recalled that American Olympic gold medallist Joan Benoit's program consisted of mainly solid medium to long sustained running, with little if any repetition work or other structured training. She hadn't done too badly on that program had she? So why not Nickey?

There were plenty of days of missed training with minor problems, but from what I could gather, mainly due to the intensity of her training, the rationale of recovery running was always difficult to explain to this girl. However, as we were to learn down the track of Nickey's unusual and abbreviated career, missed training days were the early symptoms of gradually escalating health problems which became more evident over ensuing years.

Racing was not something that Nickey looked forward to. It took the fun out of running, and, I suspect, raised the possibility in her mind that a poor performance would disappoint partner Don, me or herself. With a reluctance to race, even locally, I decided to set a marathon goal for my new runner; a non-negotiable, non-refundable set in stone marathon. I chose Paris. Australian half-marathon record holder Darren Wilson, whom I had coached for several years when he lived in Canberra, was now living over in France preparing to run Paris. Although I was no longer in charge of his program, I was very keen to see him run and the timing fitted in perfectly with Nickey's program. And I love Paris.

I called my friend Derek Froude, a New Zealand marathon runner and post-graduate Geology student in Canberra in the 80s. Derek had somehow reasoned that his master's degree at one of Australia's best universities set him up nicely for sports management. He was now a Florida-based Posso Sports manager of marathon runners from all parts of the world, and I asked him if he might be able to organize Nickey's entry into the Paris Marathon. He did this for me, but with a once-off 2:33 personal best and little race experience otherwise, the organizers weren't able to provide any assistance. Derek helped out enormously here because his Paris Posso Sports contact and running enthusiast Claude Minni kindly offered us his outer suburban Paris apartment, not far from Orly airport, for the week before the race. At that stage I was mentoring Scott Steele, a young aspiring distance running coach, and I asked Scott whether he would like to experience Paris and a big city marathon. A silly question really. Within a couple of months Nickey, Scott and I were in gay Paris in Claude's apartment.

There weren't too many places to run out near Orly airport other than around the streets, but it didn't matter. Nickey was simply too nervous to run. This was going to be an easier taper than I had planned. There was a track near the village centre and I had anticipated a few repetitions run at a well-controlled pace in this taper week. Scott and I soon realized anything timed or controlled was out of the question for our marathoner. I had also envisaged some easy jogging but Scott and I ended up going out by ourselves.

We were of course concerned about how nervous this girl was but we decided not to worry, rationalising that a week off running before a marathon is not such a bad thing so we assured Nickey this was fine. I told her that Ralph Doubell had not jogged a step for a week before he won gold at the Mexico City Olympics. We reminded her of the value of glycogen storage and the energy value of fresh baguettes, salads and fruit, punctuated with a visit or two to the local crêperie down the road, and Nickey topped up with some chocolate and sweets in the last couple of days. At least we were assured her muscle glycogen was filled to the brim.

The stress Nickey endured in those lead-up days to the marathon was obviously immense, but apart from it confining her taper week to some easy walking she disguised it well, never once complaining about anything and always maintaining a happy disposition. We kept her busy, diverting attention away from the marathon when at all possible. I diverted my attention too in visiting the city, taking great delight in showing Nickey and Scott the Paris I love, especially the delights of the Quartier Latin, and le Jardin du Luxembourg.

Finally race day came and our host Claude drove us to the start. I don't know whether she would have got any sleep that night, but we were very surprised and very impressed with her pre-race composure, knowing how her stomach must have had more butterflies than an Amazon Jungle summer as we drove up the Champs Élysée.

All went smoothly enough getting to the starting line. I coaxed our runner to join me in a 10 minute warm-up jog which she did at close to walking pace as she watched her rivals seemingly jogging for an eternity then doing their 100m strides. 'That's ok Nickey,' we rationalized again, 'Why would you need to warm up for 30 minutes and do those strides? You'll warm up in the first couple of kilometres, and save energy anyway.' In reality, the Carroll minimalistic approach was a worry because it was quite cold and the runners always take off like cut cats at the start to remove themselves from the throng and danger of being jostled or tripped. But there was no option.

As you might imagine, I was more than a little relieved when that race got underway with Nickey a few rows from the front in that huge sea of bobbing heads. I took a deep breath and I always move into a different mood state when the gun goes as there is nothing more I can possibly do to assist my runner. I wondered how Nickey felt; I imagined something similar to how Burke and Wills must have felt as they began their final journey.

Scott and I walked over to the official race hotel to see if we could find TV coverage of the race. We'd decided on the TV coverage rather than trying to get to any of the checkpoints. Getting out to checkpoints along the course didn't make sense. We could easily miss seeing Nickey (and Darren) along the way, and the chance of her seeing or hearing us was even more remote. In the early parts of the race, as is often the case, we didn't see much of the women on TV, but mobile phone reports from Claude and Derek indicated that she was up in the front pack of women. Our hopes that Nickey would see out a good part of the race heightened. We were elated when we got a glimpse of the leading women at the half-way mark to catch sight of Nickey still running, not too far away from the leaders who were on sub 2:30 pace at that!

We saw the lead girls again at 25 km. Nickey was hanging in there! We began to get excited, and thought about a top 10 finish. The opposition now became of interest as our runner now loomed as competitive. We noticed another girl, the Romanian Tecuta Alina, running alongside a man, and realized that Tecuta and Nickey were at least 100m ahead of the next female, Japanese runner Tada Tami. As coaches of marathoners know too well, waiting for another glimpse of the front running girls on the TV coverage seemed like an eternity, but we got one at around 30 km. Nickey was still there!

The Romanian girl was there too, still running along with her private pace-maker. We were to learn later that they were surging and slowing to try to drop Nickey. Not a bad ploy, and within the rules. They were not to know their tactics with the young and inexperienced Australian were to have an effect exactly opposite to that intended.

Nickey sensed direct combat with the Romanian girl and her male accomplice. It fired her up, and soon after the 30km mark she decided to turn the tables on the pair by putting in her own strong surge. The pair tried to respond but couldn't. The competitive side of Carroll was not well known to me, but I had heard later that she liked to make the pace in the training group during the long Sunday morning runs. Of course this annoyed the hell out of the better runners in that training group, especially if they were struggling to go with her. And especially if they were male.

Herein lies a paradox; Carroll the shy and retiring young lady and Carroll the leader of the pack. The key to understanding this paradox is the environment. Sure, in a social setting she is shy, but in a running setting, never; that's her territory. And in Paris, Nickey was in that favoured setting and in the zone. At 30km there were now only men ahead of her and Carroll's task now was to pick off as many as possible.

What a sight it was to see Nickey running up the Champs Élysée toward the Tour d 'Eiffel. She had lost her usual fluency, and her racing shoes didn't prevent a noticeable fatigue-induced pronation I hadn't seen before, but Scott and I didn't worry too much about that!

'La premiere femme, Nickeee Carrooolle, Australie, deux heures, vingt-sept, et six secondes ... Bravoooo' was the call. Imprévu, to say the least! A race record or 2:27:06 and a group of coaches near us turned to each other, 'Who's that girl? Where'd she come from? Can't even find her in our press release.' Scott and I smiled to ourselves.

Managers Derek and Claude were as amazed as anyone, and pretty pleased of course with this unexpected win. Scott, Nickey and I all went for a trip down the Loire Valley to celebrate, and on the way back to Australia, the Paris Marathon winner's trophy just fitted nicely into the on-board overhead locker.

Fast forward 17 years, and just to remind me to keep my feet on the ground, here's another story ... !

Not everything goes to plan

I'm sitting in the elite athletes' tent at the 2015 London Marathon. Commonwealth Games gold medallist and London Olympic marathon 16th place getter Michael Shelley is lying on a mat in front of my chair. All of the runners in this Elite Runners tent are in the same boat; quiet and nervous. It's the usual calm before the storm. In just under two hours Shelley will be testing our last 6 months of training. This is his profession, although when it comes down to it, it's more his passion, as the money is not great for a marathon runner unless you are capable of threatening the world record, in which case race directors and sponsors pay you handsomely.

I have a quiet word to Glenn Latimer, the race director to confirm the pace of the third group of pacemakers at 2:10 pace. Shelley's PB is 2:11, and his aim in this run is to become Australia's 6th ever sub 2:10 marathoner to accompany his gold and silver in the Commonwealth Games and top 16 in the Olympics. I see former managers of athletes I've coached, the highly respected Jos Hermens and Luis Posso, making sure their athletes are in the right spot at the right time.

My work is done so I'm not nervous; that's the way it usually is for me on race day. Shelley is fit and healthy and he knows what he has to do. Anyway, he's got enough butterflies in his stomach without sharing any of mine. I get in the bus and head to the finish. Frustratingly, we only see the front-runners and rely on my phone to get splits. He runs well, but not what we were after. Just outside his PB of 2:11. Solid we agree, but mission not accomplished. It didn't help that he ran most of the race by himself. His 2:10 pace maker dropped off the pace, apparently with a sore hamstring but Michael admits he made the wrong choice opting more conservatively for the 2:10 pace rather than the 2:9:30 pace maker. It's not an excuse though; the specific fitness just wasn't quite there on the day.

Later that afternoon we discussed areas of training we can improve on. The plan is already in motion well before going home. That's important. We live and learn and we need to. But for now there has to be recovery time. It's so important to take time to recover properly to avoid increased risk of illness and injury. Problems can arise when training is resumed before body and mind have recovered, not just from the race but from the stress of the build-up over many months. We'll need 6 months for the next marathon campaign. Only then will we find out if we have indeed learned from London.

Chapter 15, Pre-race tapering: the mind

'I'm very brave generally' he went on in a low voice 'but today I just happen to have a headache'.

Lewis Carroll

Some athletes don't know how good they can be. So they aren't

Given their interaction, there are strong arguments not to separate discussion of mind and body, but in this instance I will separate them as it helps me explain the sorts of things worth considering when preparing athletes for competition.

Sports psychology has evolved over recent decades to assist sportspeople cope with associated pressures and to perform at their best in competition. Before psychologists came on to the scene, coaches, friends, parents, and teachers all contributed in this role, albeit in their less formal manner. They still do. Even now, along with professional sports psychology well entrenched into elite sport, the day-to-day people skills of the coach and other mentors play a particularly important role. After all, and particularly in distance running, they are closest to the athlete and always there, in person or via phone or email. Our best coaches have a street-smart understanding of how their athletes tick. The right word at the right time is part of the art of coaching.

Physiology or psychology; what's most important?

A hypothetically interesting but practically irrelevant question often posed is 'what is generally more important in an elite runner, the physical or mental characteristics?' The easy and common answer is 'Both are equally important.'

But inference of equality may not be quite right. The evidence to date (as outlined in Chapter 6) has physiology as the front-runner, because in a line-up of top runners, we can predict race placing with astonishing accuracy from the size and efficiency of their aerobic power plants without any consideration of their psychology. On the other hand, there are no decent data to suggest we can predict the race outcome of a group of runners purely from psychological attributes without reference to their physical fitness.

However, (and there is always a 'however' in these sorts of hypotheticals), the development of psychological fitness in an athlete is extremely important in preparing for big events. Psychological instability can put a spanner in the works of even the biggest and most efficient motors.

In the right mind to race

Ever gone to the track for a race with the nerves raging and thought 'why the hell am I putting myself through this?' That's part of competition that has to be expected. After all, the enjoyment and satisfaction of doing well is directly proportional to the pre-race stress.

It may not be as sharply predictive as an athlete's physiology, but the mindset of a runner in the lead-up, immediately before and during the race will each affect performance. It has to; and as I like to remind everyone, the way we think affects the way we move and the way we move affects the way we think.

For a start, in the lead-up to a race, the best training adaptation occurs in athletes who are generally happy with life. Athletes experience the effect of life's daily psychological stressors like the rest of us; relationships with other athletes, coaches, family, friends, athletic officials, accountants, and teachers are all potential psychological stressors. Failure to meet personal expectations or the expectations of others is another common psychological stressor, particularly in athletes. Then there are physical stressors; the races, training, environment, travel, infections, and injuries, which interact with the psychological stressors to magnify the resultant effect.

We're all too aware of pre-competition, pre-performance or pre-confrontation 'nerves' where our mind seems to take little notice of what would prefer to think and feel at the time.

To a large degree this is exactly what is happening; the phylogenetic 'older' and automated parts of the brain trump our more recently developed grey matter thoughts. This is a survival mechanism, for if we took time to consciously think about our 'fight or flight', it may be too late, gobbled up by a sabre-tooth tiger or speared by a mammoth tusk! We human beings are hard-wired to charge up our systems automatically in response to a perceived physical or psychological challenge. The mere thought of an impending challenge can bring about those butterflies in the stomach and thumping heart, and blood vessels around the running muscles open up as sugar is pumped into the bloodstream. It's all systems go.

A problem creeps in when this effect occurs too often. When that tiger is always on the prowl, and that autonomic adrenergic response hangs around too long. The effect of the chronic stress response is upsetting all round, exacerbating discontent, unhappiness and, in turn, sub-standard training and adaptation to training. Should this proceed unabated there is the increased likelihood of a general fatigue and depression of the autonomic response; an athlete might even lose desire and motivation and the ability get 'fired up' for high performance training and competition. Clinical depression is not uncommon in elite sport.

Harnessing the stress response

The trick is to harness this alarm system, to control its timing, so that stressors are kept under control to prevent stress getting out of hand

and causing distress. Pre-race nerves are acceptable, even beneficial just prior to the race and on the start line, but lack of control over this response in the days and nights before the race will detract from performance. An athlete with this kind of prolonged pre-race autonomic nervous system activity is likely to become emotionally 'drained' with negative physical consequences. Consistent performers in international events are able to optimize stress reaction; to divert their attention away from the impending competition stress in the preceding weeks and days.

A coach's role is to optimize the physical and psychological stress experienced by their athletes. This is not a straightforward task for any coach, and often more difficult to balance when athletes don't feel like opening up about how they feel, perhaps perceiving, mistakenly, that this is being weak. Here is where fortunate sportspeople can employ a sports psychologist as part of the team. Professional, experienced sports psychology has much to offer athletes, and in particular those more sensitive and vulnerable individuals.

Interestingly, optimal pre-race stress response is not just individual-specific but race-specific. While middle-distance runners looking for a powerful surge of energy may benefit from heightened pre-race arousal with its enhanced glucose metabolism, for marathoners it's best to avoid any early excessive use of glycogen and start the race in a relatively calm state of mind at the gun.

The group effect

Some athletes prefer to train by themselves and thoroughly enjoy it. Being all alone on a bush trail or even on a synthetic track might suit some athletes perfectly, away from the hustle and bustle of competition. And it's true that some runners, in seeking that competitive edge, don't like anyone seeing or measuring how they train, let alone have anyone train alongside them. However, it's my firm belief that most, if not all runners, no matter how individualistic or independent they believe they are, would benefit from training with others at times. There is a 'group effect' well known to distance running coaches and one that seemed well demonstrated during an altitude training study, as outlined in Chapter 22.

We human beings thrive on social interaction, and socially comfortable runners who enjoy the company of their running buddies, competitors included, seem to stay in the sport longer. A 'highly competitive' lone runner is less likely to continue on in the sport. It's probably something to do with being comfortable and happy amidst fellow runners, feeling linked to a group. But it's also probably something to do with learning how to compete with optimal stress. There is no point in disregarding common rules of comradeship with a fellow athlete just because you might be competitors. Competing with the highest degree of intensity and engaging in positive off-the-track social interaction with your competitors are not mutually exclusive; nor should they be. There is enough stress involved on race day without introducing more by refusing to talk to or even acknowledge the presence of other runners. There's a weakness at the athlete-coach level if the highest level of competitiveness on the track or road precludes polite social interaction with fellow runners. Competitive running is an important subset of life for distance runners, and should reflect the kind of social interaction we all enjoy in everyday life.

The group effect in full swing at training in the bush in Canberra's north.
Image: University of Canberra

As a very keen runner in my 30s and early 40s I loved running behind the AIS Clohessy scholarship holders and other top local athletes. It was a privilege to run with the likes of Rob de Castella, Shaun Creighton, Pat Carroll, Gerard Barrett,

Dave Chettle, Graham Clews, Ken Hall, Simon Doyle, Pat Scammell, Andrew Lloyd, Nick de Castella, John Andrews, Steve Austin, Wayne Larden, Steve Spiers, just to mention a few I trained regularly with over those early AIS years. Our Sunday long run started and finished at the home of running enthusiasts and author Brian Lenton and his wife Linda, just over the road from Stromlo Forest. Sadly their house, along with that of Rob de Castella, and the forest in its entirety were razed by the fires of 2003. Our traditional Sunday morning long run from the original Deek's Drive (officially Clohessy signposted and certified) was at that stage 10 years old. A few months later when the shock of it all had passed for some of us less directly affected, it was an eerie feeling to retrace the trails we had known like the back of our hand. All was entirely foreign in a forest without trees.

It's now 13 years later and out of those ashes we've grown a new and official Deek's Drive and a splendid new Deek-designed Stromlo cross-country course. And we've got a pretty good start to a brand new forest that includes the early makings of a magnificent arboretum with hundreds of foreign species of trees in what seems to be a striking tribute to Australian multiculturalism. We old-timers will always miss that pine forest but things are looking positive for the new generations; and I do hope in more ways than running.

Race week

What needs to be discussed in the week leading up to a big race? In many cases, not a lot; it's all pretty obvious for most runners, experienced or novice. For many of our top runners it's usually best to divert attention away from their race and find other things to talk about. There are very few runners who need to be 'revved up' in the manner of a football coach trying to get the best out of his team members week after week.

Some runners like to have things perfectly planned; exactly when to do their session, what to do during the day, who and when to meet for coffee, when and what to eat, when to go to bed and when to have breakfast; all written down and ticked off as the pre-competition days pass. This is how they feel most in control and so relaxed. Others are happy to play each day more 'by ear', with only a rough daily plan of where they will be, who they'll be hanging out with and what they will do. These characters are usually more laid back, and used to doing things more as they please. So apart from setting training times with their coach, they're happy to coast through each day playing it 'cool'.

Irrespective of personality types and their preferred daily routines, self-confidence and self-belief is an essential component of a distress free final week before a big competition. Hence the importance of a coach's well-chosen and well-timed words during this period. But it's not just words. Perhaps even more impressive and comforting to an athlete than words is an air of relaxed confidence displayed through a coach's body language. Strong aspects of the preparation can be reminded and reinforced without a spoken word.

It's natural for a coach to have pre-competition nerves with so much emotional and physical energy involved in the preparation. But there is no point in showing it. Coaches must exude a calm confidence at all times. Anything else will immediately be detected by a super-sensitized athlete in the pre-race period. If you reckon that seems incongruous with a person of your emotional sensitivity then maybe some acting lessons are in order.

Teamwork

Many athletes just like to chill out on race day. Listen to music or watch a movie, whatever best diverts attention away from the race. But there comes a time where race tactics, having been discussed in basic terms, need to be crystallized.

For most athletes, a good time to review and reinforce specific tactical thoughts for the immediate race is in a quiet period in the waiting time prior to the warm-up. This presents an opportunity to review the effect of the prevailing weather conditions, especially the wind; to summarize key tactics, and to modify the arousal, usually down.

In major international championships there may be a two-hour wait after arriving at the warm-up track before the warm-up begins and another 45 minutes or more after the warm-up prior to the gun. At this stage it's usual for coach and athlete to seek out a spot around the warm-up area where the runner can lie down and relax with headphones and favourite pre-race tracks. This is a potential pressure-cooker situation as all the competitors are there. Coaches don't need to be right in their athlete's pocket, but being around is important. Coaches usually don't need to keep a conversation going either, but the right number and right choice of words are equally important. The value of an enduring coach-athlete relationship is rarely more evident.

Now here is another story. One I have relayed to very few people I suppose, but one that got stored away in my learning bank. It's a swimming story but it's one of those athlete stories that became indelible in my coaching mind.

Last minute teamwork

It is the Seoul Olympics, and I'm not an official member of the Australian team, but personal coach to Lisa Martin (Ondieki) who is to run the marathon and Carolyn Schuwalow and Andrew Lloyd both of whom are to run on the track. I'm also swim physiologist at the Australian Institute of Sport working with Head Coach Bill Sweetenham, so have a huge interest in the Australian swim team. But there were camps at the AIS and elsewhere and I had developed a strong relationship with Queensland head swim coach Laurie Lawrence, especially after working with him prior to the Los Angeles Olympics 4 years prior.

Duncan Armstrong had gone into the Olympics ranked 25th in the world on times in the 200m. Surprising the swimming world, but not his coach, he pulled out a great PB swim in the heat of 1:48.86 to qualify for the final in, as Lawrence was to tell everyone over and over, 'lucky lane 6.' This was in fond reference to rank outsider Jon Seiben's Atlanta Olympic gold from lane 6 as described elsewhere in this book.

I had told all the swim coaches about some trials we'd been running at the AIS with new pre-race nutrition and warm-up procedures and that there may be an advantage, but it wouldn't be a big one, if at all. Now I can't recollect exactly when and how our conversation before Duncan Armstrong's final was initiated, but Laurie and I decided, rather astonishingly in retrospect, to ask Duncan if he'd be prepared to undergo these modifications before the final. Astonishing, firstly because it was the biggest arena in the world, the first Olympic final Duncan had made; secondly, because he had never tried this pre-race regime before!

Just as astonishing was Duncan's reply when we approached him. Laurie asked me to explain how and why I thought it would help. Duncan just looked at us and unquestioningly said, 'Well if you think that is what we should do, then that is what we'll do.' I must admit I appeared much more confident about our plan than I let on. But one thing was vital; that physiologist and coach expressed absolute confidence that this was the way to go.

The time had come. All went to plan. Modified diet, modified warm-up. Duncan was obviously incredibly nervous; Laurie was even more nervous. His race plan was for Duncan to try to stay in the wake of the champion US world record holder Matt Biondi, a man of great stature physically and mentally. This would provide a type of aquaplaning advantage if the Australian could maintain the speed for three laps. The last lap would tell the story. Coach Lawrence left Duncan and me alone and asked me to speak to Duncan before our swimmer stepped into the watery Coliseum. I had chosen my words already.

'Duncan, you've done all the work that Laurie has thrown at you and you know that's more than anyone in the world could conceive. You have a great coach. You have a perfect race plan. You are rested and ready to swim the best race of your life. So you'll turn behind Biondi with 50m to go feeling like you always do, lactic and aching. But now you know you'll have the strength to come home faster than you ever imagined possible.' Duncan nodded and off he went.

History has it that is exactly what happened. the Lawrence-Armstrong combination got it precisely right. Duncan turned in the wake of the big man from the US, and swam past him with a huge last lap to take the gold medal in world record time of 1:47.25, 1.61 faster than his big PB in the qualifier.

Coach Lawrence, not known to hold back any emotional energy (and having coached an underdog to a gold medal in world record time, who'd try to hold back anyway?), was in no condition to take Duncan to the drug testing venue or the Press conference. At the Press conference, a reporter asked Duncan what he was thinking when he turned behind Matt Biondi in that last lap. To my amazement, Duncan repeated, almost word for word, what I had said to him just before he left the warm-up pool to race. 'When I turned I was hurting but I knew I'd have the strength to come home faster than I ever had before.'

When it had all quietened down a bit, the drug test and the press conference over, I asked Duncan about what he had said in answer to the reporter and why he had chosen those words. He told me 'I've no idea Dick, those words just came out. It's what I felt ...' I smiled. There was no way the new world record holder had any recollection of what I'd said to him before the race. He was in the zone, in a kind of pre-coliseum trance. But his coach's plan and his physiologist's words were well and truly embedded in that intensely focused pre-race brain.

Now, did this last minute change help Armstrong at all? We'll never ever know. But does that matter?

Combatting anxiety

Learning how to deal with success and failure at an early age is of great advantage to an athlete. With the right guidance through both pre- and post-teenage years athletes can (almost) enjoy the experience of competition rather than fear it. I can't help thinking about the short but brilliant career of one of the world's greatest ever middle-distance runners, Herb Elliott. Elliott was undefeated in the 1500m and mile over his senior career, winning gold at the Rome Olympics running away from the field in world record time. He retired at the age of 23.

I wonder how much influence his coach Percy Cerutty had on Elliott's decision to retire so early. I suspect that Herb's remarkable record was probably accompanied by more than his fair share of pre-competition stress, one intensified by a progressively strong fear of losing a race. I also suspect that this fear was likely to have been shared, perhaps even promoted by his coach. I suspect that the stress in the weeks, days, minutes and seconds before he placed his toe behind the starting line proved difficult to accept for a young man running as an amateur with many other more pleasant things to do in life.

So was it Cerutty's fanatical approach to winning that led to Elliott's remarkably early retirement? Or did Herb impose such stringent expectations on himself that failure to cross the line first presented itself as a failure in life too difficult to contemplate? In my brief but treasured conversations with Elliott, my guess is that it was likely to be a bit of both.

In Herb, Percy recognized a young man capable of beating the world, and that it was not only his challenge, but his duty to take Herb to the very top. Cerutty knew the Elliott genes were necessary, but not sufficient in themselves to conquer the world, although the coach may not have described it in this way. Again, perhaps not quite in these words, Cerutty knew he had to create the right environment to maximize expression of those genes. The environment he did create was probably the most intense middle-distance training a human being had ever undertaken; an environment that would require correspondingly intense levels of motivation.

I have the impression that Elliott the teenager was not one who freely enjoyed expressing his talent, and that even as a lad he was not overjoyed by the thought of personal combat on the track, even in training. As his reputation grew so did expectations, firstly of himself and by Percy, rapidly followed by all Australians, and the world. So for our greatest middle-distance runner ever, it was a case of proving conclusively to the world who was the best, and then calling it a day.

So back to that question of whether Cerutty's fanatic approach to winning contributed to Elliott's early retirement? One might argue this way, but like Tensing and Hillary, our legendary coach-athlete combination had climbed their highest mountain, and what really was there to gain by doing it again?

A lesson for young players

Irrespective of the underlying psychology of the Cerutty-Elliott relationship it's important for young athletes to realize that outcomes other than winning are not only acceptable but vital along the curve of personal and athletic development. In a modern climate of 'winner take all, loser be forgotten or sacked' this kind of acceptance might erroneously be perceived or described as an unwelcome competitive 'softness.' To the contrary, a view of the number on an athlete's back crossing that finish line is an experience from which to learn, be motivated and profit.

Competition is not something to avoid, but embraced and enjoyed. In recent decades there has been a move to 'protect' children from competition, presumably because they might not do as well as others, creating problems with self-esteem or attitudes to physical activity. In direct contrast with removing competition, it makes far more sense to ensure that children participate in competition early in life and learn to enjoy and profit from the outcomes whatever they be. Organized modified games early in the school years are ideal ways to teach 'competition', developing the attitudes and responses that will apply over a lifetime in more ways than just sport. 'Competition education' should be a mandatory inclusion in every school's physical education curriculum. But we need enlightened teachers to create situations where all children are engaged and derive enjoyment, irrespective of the outcome. And we need to modify games so that the outcome is not always predicted. Consequently what many might grow up to accept as the unavoidable win-loss scenario of competition becomes a win-win scenario in the competitively literate child's mind.

Athlete independence

In the best kind of athlete-coach relationships athletes hope, but don't expect their coach to be with them at every training session and competition. Sometimes coaches just can't be there. That's why confident and competent coaches develop independence in their athletes; athletes who can train and compete at the highest level, whether the coach is there or not.

This becomes very important during overseas competition where the semi-professional and often fully amateur nature of track and field coaching makes it difficult for coaches to attend. The European IAAF track and field circuit sounds exciting, and it is; it can also be stressful. Athletes trying to break into to the upper echelons of competition in Europe sometimes have to wait right up to a day or so before the race to find out if they've been accepted into the meet. That's the way it is in Europe; race meet directors have to concentrate on putting 'backsides on seats' in a sport not known for attracting large crowds outside the very biggest of meets. And because only the 'big names' bring in the big crowds, meet directors are mainly concerned with the deals at the big end of town.

Take the case of Olympian and one-mile Australian record-holder Lisa Corrigan who found herself in this situation during the European circuit on one occasion. Lisa, like others had to be both mentally flexible as well as independent in carrying out her racing and training programs.

That particular year, I got tied up in London working, and Lisa was on the continent. Not quite fast enough to secure early entry into the Diamond League races, there had to be a plan A and plan B, perhaps even a plan C drafted out with the Australian manager helping her at the time. The young Australian champion got a last minute phone call, and a last minute flight found her at an airport late at night with no-one to pick her up. Eventually, after a few phone calls the situation was resolved, but it was a very late night before a race the following evening. Lisa learned to remain patient and calm. She also learned not to expect things to go as planned, so that when they didn't, the stress reaction was controlled.

Uncertain race schedules interfere with training too. It's natural for any athlete to want to prepare the way they always do before a race, and that's the way it happens at home. But not in Europe. On one other occasion, just two days before a scheduled race meet, Lisa Corrigan was told that she no longer had a run. Plan B was put into action, a race four days later. The previous few days of taper were to no avail, and now we had another four days extension. When this occurs on more than one occasion, as it often does, fitness begins to diminish, and coach and athlete have to do their best to offset this with newly devised sessions; careful not to do too much before the race but not to do too little either. An athlete's mental flexibility and willingness to accept that this is all part of the game are valuable assets.

I've often thought that athletes going into combat on the world stage, learning to cope with new and potentially stressful situations might explain why many, if not most, do very well in their post-athletics business exploits.

The psychology of physiology

Sometimes athletes don't know how good they can be. So they aren't. One runner who seemed to be in this category when I first met him was the Welsh runner Jon Brown, now a successful coach in Canada. I remember Jon as a quietly spoken, polite 22 year-old who had come over to Australia to participate in our altitude training study in 1993. At the start of the study, Jon was generally considered a good athlete although not at the truly elite level, and this was consistent with his self-assessment. He was randomly selected to train in a sea-level control group in the northern Sydney sea-side suburb of Narrabeen.

By the end of the three-week camp his 3km time trial had improved markedly, more than any other runner in a group of about 30. I noticed a new level of respect for Jon among his training group, who were more than impressed with the quality of his training. I have a feeling that Jon's unexpected increase in form at sea-level may have been related to the following.

All the runners undertook pre-camp treadmill testing for physiological characteristics and Jon's results had surprised me, prompting me to comment to him, purposely casually, that his results suggested better performances than his personal bests indicated. We had measured many world-class athletes in our lab and Jon's profile was up there with the best of them. I remember how this rather quiet and unassuming young fellow took particular notice of my comment.

Now I might be wrong, and I never did discuss this with Jon, but I suspect that the realization he had untapped potential unlocked a new set of self-expectations. I think rather than just hoping, he began to believe that he could do something special as a runner.

And something special he certainly did! He never looked back from that camp, continually improving to break the coveted UK 10,000m record (27:18 in 1998) and going on to prove himself as one of the world's best marathoners, finishing 4th twice in the most prestigious 26 mile race in the world, the Olympic marathon, in Sydney 2000 and Athens 2004.

Might that simple relaying of his lab results have been the catalyst for Jon's improvement? No doubt his relationship with his coach George Gandy, and his dedication to his sensible training regimes were the dominant causative factors; but yes, I feel that his realization of what he was made of may have kick-started a new positive line of thought and self-belief, and a new era in the Jon Brown career.

The Jon Brown story is not unique. During my 25 years at the AIS I felt there were many occurrences of a similar nature. The psychological effect of a physiologist's factual report lies within its subtle, unanticipated nature. An athlete being briefed on their physiological assessment is not there to be motivated, and does not expect to receive any confidence boosting therapy. That itself enhances the potency of an insightful physiologist's words. If the reports on the athlete's power-plant are indeed favourable, either in in comparison with elite levels or in terms of personal improvement, the boost to confidence and motivation is likely to be of an order of magnitude of which any sports psychologist or coach would be particularly proud!

On the other hand, if results are less than encouraging, care has to be taken in how they are described. A sensibly sensitive physiologist can point out truthfully that there are always unmeasured physiological (or biomechanical) characteristics which may more than compensate for any less favourable outcomes that happened to be measured on this occasion.

When a little white lie didn't hurt

Lisa Ondieki had been training consistently over the past few months of late 1987 and now it was the January of 1988. We were working toward the Osaka marathon and the weather in Australia was pretty warm. Hot in fact in Canberra. Training was tough in this dry heat, although at least it cooled down at night so sleeping wasn't a problem. Osaka would be cool, probably cold. Now Lisa wasn't feeling too well in the lead up weeks, but as far as I could work out, there wasn't a lot wrong physically, the hot conditions were slowing her training runs down. She'd done the miles, she looked good, her quality sessions of 400s and miles were solid. Lisa had recently settled on a new life in Canberra and I figured that this was a contributing factor to some pre-race anxiety, especially after not being able to finish the World Championship marathon in Rome the previous year.

The Edinburgh Commonwealth Games gold medalist and LA Olympian had obviously thought about her condition long and hard and was adamant, 'I don't think I'm fit enough to run well over there Dick, and don't think we should go.'

I also had a long hard think about her training, and could find no reason to suggest she lacked race fitness, and decided to stick my neck out.

'All right, Lisa, let's test your fitness. Let's do a series of mile reps at your usual pace and check how well you handle it. I can measure this by how you control your lactate level. If you don't come up trumps we don't go. But if the readings confirm that you are fit enough, then we go. Fair enough?'

Reluctantly and hesitantly, she accepted the deal.

Lisa's marathon career had been kick-started over in the US by well-known physiologist and coach Jack Daniels. She knew about blood lactates and the old East German concept that a measurement around 4-5 mmol/L after a series of satisfactory efforts would be a good sign, indicating she had good aerobic control and was in good shape. Lisa also knew that the Eastern Bloc concept of lactate controlled training was that if the lactate was greater than 5, the pace was above her so-called anaerobic or lactate threshold, and not likely to be sustained for too long.

The next day, a week before we were scheduled to leave for Osaka, I set Lisa four four-lap efforts at around 76 sec lap pace, that's 5.04 per 1600m. I re-confirmed our deal.

'If your lactates indicate you are in good control at that pace, then I reckon you are in shape and ready to run in Osaka ... Okay?'

'Okay ... ' I think I heard Lisa reply, head down, not happy.

It was a pleasant afternoon at the track, mild temperature, and little wind—a good start. Lisa looked concerned, to put it mildly, and didn't say much as she put on her spikes. Not good, I wanted to avoid pre-effort stress as this sort of tension wouldn't do those mile times much good. I assumed an air of confidence, as though the result of this track test was never in doubt. I was very pleased to have two positive pace-makers at the track, Lisa's brother Danny O'Dea and Chris Cook (a long striding and extremely popular runner who, sadly, some 10 years later was to die following a heart attack doing what he loved, mountain running).

Away she went, in her usual efficient style. Good solid posture, elbows out a bit, head down, minimal knee lift. I watched carefully; no real signs of stress, although running those four-lappers at the end of a 160km training week was never going to be a walk in the park. The first one was 5:00 min flat, quicker than what I'd set; a good sign. That's 31:25 10km pace and a bit faster than what I estimated to be her threshold pace at that time on big mileage. I took a blood sample from her earlobe and checked her heart rate. It was around 180 and that was all right too as Lisa generally had a high heart rate for a marathon runner, her max being close to 200.

Lisa Martin perfoming a 1600m time trial at the AIS before competeing at Osaka marathon.
Image: Australian Sports Commission

The key to this exercise though was that blood lactate reading. In those days, we had to put the samples on ice, and run them back to the lab for testing, so there was no immediate feedback. I asked Lisa to slow down to 5:04 min, to which she complied in her usual uncanny in-built clockwork fashion. We got through the second, third and fourth miles. Lisa complained of it feeling tougher than it should, but I chose to ignore that comment, as the stress of the situation was going to give her that impression anyway. That she held the times off only a minute and a half, recovery showed she was well under control, and I reckoned she could have reeled off another couple. I was even more convinced now that if we could free her mind up she would run well in Osaka.

I walked back to the lab, and a technician handed over the blood measurements. 7.0, 7.2, 7.6 and 7.4 mmol/L. I had a problem. These values were higher than I expected, but this was the very first time I had taken blood lactates from Lisa and I had to do some pretty quick thinking. First of all, the concentrations of lactate were stable, supporting the reasonably stable heart rate out on the track; and all four repetition times were spot-on and well-sustained. Secondly, we humans are not machines. In the absence of any prior testing, her steady state lactate may well be 6-7 mmol/L, not the 4 mmol/L popularized by East Germans during the 1970s. After all, we knew her steady state heart rate was higher than expected. I recalled a lab test with extremely well-performed Australian cyclist Stephen Hodge, who who held a blood lactate level of around 6–7 mmol/L for close to an hour! In any case our marathoner was running in hot conditions at somewhat faster than her threshold speed and we might expect lactates to be a bit on the high side.

Although I had been coaching Lisa for a relatively short period of time, I had got to know her pretty well. Despite her considerable success to date she was not over-endowed with self-confidence. The last thing I wanted to do was to tell her that her average lactates were 7.4 mmol/L, a lot higher than we would expect, and then try to convince her that these results were fine and the textbooks were wrong. The chances of her accepting that were slim.

I had twenty minutes to think about this while Lisa warmed down before coming over to my office. While her blood lactates were steady they were around 3 units higher than the textbook figure Lisa would be aware of, I had also found this new marathoner of mine to be 'different' in other respects. For example, her red blood cell concentration was lower than any other athlete previously measured in our lab. Going on those results a lot of people would have written her off as anaemic and lacking in oxygen transport ability. Yet the opposite was obviously the case; she was a superior oxygen transporter. My conclusion was that Lisa's higher lactate levels were not indicative of poor metabolic control.

She walked in, head down in negative expectation. 'Lisa' I found myself saying.

'It's good news, your times were good, your heart rate was steady throughout the session, and so were your lactates. I reckon you are set to run well in Osaka.'

'Well, Dick, what were they?' I was desperately hoping she wouldn't ask about the bloods. But she had and I instinctively responded.

'4.7 Lisa.' I must have mumbled because she asked me to repeat it and I had to. Lisa's eyes raised and lit up. 'Yep' I said. 'We're going! See you tomorrow.'

That was the only time in twenty-four years of science and coaching at the AIS that I falsely reported a lab result. My rationale, albeit not strongly defensible on ethical grounds, was that I was not misleading the athlete in an overall interpretation of her fitness. To convince her that 7.4 mmol/L was good would have not been easy, in fact I'd say impossible at that stage.

In Osaka, less than two weeks after that infamous track session, Lisa ran 2:23:51, running away from a good field in a personal best, Osaka race record, Australian record and a deservedly good purse.

An unusual aside: colour therapy

It's funny the things that crop up from time to time. I was getting a watch fixed when the jeweller recognized me as the 'the AIS guy in the Corn Flakes ads'. As I politely explained that the cereal we designed at the AIS was *Sustain*, he told me that he grew up in New Zealand near the famous Peter Snell.

'Peter attended the same chromotherapy clinic as my mother' and in response to my quizzical expression the jeweller informed me that colour therapy was popular in New Zealand at the time as a treatment for some infections. I later read about the chromotherapy theory of matching the light frequencies with frequencies associated with particular microbes; and that exposing these microbes to these frequencies can knock them off. A quick internet search at that point in time a few years ago now revealed the existence of the Peter Snell Institute of Sport in Cambridge, New Zealand, and indeed, a couple of colour therapy clinics were listed there.

Actually that wasn't the only time I'd heard of a kind of colour therapy. A couple of years previously a couple of Russian coaches told us about the way they used colour to influence the mood of their athletes. This to me was somewhat easier to grasp; after all, Monet and his water lilies at L'Orangerie gallery in Paris certainly do wonders for my mood. Primates, the Russian visitors had explained, were attracted and buoyed by greens of nature, and that lighter, brighter colours improved mood and motivation to train. Interestingly consistent with this premise, was that one or two AIS swim coaches told me that when the sun was shining through the large glass walls of the AIS swimming pool, the swimmers seemed to train with increased enthusiasm. Maybe they were buoyed, so to speak, by the lighter colour of a sun-sparkled pool surface, as distinct from the darker murkier water on a sunless day.

Following his stellar athletic career, Dr Peter Snell became a respected exercise physiologist and I wonder what he thinks of colour therapy these days. I still know little about colour therapy, but if a runner or anyone else believes a treatment works, then that treatment certainly has a flying start.

Chapter 16
Race Tactics

Begin at the beginning and go on 'til you come to the end: then stop'.

Lewis Carroll

We all love a front-runner who makes the early pace but many would argue the only thing that counts is the runner who's in front at the finish.

Pure and paced racing

Track and road racing comes in two forms, pure racing and paced racing. In the pure form everyone races to win. In paced running 'rabbits' are in the field simply to set up a fast pace, then jump off the track. The pace may be set to achieve a championship qualifying time, a meet record, or even a world record. The two forms of racing require a different mindset and even a different slant on training.

In pure championship races, tactics have a more significant effect on the outcome. Typically in these races, runners are reluctant to lead, expecting or at least hoping that someone else will do the work up front. By 'work' we mean that more physical energy is involved in taking the brunt of the air resistance, especially in windy conditions. And there is more psychological energy involved up front as well with a pack of lean and hungry runners breathing down the front-runner's neck preparing for the kill.

So championship racing tends to favour runners who can 'kick' home the fastest; and this usually translates to those who are faster over shorter distances. Based on this line of thinking, runners preparing for a 5000m championship might do well to emphasize the anaerobic end of their training spectrum, focusing more on their 1500m race fitness rather than their 10,000m fitness; and similarly, 1500m runners emphasize their 800m specific work. But coaches and their runners have to be careful because focusing on the high-end anaerobically generated speed risks losing some aerobic fitness. It's no use possessing better top end speed if a loss of aerobic fitness leads to diminished homeostatic control at the bell. And that risk is increased if a front running championship finalist decides to go out hard with the intent of, breaking up the pack early (i.e. force runners into early anaerobiosis), with the intent to take the sting out of the legs of the sitters. So, as usual for middle-distance running, balancing training to suit the event and the individual brings out the art as well as the science of coaching.

One tactic employed by aerobically superior front-running athletes is repetition surging, changing speed for varying durations during the middle sections of the race. The aim is to repeatedly take the pack into their discomfort zone, over their 'red-line speed', forcing runners to drop off the pace and lose the drafting and psychological advantage of sitting in on the lead pack. Aerobically fitter runners will better cope with mid-race surging tactics, and practising pace changes in training is likely to help runners either administer or cope with such tactics, both from a psychological as well as a physiological standpoint.

The front-runners

There are coaches and runners who strongly belong to the school of thought that successful running is not just about running and winning, but about running as fast as possible. We all love the attitude of the brave front-runner who makes the pace of a race and tries to hold the pack off right to the very end, and there is no doubt about the contribution these runners make to the sport as they set up fast times.

Then there are those who care little about the ultimate race times and records, but feel that a race is just that; it's who crosses the line first, end of story.

Some runners can do both, and when a front-runner has the ability to make the pace as well as hold off the pack of sitters it's fantastic; he or she has demonstrated a clear and present superiority over the field. In the Rudisha London Olympics 800m we saw a perfect example of that.

But what about the front-runner, who having led a race for 24 laps is outkicked in the final 200m? Athletically literate crowds will stand as one to support a beaten front-runner, along with the winner. In some instances, the front-runner may even attract more applause than the winner. Indeed, there a many legends of the sport who would not run any other way but flat out and at the front of the pack and were loved for it. John Landy once said that he'd rather lose a race in 3:58 than win in 4:10 (I don't ever recall or imagine Herb Elliott making any similar comment but Herb often ran from the front anyway). Vladimir Kutz at the Melbourne Olympics was the first front-running champion I ever saw; Ron Clarke always raced courageously out in front in Australia and Europe and Steve Prefontaine epitomised classical front-running in America.

But the other side to the story is that a race is a race, and it's there to win. Elliott and indeed most runners who come readily to mind do what they must to maximize their chance of winning. Front-running in the real world is not always a chivalrous selfless offering to the sport, but sometimes a carefully considered tactic to create the best chance of winning. In a championship event, no runner would or should ever feel any guilt in not 'doing the work' up front. After all, every runner has the option of racing any way he or she likes.

It's often simply a case of common sense. Take Andrew Lloyd's unlikely victory in the Auckland Commonwealth Games 5000m as described later in this chapter. Any pre-race plan to take the front running away from runners with clearly superior staying power, in this case the Kenyan champions Ngugi, Ondieki and Tanui would not only have been brave, but delusionary.

But right now, as I check through a draft of this chapter, I'm sitting in Rob de Castella's 'Deek's Café' in Canberra chatting about our plans to increase the physical activity and health of Australian kids when we take a little time out to remember Ron Clarke who had died a month previously. Rob's eyes lit up as he remembered Ron as one of the truly great Australians, who not only led the pack on the track, but off the track in business as well. 'A great man' Rob reminisced, 'I've often wondered whether being a front-runner on the track is an inherited personality characteristic that goes with taking initiative and perhaps even risks in business? Or was it something that Ron learned during his running days and applied to business?'

I wonder too, because famous front running athletes like Clarke, Landy, Elliott, Moneghetti, and Deek himself have all gone on to contribute enormously to community ventures designed to get Australia moving, and to do their utmost to stimulate a healthier and happier Australia. Whether it be nature of nurture or a combination of both, there's definitely something special about front-runners.

The most famous pacing ever?

The world's first sub-four minute mile at Oxford in 1954 nearly didn't eventuate because of the wind—but in the end the wind was a blessing in disguise.

Those at the Iffley Road track in Oxford on May 6th 1954, were witness to the most famous case of paced running in athletic history. Medical student Roger Bannister became the first human being to run a mile in under 4 minutes, paced by colleagues Chris Chataway and Chris Brasher. Nowadays world records in middle and long-distance running are invariably set using a careful selected set of pace-makers so nothing much has changed. Well, except for the huge pay bonus current professional athletes receive when records are broken; an unimaginable feature of athletics for the Oxford trio in those purely and fiercely policed amateur days of British and indeed world track and field.

Bannister, Landy and 4 minutes

It's well-documented history that Bannister's team at Oxford almost postponed their attempt on the 4 minute mile due to strong winds, only deciding to go ahead when the rain stopped and the wind eased. No doubt the decision to run was influenced by John Landy's great form on the other side of the Channel, threatening the 4 minute barrier on several occasions.

Bannister's training partners Chris Brasher and Chris Chataway were two excellent, strong runners and they provided the 'pace'. Brasher ran through the half mile in close to 2 minutes on that cool breezy day, peeling off for Chataway, who like Bannister had to this point been shielded from any wind, drafting as we call in now, allowing him to take up the running through to 3:00.04 at three laps.

Bannister took the lead with 350 yards to go and crossed the line in 3:59.4. How that crowd reacted when they heard the announcement ...

'Here is the result of event No.9, the one mile: No. 41, R G Bannister, of the Amateur Athletic Association and formerly of Exeter and Merton Colleges, with a time that is a new meeting and track record, and which, subject to ratification, with be a new English native, British National, British all-comers, European, British Empire and World Record. The time is 3 ... ' the rest being drowned out by the noisy elation of the crowd and a thrilling moment in athletic history.

A notable absence at the track was an Oxford Rhodes scholar who had opted for a beer or two or three in a nearby hotel. He felt that Bannister's attempt would not be successful and that more satisfaction was likely to be obtained at the pub. Not one of his best decisions; but many consider his judgement tended to improve in later years following the appointment of this gentleman, one Robert Hawke, to the position of Prime Minister of Australia. One of the time-keepers at Oxford that day was a former Olympian, well known locally at the time but who only assumed his legendary status 27 years after Bannister's feat. The time-keeper was Harold Abrahams, whose preparation and participation in the 1924 Olympic Games inspired the movie *Chariots of Fire*.

The Oxford wind: friend or foe?

Should Bannister and his team have interpreted that wind as a threat to their 4 minute mile attempt? Yes, early on when it was described as a 'tree-bender' but when it subsided to a stiff breeze, it was likely to have become a friend rather than foe.

The wind was reported as around 15km/h gusting up to 25 km/h, of a direction that seemed mainly across the track. Race film shows the considerable movement not only in the trees surrounding the track, but also in the hair of the three runners, Brasher, Bannister and Chataway. For the first two laps that wind would certainly have been a net negative factor on Brasher, but the pace of 1:58 was perfect. Chataway then took up the running shortly after half way until Bannister decided it was time for his final all-out effort in the run to the tape about 300 yards out.

Whether Bannister and his team knew it or not, in contrast to being a hindrance, moderate wind has the potential to create even more favourable conditions than still air. That's providing the pace-makers are able to cope with doing the work into the wind and sustain the desired pace. The protected runner will be shielded by the wind when running into it, and benefit from wind assistance when running with it. In the case of this historic race the tailwind assistance didn't seem to be a significant factor because Bannister ran in second place for most of it. It was the second phase pace-maker Chataway who would have received that wind assistance for the first two laps. In any case, it was Brasher, then Chataway who set up a beautiful drafting effect for Bannister through the first 1,450 yards, an effect significant in still air and amplified every time they turned into the wind.

The training and planning of that run was superb and the world was thrilled not just with first sub-4 minute miler but with the extremely well-orchestrated team effort. I can distinctly remember the headlines in our morning paper, the *Melbourne Argus*, that next day in 1954. There is little doubt that Coach Franz Stampfl played a decisive role, despite Bannister's refusal to acknowledge any assistance from a professional coach and Austrian immigrant. Bannister may also have Stampfl to thank for encouraging him to run that day rather than wait for a 'better' day.

History has it that Sir Roger did acknowledge Stampfl's support several decades later, and at the same time revealed his motives in not recognizing Stampfl at the time of the race.

He was to write 'I thought it would be right for Britain to try to get this. There was a feeling of patriotism. Our new Queen had been crowned the year before and Everest had been climbed in 1953. Although I tried in 1953, I broke the British record, but not the 4-minute mile, and so everything was ready in 1954.' And decades later, Sir Roger again acknowledged Stampfl when he recalled responding positively to the coach's call of 'Relax' at a point in the race where he may otherwise have attempted to increase the pace.

It's also history that John Landy did it his way 46 days later in Turku, Finland. Chris Chataway was there to win this time, not to make the pace. Landy characteristically took up the running after a lap and a half, and at the bell Chataway remained within striking distance, spurring Landy onto the second ever sub 4-minute mile, racing to a world record at 3:57.9, a record that was to stand for 3 years. That day, Chataway ran a fine personal best time of 4:04.4 in a race Landy has treasured for the rest of his life.

Bannister and his team won the race to that very first sub 4 minute mile; a feat that was once considered superhuman and is now part of athletic folklore. The Bannister team was ahead of its time in orchestrating that race-pace assistance, but possibly fortunate that the British Amateur Athletic Association turned a blind eye to manipulating a race in this fashion. Runners rarely escaped anything from the BAAA in those days.

Following Landy's world record, the world debated the question as to who was the better miler. The two champions did go head to head in the Vancouver Empire Games mile later that year. Bannister reigned supreme, putting together another well executed plan. He would not lead, and Landy, being Landy would. The sitting cat pounced on that leading mouse in the home straight as Landy turned his head to check Bannister's position. In effect Bannister had placed Landy in the same kind of pacing role previously undertaken by Chataway and Brasher at Iffley Rd.

Does that sound fair? Most definitely. That's racing. Both runners tried to win using fair tactics they felt gave them the best chance of winning. One runner tried to break away enough to offset being outkicked at the finish. The other hung on, got the sit, and did the kicking. All's fair in love and middle-distance racing. Well, nearly all anyway ...

Have often have you seen a top Ethiopian lead in a big event? How often have you seen a top Kenyan sit back in the pack? Rhetorical questions with an answer of 'rarely' on both counts. Is it Kenyan pride that makes leading a race irresistible? Possibly, but it's also likely that controlling the pace and endeavouring to break away from the field provides many a gifted Kenyan with the best chance of winning.

By the way, if you want a good read about the days when the mile was king, my old mate Jack Pennington (war veteran, English cross-country runner, author, Australian champion veteran runner and coach) gave me a copy of Keith Miles' well-crafted tale of the personalities and drama of mile racing leading up to the Bannister and Landy Empire Games duel in 1954. Jack wrote inside the cover that 'this may be a novel, but is historically accurate and depicts Percy Cerutty especially close to the real Perce as I knew him ... and the book is a true reflection of what the mile was all about in the good old ámateur days.,'

A champion's take on front running and the wind

Following Ron Clarke's death, tributes flowed in from around the globe. One tribute came from Chris Wardlaw, Olympic athlete and Olympic coach who kindly sent it to me, as he wasn't sure whether it would get a run on the Athletics Australia website. Wardlaw remembered the motivation and support Clarke provided to aspiring young Australian runners, both in spirit and philanthropically.

Interestingly, I was reminded of the Stampfl-Bannister story above when Wardlaw recalled one particular conversation with Clarke early in 1976.

> 'I had improved quickly and suddenly qualification for the Montreal games was realistic. But I was running out of time before Nationals. I organised a 10km at Olympic Park (after a pro meet) with Steve Austin and a couple of others who in the end did not start. It was just before 10 pm and quite windy. I confided in my coach Pat Clohessy that perhaps we should try for another time. Clo, as is his way, recognized my reticence and panic and called in Clarkie, who was one of about a dozen people there. When Clarkie talks to you, you listen; so he suggested the wind, rather than a hindrance, was actually a help! " ... you use the wind behind and relax with it, then when you hit the wind in the straights it concentrates your effort ... " I ran a significant PB and qualified, ready for Nationals.'

Wardlaw went on to run 28:15.6, which was equal to Clarke's fastest 10km in Australia. The middle clock of the three timing him was 28:15.5. Without hesitation,

Wardlaw and the three timekeepers rounded up the official time to 28:15.6. Such was the respect the strong Victorian running fraternity had for the the greatest track distance runner Australia has ever produced.

Paced racing in the Grand Prix circuit

In modern track and field meets involving internationally recognized runners, almost all of the distance events are paced. In relatively low populated countries like Australia, and particularly in a country where track and field plays second fiddle to a variety of professional ball sports, finding suitable pace-makers for middle and long-distance races is more easily said than done; the limited number of sufficiently fast and experienced runners want to race, not make the pace for others. Countries without any great depth of competition are behind the eight-ball in setting up fast races. However, this is not going to change in most events, so it's the norm for Australians to go to Europe and USA to achieve qualifying times.

Some would argue that if an athlete can't run a qualifying time in their own country without a rabbit leading the way, it is almost certain that they will not be competitive internationally anyway. There might be some truth in that but venturing abroad to race often facilitates sizeable improvements. That said, runners in Australia and similarly athletically undernourished nations would do well with a change of attitude to racing in their own country.

There is a need for our top runners to take on the responsibility of hard fast front running. Fair enough, we don't expect runners to take up the pace when a national championship is on the line, but unfortunately it is commonplace for even our best runners to expect everyone else to go out and do the work in races on the domestic circuit. That attitude is clearly counterproductive to the sport, races are run in slow times, and everyone loses in my view, including the winner.

But let's not just blame our runners. We coaches need to understand that fast times require collaboration between coaches and athletes to share the work in the early laps. And perhaps a suggestion for Athletics Australia? If fast races are what everyone wants, why not provide decent incentives for times, rather than podium finishes? Perhaps even consider incentives for placings and times partway through the race? I think in the long run (and even in the short) something along these lines is needed to create faster races in Australia.

Ironically, and perhaps unexpectedly, an individual's best 800m or 1500m time is likely to occur when the first lap is faster than average race-pace, so-called positive pacing. Sports scientist Kevin Thompson alludes to this phenomenon in his book devoted purely to pacing in all sorts of sports (Pacing: Individual Strategies for Optimal Performance). He refers to evidence that starting fast can actually increase the total aerobic energy contribution in an 800m race, resulting in more overall power and a faster time. The rationale is that if a runner can get to the 600m mark in a given time but with greater aerobic contribution then he or she is in better shape to resist the feared 'lactic' legs in the final 200m. On the other hand this is not straightforward as any runner knows. It requires careful management. Going out too hard will induce excessive use of anaerobic power which may over-ride the potentially positive effect of the increased aerobic contribution with a net negative effect. Herein lies a challenge for coach and athlete to get the balance right.

The 'front-runner's dilemma'

The pre-race coach-athlete brief will often include specific details of how to run the first part of a race, taking into account the athlete's and competitors' strengths and weaknesses.

For example, if a 1500m runner A is faster over 800m than runner B, but is not as good over 3km (or even if he is), then an advantageous tactic for A might be to trail B until such a time that his or her greater finishing speed can be put to advantage. But runner B will anticipate or at least soon realize the tactic A is applying and has two options, which might be coined the 'front-runner's dilemma.'

Runner B can speed up to try to shake A off, but this is not easily done, because A is drafting off B, so running at the same speed is physiologically less demanding; and even more so if there is any wind about. On the other hand B can slow down. A may refuse to pass, the race slows down and runner A is in an even stronger position to outsprint B in the final stages. Alternatively if runner A does decide to pass, he or she is now in control of the pace, and again in position exploit a superior finishing speed.

So what to do?

B may even have the fastest personal best, but has a history of losing to A. B's best chance is to try to take A into the extreme discomfort zone by breaking away at a speed that is well above the threshold pace, forcing metabolic and respiratory discomfort in both runners. But the discomfort is likely to be higher in the more anaerobic runner A who will also have more difficulty in recovering. The break is secured, and B is likely to be out at the front of a chasing pack, but if runner A in that pack is to catch B it has to be done without any drafting assistance.

The trick for B is to get that decisive break but it involves a risk. Exceeding threshold to the extent required in this breakaway might prove too demanding, necessitating a slowing of pace and increased risk of being caught by the pack. Here's where running teamwork comes into play. If there are two or more outstanding front-runners from the same club or country, they can arrange to stage that breakaway together and share the work done by alternating the lead. We see the top Africans doing this in the big events. Sometimes there is a designated runner whose role is to go out and do the work, to sacrifice himself for his more favoured team-mate, as is the case of the 'domestic' in cycling.

There have been some extraordinary applications of the brave but sometimes kamikaze front running break away. One memorable display was delivered by Kenyan star Yobes Ondieki at the 1991 Tokyo World Championships. I was sitting in the stand with his wife, Lisa, as Ondieki made a break of what I recall as around 50-60 meters (don't quote me on the distance) in an early burst that took everyone by surprise with its seemingly suicidal intensity. He had no team mate to help him out and had kept his plans very much to himself. But Ondieki had carefully considered the 'front-runner's dilemma' and the prospect of being 'sat on' through the race and being out-kicked by runners with faster finishing speed. He applied the tactic described above and threw his cards on the table with that breakaway move. History has it that he was almost swallowed up by the chasing pack in the last lap but 'almost' is the critical word and the gold was his. Sure, another 30 meters in that race and he may not even have got a place, so fatigued was Yobes, and so fast was that pack bearing down. But that medal around his neck signified that it's the runner who gets to the tape first that counts for everything, not how fast he or his chasers are running when he gets there. One of the all-time great tactical performances.

When a pace-maker goes further

Pace-making in some events has produced some unexpected victories. For example in the Beppu marathon in 1995, Australian Pat Carroll was employed by the race committee to pace through halfway at least. This he did, but to his surprise, when he got to the half-way marker he felt surprisingly good, and ventured on. At 25km he still felt strong, so on he continued on his merry way, making the most of the 'at least' aspect of his contract. At 30 km, Carroll decided to finish the race at the designated pace; one by one the pack dropped off the pace. Pat didn't and ran through the finish line to win the race in his lifetime personal best of 2:09:39.

Nowadays, race organizers often set out contracts which render pacemakers ineligible for prize money. Sometimes it goes even further; that their professional pace-making fee is withheld if they continue past the maximum pre-determined distance. But this wasn't the case for Pat, and I'm sure he wasn't too concerned about forfeiting a modest pace-making paycheck and replacing it with the winner's prize-money and winner's trophy. Best of all though, he'd run sub 2:10 marathon, a feat still only accomplished by five Australians: Rob de Castella in 1986, 2:07:51, Steve Moneghetti in 1990, 2:08:16, Derek Clayton, in 1969, 2:08:33, Carroll in 1995, 2:09:39 and Lee Troop in 2003, 2:09:49.

Perhaps Pat's relaxed attitude going into this run had something to do with this unsolicited excellent run. Marathons are stressful. Apart from the combat of the race, there's the stress of putting the totality of the previous 6 months training to the test in one fell swoop. Fear of failure builds up and plays with emotions, sleep and performance. As pacemaker, Pat would have gone into that race in a more relaxed state than any other elite marathoner lining up that day.

This same relaxed state may have operated to the advantage of a pace-maker in a more recent race as well. Lee Troop asked his friend and emerging marathoner at the time Michael Shelley to pace him through 15km or so of the Gold Coast half-marathon. Michael agreed and went into the race in a relaxed manner, with a high quality training run to 15km or further if possible on his mind, and a good preparation for his first half-marathon which we had planned later on that year. However, at 15km Shelley, like Carroll, felt good, so he continued on, maintaining the pace 'Troopie' had requested. Unfortunately, in a similar scenario to the Carroll run where the pack dropped off his pace, Troopie fell off the pace too. Shelley, in the excitement of realizing he was feeling fine in his first half-marathon, made a decision to finish. This he did, winning the race in a promising debut half of 62:40.

On the surface this shouldn't present a problem. The pace-maker does the work up front; is more than happy to do more work and continues on the agreed pace; and goes on to win the race. However, a problem does arise when runners don't consider the pace-maker as their competition but purely as a helping hand. On discovering otherwise in the final section of the race, the element of surprise must present as disconcerting at least, and potentially upsetting to the leading pack when it's realised that the friend out front has declared himself a foe.

In the Troop-Shelley case, there was no pre-race contract, just a general friendly agreement that Shelley would make the pace, and it was not really expected that the inexperienced young Gold Coast resident Michael Shelley would be able to continue on past 15km, especially doing the work up front. Despite there being no agreement that the young runner had to withdraw from the race, it was understandable when he felt uncomfortable in relegating his friend and race favourite Lee Troop to 2nd place that day. He told me later continuing on was a decision he made during the race and that he would have been more than pleased (and even more pleased) had Troop been able to hang on and kick past him near the line to win.

When everything falls into place, literally: Andrew Lloyd in Auckland

I've already introduced Andrew Lloyd story, his fun and his tragedy. Here's my side of his Commonwealth Games 5000m gold medal; his career highlight through his coach's looking glass.

We thought there might be an outside chance of a Commonwealth Games medal in that 5000m in Auckland. And for international readers outside the Commonwealth countries, that is a pretty big deal in Australia. Being realistic we reckoned a medal the colour of a two cent piece would be a fantastic achievement for Lloydy or either of the other two Australians in the race, Pat Carroll and Malcolm Norwood. With Kenya and Tanzania being Commonwealth nations, and their best runners in that 5km, what might otherwise have been viewed outside the Commonwealth as relatively low profile event, had a world class field.

It included Kenyan John Ngugi, the reigning Olympic 5000m champion and five times winner of arguably the most competitive distance race of all, the World Cross-country Championship. Then there was Yobes Ondieki, Tokyo World Championships 5000m gold medallist and a runner I knew pretty well, as he was married to my runner, Lisa Ondieki. Both runners had run 5km about 25 seconds faster than Lloyd. Making up an incredibly strong Kenyan trio was world cross-country silver medallist Moses Tanui, who the following year would take the World champs 10,000m title and later become the first to run a half-marathon in under 60 minutes. Bearing in mind the better personal bests of several runners from UK, Canada and NZ, if any of the Aussies ran well, a realistic outcome would be a top 5 finish, but the bookmakers would still have had Lloyd at long odds on that.

Lloyd and I had some serious work to do and I invited him to sit down and set out a strategy that might get him into the top 5 in Auckland. He looked at me quizzically for a second or two and delivered a statement that would define our coach-athlete relationship for the remainder of his career.

'Dick, I'll do the running. You do the thinking!',

Coming from this street-smart athlete who could match wits with anyone, in his own way he was telling me he had confidence in me as his coach and that I should have confidence in him as an athlete.

'Fair enough' I remember replying, but the nonchalance of my reply belied the importance I had placed on his point of view. I was not a highly experienced distance running coach in 1990 and assuming the responsibility for an Australian athlete's career was not to be taken lightly.

Andrew would be ranked about 10th in the final if he made it. His best time wasn't far off half a minute slower than the top Kenyans, who were even more superior runners than Lloyd over 10km and 12km. To be realistic if these runners went out at 13:15 pace over in New Zealand then they would be running by themselves after 6 laps. However, championship races produce strange mindsets and strange tactics, although we all knew that the Kenyans would have just one tactic in mind. They'd break up the pack early, shake off any hangers on with a surge or two and then fight among themselves for the colour of the medals.

As is often the case with coaches, several optimistic race scenarios went through my head. No point in contemplating the pessimistic ones. What if Ngugi, Ondieki, and Tanui in anticipation of their three-horse race, decided to play cat and mouse with each other, rather than work together? The race might end up being slower, permitting lesser mortals like the Australians to stick around. What if they hadn't prepared all that well, or were a bit off-colour, jet-lagged or had suffered injuries following a hard race campaign in Europe? Then there were the vagrancies of the weather. What if there was a strong wind, or even a storm that made even the Africans think twice doing too much too early, opting to delay winding the pace up with a few laps to go?

One thing I had learned over the years was that championship races are different and the race could be slow through the first 9 or 10 laps. And if so, how best should we prepare Lloyd to exploit any such occurrence?

Here was the line of thinking. Let's assume for some reason the top boys only average 13:30 pace for the first 10 or 11 laps, right on Lloyd's red-line. He was training well and fitter than ever and if this continued 13:30 pace would certainly have him in the mix with a lap to go. Then it would come down to a big kick-down finish. So in the final few weeks of training, it was important to ensure that Lloyd's finishing speed, a feature of his running was well-honed. On the other hand we couldn't risk losing any of his precious red-line cruising speed, as this might have him off the pace and well out of contentions after 10 laps. So the program over the lead up 6 weeks must continue with strong aerobic threshold and race-pace work, but also incorporate increased speed work, especially following the aerobic power training within the same session, while tired.

Training went without a hitch. That happens sometimes, and instils confidence in an athlete. It had Andrew telling me at times, but not complaining, that he was 'lactic and legless', in which case we backed off a little to allow more time for adaptation. The well-earned taper would be a little lengthier than usual.

We arrived in Auckland. The 5000m heat represented the final hit-out in our slightly extended taper. All went like clockwork. No sore throat, legs felt springy, no tiredness. He was a happy underdog in the final. Very pleasing to me and for Australia was that Malcolm Norwood and Pat Carroll both got through as well.

Race-day; the favourites Ondieki, Ngugi, Tenui and fine Welsh runner Ian Hamer were all there. It looked like we could rule out the sickness or injury scenario in those top boys; they looked healthy but one never really knows. And no big wind or storm to slow proceedings down. 'Oh well', I thought from the stand after leaving the runners as they went to the Call Room, 'if all goes to schedule now, a top 5 was still a distinct possibility and an outside chance for a medal, although forcing one of the Kenyans off the podium looked unlikely. A bonus though was that Moses Tanui had run the 10,000m a couple of days previously, winning silver, and that had to take the edge of him at least.

I normally relax a bit when I leave an athlete to face the music in the big arena, as there is nothing more I can possibly do. This time as the athletes lined up in the big arena I found myself a bit more 'toey' than usual. Should we have concentrated more on endurance? Two laps went by and my eyes were glued to the runner I coached, as coaches do, to get a sense of how he was moving and feeling.

Then came gasp from the crowd. I looked behind the pack to see Ngugi picking himself up off the track about 30m in the rear. I knew this wasn't the end of things for this champion, but what happened next was nothing short of astounding.

The pack was moving along at around 65 sec lap pace, but it was made to look pedestrian as Ngugi nonchalantly ran up to the back the pack within what seemed like only 100m or so. That was a feat in itself, but Ngugi wasn't satisfied. In a demonstration of his superman status the clearly adrenalized Kenyan continued on his merry way past the pack to adopt a lone ranger running figure 40m up in front!

I had barely caught my breath, checked Lloyd's position and technique as the Ngugi show proceeded, when I heard the crowd gasp again. What now? I looked back behind the chasing group and déjà vu, Ondieki was prostrate on the track. I wondered what the hell was going on, and was glad that Andrew at least was not implicated in either fall. I checked his progress again. He was still there in that pack 40m or so behind Ngugi, and as far as I could see had kept well clear of both of the crash landings. With that Ondieki fall I had mixed emotions. It certainly increased the chances of the Australians placing higher but knowing Yobes well, I wanted him to run without misfortune. Unfortunately, unlike Ngugi he struggled to get back on the pack and it was soon clear that the fall removed him as a serious contender for a medal.

Three laps to go. I surveyed the pack again, looking for tell-tale signs of fatigue in Andrew's action, but saw none. Ngugi was still out front, with British Olympic steeplechase medallist Mark Rowland and Canadian Williams 30m or so to the rear, reducing Ngugi's margin slightly. Then came a pack of four or five runners a further 10m back, including Lloyd. The other two Australians had dropped back. Of significance at that stage was that Tanui seemed to be struggling to stay in that trailing pack.

It was at that point that I knew Lloyd was going to have a good one, looking comfortable in the chasing peloton. Ngugi still loped along 'like John Ngugi', but then, for the first time he looked back at the chasing pack. When he looked back again a couple of hundred meters hence, he sent out a signal to the crowd and the runners that he was doing it tough out front. Almost like a mere mortal.

The bell sounded at just around 12'23" for Ngugi, about 12'27" for the Englishman Mark Rowlands and Canadian Paul Williams who were a few meters on from the main chasing peloton which included Hamer and Lloyd. The enthralled crowd in that packed Auckland stadium knew the fight was about to start in earnest for the silver and bronze. The gold medal was out of reach. At this stage the Kiwi Kerry Rogers was looking strong. Hamer was sitting behind Lloyd. Ngugi was still out front by 25m, loping along but clearly hurting.

That crowd was now at fever pitch and I think I was too, but my fever was a quiet one.

'Okay Andrew, what have you got left? Are you too stuffed to exploit that speed? If you are 'legless,' you are hiding it well. But what are you waiting for? ... Go now, don't wait man!'

Then came the critical move a bit more than 200m to go, but not from Lloyd. Hamer, with an explosive change of pace took everyone by surprise. A split second after Hamer, Lloyd kicked hard to stay right on Hamer's tail! Within a couple of seconds there were only three runners in contention for a medal!

Ngugi looked around again to see Hamer bearing down still 20m back. He may then have glimpsed Lloyd, who with a little less than 200m to go had unleashed a secondary burst of speed that left even the fast finishing Hamer in his wake. A silver was up for grabs.

Then comes the final twist in this 5000m tale.

Ngugi looks around yet again with only 80m to go, to see Lloyd blistering into the home straight. Lloyd now senses a medal that wasn't silver or bronze but later tells the press that at that stage it was 'Bugger the silver, I'm going for the gold.' Ninety meters to the line and he's running as fast as I'd ever seen him at the end of a race. Fifty to go and everyone in that capacity crowd is on their feet. Ngugi couldn't be caught now ... could he? Twenty meters to go and Lloyd is only 5m back. The gallant, but absolutely spent, Kenyan wills the finish line closer but it must have seemed a mile away. Lloyd steams alongside John Ngugi a metre out, to take the lead for the first time in that race 50cm before the finish line.

An estimated 26 second final 200m topped off the most important race of Lloyd's career. A gold medal for his country and a personal best 5km executed at precisely the right time. Most importantly for the sport, it was one of the most memorable ever Commonwealth Games races.

Andrew jogged around to see me as I got down near the track. I will always remember the look on his face. That's why I coach.

Andrew Lloyd training at the AIS Canberra.

Image: Australian Sports Commission

Chapter 17
Recovery

'Speak English!' said the Eaglet. 'I don't know the meaning of half those long words, and I don't believe you do either!'

Lewis Carroll

Just why is it that some runners bounce back from a hard race on Saturday to train the house down on a day or two later while others are too sore or tired? Why can some runners benefit from the preliminary rounds of a championship 1500m and run their best in the final, while others run well in the first round or two but struggle in the final?

A hard run requires time to get our physiology, biochemistry, anatomy and sometimes our psychology back in usual working order, to restore homeostasis. But the most common reason for our impaired performance is likely to be anatomical, the damage sustained by our muscle cells to unusual running stress; faster, longer, steeper, hotter or more hypoxic.

That muscle fibre damage occurs after unusual running efforts is consistent, firstly with the soreness runners feel and secondly with increased blood concentrations of certain markers of muscle damage. Creatine kinase (CK) is one such marker. CK is an enzyme involved in the formation of phosphocreatine, a kind of energy storage and transfer unit within the muscle cell. It's a fairly bulky molecular unit as molecules go with little chance of escaping through the muscle cell membranes under normal circumstances. Following the muscular trauma of a hard race, CK molecules spill into the bloodstream; indicating damage or at least a loss of integrity of the cell wall. So the blood CK concentration provides a biological gauge of muscle damage.

To illustrate and help us understand why runners recover at different rates, consider this (unpublished) observation of runners at the AIS in Canberra in the 1980s. We measured the CK levels of 5 highly trained distance runners 3 days and 11 days after competing in the Sydney marathon. Each had averaged approximately 100 miles (160 km) per week during the previous 3 months and our findings are summarized in Table 17.1.

	Wt (kg)	Ht (cm)	June 12 m'thon Time (h:m:s)	June 16 CK (IU/L)	Distance run post m'thon (km)	June 23 CK (IU/L)	Distance run post m'thon (km)
Derek Froude	64	182	2:15:19	546	27	315	170
Graham Clews	85	190	2:18:35	983	22	1434	99
Garry Hand	64	172	2:17:18	420	32	190	120
Jim Murphy	62	170	2:23:34	499	24	590	122
Colin Neave	68	178	2:31:46	478	24	547	108

Table 17-1: Creatine Kinase (IU/L) following the Sydney marathon June 12, 1983.

Three days post-race the runners reported to the AIS lab for their post marathon blood test. I asked them how they felt before we measured their blood CKs.

Clews was 'very sore, jogging, but very slowly indeed' with a CK of 983; Hand indicated that he was 'still a bit tired, but not sore at all really' with a CK of 420; Froude was 'a bit sore but jogging ok' with a CK of 546; Murphy was 'still fairly sore and tired' with a CK of 499; Neave commented similarly to Murphy and his CK was 478 so all these CK concentrations were roughly in line with the perceived soreness.

Eleven days post-race, and the runners were all keen to get back into training as soon as they could. Their efforts toward this are outlined in the table. At this stage Graham Clews was 'still sore and struggling' and in resuming training his CKs increased to 1434! He was advised to ease right back on any running, and consider substituting water based work or cycling. Derek and Garry had 'no soreness' at the 11 day mark. Their CKs had decreased, despite the 160km plus of running they had done. Both runners commented they were being 'conservative' in their approach to getting back into training, and 'felt okay running.' Colin and Jim, whose CKs remained elevated were feeling 'a little soreness still and still a bit tired' and felt they could carry on with the running but commented that they needed more days of easy work.

All right, so muscle damage seemed to be the cause of the tiredness and soreness, but why did Garry Hand and Derek Froude have more muscle damage than Jim Murphy and Colin Neave, and why had Graham Clews suffered so much damage? Race speed did not appear to be a major factor; nor did training volume as all runners were running around 160-180km per week. However, the answer may be related to their size. The two runners who differed most markedly were Clews and Hand; Clews was about 190 cm and 85 kg and Hand was 175 cm and 65 kg. Body weight was indeed a plausible contributing factor to muscle damage, as in general the heavier a runner the greater the ground reaction forces. Couple this with the fact that the Sydney marathon involved some hills, not steep, but hills nevertheless, and the heavier runner would be doing more of the damaging eccentric work on the declining regions.

However, referring again to the Hand and Clews case study, one other potential factor stood out. Their running techniques differed markedly. Clews had a long stride, even relative to his greater height, whilst Hand had a very short stride, again even relative to his smaller stature. Two potential effects come to mind, the magnitude of the ground reaction forces at footstrike, and the number of footstrike forces exerted during the marathon. Every airborne part of the stride involves the centre of gravity moving in a parabolic curve. With a longer stride a runner is in the air for a longer duration. And with a greater vertical displacement of the centre of gravity there is a bigger ground reaction force and stress through the body at footstrike. On the other hand (so to speak) a shorter stride means more footstrikes over the course of the marathon, which again would be expected to increase biomechanical trauma. At least in the case study presented here, with Clews being heavier and with the greater stride length but hitting the ground fewer times during the marathon than Hand, the size of the footstrike force, rather than the number may have more to do with the soreness and slower recovery.

There are two other considerations when discussing the correlates of recovery. Rather than mechanical, it may be a biochemical cause. With the huge and constant production and flux of oxygen through the muscle cells, and the known proportionate increase in harmful free radicals, oxidative stress is a potential, even likely cause of delayed onset muscle soreness. Notwithstanding the mechanical differences we've alluded to, some runners, like Hand and Froude, may inherit a set of 'resilience genes' promoting development of soft tissue that is more resistant to oxidative or even mechanical stress.

The other consideration is that resilience may be trainable. We're all aware of the first session on a synthetic track in spikes which induces soreness around the calves and Achilles especially; and that after a session or two, the soreness disappears as the legs 'toughen up.' The same seems to be true of running on the road, although not quite as obvious. This suggests that road racers may benefit from training regularly on the same hard surfaces they will compete on, with the usual precaution of not overdoing it, especially for runners susceptible to overuse injuries.

A similar situation arises with footwear, as lighter less cushioned racing shoes will do less to buffer the footstrike forces and so tend to induce more soreness. An important part of marathon preparation is acquiring adaptation to the lighter racing flats. In Clews' case, he did train in spikes occasionally on the track, but more often than not opted to train in heavier shoes, fearing that to do otherwise would lead to injury. The 'catch 22' situation is that if he trains in light shoes too often and on the road too often, injuries are more likely. If he trains on softer surfaces and with heavier shoes too often he is not well prepared for the stresses of marathon road running, and may suffer more muscle trauma during the race and more difficulty recovering. Individuality as well as specificity of training are both important coaching considerations. Coaching runners wasn't meant to be easy.

Clews' CK levels were as high as I had seen up to that point; but a year or so later a veteran runner changed my idea of what 'a high' CK level was. The runner was attempting to break the world record 24 hour distance record on our AIS track, but after a colossal effort, didn't make it, collapsing at 18 hours. I spoke to the cardiologist who treated him and he told me his CK levels were 98,000! How much of that was from the heart muscle I don't know, but that order of CK must surely have indicated life-threatening muscle breakdown. Fortunately the ultra-distance runner survived the ordeal. There have been cases where a combination of heat and running have induced similar muscle 'meltdown' even in races as short as 10 km. This rarely encountered trauma is known as rhabdomyolysis and predisposition to this dangerous predicament is thought to have a genetic basis.

Now for a final consideration, one that, may supersede much of the previous discussion of the effects of weight, stride length, oxidative and mechanical stress on muscle trauma. A longer stride length in any individual generally signifies better elastic energy. This in turn promotes better economy and speed, which is a real bonus for a middle-distance runner because speed and economy trump any negative effect of muscle trauma in short events. But if a marathoner has excellent elastic properties and a good stride length, and at the same time is relatively resistant to ensuing trauma, at least during the race, then this is clearly advantageous. Such a runner will be more economical, and make better use of the two major limitations to marathon running performance, oxygen and glycogen. And that seems to be the trend in elite marathoning these days. Nowadays the world's best marathoners run like track runners, light and elastic; very different to the traditional low knee-lift style we are accustomed to see in our former marathoners. The athlete who runs the first two-hour marathon will be light and elastic every step of that 42.195 km; he will be a superb 10,000m and 5000m runner and a very good 1500m runner. He will be running 200km a week consistently in his 6 month build-up, much of it with high quality, and he will have trained up his muscle resilience to deal easily with the sharper forces he produces at each footstrike. He will be of east African heritage and living at moderate altitude and warm climate.

When recovery becomes critical: track heats and finals

Rapid recovery following a race becomes extremely important when that race happens to be a preliminary heat in a championship, because any runner who makes it through has to back up for the final two or three days later.

Such was the case with Carolyn Schuwalow. Carolyn had exceeded most pundits' expectations in running an Australian record in the heat of the Seoul Olympics 10,000m. Backing up though presented a problem. Carolyn's huge lifetime best physical and psychological effort over those 25 laps took its toll. The final was a struggle.

Why had she paid more of a penalty than other women who made the final? In short, on that occasion Carolyn was not prepared well enough for running on the track. Training had been a balancing act, continually adjusting training with the threat of injury hanging over our heads. We did a lot of work on softer surfaces, running on the track often causing niggling soreness, indicating that it was a risk to run any more than once every week or two weeks on the synthetic surface. Running in spikes was also problematical in the months leading up to the Olympics, spikes confined to two or three lead up races. Our main concern was that she got to the Olympics in good health and without any injuries. And that balancing act wasn't made any easier by the exercise-induced asthma Carolyn endured throughout her competitive life.

Carolyn's lack of specific track work in spikes had her competing at the Olympics with a minimal level of muscular resilience; a muscular system more susceptible to damage, inflammation, soreness and diminished function. Her final, in reality, took place in that preliminary heat. Making an Olympic final was, and still is not a common occurrence in Australian distance running, and an accomplishment to be proud of, but to be a real contender in a championship final it's important to have had a good set of lead-up races. That specific race-fitness is hard to come by without racing.

Training to recover

Mizan Mehari competed in the World Junior Track and Field Championships in Sydney in 1996. He had trained with Haile Gebrselassie, and as I understand held his own in that training group in some of the sessions. Mizan came to Australia as a16 year-old prodigy with a personal best 5000m of 13'36". He and his team-mate Sisay Bezabeh decided to seek asylum in Australia and after this was granted, a representative of the Ethiopian society in Sydney contacted the AIS to ask if they could come down to Canberra to train. That they did, and I was soon to discover that Mizan, with his big motor, little body and huge motivation, had a propensity to ignore common training sense and any advice we had to offer.

My plan with young runners was, and remains, simple. It was 'all in good time, let's build up gradually over a period of years' but there was no long term mentality in this youngster. I wasn't surprised to hear that Mizan's early teenage training in Ethiopia was interrupted by back and leg soreness. It was sad that this precociously talented runner never reached the heights of greatness but becoming a champion requires more than a big engine. Having said that, by the time he was 20 he became an Australian Olympian in Sydney and a World Championship team member in Barcelona. That should have only been a start for Mizan, not the end.

Downhill running and resilience

One of the many aspects of the teenager Mizan Mehari's training that worried me was his uninhibited fast downhill running during our hill sessions. This was how he did it back in Ethiopia, and despite his susceptibility to injury, and strong advice to moderate this part of his training, he wouldn't or couldn't change. The forces generated in fast downhill running can be particularly damaging not just because of the required resistance to gravity but also because of the posture developed runninng down a hill. In addition, the running muscles are stretched as they contract which can be thought of as an increased tendency be 'pulled apart.'

But is fast downhill running always something to be avoided? I think not. Systematically increasing the eccentric load of hill running by increasing the gradient, speed, distance of the downhill sections can actually help athletes train to resist muscle damage. It is, after all, a form of plyometric training, and more general forms of plyometric work may also help muscles resist damage. The eastern African runners don't seem to have any problem recovering from the heats in championship events, and one reason might be regular fast downhill running, either during the long runs or in specific hill sessions. Of course, their light frames, and ability to run their heats at lower percentages of their personal best will help recovery too.

Recovering from a hot marathon

The New Delhi Commonwealth Games marathon, run in 25 to 30 degrees C heat is as good as any to check how top athletes recover from hot summer marathons.

Well, Michael Shelley (silver medal in 2hr15'28", winner John Kelai ran 2hr14'35") recovered considerably faster than Lisa Weightman (bronze medal in 2hr35'25", winner Irena Jerotich ran 2hr34'32").

Given that more muscle damage is expected the faster the pace and bigger the runner we might have expected Lisa to recover more rapidly, but she didn't. While it took several weeks before either runner was able to resume proper training after that torrid marathon, Lisa took about 3 weeks longer. Michael was back into easy running after 2 weeks, into moderate training after 5 weeks and in full training 9 weeks post marathon. Lisa was back into easy running after 4 weeks, into moderate training in 9 weeks, and resumed full training in 12 weeks.

We might be able to explain the variation in recovery in three ways; the way they ran their races; the volume of training in the lead-up and finally the climatic conditions of their training environments.

As far as the influence of the way they raced, Michael ran much of the race by himself at his own controlled pace, which enabled him to pass five runners in the final few kilometres to grab second place. He obviously ran himself right out in that oppressive New Delhi heat, but was still able to maintain an upright position after he'd run through the finish line. Not so Lisa, whose legs decided that 42.195km plus the warm-up was more than enough work for the day in that heat; team doctor Adam Castricum providing a welcome shoulder of support into the recovery tent. But Lisa didn't have the control of her race-pace like Michael.

This was determined by the lead pack of four runners with which the Australian kept within reach but under constant pressure to hang on to a series of surges by the front-runners. This forced her to drop off the back and fight back on several occasions, although it was interesting that Lisa was to tell us after the race that she really didn't change her pace very much as the Kenyans surged and slowed.

Then there were the differences in the preparation of the two medallists. Lisa averaged a little less than 160km per week over the three months leading into the race whereas Michael averaged close to 200 km. Increased volume of training might have increased Michael's general 'resilience'; his ability to reduce the muscular damage incurred from racing 42 km. And in contrast to Michael, Lisa ran no hills. We removed these from the program after she developed hamstring soreness during a hill session, and we've already discussed the potential value of hills in promoting running resilience.

Finally, although Lisa paid careful attention to preparing for the hot conditions of New Delhi by acclimating with indoor training at the Victorian Institute of Sport in Melbourne, and moving to Cairns in the weeks prior to the race, all Michael's training over the previous months took place in the semi-tropical conditions of the Gold Coast before moving up to Cairns. Living and training in warm to hot conditions the year round may well afford an advantage not fully realized by shorter duration acclimation and acclimatization.

In any case, of concern to me as their coach was that both athletes had recurrent periods of unusual tiredness for several weeks post-Delhi, which necessitated a very close watch on proceedings. The gradual resumption of full training was based on how the athletes felt during training and how they responded to easy running. Perceived weakness or soreness was the signal to delay any sort of serious progression. All-out efforts of 26-and-a-bit miles need to be highly respected, and even more so in the heat, humidity and pollution. Athletes' brains need to recover just as much as their bodies before entertaining any thoughts of the next marathon campaign. Following lengthy discussion with the two athletes, and in the interests of their health and following careers, we collectively decided to withdraw from the World Championships in Moscow when we discovered it was scheduled at 3pm in the afternoon at an average temperature for that time of the year of 25°C.

The downside of not being available for major championships is that any modest financial support for training, competition and medical expenses received from Athletics Australia was reduced, but to my mind the decision was an easy one, especially with the huge physical and psychological commitment of preparing for the London Olympics on the horizon.

Corollary

Massage, cold therapy, heat therapy, and immediate post-training nutritional supplementation may provide additional benefits to the age-old regime of light jogging, easy stretching, sensible fluid replacement and a decent meal with plenty of good quality carbohydrates and adequate protein and fat. If the former aids to recovery are available, conveniently located, and within your budget and time commitments to training then take advantage of them. By trial and error, in the long run, you'll discover what suits you best.

Chapter 18
Running in the heat

Alice: 'This is impossible'.
The Mad Hatter: 'Only if you believe it is'.

Lewis Carroll

If you want to win in the heat and humidity then train in the heat and humidity.

Preparing to compete in hot climate championships

The big championship races of the Olympics, World Championships, European Championships, Commonwealth Games, World Student Games, World Junior Championships and national championships all over the world are held in summer. The weather is typically warm, even hot, and sometimes humid. Hot weather is welcomed by the sprinters, not of great concern to the 800/1500m runners, challenging for the 5000m runners, difficult for the 10,000m runners; and potentially distressing for the marathoners.

Distance runners need to incorporate some form of acclimation (artificial environmental adaptation) and/or acclimatization (natural climate adaptations) to heat in their training programs leading into most major championships. The problem is greatest for athletes who have to come from a southern hemisphere winter into a northern hemisphere summer to compete (or more rarely vice versa). It's only a minority of athletes who are sufficiently financially independent to afford the cost of relocation to countries that offer timely appropriate conditions for acclimatization.

There's a decent amount of literature on how human performance is compromised in hot weather. Coalmines, offices, and classrooms have been venues of investigation. Exercise in the heat adds another dimension to coping with hot conditions, because muscular work produces its own additional source of heat. Good studies on how our elite athletes acclimatize were few and far between a couple of decades ago, so with a view to determining how best to acclimatize our runners for competition in the hot and humid weather of Atlanta prior to the Olympics in 1996, my team at the Australian Institute of Sport conducted an acclimatization camp in 1995 exactly one year prior to those Olympics.

The Atlanta trial

The findings of this study were presented to coaches at an Athletics Australia Coaching Convention in 1995 and to scientists at the Exercise and Thermoregulation Conference in Sydney in 1996. However, as was often the case in the very practical and busy environment of the AIS, we didn't get around to publishing the findings elsewhere.

Given that some of our best runners were keen to stay in their own training environment in Australia for as long as possible before the Olympics, we decided to investigate the effectiveness of a 3 week acclimatization period in Atlanta. Ten highly trained middle and long-distance runners met the criteria of being in solid training for the previous 8 weeks, injury free and available for the five weeks of the study. The runners had been training well for the previous two months and the 3 week period in Atlanta was designed to replicate the volume and intensity of training prior to the Olympics 12 months later; solid with some good sessions but moving into a more conservative taper period.

We conducted two tests in the AIS climate chamber before the athletes travelled over to Atlanta for the three weeks and conducted the same two tests on their return. Both tests involved running for 15 minutes at 18 km/h. The first test took place in our normal moderate laboratory climate, 21 °C and around 50 percent humidity. For the second run, the temperature was 30 °C, 50 percent relative humidity; typical of a pre-Olympic afternoon in Atlanta. Our measurements included heart rate, blood lactates, core temperature, and body weight change to determine sweat loss.

You may be wondering why the two running tests? Well, increases in cardiovascular fitness and adaptation to heat share common characteristics. For example there tends to be an increase in plasma volume with increased fitness as well as with heat adaptation. We were keen to determine whether any improvements in the running assessments observed after the Atlanta trip were the result of heat acclimatization or simply increased endurance fitness. Any increase in endurance fitness would be reflected by a lower heart rate and lower lactate during the run in the cool conditions. Should the heart rate and lactate be reduced to a greater extent in the hot conditions then we could infer an acclimatization effect.

During the three weeks the weather in Atlanta did not let us down; the average temperature and humidity were typical for this time of the year. In the afternoon it was 28 °C with 56 percent humidity, and in the morning the average was 21 °C and 78 percent.

So what did we find?

The increased stress of running in the climate chamber in the hot conditions was evident. At 18 km/h, mean heart rates were 176 in the heat and 154 in the cool; blood lactates were 2.9 mmol/L and 1.0 mmol/L respectively.

All went well with our travel and our accommodation was good in Atlanta, with no problems getting to good training venues including the track at Life College. The three weeks over there went without a hitch. Obviously the travel and the heat took a while to get used to, but by the end of the three weeks the group without exception said they felt a lot more comfortable training in the heat. The group stuck to the plan to maintain their current training program without pressing hard to increase their fitness.

The runners flew back to Canberra for the repeat tests. As expected, the test in the cool conditions of the climate chamber showed no evidence of any change in fitness. Steady state heart rates at 18km/h in cool conditions were essentially unchanged (means 154 before and 155 after) as were blood lactates (1.0 mmol/L before and 1.4 mmol/L after).

On the other hand the repeated tests in the hot and humid conditions of the climate chamber showed a small but statistically significant reduction in heart rates (176 to 173, a small reduction occurring in every runner) and a more substantial decrease in the blood lactates (2.8 mmol/L to 1.9 mmol/L, and again a drop occurred in every runner).

Probably the most interesting aspect of the way the athletes acclimatized to the heat and humidity of Atlanta concerned their sweat rate and fluid loss. The athletes sweated a lot less in the 30 °C and 50 percent relative humidity run in the chamber on return from Atlanta. The first time they lost an average of 1.1 L, but post Atlanta they lost only 0.7 L; a statistically and certainly a practically significant difference. On presenting these results, a physiologist colleague from Sydney suggested to us that the results didn't make sense, and that we must have made a mistake. 'During heat acclimatization we adapt by sweating more, not less, as sweating is a mechanism that facilitates cooling' he reminded me.

We acknowledged that this is certainly true, and we suggested that it may well apply to maximal sweat rates. But if, following acclimatization in Atlanta the runners were able to complete the 18 km/h run in the hot and humid conditions with an attenuation of core temperature then we might expect a reduction in sweat rate, not an increase. We would have nailed this explanation on confirmation that core temperature was reduced following the acclimatization. Unfortunately our attempts in those days to measure core temperature were not sufficiently technically proficient to produce reliable results.

I have noticed on many occasions that some of the fittest athletes I have run with in the heat seem to sweat less, not more than accomplished runners. On first thoughts, sweating less might seem a disadvantage because sweating cools us down. But what this lower sweat rate might be telling us is that fitter runners are controlling their body temperature better. Perhaps this is through better efficiency, or by more effective non-evaporative forms of cooling, the latter influenced by body shape and size. Staying comfortably cool and losing less fluid would certainly be of considerable advantage to any marathoner competing in humid and hot conditions.

I've always been impressed, and sometimes amazed at the way some runners are able to perform in hot, humid conditions. Carlos Lopes and Joan Benoit in the Atlanta Olympics were two remarkable examples that first came to my notice. And Kenyan Sammy Wanjiru ran the astounding time of 2:06:32 in the heat and humidity of the Beijing Olympics, while the other best runners in the world understandably fell away. What amazed me more was that as he passed my vantage point in the final kilometres of his Beijing run, I saw no evidence of sweat on his body or face, and no evidence of distress on his relaxed face. Sammy was obviously in better control of his body temperature than any other runner that day and probably in better control than the spectators standing on the sidelines, including yours truly. I remember very slowly jogging a couple of kilometres down to the marathon course to watch him, then having to change my shirt, wringing wet with sweat, before I left for the airport.

As I jogged through the Beijing streets that steamy day I thought about the Atlanta study 9 years before. It's got to be the runner who sweats less at race-pace, not more, who is the best adapted to run in humid and hot conditions. Sweating may cool you down, but prevention is better than cure, and it's by far better if you don't get too hot in the first place. Sweating also means loss of body fluids and greater risk of a dehydration effect on running control. And the more humid the environment, the less effective sweating becomes as a cooling mechanism. Given fluid loss of around 3 percent can lead to loss of performance the net effect of sweating on performance in high humidity is likely to be negative. Rob de Castella, found this out the hard way, as described below.

Anyway, the Atlanta trial told us that three weeks of steady training of the type we might expect in a three week period leading into and tapering for an Olympic marathon in hot and humid conditions, was coincided with stress free, illness free and injury free training and facilitated acclimatization to heat and humidity.

What it didn't tell us, and what we still don't know for sure, is whether longer periods of time are likely to bring about greater effects of acclimatization for our elite runners. My guess, with the advantage these days of many years of hindsight, is that for hot, humid marathon competitions, a period of at least 3 months, not just 3 weeks acclimatization might be required, and although there may be diminishing effects after 3 weeks, the increased adaptation over the longer period is likely to be very important in elite competition. The training environment doesn't have to involve extremes of heat and humidity; not with the amount of self-generated heat of the runner. Indeed, with an analogy to altitude training, a moderate level of heat and humidity would seem sensible to permit the desired quality of training. It goes without saying that care has to be taken to ensure gradual adaptation in any new environmental conditions.

Los Angeles

History has it that in the Olympic Games marathon of 1984 in LA, Rob de Castella did not perform at a level commensurate with his clear top 3 world ranking as world record holder. But it was a summer marathon, and hot. De Castella trained for 6 weeks near Stanford University prior to the Olympics. Stanford wasn't quite as hot as it was likely to be in LA, but temperatures reached the high twenties C. We wouldn't have wanted it much hotter really, as the sweat poured off Rob and his training partner, brother-in-law Graham Clews.

Marathons in hot conditions are one of the anomalies of Championship events, as nearly all the prestigious big city marathons around the world are scheduled when the weather is either cold or moderate. With some runners better suited to running hot weather marathons than others, big city marathon place-getters may not enjoy the same success at the Olympics.

Dealing with humidity on top of, and independently of heat alone may also be factor determining success in championship races. Runners with years of training in countries with humid and hot conditions have a history of doing well in championship races when these conditions prevail. Their adaptation is likely to be psychological as well as physiological. As indicated by our Atlanta project, adaptations to the heat and humidity coincided with a lower sweat rate during a run of given speed and duration, although the mechanism of any adaptation was not clear. Runners with better running economy have lower heat production at any given running speed, offering a line of speculation that adaptation to these conditions might involve an improvement in running economy.

In de Castella's case, the question might be asked as to whether the lack of humidity in Stanford during those 6 weeks of acclimatisation in 1984 provided sufficient specificity of acclimatisation. Rob certainly acclimatized well to the heat but he was a free sweating athlete at the best of times, and I wonder how much advantage the training camp afforded if it enhanced this characteristic. LA was much more humid than our training camp venue, an atmosphere not aided by the millions of internal combustion engines in this city of freeways. But 'Deek' had one aspect of history in his favour. In the 1982 Commonwealth Games in Brisbane he emerged victorious with a wonderfully paced raced race in temperatures in excess of 20 ° and 60 percent humidity during the race. His strong finish in 2:09:18 proved he could run well in very warm conditions.

However, LA was a different story. Rob was to tell me after the race that the humidity and heat seemed to rear up from the bitumen, and a lot hotter and steamier than his Brisbane race. 'I sweated so much that I had to drink in between drink stations, something I'd never had to do before.' He was still suffering when he got 'home' to our rented house in Santa Monica several hours and several litres of fluid post-race.

As might be expected when the world record holder (2hr08'18" at the time) doesn't participate in the medal ceremony, Australians were disappointed. Naturally we in the de Castella camp and Rob himself were disappointed too, as a medal was a realistic expectation. But a little later on when the heat of the moment had subsided we all recognised that his 5th place in the world on that hot and humid day was a truly great performance. And an Australian Olympic male marathon placing only matched by our wonderful four time Olympian Steve Moneghetti from the very cool climate of Ballarat, Victoria who was 5th in the hot, humid un-marathon friendly conditions of Seoul. It's important for us not to lose sight of the enormity of the de Castella-Moneghetti achievements in those conditions in an event open to every man on earth, unrestricted by socio-economic status or lack of facilities and equipment on the world's greatest sporting stage.

L.A. When the big guys suffered

De Castella was at a competitive disadvantage; one he overcame in Brisbane, but one he never had to overcome in his many great cool marathon victories; his body size. The winner in that LA Olympic marathon, one Carlos Alberto de Sousa Lopes of Portugal was not only well used to training in humid conditions, but he also enjoyed a somatotype advantage. Small, light athletes are able to control their core temperature more effectively than their bigger and heavier competitors. De Castella was 180 cm and 70 kg; Lopes was 167 cm and 55 kg. The amount of energy required to run at any given pace, and so the amount of heat generated, is greater in heavier runners. De Castella, being 27 percent heavier, would have required substantially more energy and so produced considerably more heat than Lopes at the LA marathon race-pace.

One of the main ways of getting rid of body heat is through the skin, via convection from the muscle bellies and by evaporation. So release of body heat is to a large degree dependent on body surface area. We can estimate body surface areas of the two athletes of interest using what's known as the Mosteller formula: BSA (m^2) = SQRT[Height(cm) x Weight(kg) /3600].

Deek' surface area was about 17 percent bigger than Lopes'. This in turn tells us that de Castella's natural 'radiator' was likely to be about 17 percent better than Lopes'. Herein may lie the problem. Let's assume that the aerobic engines of de Castella and Lopes were similar relative to body weight, say a $\dot{V}O_2max$ of 85 mL/kg x min. Considering the body weight difference of 27 percent and assuming similar running economy de Castella's heat production would be around 27 percent greater than Lopes'. With a radiator only 17 percent more effective than Lopes, de Castella is at a distinct disadvantage when it comes to controlling his body temperature. Moreover, because part of the advantage of the bigger surface area is the possession of more sweat glands, much of de Castella's surface area advantage was lost in very humid conditions where sweat evaporation was restricted. All in all, the smaller athlete, in this case Lopes, holds a clear advantage in championship marathons held in the heat and humidity of summer. Interestingly, the arithmetical inferences on the heat control for Rob de Castella were not all that different for Alberto Salazar. Alberto, like 'Deek', was considered a strong podium chance, but at 180 cm and 64 kg, he too was at a weight disadvantage to the likes of Carlos Lopes in LA. Alberto finished 15th in 2hr14'19", de Castella 5th in 2hr11'09" and Lopes' winning time was 2hr09'21".

Derek Clayton was another Australian who has held a world record in the marathon (2hr08'33" which stood for 12 years). Like de Castella he was big for an elite marathoner (187cm and 72kg), and again like 'Deek' he didn't really perform in summer championship marathons as well as his world ranking would suggest. In the 1968 Mexico City Olympics it was hot, although not humid, and the 3pm start where the average temperature is more than 21 °C suggests the program planners cared little about marathon runners, or ignorant of the two-pronged threat the heat (anything above 18 °C is 'hot' for a marathon) and reduced oxygen pressure. These things considered, Clayton's 2hr27'23" for 7th place was an excellent run. And in Munich four years later, while again not performing as well as his world ranking suggested, 13th place in 2hr19'49" in an Olympic marathon in 27 °C heat was another wonderful achievement, especially for his size!

KL: the girls get it right

One of the most satisfying hot and humid Championship events I've been involved in as a coach was with Australians Kate Anderson (5000m) and Kylie Risk (10,000m) in the Kuala Lumpur Commonwealth Games in 1998. Both these women came from the southern states of Australia, Kate from Melbourne and Kylie from Hobart. The winter had been cool to cold and wet and windy at times, in contrast to the (30 °C) hot and humid conditions expected in Kuala Lumpur.

The Australian pre-KL Games camp was held in Darwin, where the temperature and humidity during the day were not far off those expected in KL. On arrival in Darwin both girls had trained well in the weeks and months prior to the camp. Most importantly they were already well acclimated, having trained indoors on treadmills twice a week for a couple of months. With no fans at 22°C, and the absence of any relative air movement one gets from running outside even in still air, this type of training certainly challenged these runners' cooling systems. Another runner, Heather Turland from Bowral, New South Wales, whom I'd spoken to as the AIS physiologist, did the same thing but went even further. Heather turned on heaters in one of the rooms of her house and ran two or three times a week, including her long 2 hour plus long run on her treadmill in 25-30°C heat.

With the humidity these conditions evoked, sweat didn't just drip off these three women, it flowed off, and they were forced to cope with little help, if any, from evaporative cooling of their sweat.

The speedier sessions each week were performed outside in the cool, allowing high quality training to accompany the treadmill acclimation work. A couple of weeks in Darwin to get the feel of living as well as training in a hotter and humid environment, then a week or so in KL had the girls feeling confident and looking forward to running well in KL.

Confidence in their preparation clearly played a part. During the days preceding the races and even in the warm-ups for the races, I overheard some competitors from other countries, including the Kenyans, talking about the 'atrocious conditions' they were to race in. I was more than pleased to pass on the concerns of these runners. There was no fear of the conditions in the three Australians who were actually looking forward to putting their acclimation and acclimatization processes to the ultimate test.

And run well they did. Kate won gold in the 5000m and Kylie silver in the 10,000m, and Heather took gold in the marathon. What made these performances especially satisfying was that these girls were relatively unknown internationally, and not ranked particularly highly in terms of personal bests before the race. Kenya and Tanzania always provide classy competition, and the UK countries, Canada and New Zealand have had more than their fair share of world-class distance runners over the years. Heather Turland, as a mother of four and 40 years-of-age, received a lot of well-deserved public adulation. I always felt that Kate and Kylie's exceptional performances weren't given their due credit. After all some of the greatest runners Australia has produced have not won gold or silver in the Commonwealth Games, a championship highly regarded in Commonwealth countries. These girls may not have been world record holders but they got it right at the right time.

A warm weather marathon well executed

In 2009 for the World Championship marathon in Berlin the temperatures were forecast to range from 18 °C to 27 °C, but humidity was not a problem. This may not be hot by normal living standards, but add to the heat my marathon runner Lisa Weightman produces in running 3'15"–30"/km, this environment, especially with the direct sunlight, presents a huge challenge to body temperature control.

With Lisa's Melbourne hometown training environment presenting typical maximum winter temperatures of around 15 °C, we engaged in an acclimation program at the Victorian institute of Sport consisting of cycling and running in a room heated to between 25° and 30 °C and around 50 percent relative humidity. With two or three sessions each week, Lisa reported how much easier the exercise became and her lowered heart rate response vindicated her perception.

The plan was to run according to feel, not to any pre-determined speed. And when I say 'our' race plan, I include Lisa's husband and training partner Lachlan McArthur and father Peter, whose carefully considered input is invaluable. And in the first half of the race we agreed that the 'feel' should be comfortable. Our marathon runner was well practised in running as fast as possible while feeling 'in control'. In this race the placing rather than the time was our highest priority. Taking any risk to run a personal best in very warm conditions was simply not on. We knew there would be others who would underestimate the effect of the conditions, but also knew that most of them would pay the price. So in essence we adopted a 'biological feedback' tactic, for our runner to adjust her pace according to the messages she received from her legs and lungs.

So the plan was not complicated. It was a 'comfortable first 10km **; a solid but still well-controlled second 10km**(*); an up-tempo effort third 10km*** working harder but still feeling in control; then an all-out last 12km ****.

I included those asterisks to link this race with her training and help her understand how she should feel during the race, because those asterisks were used to describe the effort in her daily training over the previous 6 months.

- * easy recovery, no stress
- ** steady effort, well in control, breathing is strong but steady, certainly no lactic feeling in legs
- *** best training effort, working hard but judged so that there always a bit left in the tank
- **** all-out effort to exhaustion

At 5km Lisa Weightman was not in the top 50, and even in this world class field Lachlan and I wondered if she had taken our race plan instruction to feel comfortable in the first quarter of the race too literally. Being so far back at 5km was concerning. But any concern we had subsided when we saw her go past at the half-way mark. She looked exactly as she had at 5km; breathing controlled, technique and cadence maintained and face relaxed. And she had picked up more than 15 places. She continued on at her perceived 'up tempo' *** effort. Many of her nearby competitors had indeed underestimated the combination of their fitness and the conditions and our marathoner continued to pass runners. Lisa finished completely exhausted but extremely happy with a personal best in trying conditions and 15 places higher than her pre-race ranking by times; a good example of a plan well executed by a a runner who can think on her feet, and with belief in the plan.

Kerryn and the heat chamber

Recall that as part of the Atlanta trial we set out to measure core temperature, heart rate, sweat rate in a standardized treadmill run in the AIS Climate Control Room, both before and after a three-week acclimatisation period in Atlanta. Kerryn McCann was one of those athletes. In those days she was a promising athlete and history has it that she became one of Australia's best ever marathon runners, guided throughout her career by renowned coach Chris Wardlaw. In 2006 she won the hearts of the nation with a courageous Melbourne Commonwealth Games marathon victory. Tragically, in 2008 she broke the hearts of the nation when she passed away after a battle with cancer.

Back in 1995 Kerryn impressed the AIS lab staff as a delightfully unassuming runner of grace and excellent potential who loved running and loved life. That Melbourne Commonwealth Games marathon epitomised Kerryn's courage and talent, and she is missed very much by us all.

Kerryn contributed well to that camp, not only in terms of her dedication to training and commitment to the study, but with her light-hearted humour. One incident in the lab stands out.

If core temperature is to be measured properly it's not under the tongue or in the armpit; it has to be measured at the runner's core, literally. The runners were briefed on the importance of measuring core temperature properly and they somewhat hesitantly went off to the bathrooms to set their thermometer probes in readiness for their treadmill run.

Kerryn was in the heat chamber, about 5 minutes into her test run when lab technician Hamilton Lee, whose role was to monitor Kerryn's core temperature via a remote control unit from outside the heat chamber, noticed a sudden drop in temperature. He deduced that the rectal thermometer had become dislodged and asked Kerryn to return to the bathroom to make sure it was secure. In resuming her run, Hamilton was delighted to find that Kerryn's temperature had now risen back into the normal range.

'Kerryn, that's great, it's up again' Hamilton called out, referring to the temperature reading on his monitor.

But Kerryn, now getting pretty hot and bothered, having run for about 10 minutes already at 18km/h at 30°C, turned to Hamilton and informed him quietly, 'You're damn right about that ... and it's not going up any further!'.

We immediately realized that Kerryn had linked our young technician's comment to the actual position of the thermometer probe rather than the temperature, and we later suspected that Kerryn did so for some mischievous fun, rather than through any misinterpretation.

Kerryn, I and one or two other staff got a great chuckle out of this incident, but not so our conscientious young technician Hamilton (who by the way now is a highly experienced physiologist still working in the lab at the AIS). Hamilton continued to concentrate hard on his remote control and the temperature, oblivious to any frivolity.

Chapter 19
Food for a runner

'Then you should say what you mean' the March Hare went on. 'I do' Alice hastily replied; 'at least – at least I mean what I say – that's the same thing you know.'
'Not the same thing a bit' said the Hatter. 'You might as well say 'I see what I eat' is the same as 'I eat what I see'!'

Lewis Carroll

Distance runners are fortunate really; they can generally eat a lot and remain lean. Except females.

With apologies to Lewis Carroll

General nutrition

Runners and coaches don't need a degree in nutritional science any more than in sports psychology, biomechanics or physiology, just some basic knowledge and common sense.

After all, despite what some would like us to believe, a runner's nutritional requirement is not much different to anybody else's: a good variety of fresh vegetables and fruits, meats, fish, dairy products, cereals and nuts. Eat this way and make non-sweet carbohydrates the majority of your kilojoule intake then you'll be on the right track. Variety is the key, and nowadays there's more than ever, as countries become more multicultural, and food is sourced from different soils all over the country and the world, so minimizing the chance of missing out on any essential nutrient.

Runners are lucky, not so our kids

In general, when it comes to fuelling up, we humans are extremely flexible and runners are no exceptions. None of us need to meticulously gauge the proportions of fats, carbohydrates and protein we consume. While runners and non-runners alike are well-advised to get most of their kilojoules from sensibly cooked or prepared carbohydrates in the form of vegetables and grain products, it just doesn't matter if the percentages vary from time to time. We've got a system well-accustomed to coping very well indeed. This is fortunate because we seem to have survived quite well despite being lured into a new 'research proven' super-diet on a weekly basis by a creative nutritionist with marketing manager in tow.

The majority of consistently well-performed runners I've known over the last few decades are far from finicky when it comes to food. Most runners enjoy eating well, to their satisfaction, day after day. It's remarkable really how runners are able to balance large quantities of energy in and out to maintain a lean body over extended periods of time. Athletes aside, physically active people in general enjoy better control of their energy balance and body composition than those who don't move very much. This might have something to do with physically active people being better able to control blood glucose and, in turn, develop an appetite centre of the brain better able to match food intake with energy expenditure.

That reminds me of one of our publications in our Lifestyle of our Kids (LOOK) longitudinal study. The leanest 8 to12 year-olds in our cohort of 850 typical Australian children consumed no more kilojoules, sugar or fat than fatter children. In fact they actually tended to eat more than their fatter peers. This may surprise some people, as there is a tendency to become myopically focused on dietary intake when it comes to tackling the problem of childhood obesity in the general community. The leaner kids were simply more active. The pre-smartphone/iPad/computer generations have fond memories of running around outside kicking or hitting a ball until it got dark, and eating whatever we liked, but remaining as skinny as the drover's dog. Those same leaner more active kids in the LOOK study were more sensitive to insulin and better able to control their blood glucose than their less active and fatter friends. This feature is consistent with the premise that the appetite centre control of a more active child is better regulated; and that the role of physical activity in controlling body composition exceeds that of simply interpreting energy output in terms of 'burning' fat.

A coach's role

So how might we coaches routinely advise our athletes on what to eat and drink? In general, advice should given the way we cook a good steak; fairly rarely and simply. Coaches don't need to talk about dietary intake too often, but a gentle reminder is warranted now and then that quality food is required to generate quality power.

I like to explain the variety principle in different ways. For example, that eating plants with a variety of colours signifies a variety of minerals and vitamins. I remind my athletes that steaming vegetables is a good idea, as is preparing them in a wok taking care not to overcook and upset the vitamins. And I like to point out that we need some good quality protein each day such as that found in cheese or meat to ensure we recover well from hard training. I like to ensure my runners that fad diets condemning carbohydrates might be attractive to a sloth-like lifestyle but a running or generally active life thrives on carbohydrates; and that includes a variety of cereals and other grain products, preferably not cooked to a crisp.

Interestingly one former champion runner disagrees with the latter point.

The marathon man's grain free bread shop

Francois Robert de Castella always enjoyed plenty of bread and cereals through his stellar running career. Following his running years his athletic ambitions turned to martial arts and typical of his commitment to (and talent for) anything he takes on, he progressed to a third dan black belt in Okinawan karate.

During this post running period he met clinical immuno-biologist, Bill Giles whose research suggested that many of us may benefit from a grain free diet. Bill introduced Deek to this modified diet, and soon our martial arts expert felt a lot better both generally and during his new form of training.

So much has de Castella believed this grain free approach helped him achieve best health that he and colleagues developed a method of baking grain free bread, the flour based on seeds and nuts. Putting his money literally where his mouth is, Rob now runs a successful chain of 'Deeks' bakeries specializing in all sorts of grain free breads and and pastries. His wares are popular, and Bill Giles has run a busy practice over many years, suggesting that a grain-free diet may be of benefit to many people.

What if de Castella had discovered his grain free diet during his marathon days? Might he have improved on his superlative record of marathon running through the 80s? His Helsinki World Champs victory; his Fukuoka (later recognized) world record of 2hr08'18"; his legendary Rotterdam head to heads race against Alberto Salazar and Carlos Lopes; his Commonwealth Games gold medals, his 2hr07'51" Boston triumph? And the rest. Mmmm—I'll leave that kind of speculation to you.

Fat ain't all that bad

It has become fashionable to remove fat from our diets. It's certainly fashionable in several of my female runners. This is because fat is energy dense and is reasoned to make its consumer 'fat', and a diet high in saturated fats has been linked to cardiovascular disease.

Yes, these are plausible reasons to limit ingestion of fat, but we shouldn't forget that fat is an integral part of our normal diet. We have been programmed to enjoy the taste, to digest it, to metabolize it; and we can't do without some 'essential fatty acids'. Even different types of essential fatty acids need to be balanced out and this can be achieved by eating fish (especially deep sea fish), some vegetable oils like olive oil, avocado and nuts (not cooked and salted!), and meat contains its fair share as well. In case you're wondering why 'deep sea' fish, essential fatty acids are a class of unsaturated fats (meaning all of the carbon atom skeleton of the fat molecule are not 'saturated' with the maximal number of hydrogen atoms). Unsaturated fats don't actually freeze as easily as the saturated ones so fish from cold deep waters tend to grow a larger proportion of unsaturated fats to avoid freezing to death.

But then again, I see no reason to remove saturated fats from your diet if you are a runner, or even if you aren't. Sure, limit their intake, but there's a place for some saturated fat in meat, cheese, butter, cow's or coconut milk.

I always remember the look of surprise on the face of one of my long term ex-Ethiopian athlete Sisay Bezabeh when I said I was going to trim the fat off a steak we were about to consume at a barbeque.

'Why would you want to do that Dick? In Ethiopia we reckon that part of the meat is the best!'

Of course things are a lot different in the less affluent countries. Why would you waste some of the meat when it's in such short supply? Here in our 'Western world' many of us consume too much saturated fat in hamburgers, potato chips, sausages and the like. A dangerous practice, particularly as food deep fried in re-cycled fat offers a carcinogenic threat as well. Consumption of food prepared with this kind of assault warrants a sensible minimization tactic, and abstinence makes the most sense. The same applies to commercially processed cakes, biscuits, pizza bases and the like where physiologically damaging artificial trans fats are created as manufactures tempt the tast buds of the masses in economically profitable ways. Alas, millions of us flirt with this deadly double whammy of metabolic disorders predisposing Type 2 diabetes and heart disease and some forms of cancer; and even gamble with a triple whammy by opting for a physically inactive lifestyle. So while runners obviously benefit from an active lifestyle, the evidence is clear that refusal to heed the warnings scientists provide about trans fats is a health risk; and a healthier runner is a better runner.

A bit of sugar won't kill you, but get the timing right

Common table sugar, or sucrose, extracted from sugarcane, is a complex of glucose and fructose. Fructose can be converted to glucose in the liver and glucose is the form of sugar that has to be carefully controlled in our bloodstream by a series of hormones working in concert with physical activity. Glucose is also a fundamental molecule (with the fatty acids) from which we extract energy through systematically dismantling it with some clever biochemistry, trapping the energy bit by bit in the form of ATP. Glucose is in one sense more versatile than the fatty acids, in that we can extract its energy both with and without assistance from oxygen; not so for fatty acids where we need oxygen.

So what's all the fuss about sugar? As I write this, sugary drinks are being banned in schools, and nutritional gurus are damning it as a threat to mankind. Well, consuming too much of anything for extended periods can cause highly problematic imbalances in our biochemistry whether it be fat, protein, water or oxygen. Sugar is no exception, as loading up repeatedly with concentrated sweet stuff places our blood glucose regulation process under pressure. But that doesn't mean we need to avoid it altogether.

Consider the following. One of the poorer design aspects of Homo Sapiens is our blood sugar control system. While we've evolved with numerous hormones to increase blood glucose, we've got only one hormone that lowers it, insulin. This puts us in a vulnerable position because if for some reason insulin is not available we are in deep trouble. Over millions of years of evolution how could such a basic flaw go unnoticed and uncorrected? Well, it's simple really. It's because we all possess another perfectly fine and natural alternative way to lower blood glucose, even without help from insulin. It's called exercise. The problem lies in Mother Nature's absence of soothsaying prowess. She never envisaged a day would come whereby Homo Sapiens could get through a day hardly flexing a muscle. This places huge pressure on our insulin supply until a point that it cracks and our pancreas' ability to secrete insulin in sufficient quantities diminishes. At that point we are developing what is now widely known as Type 2 diabetes.

So, while sugar's reputation is as a villain, physical inactivity has certainly emerged as a clear and present danger, an accessory to the crime of modern manslaughter. Physical activity, i.e. using muscles energetically, facilitates control of blood sugar, so it stands to reason that active people can consume more food, including more sugar than their inactive counterparts and still maintain good metabolic control. But considering that the majority of humans in rich countries and an ever-increasing number in the poorer countries lead sedentary lifestyles, the taste bud targeting strategies of sugar-based food and beverage manufacturers might reasonably be suspected to accelerate what is now recognized as a global epidemic of Type 2 diabetes.

Sugar for elite runners

Can the regular consumption of sugary foods and beverages detract from running performance? Probably not in most runners; but possibly in some. Let me explain. As outlined above, training daily, and sometimes twice daily, have the advantage of regular vigorous physical activity which assists insulin in its work, day in and day out. Snacking on a candy bar or consuming a sugary beverage during the day is not likely to cause a problem in the vast majority of runners. In fact this practice offers a quick and easy way to replenish glycogen in preparation for the next training session often just a few hours later.

However, (and there's often a 'however' when discussing human performance), my preference for distance runners is not to make a habit of taking a sugar hit on an empty stomach, for at least four reasons.

Firstly, it makes more work for the pancreas (which sends out the insulin to control blood sugar) and some runners may have a genetic predisposition to pancreatic dysfunction leading on to Type 2 diabetes in their later non-running life. Secondly, it's best to let the liver do the job of controlling blood sugar, rather than receiving regular sugar direct from the gut, and a liver well-accustomed to doing the job it was designed for will assist runners in the long run, when the pressure is on to maintain blood glucose. Thirdly a candy bar contains few micronutrients, and a slice or two of wholegrain bread and honey is a far better choice. Fourthly, an apple a day might help keep the doctor away but chewing candy and drinking sugary soft drinks regularly just serves to line the pockets of your dentist.

As usual running related stories crop up in every area of consideration. In this instance my mind goes back to Townsville, prior to the Atlanta Olympics in 1996 when I had the pleasure of joining the Australian team in its final stages of preparation.

Among our athletes was champion marathoner Steve Moneghetti. He was well known to be sponsored by a prominent candy manufacturer at the time, and I wondered whether he took advantage of his free supply. Steve, some team-mates and I (trailing) had just completed a 2 hour plus run and we were chatting in his room. I soon had no doubt about the marathoner's ambassadorial approach to his sponsor; his fridge housed an excellent supply of the candy bars. As he took the wrapper off one, Steve did the right thing and offered them round. As I recall no one declined (I know I didn't), and after the 2 hour run, the sugar and fat of that candy bar not only tasted good, but was rapidly deposited into the muscle storage bank. Fat stores around the tummy would not have got a look in amongst that lean and hungry group. There's a time and place for everything—but it does make sense to make those sugar and fat hits of candy bars a rare treat.

For joggers

But what about those of us who like to get out for a regular jog? Can we accommodate the occasional candy bar or sugary drink without increasing the risk of chronic disease?

Yes, to a degree we can, but in the absence of experimental evidence, and relying somewhat tenuously on observation and basic physiology, my feeling is that the 'as a treat occasionally' rule holds up pretty well here. Like fat, an occasional treat of a candy bar is likely to be physiologically well tolerated in one who jogs with sufficient volume and intensity. What is 'sufficient' will vary individually, but if you want an indication, my guess is that a daily run of 5km, which includes at least 10 minutes of effort to induce some strong but not stressful breathing at least twice a week, is in the ball park of being 'sufficient'. I haven't considered the effect of adding dietary kilojoules to an energy-balanced lifestyle. To do so will clearly result in body fat storage and weight gain. That's common sense.

And there is one more consideration. Like a lot of things in sport and life, timing is the key.

A preferable strategy to enjoy sweet food is to do so following, not before a nutritious meal. This will slow down absorption of sugar and make life a bit easier for insulin to do its job. Choosing your sweets well will also help. For example, let's say you really enjoy a dessert of chocolate mousse following your meal. A sensible, and for mine even more enjoyable strategy is to enjoy the chocolate mousse as the minor complement to some fresh fruit, rather than the other way around. And for an 'after dinner mint,' try some dark chocolate, with 70 percent or 80 percent cocoa content and sweetened to taste with some dried fruit or cashews (which can taste quite sweet if you get them fresh). That sort of sweet snack can actually be good for you!

Glucose and middle-distance running

A gram of glucose is not as energy rich as a gram of fat, but despite its power to body weight disadvantage, glucose has a couple of distinct advantages over fat in the running game. Firstly, glucose, through its exclusive involvement in the anaerobic pathways, permits more power production than fat, so faster running. Secondly we can generate more energy from glucose per litre of oxygen than we can from fat, and this has implications for runners, because getting oxygen into our system quickly enough certainly is a limiting factor.

How can we exploit this knowledge? Well, if we reasonably assume oxygen uptake to be a limiting factor during a race, the more glucose an athlete metabolizes in a middle-distance or distance race, the more power is derived from that limited supply of oxygen and the faster the athlete runs.

But can we increase our use of glucose (and decrease fat metabolism) in a middle-distance race? Yes, because consuming carbohydrates has this effect and distance runners do this as a matter of routine before races. A typical pre-race is diet high in easily digestible carbohydrates and athletes often supplement this by sipping on sugary sports drinks or glucose gels before warming up. This will have blood glucose rising in minutes and stimulate insulin secretion which in turn will promote a metabolic preference for glucose in the muscle cell.

As far as I know the effect of a more specific strategy of pre-race glucose supplementation hasn't been scientifically tested but seems plausible. The trick would be to ensure that the timing was right; that the blood was high in sugar at the start of the race. Timing is critical because if the sugar was consumed too early, insulin may have done its job and restored blood glucose to normal levels. In any case the 'nerves' and adrenaline release of the pre-race 'fight or flight' reaction also incites glucose release from the liver and that poses a relevant question. If indeed pre-race blood glucose ingestion did promote glucose utilisation during a track race, might our normal pre-race 'nervous' reaction be enough in itself to promote maximal glucose metabolism, dampening or removing any effect of pre-race glucose spiking? Perhaps this is a topic worthy of experimental investigation by a bright young sports scientist.

Glucose and marathon running

When it comes to thinking about glucose and marathon running, we have a very different proposition. In marathons 'running out' of glycogen is a major concern. Anyone who has gone out at too adventurous a pace knows how debilitating 'hitting the wall' of glycogen depletion can be. In contrast to our middle-distance running proposition, we want to conserve our muscle glycogen supply during a marathon; and this presents somewhat of a dilemma.

On the one hand it is beneficial to get as much energy as possible from every molecule of oxygen, and this favours glucose as the fuel of choice. On the other hand a marathoner will benefit from reducing glucose utilisation to ensure that muscle glycogen stores don't become critically low, and this means not trying to run too fast, because the faster the pace, the more glycogen used per kilometre.

Experienced marathoners learn by experience to run their race at sufficiently lower than 'threshold' (i.e. best 10 km) speed so as to optimize glycogen utilisation in the fuel mix. The 'perfect' marathon would have the glycogen tank almost but not quite emptied at the finish line, so that speed can be maintained through the finish line. Judging that optimal pace is not an easy task, but one coaches and runners need to do their best to estimate prior to the race, based on their preparation and prior experiences.

In a different role as designer of a breakfast cereal, named Sustain. Revenue from the product created funds for many new scholarships.

Image: Australian Sports Commission

So, should marathoners take in some last minute sugar in the hope that it will 'top up the tank'? Might this help prevent muscle glycogen depletion late in the race?

Probably not, but we don't need to worry too much about any so-called rebound hypoglycaemia (low blood sugar) as some have suggested might result from pre-race sugar ingestion. In the real world of racing, and the preceding warm-up, as distinct from the laboratory treadmill, most marathoners will experience sufficient pre-effort neuro-endocrine reactivity (read 'nerves') to ensure blood sugar is well sustained. I've observed plenty of good performances both from marathoners who sip sugary sports drinks or suck on glucose gel in the hour before the start; just as I've observed many good performances from those who don't.

Regarding the possibility of a last minute contribution to our energy stores, it might seem sensible to top up with some sugar just before starting the marathon. However, in a well-tapered runner, ingestion of glucose just prior to the run, after a well-controlled warm-up, is highly unlikely to find its way to a fully loaded muscle, and probably has little to do with maintaining blood glucose during the run when the liver supply of glycogen is unlikely to be exhausted. It's a bit like trying to squeeze an extra squirt of fuel into the tank of a car after you've filled it up to the brim, driven round the block and returned to fill it up again; might not be worth the effort.

Carbohydrate loading

Carbohydrate loading refers to filling up the muscle (and liver) glycogen stores by reducing training and increasing dietary carbohydrate intake over the few days prior to the event.

It's based on the premise that the higher the glycogen stores prior to racing a marathon, the better the performance. This is probably true for most marathoners, although the fittest runners make greater use of fatty acids at any given speed than less fit runners, suggesting that increasing intra-muscular, readily available fat (as distinct from other irrelevant fat depots) may also be important.

In any case, work a few decades ago by Scandinavian physiologists indicated that marathoners can load more glycogen into muscle if they markedly lower their muscle stores first. They called it glycogen super-compensation. The 'depletion' was induced by a long run a week out from the marathon, followed by a low carbohydrate diet for three to four days, then three days of high carbohydrate consumption prior to the race.

This regime appealed to many marathon runners, but didn't suit everyone. Many runners, and probably most these days like to forego the depletion phase, believing that they can store glycogen maximally without emptying the muscle out first. Concern about the depletion phase is understandable. After a commitment of months or even years to training for a marathon, many runners are not happy undertaking a 25 or 30km depletion run a week out from the big race. And many are uncomfortable changing their diet dramatically during the race week, particularly on to a low carbohydrate regime which contrasts sharply with their usual food mix. This can be uncomfortable for both mind and body, and any additional pre-race anxiety or heavy leggedness in the last week is not welcome.

The coaching practice I have encouraged over the years has been to gently encourage marathoners toward a partial depletion and repletion of glycogen stores, to a degree that suits their physiology and psychology. I like to explain the pros and cons and I think the former outweigh the latter.

Our regime is as follows:

Assuming the marathon is on a Sunday the long run on the previous Sunday is usually modified to a moderate 20-25 km. It serves to lower the glycogen stores, and for a very fit and already tapering runner, this run is not at all demanding. The low carbohydrate diet begins after this run and continues over for three and a half days through to and including Wednesday evening.

We continue to train easily during the low carb days, with the exception of our quality session on Tuesday (see the section on marathon taper) and this presents no problems, although some runners do feel a little less energetic than usual. This seems more the case in males, females usually reporting little or no effect of the lowered carbohydrate intake. In any case, it's important to remind runners that they'll feel great in a few days when they begin the loading regime.

On the Thursday morning prior to the Sunday race, and before breakfast, (after which we begin the high carb phase), we go out and do a series of six or eight, 200m strides at around 1500m pace. I started this practice first with Lisa Ondieki in 1988 after she felt that she'd feel better doing a set of good solid strides at this stage. I had no problem with this, and thought that it might even help a bit in depleting the faster fibers just prior to the first high carbohydrate meal. In any case, given that Lisa felt remarkably strong before and during that particular first marathon, and ran her personal best, I have continued this practice with most of my other marathoners over the years.

Typical pre-marathon low-modified carbohydrate food choices

Breakfast: scrambled eggs, or eggs tomatoes and bacon; steak and eggs, with a piece of toast and butter; plain yoghurt with some blueberries

Snacks: piece of watery fruit, apple, orange, watermelon, tea, coffee, water

Lunch: Choice of cheese or meats and poultry, ham, salad, avocado and one or two thin slices of bread or a small portion of rice or pasta

Dinner: Fish, meat supplemented by steamed vegetables (broccoli, carrot, beans especially, and small portions of potato or pumpkin; dessert watery fruit and yoghurt (sweetened with the fruit), after dinner chocolate (70-80 percent cocoa).

Typical pre-marathon high carbohydrate food choices

Breakfast: Toast, bread rolls, honey, fruit spread, cereal, tinned fruit, bananas, rice

Snack: Muffin, bread, banana, fruit juice, chocolate (50 percent cocoa).

Lunch: sandwiches, pasta, pizza (minimal cheese), rice.

Dinner: Pasta, rice, vegetables (potato, pumpkin especially) supplemented by small servings of meat, poultry or fish. Desserts of fruit and ice cream.

My runners consume mainly complex (non-sweet) carbohydrates on the first couple of repletion days, supplementing with more of the sweeter snacks during the last day when 'topping up' the glycogen stores. The rationale here is that runners might squeeze in a bit more glycogen following the sharper insulin response typical of foods with higher sugar content. My runners have been delighted when I've suggested that chocolate might be a good snack during the repletion phase. Variety is important to ensure that appetite is stimulated. It may well be that the mono-saturated fat of good quality chocolate (preferably in chocolate of around 50 percent or more cocoa) assists building a good intramuscular fat supply as well.

One of these days we are going to find a way to store enough glycogen to fuel a marathoner throughout a race without worrying about running out. Marathon pace will then approach the runner's best half-marathon pace, and a sub-2 hour marathon a realistic proposition!

A real example of pre-marathon preparation

Here is an example of some notes I wrote for a runner. Modifications are always made according to personal preferences of athletes.

Sunday: 24km easy

Monday: Modified low carb diet regime; am easy 10km; pm 8km

Nutrition note: emphasis on meat, fish, cheese, nuts, eggs, watery fruit, vegetables but not a lot of pumpkin and potato...some ok of course. Remember this is a 'modified low' carb regime not a 'no carb' regime.

Tuesday: am low CHO 1 x 2km (2'30"), 3 x 1km (1'), 6 x 200m (30") a good solid session but never forcing it; pm easy 8km.

Wednesday: am low CHO continued. Travel overseas. Easy 10km.

Thursday: am easy 10km including 4 x 300m (1'jog) steady and 2 x 200m (1' jog) good solid strides; start high CHO after this run at breakfast, and continue through to the race on Sunday.

Nutrition notes: emphasis on good quality complex CHO (rice, vegetables, bread, pasta, plus bananas and fruit, cereal all fine... just take sweet foods as your palate directs you.

Friday: am 8km with 6 x 150m strides at race-pace.

Saturday: am 8km including 6 x 100m at race-pace .

Nutrition notes: A little more emphasis today on sweeter foods today if you feel like it ... snacking with some sweets as you feel.

Sunday: First 30km on PB pace; then a PB is your likely outcome.

Result: This athlete felt good at the start of the race, and ran a personal best with a podium finish.

However, there are always individual exceptions to the text book rules of best practice. Take the next example.

One track superstar gets it wrong in the long run

Lasse Viren, the great Finnish distance runner took out the 5 km/10km Olympic gold double in Munich 1972. Incredibly he did it again in Montreal 1976. Training prescribed by Coach Rolf Haikkola always involved plenty of volume given his Arthur Lydiard inspired methodology, and at the Moscow Olympics in 1980 a leg injury hindered his preparation although he ran extremely well for 5th in the 10km. The marathon was clearly in his mind in the lead-up to Moscow and he ended up pulling out of the 5000m to give himself a better chance of success in the marathon. Rob de Castella, a 23 year-old starting out on his own marathon career, found himself sitting adjacent to Viren during the pre-marathon breakfast. All marathoners are keen to see what champions do, and without making it too obvious he took a mental note of Viren's breakfast. He was surprised to see it consisted of 2 boiled eggs and a small tub of yoghurt. That's the kind of low carbohydrate high protein low kilojoule diet we might expect a bodybuilder to employ as he or she 'cuts' for a competition. At around 25km or so, Rob was next to see Viren up ahead in the distance so Viren had obviously run very well at this stage. But de Castella was soon to overtake him as the Fin was forced to duck off into the bush for a 'pit-stop.' Needless to say the young Australian never tried the eggs and yoghurt breakfast as his immediate pre-run nutritional choice.

Mind you, it's not out of the question to run extremely well on this sort of breakfast, providing it's consumed with plenty of time for the digestive process to have taken place. And provided the previous few days have included plenty of carbohydrates and little training. A more sensible pre-marathon breakfast is a light easily digested breakfast of some toast or rice with honey accompanied by fluid in the form of sports drink, water or tea or fruit juice.

In-race nutrition during a hot marathon

Many of my runners have been involved in hot weather marathons. Here I select one instance where a male and a female ran the same race. Let's call them M and F. Here's a summary of what they consumed during that marathon. We had a plan of course, but as all marathoners know, getting drinks doesn't always go to plan. After the race, I asked them to tell me exactly what they consumed. Both runners ran extremely well.

Team mates Lisa Weightman and Michael Shelley work together at the London Olympics.

F: I got 1/2 of each of 3 glucose gels, took extra water and tipped it on my head at the water stations at least once per lap, and about 100 ml sports drink at the personal tables when not taking the gels.

5k -, 100 ml sports drink (diluted to 4 percent sugar)
10k - 100 ml sports drink (diluted to 4 percent sugar)
15k -, glucose gel and 100 ml water
20k - 100 ml water
25k, - glucose gel and 100 ml water
30k -, glucose gel and 100 ml water
35k - few sips of flat coca cola
40k - nothing
And a few gulps of water at three water stations.

M:

5km - 100-150 ml sports drink (diluted to 4 percent sugar)
10km - 150 ml
15km, - glucose gel nearly all plus 100 -150 ml water
20km -, 200 ml
25km -, glucose gel plus 150-200ml water
30km -, 250 -300ml sports drink
35km - glucose gel plus flat coke 150ml
40km - No drink

Everyone knows that we have to replace fluids during marathon running, and that replacement becomes more critical when we sweat more in warm or hot conditions. During this hot and humid marathon, M reported that he had taken close to 1.3L of fluid, and F reported about 600mL.

In that temperature and humidity, M would probably have sweated in the order of 2.5L and F about 2.0L. So M's estimated fluid deficit was likely to be around 1.2 litres and for F 0.9 litres. This would suggest a negative effect on performance, but both finished the race very strongly and extremely happy with their performances.

Sure, they certainly enjoyed a drink at the end of the race, but on top of water in and water out another variable enters the equation. It's not just camels that have an inbuilt water supply. Runners do too, and fitter runners have a bigger supply. Glycogen in storage hangs onto water, the usual figures cited being about 1.3 ml water per gram of glycogen. Assuming M and F metabolised around 400 g and 300 g of glycogen respectively, this would free up around 0.5 and 0.4 litres of water. We also produce H_2O in the metabolic process as protons (H^+) combine with O_2 and the amount of water produced over the course of a marathon is likely to be another 0.25 L and 0.2 L respectively.

Adding these last two inbuilt water supplies, M's total inbuilt supply was 0.75 L and F's 0.6 L. So the within-race fluid deficits we calculated above (sweat loss–fluid intake) of 1.2 and 0.9 litres for M and F respectively are reduced to 0.45 L and 0.3 L.

Now these back of the envelope calculations are estimates, but the point of this little exercise is to show that although the two runners consumed only about half and a third of the fluid they lost as sweat, they were likely to have only been one third to half a litre down at the end of the race. Both runners were exhausted but did not seem dehydrated. Many of us would have experienced going out for a long run without water, coming back 0.5 to 1 kg lighter indicating a net loss of 0.5-1 L loss of body fluid, but still finish off the run pretty well, even if a bit thirsty.

We are all well-advised to make sure we have access to water in these long runs, as the level of dehydration is likely to proportionally hinder recovery for the next day's training. On the other hand I've always wondered whether partial dehydration and repletion during long runs might fast-forward heat acclimatisation in distance runners. Repeated bouts of exercise in the heat with associated water loss followed by restoration might exert a stimulatory effect on plasma volume, increased plasma volume is in itself being a well-known adaptation to hot conditions.

Body composition and the elite runner

Best middle and long-distance performances do coincide with both low body weight and percent body fat, but not necessarily with an individual's lowest. Nonetheless it is common for runners to lose muscle mass around the trunk, arms and shoulders during extended periods of distance running training. Champion runners carry minimal muscle or fat mass above their navel, exceptions being the heart and diaphragm. Extra muscle weight in the 'pecs, lats, or traps', to borrow the body-building jargon, has little role to play in long-distance running. Highly trained distance runners are certainly unprepared for kayak canoeing where nearly all the aerobic and anaerobic power is developed from musculature above the navel!

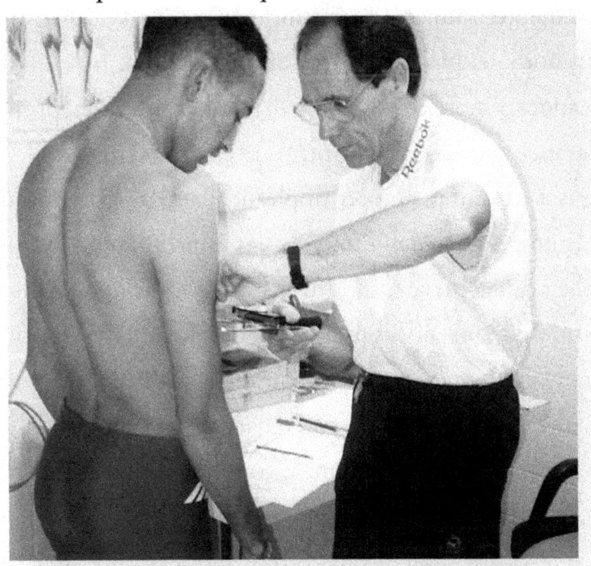

Checking the skinfold of Seoul Olympics 10,000m gold medallist, Moroccan Brahim Boutayeb.

It's harder for girls

Distance runners of the fairer sex have drawn the short straws in the body composition stakes, because, unlike their male counterparts, optimal percent body fat for fast running is less likely to coincide with best health. Nature encourages women to maintain a state of readiness for reproduction; a body well-endowed with energy reserves.

During the eons of our evolution, extreme leanness in a woman would have signaled famine or unavoidable excesses of physical activity as might occur in tribal feuding; unsuitable environments in which to produce offspring. As about half of all serious runners are very well aware, extremes of leanness and training tend to turn off the female reproduction system and switch the female physiology to survival mode. Disruption to the menstrual cycle certainly reduces risk of pregnancy in perceived hard times, but there is evidence that an associated reduction in oestrogen secretion might detract from bone health, as discussed in Chapter 21.

In contrast to many female runners, males can usually train and eat well without constant attention to restricting energy intake, and still develop an optimally lean body within the realms of good health. In evolutionary terms, male leanness appears more consistent with good health and reproductive power; leanness, endurance and speed being protective of the clan.

Running is a natural promoter of physical and psychological health in us all, but there is no point in deluding females aspiring to international running success that they can achieve their dreams with the kind of body composition normally considered most appropriate for good health. Across our population females naturally carry more fat than men, and a healthy percentage of body fat in a woman may be 30 percent compared with a male equivalent of 25 percent. However, many top international female competitors have only slightly higher proportions of body fat than top male runners; in some cases under 10 percent. Normal distribution of human physiology and anatomy suggests that some women will be genetically more fortunate, and so achieve low body fat levels with reasonable safety. For others, the process of developing unnatural leanness is more of a struggle, and must be considered a risk, not the least being the risk of developing eating disorders and compulsively excessive training schedules.

At the back of a coach's mind

Coaches of highly motivated distance runners, and in particular female runners need to be aware of the threat of eating disorders. Anorexia *per se* (meaning a loss of appetite for food) is in one context, not a common problem with runners. Runners in general are very good eaters; they have to be. However, it does remain that some runners, in trying to develop or maintain a body composition they believe necessary for success, develop unusually selective and restrictive eating habits. Sadly, some of these runners go on to develop clinically diagnosed eating disorders, a grave risk to anyone's health.

Eating disorders are sometimes difficult to pick up in runners, as they can be disguised in many ways, but sooner or later tell-tale signs emerge. Sometimes these emerge later, following a 'honeymoon' period in the early stages of weight loss, with increased power to body weight ratio coinciding with good race performances. However, the associated poor nutrition inevitably leads to a reversal of form as strength and aerobic power decline. Anorexia nervosa is an extremely serious illness, triggered at times in runners by psychological factors other than those emerging from athletic motives, and careful specialist medical attention is essential; the sooner the better.

The de Castella tuna salad

Yes, running performance is directly related to the aerobic power to body weight ratio. And yes, increasing the numerator or reducing the denominator body fat will increase the aerobic power to body weight ratio and running performance. But these are gradual and natural human being adaptations to sensible training and sound nutrition which aren't conducive to being forced or fast tracked.

We were in Tirrenia, Italy, not a long way from Pisa, and Rob de Castella's final training camp leading towards the 1992 Barcelona Olympics. Rob's stellar marathon career was drawing to a close. He was determined to do everything he could to uphold his reputation as one of the greatest marathoners ever, a former world champion and at one point the fastest marathoner in human history.

One thing that had changed a little bit since his very best performances was his body weight and the amount of body fat he carried. It wasn't as though there was much difference, and at 5'10" tall (178 cm), he was still as lean as a pin. However, at 72.5 kg and 38 mm of skinfold sum for 8 sites, he was not quite the 70-71 kg and 32 mm that coincided with his very best runs.

It was at this point that I made an error as his physiologist and nutritional consultant. Even though I mentioned it in a purposely casual manner that it would be worth making sure that his skinfolds did not increase before the Barcelona marathon, and even nudge them down slightly, it was a comment I later came to regret. You don't get to be the best and most consistent marathoner in the world without being meticulous, almost fanatic, about an Olympic preparation. This man could not tolerate the thought of leaving any performance stone unturned.

Tirrenia is a coastal town south of Pisa with nearly as many Italian restaurants as Lygon Street, Carlton. And like most marathoners, Rob was somewhat partial to good pasta. He asked me what he should do to get his skinfolds down 32 mm. Given that he was in his last three weeks of work, I didn't want to introduce any dietary restrictions, apart from our usual modified carbohydrate loading regime in the last week.

'Let's just do the training, Rob, and if you just watch what you eat a bit, remove some of the usual snacks between meals you'll be fine'. Rob was not convinced, 'What do you think about tuna and salad sandwiches?' he asked.

'Yes, that's a good sandwich Rob, let's make some for lunch.'

That we did, and very nice they were too; wholemeal bread with tuna in spring water, tomato, lettuce, no butter and a thin supplement of mayonnaise. I must admit, I would have preferred the fresh white baguette for myself, but yes, the wholemeal bread certainly was the smarter choice.

I didn't quite anticipate his comment after lunch.

'I'm going to get these skinfolds right, Dick, and to simplify the process considering it's only a matter of a few weeks to the Barcelona, I'll have the tuna sandwich without the bread'.

That amounted to a tuna salad. I was not impressed but Rob's mind was set in stone. The tuna salad became his regular meal over the next week before we left for Barcelona. There were five of us staying in the villa in Tirrenia, Rob, his wife Gaylene, his training partner and friend Rod Cedaro, my wife, Sue and me. Rob didn't deviate from those tuna salads over that week, despite the 100 miles he ran. He was hungry all the time, but didn't care. Rob was so keen on keeping that control over his skinfolds that he added another major dietary component to his strict regime. Believe it or not, it was the baby food Farax that he'd been able to find in a supermarket. He'd read that this low fat food had to be nutritious because it was designed for infants, well-labelled in terms of calories and nutrients, and allowed him to control his diet perfectly!

I was concerned about this extreme approach to his diet but as any plan B was not on Rob's mind, we thought it only proper to help him get through it. We decided to go out in sympathy with Rob and stick to the tuna salad routine as well. This worked out all right, but every now and then, when Rob was elsewhere, we'd snack on an Italian baguette and an ice-cream. We never let on—well not until after the marathon anyway.

We'll never know whether the tuna salad and Farax regime had a net beneficial value to Rob's marathon performance but it did lead to a 33 mm skinfold sum, and the psychological value to the runner was evident. As we have discussed in some detail, being one of the biggest athletes in the event de Castella was not well-suited to such a hot humid race. At the start of the Olympic marathon, the temperature was around 29°C with 40 percent humidity; an hour later, the temperature had dropped to 26°C with a humidity of 72 percent. Our man ran exceptionally well in those those torturous conditions, finishing 26th in 2hr17'44", just 3'39" behind the diminutive Korean winner in a start list of 110 of the world's finest runners, 26 of whom failed to complete the journey.

But, you budding marathoners, please don't adopt the de Castella tuna and Farax pre-marathon diet. If your weight is a concern, work on optimising it over several months before the big day. We physiologists and coaches can do without the extra stress!

Measuring body composition in elite runners

For mine, the simplest and probably the best way to get an idea of what sort of shape (literally) a runner is in, is to take a series of skinfold measures. It beats underwater weighing (time-consuming and wet); DEXA scans (time consuming and expensive, suitable for research); BIA bioelectric impedance (quick, but not particularly reliable); and BMI (doesn't discriminate muscle and fat so is worse than useless, it is misleading). In measuring skinfolds routinely in thousands of athletes over the years, and sometimes more than 100 serial measures over many years within an individual, technique becomes well-honed and sensitive. With our resident athletes at the Australian Institute of Sport, bearing in mind the potential complications associated with body composition control, it was important that the athlete requested the check, rather than me as a physiologist or their coach demanding it. In this way, the athlete was in charge, under no external pressure to become leaner, and less likely to become obsessed with diet or body composition.

I always summed up 8 sites in the men, at the triceps, biceps, subscapular, abdomen, axilla, supra-iliac, thigh, and calf; and 7 in the women. Typically, distance runners at the top of their game, were close to their lowest skinfold sum. Of all the athletes at the AIS, the distance runners were the leanest.

I once had a coach ask me why I chose 8 sites for the males and only 7 sites for the females, and that there must be a scientific explanation, but he couldn't think of it. He was a bit surprised but also amused when I told him that I dropped the axilla measure in the girls to save time as their bra strap kept getting in the way!

In terms of numbers the best male runners, including international medallists, were usually around 30 to 34 mm for the 8 sites, with one or two regularly measured at 28 mm, but notably one of Australia's best ever middle-distance runners was never lower than 37-39 mm. The range of the sum of 7 skinfolds for the internationally competitive women was 34 to 40 mm. Over the years I came to realize that the female's mid-thigh measurement was the site with the most impact on performance. A skinfold of circa 10 mm was typical of the most successful female distance runners. Some women seemed to achieve a sub-10mm thigh skinfold without any real effort, simply going about their training and eating well. Others had extraordinary difficulty attaining a sub-15 mm thigh skinfold.

Some females, no, make that most females are worried that they are too fat. It's important for female athletes to realise that they are extremely lean by normal standards and not get too caught up about it. I like to let them know I was once asked to measure the skinfolds of a group of well-known female fashion models, who the athletes described as 'beautiful and very skinny'. As non-athletes, they certainly presented as tall, graceful and slender. Our female athletes were surprised when I told them that a typical thigh skinfold of these ladies, considered super-thin by the public, was in the order of 25–30mm, with some of the visually slender girls being measured at considerably higher!

Now the above low skinfold values mentioned are from our best runners. It may well be that these runners are (or were) our best partly because they were able to achieve those very lean bodies and remain healthy during intense training periods. On the other hand I have seen some dramatic changes in body composition, with skinfold sums of more than 80 coming down to mid-30s over a period of a year in some runners. Such dramatic reductions in adiposity were achieved during sustained periods of training and no-nonsense consistently nutritious meals. Performances improved gradually and proportionately.

My observations over the last four decades suggest that the vast majority of athletes can get down to the kind of percent body fat typical of the very best. While we do inherit a genetic predisposition to a certain body stature and shape, I've seen no evidence to refute the hypothesis that anyone can, with a bit of effort and discipline achieve a body composition conducive to best athletic performance.

Conversely, I've noticed a remarkable metamorphosis in even the leanest of distance runners who on retirement develop into very large people indeed within a few years of inactivity.

Chapter 20 Supplements and ergogenic aids

'I know SOMETHING interesting is sure to happen whenever I eat or drink anything; so I'll just see what this bottle does.'

Lewis Carroll

There are a couple of legal ergogenic aids that may enhance performance, but effects are inconsistent, minimal, and individually variable.

Vitamins and minerals

Athletes in general, like the rest of us consume food derived from a large variety of soils around the world. Even out of season fruits and vegetables are transported from one hemisphere to another and consumed within a day or two. Runners are therefore, more likely than ever to consume what is commonly clichéd as the 'well-balanced diet,' one that easily provides the necessary and sufficient quantities of all the stuff we need, the carbohydrate, protein, fat, vitamins, minerals, fibre, and fluid.

To supplement or not to supplement, that is the question

We have evolved to function effectively on very small quantities of vitamins and minerals, or 'micronutrients' found in our food, and to survive substantial periods of time without consumption of these nutrients. It's natural though for coaches and athletes to wonder whether training intensively on a daily basis results in higher rates of micronutrient turnover than 'normal humans'. And it's reasonable to wonder whether runners have greater requirements than even our evolutionary predecessors over hundreds of thousands of years whose physical activity would hardly have approached the chronic intensity of modern professional athletes. That some athletes have higher requirements of certain vitamins and minerals may have some basis, but equally likely is that these athletes' increased food intake is sufficient to maintain optimal micronutrient status.

Nevertheless some health and medical practitioners recommend 'mega-doses' of vitamins for athletes and non-athletes alike. In consuming large quantities of these micronutrients packed into tablets and pills, vitamins and minerals are likely to take on characteristics that better characterize them as drugs; and with poorly understood pharmaceutical effects at variance with their effect at the concentrations we consume in food. In accordance with the approach of ensuring any procedure 'does no harm', mega-doses of vitamins or minerals cannot be recommended for athletes. Any physiological evidence for the benefit of consumption of multivitamin-mineral complexes by athletes on typical mixed diets in Australia is non-existent.

But can we be absolutely sure that our intensely training athletes' micro-nutritional requirements are being satisfied week after week with sensible dietary practices? Probably not, so in this day and age of inexpensive micronutrient preparations in amounts deemed safe by nutritional regulative bodies, an appropriate coaching comment to hard training athletes might be as follows.

Pay particular attention to eating sensibly. Don't rely on supplementation to correct bad habits because food itself is more than the sum of the commonly known nutrient parts; the combination of nutrients may interact to influence absorption and metabolism. If you suspect your food and beverage intake may lack consistent quality then it's worth considering supplementing your diet with one wide-spectrum multivitamin-mineral tablet each week.

Antioxidants and anti-inflammatories

Despite their well-accepted biochemical properties and essentiality to human health, the literature is far from convincing of the benefit of specific high dosage antioxidant promoting supplementation such as the vitamins β-carotene, E and C, or coenzyme Q and selenium in preventing muscle trauma or aiding recovery. By recommending these substances in large doses to athletes, we may well be loading up an athlete's bloodstream, and presumably muscle, blood and other tissues with more anti-oxidative power, but is this of benefit to athletes?

Australian nutritional scientist Dr Ian Gillam is convinced of the benefit of antioxidant supplementation. Dr Gillam studied athletes at the Australian Institute of Sport and followed this with more than two decades of consultation work with professional sports-people in a variety of disciplines. Ian's solid background in physiology and biochemistry and long-term experience with his clients leads us to respect his opinions. But as a long term scientist (read growing old and grumpy), I've become increasingly sceptical about any nutritional ergogenic claim, especially when there's money to be made by manufacturers, distributors, advertising agents and advertising media.

For example, let's take the case of antioxidants protecting what we might expect to be the most vulnerable of tissues, the red blood cells. Red blood cells are certainly exposed to oxidative stress and they are vital to endurance performance. But even if an antioxidant supplemented athlete's red blood cells are better able to resist the oxidative stress and red cells live a bit longer does this necessarily infer that the supplementation is beneficial? Not necessarily, because turning over red blood cells more often, and possessing a younger population, may actually assist, not impair, oxygen transport. Younger red cells are more flexible, a feature promoting ease of flow through muscle capillary beds at the site of oxygen transfer.

I may be sceptical about nutritional supplementation in general for runners, but when it comes to iron, and to a lesser extent magnesium, I'm not. Runners have been found wanting from time to time; supplementation to prevent or rectify a proven deficiency is of course a clear, sensible course of action.

A telling blood test?

During the mid-80s the AIS benefitted from the expertise and generosity of Dr Alan McLeay, a medical practitioner from Sydney who, well before his time, specialised in the assessment of nutritional status through a series of validated assays. He was sure our aspiring Olympic athletes would benefit from his objective assessment of vitamin and mineral status, as he believed the stress of training and/or inadequate dietary intake might compromise their nutritional status. Alan graciously offered, free of charge, to measure the vitamin mineral status of any elite athlete who requested it, given it may help them achieve their goals.

Around that time, Phil King was in Canberra, coaching his wife Debbie Flintoff-King. Phil and Debbie were preparing for the 400m hurdles at the Seoul Olympics where Debbie was shaping up as a very strong contender for a medal. Nothing was left to chance. If there was any way her prospects of success could be improved it would be exercised. Phil and Debbie had become familiar with the Seoul Olympic stadium track; they had slept exactly a year previously in the Seoul hotel room they had booked into again during the Olympics; they knew exactly where they would be, what they would do and what they would eat in that penultimate week and day.

Now at the AIS in Canberra, as planned of course, they were carrying out their final preparation only a matter of weeks before travelling over to Seoul. But humans are not machines, and even the most carefully laid out plans do not always follow the script.

Phil was experienced enough to realise this. Perhaps that was why he was at the AIS, with plenty of support from all levels. A problem did arise. Debbie's training lacked sparkle; it was certainly not at its usual high standard. She told me about a lack of energy which had persisted for more than a week. With brain and body so closely tuned in to the most important period of this couple's athletic life, we needed to get to the bottom of this pretty smartly. We ran routine blood tests, including iron status in our lab at the AIS, but nothing untoward showed up. I called Dr McLeay.

In his characteristically generous Australian form, he drove down to Canberra the next day to take samples of Debbie's blood back to Sydney. He ran these tests himself. He was the all-in-one general practitioner-biochemist-technician in his setup. Passionate about his work, he found it difficult to make ends meet with no government rebate for the kind of nutritional assessments he believed critical for understanding many of the common ailments he saw in his patients. A faxed report arrived within 36 hours. Of around 20 measurements he had circled two in red; magnesium, measured in the red cells themselves as representative of tissue concentration, and vitamin B6. The relative novelty of these assessments at the time meant that 'normal' ranges were not particularly well established, but both were considerably lower than those cited in the somewhat sparse nutritional science literature. Most importantly to me was that Debbie's B6 and magnesium levels were low by the laboratory ranges Alan McLeay had derived from testing many hundreds of patients.

We prescribed oral supplementation of both magnesium and B6 immediately. Five days later Phil reported that both Debbie's training and her psyche had picked up. It was obvious that Phil's psyche had improved as well. Follow up tests two weeks later revealed that Mg and B6 status were both back in his laboratory normal range. I was of course delighted and very keen to report the good news, knowing the positive effect it would have on athlete and coach.

The rest is history. Flintoff-King won an Olympic Gold in Seoul, a tribute to a great athlete-coach combination. Did restoration of the Mg and B6 status have anything to do with removing that cloud of fatigue? We'll never know for sure. Perhaps the obligatory reduction in training restored Debbie's track training energy. Nor can we underestimate the power of a support team; the interaction between sports scientist, clinician, coach and athlete. The process worked well; the solid diagnostic evidence (blood nutritional status), a plausible treatment and its immediate implementation (the supplementation), and the post-treatment assessment (follow-up nutritional status) to clearly show things were back to normal.

I wonder how much Debbie and Phil would recall this period. It was important to me as a scientist and important to Alan as a clinician, but perhaps it is just a temporarily concerning hiccup that is easily forgotten by coach and athlete on their journey. I never did talk too much about it after that gold medal was placed around Debbie's neck; the outcome was all that mattered. Scientific method and inference are sometimes relegated to secondary importance. And now, more than a quarter of a century later, Debbie and Phil have that ultimate prize in athletics tucked safely and securely in their keep.

Iron status

It's not uncommon for athletes to limit or even omit red meat from their diet given the bad press red meat seems to attract at times. However, meat is a source of iron in its most absorbable form, the 'haem-iron', so in order to absorb a given amount of iron, vegetarians need to consume more iron. Iron is required to synthesize haemoglobin and also plays a part as a cofactor in the process of extracting energy from the molecules of food we consume. So dwindling iron stores can make us feel lethargic. This isn't good for anyone, but for a runner relying on oxygen transport to generate lots of energy, it is disastrous.

The common practice of modern day distance runners to train in hypoxic conditions at altitude or simulated altitude requires extra care to consume sufficient iron. The underlying idea behind altitude training is to stimulate extra red blood cell synthesis and that requires extra iron. This has been well recognized for many decades. I was just looking through some old notes given to me by NSW coach Jack Pross, written by D.H. Le Messurier of the Aeromedical Research Laboratory, University of Adelaide in 1967. 'Athletes taking part in the Olympics at Mexico City should be fed high iron diets before leaving ... many athletes have low iron reserves and so incapable of increasing haemoglobin no matter how long they attempt to acclimatize.' Too true.

We shouldn't point the finger at iron alone in causing anaemia, because red cell manufacture (haemopoiesis) can be the result of insufficiency of other nutrients such as protein or vitamin B12. It's possible, although unusual, for a runner to be anaemic without iron deficiency.

Understanding blood tests

When a distance runner feels unusually tired for an extended period of time, even after resting up thoroughly between quality sessions, a distance running coach's mind often turns to a blood test. More often than not, nothing shows up. 'A low grade virus' might be the doctor's diagnosis, which might reasonably be interpreted as 'I've no idea what the problem is.' A period of reduced training is the standard prescription and more often than not, this turns out to be the best medicine. Relative rest and Father Time are master healers, and often with reasonable speed in young runners.

One specific blood check that does explain disappointing training and racing is iron status. It's useful for athlete and coach to have a good understanding of how iron status is assessed, as coaches and health professionals need to work together as a team.

There are several blood indicators of iron status, and serum ferritin concentration is an important one. Ferritin is a protein that can bind and store iron and it's found mainly in the bone marrow and liver. Actually it's very important that we bind iron in this way, because free iron in the bloodstream is poisonous, inducing tissue oxidation and real damage. We can get a reasonable estimate of the status of our liver and bone marrow iron stores from the tiny amount of ferritin circulating in the blood, because the blood concentration of ferritin, tiny as it is, in the order of nanograms per millilitre, i.e.1/1,000,000,000 of a gram per ml of blood is roughly proportional to the body stores.

The pathology report sheet compares the runner's blood value with the laboratory 'normal ranges.' For example, female runners should have ferritin concentrations higher than 30 nanogram/mL and male runners above 40. Anaemia is suspected in female and male athletes when haemoglobin concentrations are less than 12 and 14 grams/dL (decilitre) respectively.

But over years of work at the AIS we learned that lumping athletes in with 'normal' people was inappropriate. One early clue was provided by some healthy and consistently well-performed female runners whose ferritin concentrations were consistently between 20 and 30 ng/ml. But iron supplementation did not nudge these levels any higher; nor were there any signs of anaemia and they were training well. We suspected that a serum ferritin concentration of 20-30 was likely to be normal for these runners. But we needed to find out. This prompted a few studies, and we found that a more accurate diagnosis needed to take a few factors other than the sex of the athlete into account.

Nuances of iron status in athletes

Firstly there is the 'sport factor'. Some years ago at the AIS, noting the large variation in blood measurements in our athletes, and wanting to improve our diagnosis, we decided to have a close look at the patterns of variation. We found (and published) reference values which showed that distance runners had lower blood concentrations of each of haematocrit (the proportion of packed red cells), red cell counts, haemoglobin and ferritin than sprinters. We then showed distance runners to have lower levels in each of these variables than all other sportspeople; even lower than swimmers, rowers, canoeists and cyclists all of whom train with as great or greater volume than distance runners. But why?

A few reasons come to mind. Firstly running, especially in hot conditions, is known to expand plasma volume, thereby diluting the red cell and haemoglobin content of the blood. Consequently even though a distance runner is likely to possess a greater quantity of total circulating haemoglobin and number of red blood cells he or she is still likely to have a lower concentration than a sprinter, or any other athlete whose training does not involve endurance activities. Secondly, and more specific to the actual iron status and ferritin measure itself, running accelerates the destruction of millions of red blood cells as they pass through the soles of their foot during footstrike. Such destruction doesn't usually present a problem because runners compensate by manufacturing millions of new cells just a quickly. But rarely is the body 100 percent efficient in any task and we don't recover all of the iron from the dead cells to make the new ones, which might have something to do with the generally lower concentrations of iron and red cells in runners.

Then there is the 'body size factor'. Slender athletes, whatever their sport have lower blood values of all sorts than thick-set athletes. This certainly holds true within distance runners. Now you might be trying to work out why that might be. If you come up with any good ideas, I'd be very interested to know myself. It didn't seem to have any relationship with levels of testosterone hormone we measured in these athletes.

There is also a 'sex factor' effect on blood concentrations, which is well known. Any set of normal laboratory values for haemoglobin, red cell counts, and ferritin will show male athletes with higher concentrations irrespective of body size and the particular sport they play. And this is despite the higher plasma volumes of males which would tend to lower the blood concentrations. Lower values in females have been suggested to be the result of menstrual losses, but these differences are observed in amenorrhoeic females as well. It is generally argued that the higher blood concentrations in males are simply a reflection of their relatively higher total body red cell and haemoglobin mass (measured by carbon monoxide rebreathing, not a normal venous blood sample, see below). But this explanation is not that convincing as blood concentrations don't necessarily predict total body content; for example power athletes such as weightlifters have high blood concentrations of haemoglobin but low total body haemoglobin mass.

Specificity of training will affect blood concentrations because endurance training increases red cell mass, but given that it increases plasma volume as well, endurance work may not have too great an effect on red cell numbers per millilitre or haemoglobin concentration.

The upshot of all this work during the early AIS days is that interpreting iron status and diagnosing anaemia in an athlete is not as straightforward as many health practitioners might assume. A much better assessment of athlete haematology and biochemistry, including iron status requires knowledge of the athlete's particular sport or event, body size and state of training as well as sex.

Higher values are not always better

We can't automatically assume that a higher haemoglobin concentration and haematocrit (packed cell volume) is better than a lower one. For a start higher concentrations don't always coincide with higher total body haemoglobin, as an athlete with a lower haemoglobin concentration may possess more circulating blood and so a greater total body haemoglobin. And blood of higher concentration of red blood cells and haemoglobin is thicker, making it more difficult to pump around and infiltrate into the capillary networks around the muscle cells.

The athletes with the highest haemoglobin concentrations for their size (as distinct from total circulating haemoglobin) are the sprinters, throwers, and especially the weightlifters. These athletes are certainly not noted for their aerobic abilities; in fact it is quite the reverse.

Not too much please!

As a word of caution, and somewhat counterintuitively, iron is actually extremely toxic. Iron atoms have the potential to play a lethal role, also counter to a runner's expectations, in partnership with oxygen. Iron and oxygen are terrific allies and vital supporters of human life. But let them off the leash together unsupervised and they can play merry hell. Especially in the kitchen; they just love to cook everything in their reach.

Fortunately (and evolutionary processes are not independent of good fortune) the gut structure evolved so as not to let too much iron make its way into the bloodstream at one time. This dampened its destructive capabilities but ironically, so to speak, restricted absorption may be problematical in runners who may require more iron than non-runners.

Many an athlete performance has been 'saved' by an iron injection, athletes reporting excessive tiredness and substandard training being rectified in as little as a day or so. Such comments might be considered representative of a 'placebo' or 'psychological' effect, but I'm not so sure. Iron containing cofactors are involved in numerous metabolic pathways including those producing aerobic power. Energy production will slow if there is a deficiency of cofactors, hence the perception of 'tiredness' and it may only take a day or so for iron delivered directly into a muscle (usually your backside) or bloodstream to rectify this situation. Parenteral iron might also make a rapid contribution to erythropoiesis when 'hungry' partially developed bone marrow cells suddenly gain ready access to iron, and waste no time in completing their final stages of development into new young red cells (reticulocytes) to be sent off for circulation duties. Then there is the possibility that the supplemented iron might increase myoglobin, the form of ready-to-go oxygen storage in a runner's muscles. Rectifying a short supply of myoglobin could also contribute to an athlete feeling more energetic within a day or two.

So, even though I'm not sure about the time required for the above processes to kick in, when athletes tell me they feel better a day or two after their iron injection, sceptic as I've been trained to be, I tend to believe them.

Iron and Louisa

Louisa Lobigs was as keen a young runner as any I have coached. A very good junior, she was going through the typical mid to late teenage 'growing up' phase in female runners where improvements are sometimes hard to come by. I reminded Louisa that she just had to be patient, keep up the consistent work without trying to force the issue and her form would return. Unfortunately Louisa's form didn't return, and she had difficulty keeping up with the team-mates she had trained alongside previously. A strongly built girl, she was not a finicky eater and ate lean meat regularly. Not a strong candidate for iron deficiency. However, one never can be really sure of anything in this game, so I asked her team-mate Dr Laura Garvican, a member of my former department, AIS Physiology, to check her iron status. Laura emailed me with the results and they took me completely by surprise. I'd seen many cases of iron deficiency in athletes over the last couple of decades, but this one took first prize.

Not only was Louisa iron deficient, she was well and truly anaemic. It's not often that low iron status gets to that stage in athletes. Low iron status without anaemia is likely to compromise performance, but throw in anaemia as well and power and endurance suffer badly. Louisa would have felt like she was at an altitude of 3000m, where oxygen transport to the muscles is also reduced, but for a different reason. At least at altitude Louisa would expect it to feel hard, at sea-level it was worrying—until the blood test explained everything.

Have a look at the table showing the improvements brought about by an initial course of intramuscular and then oral iron supplementation. This was accompanied not only by a remarkable improvement in Louisa's training and racing form, but in her general energy levels and zest for life. A few days after her first injection Louisa told me she was sure she felt better. And it showed on her face. She didn't look back and training began to pick up. Just two months after the first injection, she ran a personal best 3000m, a race heavily dependent on aerobic power.

The accompanying graph illustrates the progress. Note that Louisa's haemoglobin mass (measured by a carbon monoxide rebreathing technique) increased from 389g to 580g in two weeks and to 690g at 15 weeks. That's 77 percent more oxygen transport capacity. On this measure alone, let alone the other roles of iron outlined above, it's no wonder she felt better and performed better.

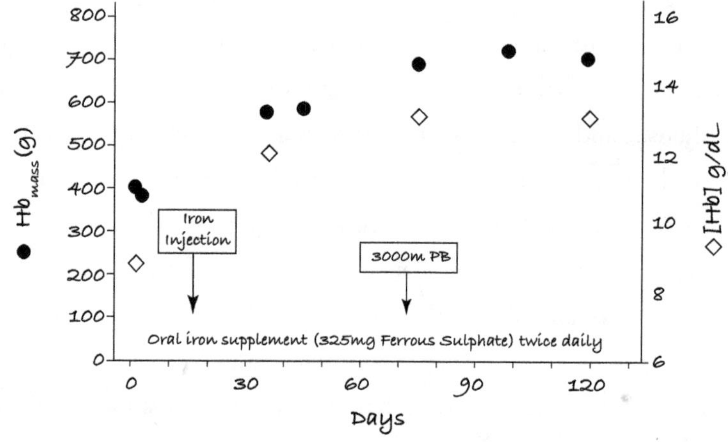

Fig 20-1: Haemoglobin mass and concentration before and after iron supplementation.

A post-script to this story is that despite considerable talent for running, a series of running injuries prevented Louisa from achieving the kind of success she yearned. During one of her cross training periods, she discovered that cycling provided the kind of physical challenge she enjoyed, without the injury risk of running's eccentric muscular activity and stress on joints.

I always had the feeling that Louisa's strong legs coupled with her highly competent aerobic motor might lend itself more to high performance cycling than to running. This proved to be true, and after not more than a year of concentrated cycling, Louisa was selected in a national training squad and continues to show promise of developing into one of Australia's best road cyclists.

As an aside ...

Louisa's change of sport raises an interesting issue. Distance running's a great sport as we all know, but when it comes to making the grade at the highest level, some runners with high levels of aerobic power are not anatomically well-suited to elite level running. Often, strangely enough, it's, because they are too strongly built, or with a skeletal set-up that is not conducive to mechanically efficient running. Through the years, many of my running friends have just loved to run and do their best, happy in the knowledge that champion status is not for them. Personal bests and better placings in races provide all the competitive satisfaction. Others, though have a burning desire coupled with an intrinsic belief that they are capable of becoming sporting champions. And when talented endurance athletes possess this sort of fierce desire to excel, it's critical to identify a sport where their physicality, as well as mentality are compatible with elite level performance. Triathlon, cycling, swimming, rowing, canoeing are all great sports reliant on aerobic power without the delivery of that power being heavily influenced by running biomechanics. These sports have served that 'sea-change' well.

P.S. Training alongside Louisa in our Canberra running squad for several years was Rebecca Wiasak, another good distance runner but, it's fair to say, not destined for Australian representation. Like Louisa, Bec always impressed both aerobically and anaerobically and with naturally strong legs was of body build more typical of our best female cyclists rather than runners. In 2009 when running just wasn't taking her where she wanted Bec decided that she might be better suited to triathlon. That led to her next progression which came when she was to find her real strength was the cycling component. Taking up cycling she responded rapidly to specific training to become a nationally competitive road cyclist. But it was the final step into the world of track cycling that Bec found her rightful place in the world of sport. Suffice to say that as I write this sentence Bec Wiasak is the reigning World Cycling Champion in the individual pursuit.

It's not just a long distance thing

Iron deficiency is certainly not confined to females running high mileages. Take the case of a 24 year-old male middle-distance runner, Phil Pelgram, a Biophysics graduate from Swinburne Institute of Technology, the same institution that provided our first technician, one Robert de Castella. Phil was a very keen young athlete, quicker than Deek over 400m and 800m, but not quite as quick over 42.195km. Although he didn't train with great volume, about 60km per week, there was as stage where Phil was very concerned about his unusual tiredness and inability to meet anywhere near expected times in training. After checking his training to ensure he hadn't over-estimated his quality or quantity and after a few days' rest the tiredness and poor training persisted. We took the customary venous blood sample.

Our initial measures confirmed our suspicions. His blood ferritin concentration was 10 ng/mL; well below the 30 ng/mL mark we generally considered satisfactory for a male runner of his height and weight. His haemoglobin, at 13.6 g/dL was a bit low; our estimation of normal haemoglobin for his body type and sport was in the 14–15 g/dL range. Compromised haemoglobin would be indicated if supplementation of iron led to an increase in haemoglobin concentration.

We prescribed supplementation of 100 mg of elemental iron per day and measured his blood again a month later. Phil reported that his training had improved immensely and it was plain to see he was now a happier athlete. His improved iron status, as shown in Figure 20-2 was a strong indication that this was the critical factor. The increase in his haemoglobin concentration to 16.5 g/dL showed that indeed his oxygen carrying capacity had been compromised.

An interesting observation of Figure 20-2 is the timing of the increase in ferritin (representing iron stores) in relation to the increases in haemoglobin and red cell concentrations. As we can see by the graphs, the haemoglobin concentration had risen to just above 14, but the ferritin level hadn't budged. One possible explanation was that as the iron was introduced into the bone marrow and liver iron stores the absorbed iron was used to

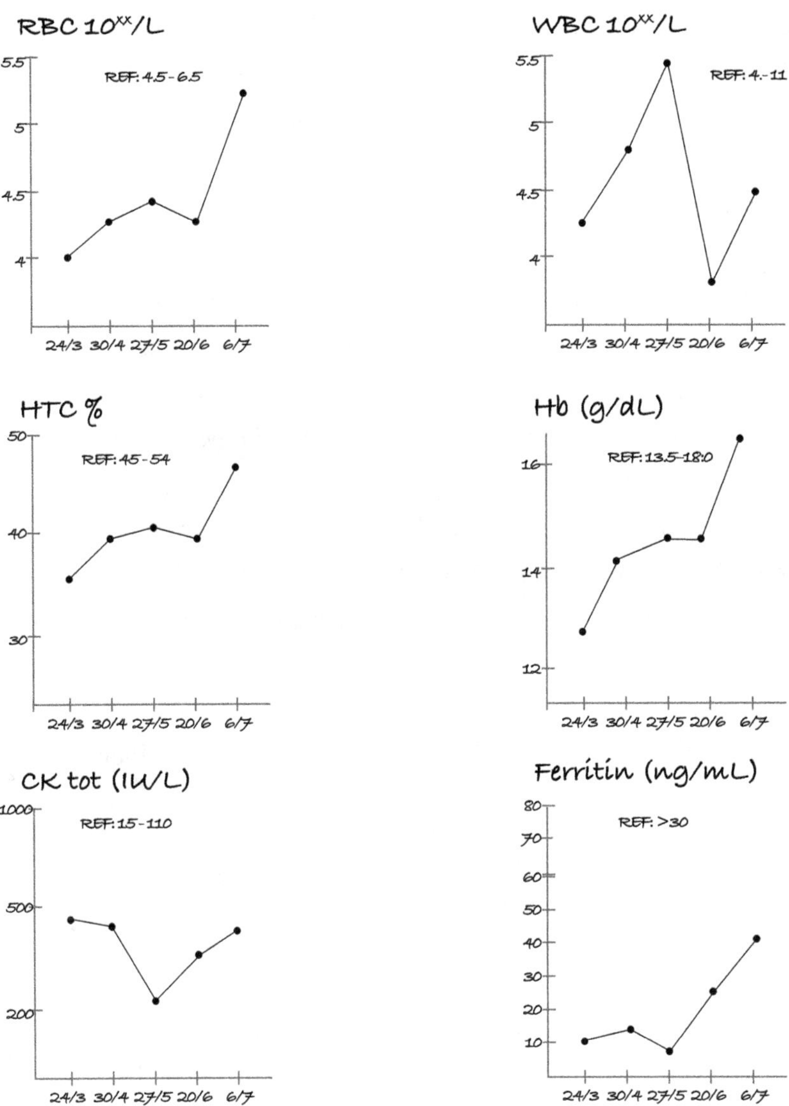

Fig 20-2: Time course of blood measures of our 800m runner PP as, iron deficiency anaemia and poor training performance were rectified by 100mg elemental iron tablets per day. REF signifies laboratory reference ranges.

manufacture haemoglobin as fast as it arrived. I was immediately reminded of the advice provided by the US researchers Jim Stray-Gundersen and Ben Levine in their altitude training studies of the nineties. They recommended that all our athletes training at altitude not only consumed food rich in iron but supplemented their diet with iron tablets as well. They felt that supplementation might actually drive and enhance the haemopoeitic (red cell growth) process at altitude.

Again referring to Figure 20-2 it's also interesting that Phil's ferritin level and his haemoglobin concentration (we didn't measure total body haemoglobin mass) improved through a 5 months period. His training did as well. He had continued his oral iron supplementation throughout this period, suspecting that his iron stores may have begun to run down again without supplementation. It seems that ongoing iron supplementation might be routinely required in some individuals just to maintain normal iron stores.

Like our case study, Louisa, it's no wonder Phil wasn't training well five months previously; his haemoglobin concentration had been 20 percent down and judging by the way that individual haemoglobin concentration tracks along with haemoglobin mass (Figure 20-2), presumably his haemoglobin mass was similarly compromised.

Lisa Ondieki and her liver

Lisa Martin (later Ondieki) displayed those similar characteristics of uncompromising dedication and determination as her good friend, Rob de Castella. She was not as compulsive about her training diary as was Rob, and would take a day off when necessary, although a day off running for Lisa was a rarity. But she was only human and I recall a worrying time where unusual fatigue was interfering with her training. We hadn't checked Lisa's iron status for a couple of months so that was the obvious first line of investigation. On scanning the outcome in our biochemistry lab I was relieved to see the low ferritin. Better something we can manage easily rather than something more problematic such as mononucleosis or that mysterious unidentified 'virus' often blamed as the cause of training lethargy.

We discussed the possibility that her twice-a-day training regime might be inhibiting iron absorption, and that consuming more red meat should help. In our discussion I mentioned that liver was perhaps the richest readily absorbable source of iron. Over the next few weeks, Lisa's training picked up nicely and I asked about her diet, especially whether she had added any red meat and any liver.

'Of course, Dick' was the reply 'I didn't want to waste any training time and you mentioned that liver was likely to work a lot better than meat or even iron tablets.'

I was pleased with this because most athletes can't stomach the thought of eating liver.

'Oh that's good Lisa, but how do you cook it to make it taste ok?'

'Oh I just throw it in the pan and cook it lightly and have it with whatever else I'm cooking at the time.'

Excellent, I thought. As a kid, I remember Mum and Dad trying to bribe me and my sister to eat liver, or 'lambs fry' as we called it. It tasted awful, even when it was drowned in tomato sauce (ketchup for our US friends).

I was pleased that Lisa seemed to have eaten it more than once over the last couple of weeks.

'And how often do you have the liver, Lisa?'

She looked slightly puzzled, 'What do you mean, Dick? I eat it every day of course.'

I should have guessed as much. That was Lisa and her attitude; the same as Rob with his tuna salad; no point in letting taste-buds get in the way of a good marathon performance. Now that her iron status was all in order and training was going well, I suggested that one or two small pieces of liver each week would be more than enough to keep iron status well catered for in addition to her normal diet.

'Okay, no problems' she replied, happy that training was back to normal.

Alkali loading

During the 80s and 90s researchers became interested in the concept of alkali loading, ingesting alkaline substances with the intent to buffer the protons derived from anaerobic metabolism. 'Re-interested' is perhaps more accurate because even as far back as the 1950s sports science pioneers such as Forbes Carlile were interested in the effect of antacid tablets in Australian swimmers, and it wasn't as a remedy for indigestion. Not a bad thought in those days, although the procedure of sucking a couple of antacid tablets was more likely to provide a psychological rather than physiological benefit.

In the 80s I had a chat with Tasmanian-based physiologist Dr Lars McNaughton, who had produced evidence that about 0.3 g/kg body weight of sodium bicarbonate (baking powder) ingestion could enhance short duration (1-5 minute) cycling and running performances. Some members of the Australian kayak team had dabbled in this purported ergogenic aid in recent times, and the coaches were keen to find out whether it was worthwhile or not. Given that alkali loading was not on the ever-growing listings of banned substances we at the AIS conducted a series of investigations as to whether highly trained athletes might benefit from alkali loading prior to competition.

Drinking a solution of sodium bicarbonate on repeated occasions is not a pleasant experience. It's taste makes it hard to get down, and can cause stomach problems and diarrhoea. This is not a welcome pre-race intervention, especially when that race happens to be the culmination of years of dedicated training a the Olympics or World Champs.

In these first trials, we found a commonly used lemon flavoured urinary alkalizing powder was more acceptable. Even then, with the quantities of fluid and alkali required to attain sufficient increases in blood pH, this process could adversely affect a competitor's physical and psychological well-being in the hour or so before the race. Finally, we found that ingestion of capsules of sodium bicarbonate or equivalently alkaline compounds was the most acceptable way to consume around 0.3 gram of bicarbonate per kilogram body weight, a couple of hours prior to the event.

Anyway, the upshot of our cross-over placebo based trial, which involved the Australian Kayak squad ingesting the tablets or a placebo prior to two all-out 4 min minute efforts on the kayak ergometer, was encouraging. Of 8 kayak paddlers, 6 did better in the bicarbonate trial than the placebo, and in 2 kayakers there was no difference. There was an average and statistically significant improvement in the order of 3 percent. Alkalizing the bloodstream did seem to operate effectively as an ergogenic aid.

A change of pre-race routine is a big decision for any athlete, and while 3 percent is a considerable improvement, not all athletes applied the alkaline loading prior to the world championships. I never got around to checking who did and did not use the bicarbonate tables in those canoeing World Championships, but the team did remarkably well. I suspect that the paddlers whose results showed the greatest margin of improvement in our trial decided to reproduce this in competition, and that those whose results were marginal, did not.

Alkalis and runners

There was no reason to suppose that the findings of our trial with the paddlers wouldn't apply to 1500m runners and possibly to 800m runners as well who also need to fight through that so-called 'lactic' muscular fatigue in the latter part of the race. But there'd be nothing worse than providing coaches with information to find that it upset the digestive systems of runners with a wasted race.

I decided to try it myself. Whilst in my 40s, I had switched over to middle-distance running from a few years of preparation for marathons. As a physiologist for elite athletes, I was never very much interested in data obtained from less than elite runners like me, but I had run a series of consistent middle-distance race times, and had a good idea of my capabilities. Any immediate increase in performance after taking bicarbonate would most likely be due to the procedure. My own case study was of particular interest because I would understand how it felt to undergo the regime of temporary lifting the pH of the bloodstream.

It did seem to do the trick. A series of my best times over 800m and 1500m followed this practice but even I can't rule out a placebo effect. At the Australian Veterans Athletic Championships in Adelaide that year I adopted the regime in the 1500m and ran well, kicking home strongly to win the title. The next day I undertook the same regime of alkaline loading before the final of the 800m. I felt very flat in that 800m and after running 600m at a pace I thought would allow me to accelerate over the final 200m, but I had nothing. That left me wondering if the alkali loading on successive days had something to do with my poor performance.

Unfortunately I never found out as I was never to undertake the alkali loading regime before races in successive days again.

In the heats of my biggest ever and last track competition, at the 1987 World Masters Championships, held in Melbourne, I decided to keep the bicarbonate loading for the final, assuming that I could get through the heats. This I did without too much trouble, and, in that last race I ever ran, it certainly didn't do me any harm, as I finished equal third in a career personal best of 3'57".

In general, middle-distance runners are not sold on alkali loading; there are some middle-distance coaches I know who encourage the practice but the majority of coaches and athletes don't think it worthwhile. My overall view? Well, given the procedure is considered legal and safe, and if, but only if, an athlete seems to have reached some sort of ceiling of personal performance, then it's worth trying.

Such a situation occurred in a young runner prior to the Atlanta Olympics.

I was one of the Australian 1996 Olympic team distance running coaches in Atlanta. In the lead-up to the Olympics, Bruce Scriven, a middle-distance coach with plenty of experience and plenty of success to go with it, had a dilemma. One of his charges, Paul Byrne, a former World Junior champion over 800m, had run a series of races but could not achieve the set target of 1:47.5 to prove his fitness for entry into the Olympic Village. He had run 4 races and despite getting to 600 at the required pace, he had faded each time over the final 200 and his best time had been just under 1:48. The selectors were sticking to their guns and he had to run the set time, otherwise he'd be watching the heats of the Olympic 800m from the stands.

We were now in North Carolina, and the track meet here was Paul's last chance to become an Olympian. Bruce and I discussed the pros and cons of alkali loading, and we decided that on current form, that Paul had little to lose and everything to gain. We spoke to Paul who had not used this procedure before and I explained how it worked, being sure to concentrate on the pros rather than any cons. He and Bruce decided it was as good a time as any to 'give it a go'. So, in this very last crack at becoming an Olympian, Paul did just that.

Apart from feeling a little light-headed during the loading regime, Paul was feeling okay, nervous, and ready to race. As he had done in his prior races, Paul got to the 600m mark in close to the target time. But he had done this three times recently. We all held our breath. To our delight the young runner didn't tie up and fade this time and ran on strongly through the finish, 0.2 seconds under the qualifying time and a season PB. Was the procedure the difference? We'll never know, as the placebo effect and the last chance situation were potentially powerful effects. All in all it didn't matter, Paul was to become an Olympian.

Caffeine

Ever since the unfortunate disqualification of pentathlete Alex Watson, Australian competitors especially have been acutely aware of the doping rules related to caffeine ingestion. The authorities have changed their rules about the legal level of caffeine consumption, but 3 or 4 cups of coffee, which might mean around 300 or 400mg of consumed caffeine has never really been an issue. It's common for athletes across many sports to have a coffee or two before competition.

Athletes have often told me that it makes them feel better in warm-up, which is interesting in itself, because athletes going into combat are already likely to be well-primed with adrenaline and other natural 'fight or flight' neuro-endocrine responses. That caffeine doesn't seem to increase pre-competition 'butterflies in the stomach' is indicative that its effect on mood is via different channels of neurotransmitter modulation than those associated with the naturally occurring stimulation of pre-competition adrenaline-charged arousal. Quite the contrary in fact, as runners sometimes tell me the coffee helps to relax them, and this may be related to reported effects of caffeine on dopamine and serotonin, neurotransmitters purported to enhance good 'mood' or psychological comfort.

Like blood alkalizers, there is some scientific evidence for an ergogenic benefit of caffeine. One or two studies have suggested that it may promote fatty acid utilisation at marathon race speed, and so conserve glycogen stores early in the race. This may be the case, but I'm not sure whether this makes much difference in a highly trained runner whose flexible metabolism is already well-adapted to maximizing use of fatty acids to spare muscle glycogen at marathon race-pace.

It's common for athletes to enjoy a cup of coffee before the race, but some don't and opt to take an equivalent amount of caffeine in tablet form. Marathoners concerned about the diuretic effect of caffeine may have a point, but I can't remember any of my coffee drinking marathoners requiring a pit stop during their race. Once the gun goes the kidneys tend to hand over their share of the blood supply to the working muscles, reducing any flow into the bladder.

And just for the record, especially for you veteran or masters runners; my best marathon time of 2hr27' (forget the seconds) in my late 30s can't be considered elite by any means, but it was run following a couple of coffees an hour or so before the start.

So with some physiological grounds and anecdotal evidence of good performances following caffeine ingestion, all we can say is that caffeine might help, and is unlikely to hinder. The same might apply to taking caffeine during the race, and it's a common practice now for runners to consume sugar gels that include caffeine at various stages of the race.

Perhaps the caffeine effect on our brain is a factor. If how we think and feel affects the way we move, and how we move affects the way we think, then caffeine's effects on those 'well-being' transmitter substances in the brain could help us resist fatigue. This might occur at both the conscious and subconscious levels. The Central Governor model of fatigue, as discussed in Chapter 8 has it that the brain will do it's best to prevent us with damaging ourselves with extreme levels of exertion. Could it be that caffeine adjusts a 'fatigue threshold' in the brain, that point at which the brain kicks in to slow us down whether we want to or not?,

Corollary

It's important not to over-read the effects of caffeine or alkalizers. Some studies show only modest or even non-existent effects, and there is little evidence of the real effects in the heat of competition, especially in highly trained runners. Furthermore, we hear much more about the studies and anecdotes which show some effect than those which don't. Studies showing little or no effect are less exciting, less likely to be submitted for publication and less likely to be published even if submitted, thereby producing a bias toward positive findings in the scientific literature. And the experiences of runners who took caffeine or blood alkalizers and didn't race well are less likely to be talked about. Perhaps more practically relevant is that many athletes in the competitive arena have tried and choose not to use blood alkalizers or caffeine, suggesting that in the real world, as distinct from the laboratory, if ergogenic effects are present, they are not obvious.

Finally, after all these years, I prefer my runners to prepare for big races using the same warm-up routine they use to prepare for any race or indeed any quality track session. And that doesn't include blood alkalizing procedures.

Chapter 21
Insights on injuries

'She generally gave herself very good advice, (although she very seldom followed it).'

Lewis Carroll

There is a threshold stress of training intensity, of training volume, and of their interaction, above which a body part or system is unable to adapt, then unable to resist, and breaks down.

We coaches and sports scientists try to design programs to put the physiotherapsts, chiropractors, sports physicians, pathologists, radiologists and surgeons out of a job. We aren't doing too well; runners are lengthening, not shortening the queues to sports medical clinics for diagnoses and treatment of damaged bodies.

This book does not deal with diagnoses and treatment; I'll leave that to the experts. However, underlying every training program is 'do no harm', or to be more realistic 'do your best to reduce the risk of harm'. In other words, coaches who want their charges to perform at their very best and at the highest level will necessarily put their charges at risk of bodily harm and all we can do is to feel our way through each session, day, week, month and year in designing programs that are less likely to produce injuries and ill-health.

By 'feel' I mean putting a toe in the water to test the temperature rather than the whole foot. Small increases in training stress must be tested and observations of adaptation made on a sessional, daily and weekly basis. All athletes, from champions to joggers possess individual thresholds of training intensity and volume, and exceeding these limits leads to injury or ill health. We call these breakdowns 'overuse injuries' and we learn from experience how to prevent or at least reduce this damage as we try to squeeze the most out of our athletes, teasing up that quantity or quality of training.

Here are some stories about injuries that remain foremost in my coaching mind, although the first story is memorable for its laugh rather than lesson.

Deek's hamstring

We were running in Stromlo Forest in the early 80s, as Stromlo used to be a fine pine plantation of various ages with numerous tracks, before the fires of 2003. (A decade later and I'm pleased to report it's on its way back to its former glory; in fact even better with the introduction of an arboretum that promises to become a national treasure.) Our pack of about eight runners included Deek (Rob de Castella) and his brother Nick. Nick was a very good runner who had earned a scholarship alongside his brother at the Australian Institute of Sport under coach Pat Clohessy.

I had Rob trying out a heart-rate monitor, relatively new in those days, and the strap around his bare chest securing the surface electrodes was a source of running group interest. It was of particular interest to Nick, who was more than a little intrigued with this new technology. With an expression that Rob would have recognized, had he seen it, as potential brotherly mischief, Nick sped up a little with quiet feet behind his brother who was leading the pack as usual.

From as close as behind him as he could get, he let out a sharp 'BOO!' directly into Rob's right ear. Rob was understandably startled. 'Let's see how your heart rate reacts to that one!' Nick chuckled, at the same time expertly keeping up the pace of the run. Nick's amusement was not shared by his big brother. Rob wheeled around and in mid-stride directed a right foot at Nick's retreating posterior. He failed to make good contact with the rapidly moving target, mistiming the knee extension phase and strained a hamstring.

Rob was confined to nothing faster than slow jogging over the next couple of days and I don't recall Nick being around too much during that period. That mistimed knee extension turned out to be an act of some significance, as it resulted in the first injury Rob had suffered since he took up residence in Canberra some years before. Perhaps not an overuse injury but a running injury at that!

Apart from the obvious moral of this story that one should not attempt to kick any other runner in the middle of a training run, no matter how annoying they might seem, this may have been one occasion where a bit of flexibility work might have been a useful. Deek was never noted for his hamstring flexibility.

A blessing in disguise

I watched Ralph Doubell run a series of 400s on the cinder track at the University of Melbourne in 1966 on my way over to cricket practice at the oval up in front of Ormond College. Little did I realize I was watching not only a future Olympic gold medallist and world record holder, but a gold medallist who almost missed his race. An Achilles injury threw a potential spanner in the works of his preparation for the 1968 Mexico City Olympics.

Recalling that old Melbourne University track, a rough surfaced remnant of the 1956 Melbourne Olympics, and the flimsy heel-less spikes even distance runners used to wear, and the 20 x 400m Ralph used do as a routine session, it's no wonder his literal Achilles heel became his proverbial Achilles heel. Three decades later, Ralph was to mention that his coach Franz Stampfl used to have a friendly dig at him as 'always injured.' I reckon with those spikes, that track and the training that Ralph got through, he did very well keep his body in one piece for the period he did.

I always knew that Stampfl was an extremely demanding coach. As a young student at Melbourne University I used to muse at the rather old guy (old then for me at that stage was anyone over 40; nowadays it's anyone over 80) who loved to take his shirt off to maintain his tanned body in the Melbourne sun in front of his office next to the pool. In hindsight he probably recognized the value of the vitamin D! Even from afar, and through my young man's eyes, I remember an air of confidence and a hint of arrogance in the man. A man who thought he had the coaching game sewn up; and as it turned out he probably did.

At that stage I had heard stories about Franz playing some sort of a part in Roger Bannister's athletic world shattering first ever sub 4-minute mile. Stampfl's reputation in Melbourne was growing, and he was to make a huge contribution to Australian track and field through athletes in a wide variety of disciplines. He already had Olympic finalists in high jumper Tony Sneazwell, long jumper Alan Crawley and miler Merv Lincoln, in addition to Commonwealth champion middle-distance runner Peter Bourke, javelin thrower Sue Howland, 400m runner Judy Peckham and Commonwealth Games medallist and Olympian, shot putter and discus thrower Jean Roberts.

But in Australia, it's his athlete Ralph Doubell for whom most Australian athletics enthusiasts best remember Franz Stampfl. Some 15 years later, I had the honour to pick Ralph up at the Canberra airport. I had invited him to the AIS for a talk to our distance runners, and it was good to hear the now legendary story of his Mexico City 800m gold medal triumph from the man himself. Ralph had suffered Achilles heel soreness during his build-up to the Olympics. In the preceding months he received treatment every day and avoided fast intensive work and also avoided any work in spikes. In effect Stampfl was forced to extend the 'base' phase of the Olympic 800m preparation, limiting his high intensity 'speed' work phase to about 4 weeks before leaving for Mexico City. As Ralph explained, the duo did not know how this preparation would stack up.

History shows it 'stacked up' wonderfully well, and the Achilles injury may have been even been a blessing in disguise.

Mind you, don't get the idea that training was easy. This enforced phase of less intense training involved plenty of work, but as you can see from his normal base work, reductions in training do not necessarily mean a light week. In the enlightening and educative book *Brian Lenton Interviews* (Brian Lenton Publications, 1997) Ralph describes a typical week during his normal build-up.

An 8km jog every morning, and 5km warm up and warm down with each session. His pm sessions were:

Monday: 50 x 100m

Tuesday: 10 x 1200m

Wednesday: 20 x 300m

Thursday: 10 x 600m

. **Friday:** rest day

Saturday: 30 x 200m

Sunday: 20 x 400m.

A ladder was often slotted in sometimes during the week well, with efforts of 1,2,3,4,5,4,3,2,1 minutes on that cinder track with approximately equal recoveries.

Franz was certainly sold on interval training. And none of this Lydiard slow long running stuff from this coach. There was usually a substantial recovery between efforts, and this allowed repetitions to be maintained at good speed but well-controlled and never maximal during the build-up phase. As an example of recovery, on Tuesday for the 1200s he might jog two laps. No such thing as a 20 minute track work-out that's for sure; most sessions were longer than an hour.

Doubell only put on his spikes on that track 4 weeks prior to leaving for Mexico City, and time-trials run over 600 and 1200m. There was no racing at all going into the most testing athletic arena in the world and an extended pre-Mexico altitude training regime wasn't considered. Then there was Ralph's real work in the city, so no extended periods over in St Moritz or Boulder. How did this regime produce the best 800m running performance in the world? Let's look at some possible contributions.

Firstly, it provided a long relatively uninterrupted run of solid interval work in flat shoes which built up a very strong base of aerobic power. I say aerobic power, not just threshold, because much of the work was well above threshold pace (i.e. above 10km pace). For example Doubell would have been running around 800m pace in those 100s, around 1500m pace in his 300s; with 1500m-3km pace work in his 400s and 3 km-5km pace work for his 600s. This provided plenty of scope for building aerobic power. The daily practice of repeated rapid increases in oxygen uptake is beautifully specific to the 800m event where ability to induce an early and rapid rise in $\dot{V}02$ reduces the early anaerobic requirement, promoting a more controlled muscle biochemistry at the bell.

There was another related blessing in disguise. The Australian team got over to Mexico City for four weeks altitude acclimatization. Stampfl, who was to arrive in the week preceding the Olympics had agreed that Doubell set his own training according to how the athlete felt. The Achilles was tender and Doubell's training was conservative, and I suspect considerably more conservative than Stampfl's likely prescription. But even then the Achilles remained a worry. In what turned out to be a wonderful coaching call, Stampfl instructed his charge to do no running at all, not even any jogging in the week leading to the first heat of the 800m. Doubell, with unreserved confidence in his coach, complied without blinking an eyelid.

The Australian felt good in the first preliminary race; just as good in the semi; and he felt strong going into that Olympic final. Interesting in itself after doing nothing in the preceding week.

In that Olympic final, the first lap was a little above 51 seconds, Doubell perfectly positioned around 4th on the outside of lane 1, no-one just outside him to impede any move. He moved into second place with 250m or so to go, and responded immediately to a kick-down through the 600m mark. He initiated the final surge himself with less than 100m to the finish, one which the world's fastest 800m runners could not match.

Doubell became the best and fastest Australian 800m runner ever, equalling Peter Snell's world record of 1:44.3. Remarkably, and perhaps sadly for Australian middle-distance running, this remains the Australian record as I write this sentence 46 years later!

PS (1) As I read through this paragraph looking to tidy up the grammar some time later, I'm up at the Gold Coast at marathoner Michael Shelley's place supervising some of his final preparation for the Glasgow Commonwealth Games. He calls out, remarkably coincidentally, that one of our young Australian 800m runners Alex Rowe just ran 1:44.6 in Belgium. With two other promising young Australians in Jeff Riseley and Josh Ralph competing strongly around that level, surely Doubell's record is ready for revision.

PS (2) As I am reading through a draft of this book, I see that Rowe has equalled the Australian record in Monte Carlo during his 2014 European race circuit. By the way, he was 7th in that race with 5 runners going under 1:43.

The Doubell story reminds me of the type of build-up I saw as physiologist with an Australian swim squad at the AIS. A very long, extremely intensive build up over several months, a four to six week period of extremely intense race-pace work and time-trials, followed by a three to four week taper that had the swimmers training with dramatically reduced volume progressing to a period of little intensity in the final week.

This seemed to work well for many swimmers, but not all of them. Some swimmers needed two or three weeks of easy work to achieve best race sharpness. This type of preparation was not dissimilar to the traditional Eastern Bloc regime, and although a few other variables may have entered the equation in the Leipzig led East German Sports Institutes methodology, it was an extraordinarily successful one.

Training was meant to be easy ... sometimes

So, about 30 years after his Mexico Olympics triumph, here I was picking up Ralph Doubell, successful international banker, from the airport. I found out he was a man of strong opinions, not prone to pulling any punches. He was severely critical of the 'light training loads undertaken by the modern group of middle and distance athletes.' I won't forget his damning criticism of versatile Australian champion Shaun Creighton's training program during a discussion seminar at the AIS; in particular the amount of slow running he did each week.

Doubell (and his former coach Stampfl) considered long slow runs a waste of time, informing the audience of runners and coaches that to be successful at world level, they needed to do something productive (read intensive) nearly every day. Shaun's coach Pat Clohessy (also de Castella's coach) certainly didn't see it this way, being proponent of the Lydiard philosophy that long slow distance running was essential to develop the anatomical resilience and aerobic base of fitness on which to build more intensive work.

History and the success stories coming from both schools of thought tell us that both the Clohessy/Creighton/de Castella camp and the Stampfl/Doubell/Merv Lincoln camp may have skinned their cats in different ways, but got the job done nevertheless. After all, of Clohessy's athletes de Castella was the world's greatest marathoner and Creighton the Australian 3000m steeplechase and 10,000m record holder. Doubell may have had a point in relation to modern

800m runners not training as hard as he did, but in defence of Australia's middle and long-distance runners in general, coaches with limited numbers of runners have to protect their runners from overuse injuries. Too many promising young runners' careers have been cut short from over-reaching on a daily program like that described above by Ralph Doubell.

Training's a balancing act for coaches. In not pushing that training envelope enough the desired performance just doesn't happen. Push it too hard and it's game over. Somewhere in the middle is 'just right', as Goldilocks once exclaimed. And putting that toe in the water to feel the temperature before jumping in makes sense for any coach of a developing athlete.

Risk taking and injuries

Perhaps greater risks are taken where there are larger numbers of talented and highly motivated athletes competing for national recognition and competition. In Eastern Africa, for example, survival of the fittest is on for young and old. There are plenty of the young and older Kenyans and Ethiopians looking for national recognition in one of their few avenues to financial security. In such a cauldron of talent and competition there has to be strong feeling among the top runners that if you can train with more intensity and/or more volume than the others, and stay in one piece, you will come out on top. Some of those willing to take the risk of exceptional training regimes do remain uninjured and healthy and do go on to become world champs. Others, despite great talent do not.

The upshot is that with their enviable genetic pool and literal survival of the fittest, the Kenyans and Ethiopians enjoy overwhelming international distance running success. The only country to have challenged the eastern African dominance over the last couple of decades is their northern African neighbour Morocco, which has also clearly and consistently punched above its weight. Take the 10,000m event for example, arguably the purist track running test of aerobic fitness. In the seven Olympics between and including 1948 through to 1976 (excluding 1968 at altitude) there were 4 runners of African nationality or heritage out of 21 medallists in the 10km. Contrast that with the Olympic period of 1988 to 2012 where 20 of the 21 medallist were African or of African heritage.

The premise that the Africans are prepared to risk the injury consequences of extremes of training volume and intensity may be true in general, especially within that developed culture of distance running along the Rift Valley. But it's never been confined to Africa. Far from it. There have been and continue to be numerous non-African runners around the world who share that fierce desire to be the best in the world and train with correspondingly risky volumes and intensity.

Ralph Doubell was a case in point. So was former world marathon record holder Derek Clayton.

Clayton was an English-born Australian in the tradition and mindset of his former country's champion distance runners Gordon Pirie, Dave Moorcroft, Ron Hill, Dave Bedford and Brendan Foster. Clayton believed he had to punish himself incessantly by training 'harder' than anyone else, in order to be better than anyone else. Punish himself he certainly did, and along came great success. Clayton ran the word's first sub 2 h 10 min marathon in Fukuoka, Japan in 1967 and the world fastest ever marathon in Antwerp, Belgium of 2:08:33 in 1969. But these triumphs came at considerable cost to his body, and his career was plagued by overuse injury.

It has been argued that his history of injuries prevented him from running at the level expected from him in championship events, but to be fair his body size may have contributed to a disadvantage in competing in warm weather championship marathons (as discussed in Chapter 18). Clayton's 2hr27' for 7th place in the marathon in Mexico City may have been viewed as a substandard performance for a world record holder, and even by the runner himself, but this effort at altitude nearly 4 decades ago should be appreciated as another of his superb and courageous runs.

Getting back to the point at whether coaches and runners should push the limits of anatomy, physiology and psychology to the point of high personal injury risk. Many modern coaches in the Western world these days would say that is sheer lunacy; that indeed it's unethical to push the envelope of a young runner to the point of it bursting. This is hard to argue against, but the tricky part is determining just where that threshold of risk lies. Clearly it varies enormously, and sometimes the threshold can only be discovered the hard way.

And would Clayton have enjoyed his legendary status as a marathon runner had he not taken those risks and trained more conservatively? I tend to think not.

Unusual training and injuries

My role at the Australian Institute of Sport paved the way for me to meet some of the track and road heroes of my Melbournian based younger years. People such as John Landy, Ron Clarke, Herb Elliott, Ralph Doubell, Roger Bannister; and I put Franz Stampfl well and truly in this category.

It was 1983, a couple of years after moving to Canberra from Melbourne and I was now a keen runner, spurred on by the de Castella successes, like many thousands of other Australians. I was extremely keen to experience personally just what has to be done to do my very best, calculating the risks involved and whether to take them; initially for the marathon, later for middle-distance racing. I had heard that Franz Stampfl wasn't a great supporter of the AIS. This was not an uncommon sentiment amongst coaches in various sports, who viewed the Canberra-based scholarship scheme in understandably parochial terms as usurping athletes away from their tutelage and state.

(Digressing momentarily, as it turned out this parochialism was a blessing in disguise for Australian sport because it needled each state and territory governments to set up their own Institutes of Sport. A highly competitive national system evolved which had the effect of magnifying the impact of the AIS and ultimately contributed significantly to the success Australia enjoyed at its home-country Sydney Olympics, 19 years after the AIS kicked off).

I was keen to meet, Franz and called his office at Melbourne University to ask whether I might meet with him for some advice on training methods, both at a personal level and to pass on to others at the AIS. I got a hint of Franz's reputed disapproval of the AIS when at first he was too busy to accept my calls; and when I did catch him, it wasn't the warmest of invitations but an invitation at least. I could come over to the Melbourne Uni track on Tuesday evening and train with his group.

I jumped at the chance and arrived to find Franz's group of runners taking off for a 12km run around Princes Park who made me feel more comfortable when they invited me to join them. Arriving back at the track and Franz's office, I introduced myself, letting him know of my extraordinarily long term association with the Melbourne University (telling him I went to a small school in the corner of the university campus for 6 years, and studied there on and off for 15 years) I very briefly mentioned my role at the AIS and personal plans to run the Canberra Marathon.

Judging by a wave of his hand, Franz had invited me to join his group of runners in a set of circuit exercises. I participated in some abdominal work, but baulked at the sets of squat jumps which followed, as I was not accustomed to these and with all my long running I knew it would make me very sore. Franz offhandedly, probably mischievously inferred that I was soft; opting for the easy road he told me was typical of most modern day athletes. Reluctantly I completed the 5 sets of 30 squat jumps, mainly to avoid showing a mistrust of his judgment and to offset his impression of me as an arrogant young know-all from the AIS.

Those 5 sets of squat jumps cost me the three days of running training and I could barely jog on the fourth. Of course Franz knew this would be the case, and the experience certainly provided me with some understanding of the Stampfl psyche. I began to understand the roots of his acrimonious relationship with archrival and fellow Victorian super-coach Cerutty and to a lesser degree with New Zealand super-coach Arthur Lydiard. Two alpha males in the same part of the jungle are never likely to be best buddies.

Patience personified

Lisa Weightman's commitment to running has been well and truly tested over the years, because for much of the time in her 20s she was injured. I got a phone call from her father Peter one day out of the blue. I had the pleasure of both playing alongside and coaching Peter as an Australian Rules footballer at Preston in the 70s. I always doubted whether any footballer could stay with me on a 5 mile run in those days, but I think Peter might have had me covered. He was a fine footballer who later became a highly respected coach. It was good reminiscing about our football days and Peter explained that his daughter Lisa was a keen runner but had suffered a series of stress fractures.

Peter told me that Lisa was being treated now by another former Preston Football Club player, Dr Bruce Reid (a fleet-footed and effective on-ball player in our dual premiership winning team) now chief medical officer at the Essendon Football Club. Peter asked if I would have the time as a physiologist to set a program in tandem with Bruce's advice. As usual I had plenty going on and I'm sure Bruce was even busier, but old football mates like to help each other out and we teamed up. Although my work was by correspondence between Canberra and Melbourne, Lisa did things exactly, and I mean exactly, as we set out. I was hopeful that she would get back into club running and enjoy herself. Within a year or so, things began to look promising, as our little team of Bruce, Peter and I gradually built up her training without serious mishap. Lisa was ready to embark on some more intensive training. I recommended that she ask Melbourne-based coach Pam Turney if she could join her squad of female runners. At that stage all I hoped for was that Lisa would remain in good health, and that she enjoyed a relatively uninterrupted few years of distance running. Little did I realize what was to come.

We remained in contact from time to time and I was pleased to hear that Lisa did remain injury free and was improving at a rapid rate, to the extent that after a couple of years, coach Pam Turney had expertly guided her to an Olympic qualifier of 2hr32' in her debut marathon in 2008. Lisa was an Olympic marathoner and in Beijing she acquitted herself extremely well in trying conditions, running another but arguably better 2hr32'. Not long after that Peter rang me to ask if I would again consider guiding Lisa's program as he felt my experience with marathoners would help get Lisa to the next level. Eventually, following discussions with Pam Turney, I did resume coaching Lisa, and continuing the progression that Pam set up, Lisa developed into Australia's most consistent female international marathoner of recent years; she's run 2hr30' or better in her last 7 (with the exception of the Commonwealth Games hot marathon in New Delhi where she medalled), with top 20 performances in the Berlin World Champs and the London Olympics, and marathon wins in Nagano and Melbourne in 2013 where she ran her PB of 2hr26'.

P.S. (1) As I continue with what might be described as my 'long recovery interval writing' habits, I notice it's now December 2014 and Lisa and husband/ training partner/mentor Lachlan have month old Peter Richard, already looking for a football to kick (and I see there's one in the cot already).

P.S (2) It's now June 2015 and Lisa's looking to get her running legs back again, aiming at Rio.

Not always smooth sailing

At first glance this looks like smooth sailing, but as most coaches, and most marathoners know, all was not plain sailing for this marathoner. Let's go back to 2011 ...

It's March 2011. I'm in the Qantas lounge at Tullamarine Airport. My phone rings. It's Lisa. Soreness in the groin has been hampering her training over the recent couple of weeks and we are due to leave for the London Marathon in 5 weeks. She has just been to see Doc Reid. He arranged an MRI and bone scan immediately after his consultation, and it confirmed his suspicion of a stress reaction in the ramus of the pubic bone. This means rest or cross training for two weeks and another four weeks of gradual build-up into full training—if things proceed smoothly. Extremely disappointing but our team of husband Lachlan, father Peter and I all agree that whilst running the London Marathon in 2011 would be great, the name of the game is preparing for the 2012 London Olympics. We cancel that 2011 London marathon.

We accept this setback as a feature of a marathoner who is striving to become a better runner each year. I accept this as a coaching error. Risks can be minimized but risks remain when training is gradually ramped up. We remain positive on the phone and begin to talk about our campaign for a European marathon in October. We rationalize that her racing three marathons in two years is probably all we should be aiming at anyway, so missing London may be a blessing in disguise. I reflect on a succession of minor setbacks Lisa has had since her courageous bronze medal effort in the New Delhi 32°C heat. She took months to recover, and still seems to be paying the price. That marathon for Australia was costly, but without doubt, a price worth paying.

Many coaches reading the last paragraph will have experienced that phone call or conversation where an athlete informs them they have pulled up sore and sorry. These sorts of phone calls or direct discussions are not unusual in distance running circles. In long term coaching relationships coach and athlete learn how to deal positively with setbacks; put them in the 'recent history' basket and set sights on the next progression. Lows are accommodated along with the highs. A line of close communication, realistic optimism, and never failing encouragement are characteristics of enduring coach-athlete relationships.

And believe me, it's not just a one-way process.

Flexibility and Injuries

In my commentary on running economy, I pointed out the somewhat counter-intuitive argument for a negative correlation between running economy and flexibility. That's ok, but there aren't many coaches or sports medical practitioners who would argue with the premise that distance runners still need good flexibility to prevent injuries.

But do they? Can distance and middle-distance runners really reduce the risk of injury by doing specific exercises to increase the resting length of muscles and facilitate hip and ankle joints to move through bigger ranges? While a high level of flexibility is essential to the performance as well as injury prevention of hurdlers and sprinters the logic of assuming it also applies to distance runners is not at all clear to me.

The hip and ankle are the joints given most attention when it comes to stretching; the hamstrings and hip flexor muscles (with their tendons) limit motion around the hip, as do the calf muscles and their Achilles tendon around the ankle. Do distance runners really need to apply the considerable forces required to stretch these tissues? After all, the range of motion and stretching achieved on the training track will at times exceed those of racing, especially as typical running training includes faster than race-pace running. So how much formal stretching do runners need?

And distance runners might also be excused in questioning the benefit of slow sustained stretching? We get plenty of dynamic stretching during running at varied speeds and on different gradients. Is it really beneficial to hold a stretch in a painful position for repetitions that last 30 seconds? Does that really lead to more resilience in a runner's tendon? Over the past few decades of coaching I haven't been convinced.

On the other hand, a few minutes of gentle stretching to let the muscles know they are going to be called into action as part of a warm-up for training or competition is an entirely reasonable approach. Maybe the value of stretching for distance runners is not so much to increase flexibility, but simply to help prepare muscles for action. Distance runners can derive certain psychologically therapeutic benefits from gentle stretching, but any euphoria is unlikely to be extended to the kind of strenuous stretching typical of sprinters, hurdlers, gymnasts, dancers and tennis players. Without any intended reflection on the well-known Cerutty philosophy of emulating the techniques of fast running animals, my dalmation used to enjoy a good stretch after our runs. However, like the runners I coach, he preferred an easy stretch routine, usually one leg at a time without a hint of a grimace. His lack of strenuous stretching didn't seem to increase his risk of injury and I don't recall him pulling a muscle at any stage during a run, even during an unexpected anaerobic effort induced by a stray kangaroo.

Australian Rules football, cricket, and kinesiology studies formed the bases of my views of flexibility. There is no doubt that increasing ranges of joint motion in many sports is a sensible part of training and can prevent injury. Footballers often find themselves in compromised postures, body parts simultaneously twisted and active. Increased joint ranges are likely to prevent or at least dampen the effect of unexpected torques on hips, backs, knees and ankles. And joint flexibility can improve performance as well. For example, tight hamstrings can restrict the follow through and therefore, the power of a kicking a football or bowling a cricket ball, and we could easily apply the same logic for a lack of flexibility interfering with a free-flowing follow-through driving a cricket or golf ball.

On the other hand, I'm not at all convinced that the majority of hamstring injuries, a most common injury in modern Australian Rules football, are due to poor flexibility. I can't remember anyone injuring their hamstring by over-stretching, at least during my time as a player, fitness adviser and coach.

On the other hand there did seem to be an unusually high occurrence of hamstring injuries in footballers. My observation was that the majority of hamstring injuries were related to fatigue. Fatigue induced in the game itself and fatigue induced by training in an unusually intensive or unaccustomed manner. One real danger lies in overloading with heavy or powerful squats or squat jumps with or without weights or overdoing the hill running. Following this kind of stress the hamstring, 'pull' often occurs in the middle of the contraction, not at the end of the stride when the muscle is in an extended position, making it most unlikely that flexibility or the lack of it had anything to do with the those injuries. More likely to be the culprit is neuromuscular fatigue interfering with the contraction-relaxation timing. If the hamstring is supposed to be in the relaxation-lengthening phase and through fatigue its neural coordination control fails so that it inadvertently partially contracts, then the muscle literally tears itself apart. Cramping is an extreme example of muscle fatigue causing involuntary contraction, mistiming of contraction and relaxation, and a potential hamstring 'pull'.

Getting back to running training, and acknowledging the anecdotal nature of this comment, the two runners I recall suffering with recurrent hamstring injuries were both extremely flexible and liked to stretch for lengthy periods.

I was interested to read what the remarkably resilient New Zealand marathoner Jack Foster thought of stretching. His running success followed a successful cycling career, and included a 2hr11' marathon at age 41 (12th fastest ever at any age at that time) and a 2hr17' marathon at 46. Jack made his thoughts on stretching very clear to Brian Lenton in his highly informative book of interviews with great distance runners, 'Off the Record'.

'I never do any stretching.'

Interestingly, Jack was a firm believer in carefully designed weight training which to him provided the degree of joint mobility he sought. Fair enough, Jack. But again, like my observations, it's all anecdotal. There aren't too many epidemiological studies of the effect of flexibility and strength work on injury prevention; although I did find one recently, and two of the authors were formerly leaders in many of the fine studies showing the benefits of physical activity carried out at the Aerobics Centre in Texas. Now they work at the

University of South Carolina and in collaboration with two other university researchers they questioned 4,610 middle aged men and women over a five year period about their incidence of back pain. Interestingly, the results were consistent with my anecdotes; those who reported specific stretching or weight training were at higher risk of developing lower back pain. Now this sort of study doesn't lend itself to any strong inferences; for a start it doesn't involve fit young athletes. But even if you're a reader in the generally active older age bracket I can't imagine it inspiring you to increase the amount of stretching and strength work you slot into your exercise programs. However, my recommendation is that if resistance and flexibility is done well with solid posture, and avoids fatigue-induced failure, then there are many compelling reasons for all athletes and non-athletes alike to participate in well-designed carefully controlled strength and flexibility work.

Getting back to running, the steeplechase is a different story because getting over the barriers introduces one or two new variables into the performance equation. Sprint hurdlers have to propel themselves forward while the knee joint of the leading leg is close to 180 degrees and the torso slanting forward. A substantial degree of flexibility is required to achieve this position without straining, and flexibility work is a fundamental component of sprint hurdling.

Our sprint hurdlers must shake their head in disbelief watching some of the world's best steeplechasers 'hurdle' over the last couple of decades. An apparent Kenyan nonchalance in regard to hurdling technique may have come about because their running fitness was sufficient to get them over the line first. Alternatively it might be because top distance runners like the Kenyans lack flexibility and simply don't like stretching activities that are routinely required in improving hurdling technique. There may be some truth in both suggestions but it has been noticeable in recent years, with competition within Kenyans themselves getting tougher by the year, that their steeplechase hurdling techniques have improved. It stands to reason that flattening the path of a runner's centre of gravity over the hurdle will not only reduce the energy requirement but get the runner back into running mode earlier, both these factors leading to faster times. All aspiring steeplechasers will benefit from, investing time and effort in learning to hurdle correctly, and development of optimal hip and knee joint strength and flexibility cannot be neglected in this event.

Steeplechase aside, in what sort of stretching should a distance runner engage? In brief, gentle, regular and varied. It makes sense to involve all joints, especially those surrounded by the running propulsive muscles, in some daily gentle flexibility work. This could be part of circuit training, requiring around 10–15 minutes or so each day, and also as a routine part of warm-up and/or warmdown to prepare for the involuntary stretch-reflex contractions of muscles around the hip, knees and ankles that accompany each footstrike. Inflicting pain on oneself is not part of the deal. Not that I'm concerned about the pain, it's just that striving for maximal joint flexibility in distance and middle-distance runners isn't necessary and may even be contraindicated.

Shoes and injuries

Good quality running shoes aren't cheap, we all know that, but we still buy them. They are our tools of trade and it's false economy to opt for second best. In terms of quantity, most marathoners assume Imelda Marcos status, as they go through a pair of shoes every 800–1000km. That's 4 or 5 weeks of training and about $2,000 a year just for training shoes for the non-sponsored elite-level marathon runner. But cost is where Imelda might have our marathoners covered, $2,000 will change hands for just one designer-brand pair of high heels.

Anyway, now that I've made a pair of trainers sound less expensive (and I declare no conflict of interest or current sponsorship from any shoe company) we'd still like our trainers to do what the manufacturers tell us they do, that is to prevent injury, and certainly not to cause it. As a rule I believe this to be the case but exceptions to rules inevitably occur.

Two instances come to mind. In the early 80s Andrew Lloyd and Carolyn Schuwalow were a husband and wife team of national distance running champions. Tagging along as their coach, I was favoured by their shoe company as well, and we all got well looked after with training shoes and other gear.

Things were going well until Andrew complained about Achilles soreness. I eased his training down to jogging. I was dismayed when Carolyn told me her Achilles was sore too. This was great coaching, 100 percent of my coaching group at that time out with Achilles injuries.

We three used to run together at times, and now the coach was the only one running! But then on a training run, and I could hardly believe it, my Achilles tendon got sore. This is just ridiculous, I recall thinking. We haven't changed anything dramatically; haven't done too much on the track and very little in spikes. The track hasn't got too hard and it's the middle of summer and pretty warm. So what was going on here? Was there some sort of Achilles virus circulating?

I walked home the last 3km of an intended 8km run, sat down, took off my shoes, and was going to dive into the pool for a swim when it all dawned on me. Andrew, Carolyn and I had all taken delivery of the latest training shoe, and we'd all changed over to this shoe at roughly the same time and we were all sore. I picked up the shoe for a close look and went up to grab a pair of my old shoes. The difference was clear. There was a markedly raised section on the heel on the new shoe. I got on the phone, rang the others and we discarded those shoes. Within a week the soreness had all but disappeared. Being brought up a post-World War 2 baby boomer where frugality was a given, I cut that raised back of the shoe with a sharp pair of scissors. The shoe may no longer have cut it for style, but it no longer rubbed and inflamed the Achilles tendon.

Andrew and Carolyn had seen their sports doctors, the heel diagnosed as an overuse injury, taken their anti-inflammatories, and hardly run for a week. All the time it was a simple mechanical problem. Another case of looking for simple solutions before those more complicated.

Just prior to the Commonwealth Games in Glasgow, marathoner Michael Shelley's foot was getting sore on the upper outside part of his during his longer easier runs. He didn't think it anything to get concerned about, but it did worry me a bit; minor 'niggles' sometimes develop into real problems. The strange thing was that when Michael ran faster it felt better, although he was still aware of some minor soreness. He went to his trusted long term chiropractic specialist who mobilized the foot and our runner rubbed anti-inflammatory gel into it, both of which seem to help, but the pain persisted in those easy runs. We were sitting in the living room of Michael's parents' house on the Gold Coast.

'Dick, I've worked out what the problem is!'

Bringing his recently acquired shoes over Michael showed me how the shoe had been modified with the addition of a patchwork of fine interlocking lacing at the side of each shoe to supplement the usual lacing at the front.

'Look at this' he held out the shoe, 'part of this fine lacing hasn't been threaded through the patchwork of loops properly and although it's hard to see, there's a small sharp bit that sticks into the top of my foot when I run. That's the problem without a doubt. It explains why I only get sore running slowly. It's because I only wear these particular training shoes when I run slowly and change into my lighter weight shoes when I do the quality sessions.'

A slick piece of sleuthing from our runner (demonstrating once and for all that distance runners are smarter than sprinters); and a relief for me when 'stress reaction' was in the back of my mind. Herein was yet another instance of looking at the basics; the simpler explanations upfront. In any case, we were both very happy about Dr Shelley's self-diagnosis!

The problem with flying

Sue Malaxos (nee Grayson) was a consistent 2hr40' min marathon runner from Perth. She arrived at the AIS on a training camp and it was then that we first formed a coach-athlete team with a mission for Sue to become an Olympian. The qualifying time was 2hr35'. At age 32, we had to make some changes to her training, perhaps take a few risks with increased volumes and intensities. We did just that, gradually upgraded the program and with a good consistent 6 months of training behind her, Sue was overjoyed to run 2hr33' and win her way onto the Australian Olympic team, to compete in Atlanta.

With only the final weeks of fine tuning to do, Sue got on the plane, final destination the Australian team training camp in South Carolina. The flight across the Pacific to LA is about 13 hours, plus another 3 hours over to South Carolina, but for Sue, the journey was even longer, as she lived in Perth, and that added another 4 hours of flying time. Sue's ankles and feet were swollen when she got off the plane, although this in itself is not all that unusual and several other athletes suffered similarly. It is difficult to prevent the accumulation of fluid around the feet and ankles in economy class, especially when the sleeping position is in a sitting position with feet well below the body's centre of gravity.

But Sue's ankles and feet were unusually sore as she tried to jog, to the extent that she could not continue. Even walking was uncomfortable. At that stage we weren't overly concerned as we were sure all would be back to normal in a day or two. Our minor concern became serious when the problem persisted over the next few days and Sue was forced into a sedentary week.

Our very popular marathon runner never recovered. Pain persisted in her feet and lower legs during the three weeks of our training camp. The medical team was unable to resolve the issue, and the psychological stress accompanying the physical stress added up to considerable distress.

Race day eventually came and nothing much changed. Sue was a devoted and tough competitor, and by hook or by crook, she was going to start that marathon and do her best to finish. With the most determined of efforts, our Olympian was reduced to a walk after a few kilometres. But Sue Malaxos, was an Olympic marathoner, a rare honour and her determined effort was one we were all proud of.

The Malaxos story serves as a warning to anyone complacent about the risks of air travel, even and perhaps especially, in finely tuned athletes who are booked into economy class for very long journeys. In those days, little concern prevailed about the effect of air travel on our blood circulation, with its extended period of sedentariness and low cabin pressure. Nowadays we are very aware of deep vein thrombosis (DVT). I wonder now whether that was Sue's problem.

Fit young athletes like marathon runners are considered low risk for blood clotting problems, and while this may be the case in general, following that Atlanta experience runners are well advised to:

- avoid any long or intense training on the day they fly out, or even the day before,

- avoid long periods in a stationary sitting position; try to find a way to elevate the legs from time to time; do some repeated short duration isometric contractions in the seated position; lift your legs up against the seat in front of you; plant your feet on the floor and lift your backside off the seat, holding for a few seconds and repeat in a set
- look around for any spare seats as being able to lie down is a huge bonus
- take the opportunity to fly Business Class of course but this is rarely available to all but elite professional sportspeople
- wearing flight stockings to assist venous return has been recommended, but I'm not convinced about the effectiveness of this procedure. Does it enhance blood flow back to the heart or act as a modified tourniquet and do the opposite? It seems to me that compression socks might be counterproductive when in a sedentary position for extended periods—so obtain the most recent expert advice here.
- get up and walk around at regular intervals and do some squats and knee raises up the back of the plane where there is a bit of space. Muscular activity is our natural venous return blood pump, so activating the pump takes pressure off the veins, literally.
- drink plenty of water, and mix in some fruit juice or sports drink to assist maintenance of electrolyte balance. There is little chance of common salt deficiency with food these days, especially airline food. In fact the opposite is the case and it makes sense to avoid over-salty food.
- postpone your travel if you contract an infection. Apart from the risk of infecting fellow team members, infections can increase blood viscosity. Increases in circulating white blood cells, often the case in low grade viral infections, can do this by themselves as we found out at the AIS some years back. The reduced cabin air pressure is enough to increase blood viscosity in itself.
- on arrival, re-introduce training gradually. Don't jump straight into a big session before homeostasis has been restored.

Core strength and Injuries

It stands to reason that injuries are more likely to occur in runners whose actions are untidy and asymmetrical. In other words, problems will occur when the direction of muscular forces pull the body in undesirable directions. A basic premise of core strength training is to stabilize the pelvis and lower back to provide a firmer base of support and therefore, a better alignment of those forces.

In my early sporting football and cricket days, we did sit-ups and press-ups, squats and high knees and we'd run up hills and we'd do some weight training to increase strength and power. The term 'core' strength wasn't part of any coach's vocabulary in those days but now it's on the tip of every fitness and conditioning coach's tongue. Probably with good reason, as core strength has been associated with both injury prevention and increased power. But how much extra core strength training does a middle and long-distance runner need to do to prevent injury?

That's not a straight forward question, because all runners practise a form of 'core stability' work. Every time we place a running foot on *Terra Firma*, our 'core stability' muscles automatically go to work to maintain our posture, ensuring we don't collapse like a rag doll. Running naturally trains our postural muscles, there being as many separate sets of postural muscle contractions and relaxations as there are foot-strikes; hundreds of thousands every month for many runners. The question is whether runners need to practise the more dynamic and higher resistance core work typical of commonly practised 'ab' routines, such as crunches and the like. We can't be sure whether more specific 'core' postural work in the form of running based drills, including bounding, skipping and hill work isn't just as, if not more effective.

Running itself and specific running drills need to be practised with what we consider to be a biomechanical efficient posture. Practice makes perfect, as they say, but only as long as we practise the right way. To do otherwise and we may finish up with a perfect mess. It might be easier to envisage this in a game like golf. Practising a faulty golf swing time after time will certainly develop an imprint of that swing in our nervous system and make it easier to reproduce that swing on call. But if we've practised a faulty swing, then the result, the flight of the ball, is painfully obvious.

The tricky part for a coach, be it of golf or running or any other sport, is to determine exactly what the 'right way' is, or in other words what is meant by 'good technique'.

Good running technique will align and coordinate movement of joints to minimize muscular activity at any given running speed, and so increasing running economy. Experienced coaches with 'an eye' for correct technique will judge this on the basis of a runner's symmetry and how fluent the movement pattern appears overall.

Back to the question of how much non-specific core work a runner needs; non-specific referring to exercises that do not involve the running locomotive action. Examples are the artificially contrived dynamic and isometric variations of 'crunches', 'sit-ups', 'trunk curls' or hip and leg raises, medicine ball rotations, and 'plank' holds. Instructors inform their charges of ways to maintain good posture while doing these exercises, such as 'flattening the lower back', 'engaging the buttock muscles' etc. The theory behind the practice of these exercises is that they permit more resistance to be applied to the trunk or core, and so increase strength, which in turn allows runners to maintain good posture when running fatigue sets in.

As to whether non-specific core strength work is of benefit to an intensely training runner we simply don't know, as there aren't any authoritative studies to turn to. A recent review of the scientific literature doesn't help us much, but the reviewers could find little support for its role in injury prevention. It must be said that researching such a topic is problematical in itself, as strong evidence requires a randomized controlled trial over a lengthy period of time in high level runners. Resorting to anecdotal evidence, I've observed plenty of successful runners who seem to maintain solid posture even when fatigued, who don't participate in non-running core work. Instead they obtained all their core stability purely from running on different terrains and gradients with different speeds and distances. These runners are typically poor at executing the traditional non-running core exercises, such as sit-ups and crunches, but the relevance of these dynamic actions foreign to the action of running has to be questioned. But let's not jump to any general conclusions that traditional core work has little to offer distance runners. Some runners may require more than running and running-related drills to develop appropriate pelvis and lower back stability.

A sensible approach to core stability work in distance runners parallels the flexibility issue. Include some non-specific core work on top of the core work of running itself, as it may assist some runners maintain a stable posture in the fatigued state.

In one of those coincidences that seem not to be just coincidence, and having just written the above piece concerning core strength, marathon runner Mel Panayiotou commented over a coffee in her home town of Mooloolabah, 'It's funny, Dick, but since you've increased my mileage and introduced those quality sessions, my body shape has changed'.

'How's that, Mel?' I asked, not having seem too much of my runner over the past 6 months, coaching her by corresponding with regular phone discussions and email exchanges.

'Well, I've definitely become more muscular around the torso as well as in my legs' she said 'and the funny thing is that since I've trained harder for running, I've not done any of the crunches, sit-ups or any other of the ab work I used to do ... but I feel stronger round the trunk region when I'm running.'

Now I realize this is pure anecdotal non-scientific stuff, but Mel's unsolicited personal observation was at least consistent with my observations over the years. The 150,000 times Mel put her foot on the ground running every week and the 150,000 times the postural stability muscles contracted seemed to exert enough of a noticeable effect to prompt her comment.

It was time to go, as we finished our coffees and headed for the car, then to the Brisbane Airport where Mel was to depart for Glasgow and her debut as an Australian marathoner in the Commonwealth Games. Not bad for someone who thought that top 6 in a local fun run would be a great result just three years previously. In that period Mel had reduced her marathon time from 3hr10' to the 2hr38' qualifier for the Games. Mel's an animal doctor at the Australia Zoo with a busy 40 hour working week. Just three days ago she could think of little else than the giraffe who was ready to give birth.

'Her progesterone levels are still high Dick, so I think my long run is going to be safe, she'll hang on until I get back'.

She did hang on, and with a shot of oxytocin, Mel induced that delivery of a baby girl giraffe, all safe and sound, so our marathon runner could get on the plane headed for Glasgow with a free mind. Following an example set by Lisa Weightman, this did at least show it's still possible to pursue a professional career and make an Australian marathon team; but not necessarily advisable, as training at 4:30am and 6:00pm each day with a full day's work in between is a tough ask.

P.S. Time has ticked on. I can add now that Mel Panayiotou ran another PB of 2hr34' for 8th place in Glasgow.

Don't get run down

Many an athlete has a sad story to tell about how consistently they trained and raced in the months and weeks leading up to a big competition, only to get a sore throat or a bad cough in the week, taking the edge of their competition performance.

In the early 90s at the AIS we tried to work out whether there was an increased risk of infection just before competition or whether it was sheer coincidence. Some of our first work was to investigate how the immune system of athletes responded to training. Do our best athletes in training have enhanced or compromised immunity to common infections? Is the problem one of high volume training, high intensity or both training? Could it have something to do with tapering off training? We were fortunate to collaborate with Dr Maurie Weidemann of the Australian National University's then Department of Biochemistry and Molecular Biology.

Our PhD students at the time, John Smith, Bon Gray and David Pyne, now all highly successful scientists in private practice, academia, and at the AIS respectively, carried out a series of studies to demonstrate several important practical outcomes. As one indication of immune response, these researchers collected a blood sample from our athletes and isolated the neutrophils, white blood cells which play an important role in our first line of immune defence. Then they exposed the isolated neutrophils to a simulated bacterial attack to test the strength of the response. Neutrophils are our front-line killing machines, destroying foreign invaders by delivering a burst of extremely reactive oxygen species. We can get a good idea of the potency of our first line of defence by measuring the power of this oxidative burst when we add a known amount of foreign material into a test tube containing a known number of neutrophils.

In one of the early studies, measures were taken before and after a steady well-controlled 10km run. The result was good news for joggers. Steady aerobic exercise of moderate intensity primed up our neutrophil first line of immune defence to be more effective killing cells. It was reasonable to assume that jogging regularly might reduce the incidence of upper respiratory tract infections, and we were pleased that different researchers found similar trends using other indicators of immune response.

But runners just don't do easy paced 10km runs all week. They train with higher intensity and volume, and the biochemical disturbances accompanying intense or extra-long bouts of training might have a completely different impact on the human immune system than a relatively stress-free bout of easy running. Unfortunately this turned out to be the case on both counts. Runners undertaking very large training volumes showed a depressed neutrophil response; and measures of immune responses before and after a bout of high intensity interval training had a similarly inhibiting effect on neutrophil response.

So moderate amounts of aerobic running seem to help us combat coughs colds and sore throats, but large mileages and high intensity anaerobic training tend to leave athletes more susceptible to infection than normal. These findings provide extra reason for caution about rapid increases in the volume or intensity of training, and the special care needed to be taken when upper respiratory tract infections are more frequent than usual in the general community.

As for being more susceptible to upper respiratory tract infections just prior to targeted competitions, it's unlikely that it's anything to do with training, as during the taper period things are generally well under control, with plenty of recovery time. But the unusual 'up close and personal' nature of air travel presents the first threat to an athlete preparing to compete overseas. A second and related threat is encountering new bacteria and viruses in foreign countries, which may get the jump on a runner's immune system, and take over for a while. Then there is residual training tiredness, runners sometimes making the mistake of leaving their shores in a fatigued state, over-tiredness being a well-known immuno-suppressant.

Finally there is the mental stress of the days leading up to the big day, psychological stress having an adverse impact upon the secretion of the very same hormones which control our immune system. Combine these factors and it's not hard to imagine why athletes may become more vulnerable to pre-competition infection.

But then again, we don't know for sure if indeed there is a real increase in sickness prior to a major competition. It's possible a sharpened awareness of wellness or lack of it plays a part; problems shrugged off back in normal training magnified by pre-competition anxiety.

The Maurie Weideman story

I can't pass this section without paying tribute to my Australian National University research colleague and part-time running partner, now deceased biochemist Dr Maurie Weideman.

My first meeting with Maurie was a jaw dropper for a couple of reasons. Firstly, he impressed me no end when he told me he was a cousin to the former Collingwood Australian Rules Football Captain, and centre half forward Murray Weideman (known as The Enforcer). I actually played for Collingwood in their Reserves team (and one senior game on the bench I add with pride) when the great man was still at the club in 1963.

Then I happened to ask where Maurie did his postgraduate studies in biochemistry. 'Over in Germany, in Freiburg, Dick.' I continued on, hoping not to become annoyingly inquisitive, but I was genuinely interested as I had visited Freiburg University not long ago.

'That sounds interesting Maurie. Who supervised your work over there?'

'Hans Krebs' was the casual reply.

Now anyone who has done any work in biochemistry at all will know Krebs' work well, too well in fact for many students, or perhaps not well enough. Professor Krebs isolated and characterized the series of reactions explaining how a runner derives aerobic energy from our food, making use of oxygen. The Krebs Citric Acid cycle. So every time we refer to terms like 'aerobic', 'anaerobic', 'mitochondria' or 'muscle enzymes' we are referring to Krebs' discoveries for which he was awarded a Nobel Prize.

Maurie was not one to boast about his background and achievements. Apart from explaining the nuances of biochemistry to me and our students, Maurie was a passionately creative and motivating scientist, which spilled over to anything he set his mind on, his brilliant photographic artistry in the theatre of opera and ballet as well as the bush, not to mention his expertise in the kitchen. And he loved coming over to visit us and our athletes at the AIS, just as we loved visiting him in his lab at the ANU.

Bones of contention

Every year we hear of top runners whose bony chasses succumb to the barrage of forces sent up through each strike of the foot.

In the early 90s at the AIS Kate Cameron from the ACT Academy of Sport and I, along with bone researchers John Hopper and John Wark of the University of Melbourne, conducted a survey of runners ranked in the top 100 nationally in at least one event. We asked the athletes about their history of diagnosed stress fractures and the training that had done. Given our strong priority in those days at the AIS was to provide information for the AIS and other Australian coaches rather than contribute to global medical science we didn't get around to publishing the results. Working on the old adage "better late than never", here's a summary of what we found.

Questionnaires were sent out to 886 athletes, and we got 550 back; 287 males of average age 25 years and 263 females of average age 22. 38 percent were sprinters, 46 percent were middle-distance (800-1500m) runners and 34 percent were long-distance runners (3000m to marathon).

Stress fractures are very common in runners, and many of you will know this first-hand. 28 percent males and 27 percent of the females reported at least one stress fracture in the last five years; and 12 percent of males and 14 percent of females had more than one stress fracture. I was a bit surprised to find that there were no differences in the incidence of stress fractures in sprinters, middle-distance and long-distance runners. I suppose it's just that I've been around distance runners more often that led me to suspect they would be more likely to be injured this way.

The stress fractures were mainly in the lower leg and foot. The most common site of the fracture was the tibia, 38 percent of all fractures and the prevalence was similar in males and females; followed by the metatarsal (23 percent), fibula (11 percent), navicular (7 percent) and femur was 6 percent.

We were of course interested in prevention, so we sought clues as to what caused the injuries. They were certainly more prevalent in athletes who trained with the most volume and/or intensity. That's to be expected. But the second and perhaps the most important message we relayed to the coaches was that the major risk was a change in training. Of all the athletes succumbing to a stress fracture, 76 percent reported one or more significant changes to training before the injury. Of this 76 percent, about a third reported an increase in distance per week, another third an increase in intensity, and 20 percent a change in surface or shoes. Training phase didn't seem to be a significant factor in the incidence because the injuries were shared equally between the build-up, the pre-competition and the competition phases. In the females, the hormonal milieu emerged as another potential culprit, with amenorrhea being about twice as prevalent in the women who had recorded a stress fracture (34 percent), compared with those who had not (16 percent).

But there was one other factor to emerge. Overall, runners surveyed averaged about 2 hours of resistance training per week. However, those with at least one stress fracture did a lot more resistance training than those never afflicted; around 40 percent and 50 percent more in the men and women respectively. This was surprising, given that we are often encouraged to participate in weight training to prevent stress fractures. It's possible that resistance training on top of all the running may have overloaded the bone remodeling cycle, but let's not fall into the trap of sublimely inferring a cause from this observation. It may well be that the increased resistance work was taken on following the stress fracture; the intent being to prevent a recurrence. Unfortunately our questionnaire didn't throw any light on this.

Bone is a highly dynamic structure, exemplified by its interactive role with the bloodstream in controlling blood calcium. In healthy bones, bone formation (incorporating calcium uptake) and resorption (secretion of calcium back into the blood) are well balanced. While physical activity does induce its own physical stress on bones, it also plays an important role in maintaining bone health through its influence on a variety of hormones. Indeed, bones become less dense and weaker when insufficient stress is applied through muscular and gravitational forces.

But as for just about every aspect of human homeostatic control, there can be too much of a good thing. Too much volume, intensity,or change in physical activity can upset the balance. Bone physiologists tell us that following an intensive training session, something in the order of 8 hours are needed for complete bone re-modelling. When runners back up for training twice a day, often adding a third session in the form of resistance training, it seems that many runners may cut things too fine and compromise the the bone remodelling processes. We all know runnerswho never seem to get injured and others who are always injured. There are many potential reasons of course, but one might be differences in the time course of bone remodelling after between training sessions or after racing.

The training threshold

It's worth reiterating here that neither physiologists nor coaches can predict the threshold of training over which an athlete is likely to break down; usually determined the hard way, by trial and error. Training is then adjusted to deal with the suspected culprit, perhaps training volume, intensity, changes in volume and intensity, technique, recovery time, surface, gradient, or footwear. Herein lies more support for sustained coach-athlete relationships, because working out the limitations of an individual athlete takes time and experience.

A couple more of my coaching errors

A change in running stress

Robbie Lynch was born up at the 'top end'. He'd been living in Melbourne and decided to come to Canberra to train with my group to see how well he could run an 800m. He moved fluently with good speed and with a 1'51" 800m and a 48" 400m and no 1500s, his training had focused on speed. With six months leading into the track season the plan was to introduce a little bit of volume to his training as a base to raise his aerobic power and complement what appeared to be some good natural anaerobic capabilities.

It helps when a runner just loves training and life and Robbie loved both, keen to see how well he could run next summer. All was going particularly well, Robbie enjoying his new style of training on bush trails and gaining in confidence. He did need some good supervision to make sure he didn't overdoing things, especially on the track where he really enjoyed running fast. One day Robbie asked if he could do a little speed work with the sprinters instead of our usual speed session on the track. I always held him back from all-out efforts, mainly by setting shorter recoveries and concentrating on technique.

I liked the idea of training with the sprinters, but it did go through my head that he might get a bit carried away in trying to match their speed in the middle of his more aerobic power oriented build-up. The sprint group was doing a set of 100s and as it turned out I had to travel interstate that afternoon so training with another group would fit in well. I had a good chat to Robbie about not getting carried away and trying to match it with his mates; that he should hold back and run in his training flats and do no more than four 100s with the group.

I saw Robbie when I got back that same afternoon, and he told me he had felt really good and his speed was terrific but he had got a little competitive and run some 100s 'pretty quick' including a couple in his spikes.

That session turned out to be his last. An Achilles soreness which developed following the session persisted during that winter. Despite the efforts of excellent sports medicine practitioners over the next couple of months he wasn't ever able to train with the intensity required of a good 800m runner. Money ran out and work took him back to Darwin.

I've often wondered what the future may have held for Robbie Lynch had I not allowed him to do that sprint session. Had I recognized that with his sprinting friends it was unreasonable to expect someone of his personality to hold back. That's coaching, that's running. We live and learn.

Robbie is of Australian indigenous heritage. Indigenous athletes have something special in the way they move. I love watching these guys play football. Their fleet of foot and general awareness of space and movement around them provides an elusiveness that is something to behold. The free-flowing movement of Sydney 2000 Olympic 400m champion Cathy Freeman was a beautiful running example (not dissimilar by the way to current world champion in this event, US athlete Alison Felix). One physical characteristic that we might expect in the multi millennium adaptations to nomadic life in indigenous Australians is endurance. But so far we haven't seen endurance running shine through the way one might expect. There may be many explanations for the absence of champion middle and long-distance indigenous runners but our ex-world champ marathon runner Rob de Castella is driven to providing opportunities to bring out this dormant characteristic. He directs the Indigenous Marathon Programme, where young aboriginal men and women train for a marathon. Not just any marathon, but the New York Marathon or the Boston Marathon. The program is a raging success with a terrific knock-on effect. Not only do the marathoners get a life-changing experience of training and achievement themselves, but they go on to become ambassadors for the program, setting up fun runs in their home districts and inspiring indigenous families to get fit and participate. The potential benefits in creating a pathway to improved health, purpose and happiness in often disadvantaged and disillusioned aboriginal communities is enormous and we are now seeing these benefits shine through.

Split leg training

Michael Shelley had reduced his 1500m time from 3'51" to 3'39" in a year and a half at the age of 19 going on 20. Not bad for someone who told me when he came down to Canberra from the Gold Coast that he 'had no speed' and 'not enough endurance for the 5000m.' He had chosen to pursue the steeplechase as a less competitive event. His junior development coach and High School PE teacher Brett Green has a particularly good eye for young talent; and for developing that talent. When he recommended young Shelley for a scholarship at the AIS, Brett obviously had more confidence in Michael's ability than Michael himself.

He was well on the way to developing into a really good middle-distance runner when we were offered an opportunity to train in the gymnasium under the guidance of the AIS strength and conditioning coach. Michael had been carrying out my preferred routine 'open air' circuit program conducted on the grassy areas at the side of the track. This involved mainly body weight resistance work; squat jumps with sand-filled car tyre tubes, high knee running with elastic band resistance to 'lactic' fatigue, varied abdominal and trunk work, stretching of most muscle groups, and partner work for 'running arms' where runners link hands, facing each other to try to exhaust each other in a vigorous running arm action.

Given the excellent improvement of Michael and the group (1500m partner Lisa Corrigan who had recently broken the Australian mile record), this circuit seemed to be suiting our needs pretty well.

However, at the AIS we now had access to a well-equipped gym and personal strength and conditioning coach supervision, and the group was keen to make use of these. Concerned though that the program included exercises that we hadn't done before, namely split leg lunges with and without weights, I expressed my reservation to the gym-based coach who assured me that he had many runners on this regime without any mishaps and that Michael would be ok.

About 6 weeks later Michael developed osteitis pubis which put him out of action for 8 months and ended his middle-distance career.

The fundamental change to split leg resistance training may not have been the cause of his injury but it was certainly the only real change in his trunk and leg training and the most plausible reason. My coaching error, and the buck stops with the coach, was to agree to changes in a program that had led to consistent injury free training and impressive improvement. There is no way any distance or middle-distance athlete of mine will ever engage in stressful split leg work with weights or depth jumps. I don't coach sprinters who may build up and benefit from such work. Again, we live and learn.

Olympian and Australian mile record-holder, Lisa Corrigan, competing at the AIS track in Canberra.

Image: Australian Sports Commission

Chapter 22
Altitude

The king was referring to Alice, believing she had an unfair advantage.
'Rule 42: All persons more than a mile high to leave the court.'

Lewis Carroll

During the era of the modern Olympics right up to the 1970s, distance runners of European and Asian ethnicity led the way. But no longer is this the case, especially among the males. The Eastern and Northern Africans, and particularly the former group living along the now legendary Rift Valley, have been taught how to exploit their talents and taken world distance running by storm.

Why these eastern Africans have done so well is a hotly debated question. Coaches and athletes will usually agree that a large part of their success is due to their living and training at moderate altitude. But it's an odds-on bet that the eastern Africans, particularly the Ethiopians and the Kenyans are more favourably genetically wired for superior endurance running.

What would Charles Darwin have thought? Even after consideration of factors such altitude, relatively greater financial rewards, harder training, within-group competition, just two sports to choose from I think Dr Darwin would be inclined to consider genetics as playing a major role. Especially if he had the opportunity to witness the likes of Haile Gebrselassie, Kenenisa Bekele, Tirunesh

Dibaba, Meseret Defar, Tiki Gelana, Paul Tergat, John Ngugi, David Rudisha, Dennis Kimetto, Wilson Kipsang and more recently Mo Farrah, Genzebe Dibaba and Almaz Ayana; just to mention a few superstars that came immediately to mind. Apologies to the other hundred that didn't.

Darwin might point to a line of ancestors who survived because they had the most endurance, the best economy and endurance to withstand famines, inter-tribal battles and predators, all in an atmosphere of reduced oxygen tension—producing a nation of slender, fleet-footed men and women with highly superior aerobic motors. I'm not forgetting the remarkable feats of the northern Africans (champions like Said Aouita, Noureddine Morcelli, and Hicham El Guerrouj) who've done their bit to put the European, Scandinavian and Asian heritage runners on the world listings of endangered species, and with a real threat of extinction.

Where are those non-African household distance running names of the past? Nurmi, Zatopek, Viren, Kutz, Ryan, Bedford, Foster, Snell, Walker, Landy, Elliott, Clarke, Clayton, Bannister, Coe, Ovett, Bordin, Baldini, Cierpinski, Salazar, Shorter, Walker, Anton, Young-Cho, de Castella, Barrios, Fiz, Moneghetti, Prefontaine, just to reel off a few that again come straight away to mind. Now how about in 2015 Galen Rupp, Nick Willis, ...?

Comparisons have been confined to the men as the Africans are less dominant in the women's distance running scene. It's only a matter of time before that changes, but Paula Radcliffe's remarkable marathon 2hr15'25" outlier of 2003 is going to take a lot of chasing down.

Now, back to where this discussion kicked off, altitude training. Nowadays just about every top distance runner around the world spends time training at moderate altitude or simulated altitude in altitude houses or tents. Despite this the African dominance continues on its merry way. So it doesn't seem that living, training or sleeping at moderate altitude is the factor separating the African and non-African runners. One could argue though that full-time, long-term living at altitude is the difference. There might be some truth in this, but there are generations of non-east Africans who've lived at moderate altitudes and we haven't seen too many champions emerge from these communities although there are a few. Mexican Arturo Barrios is a standout.

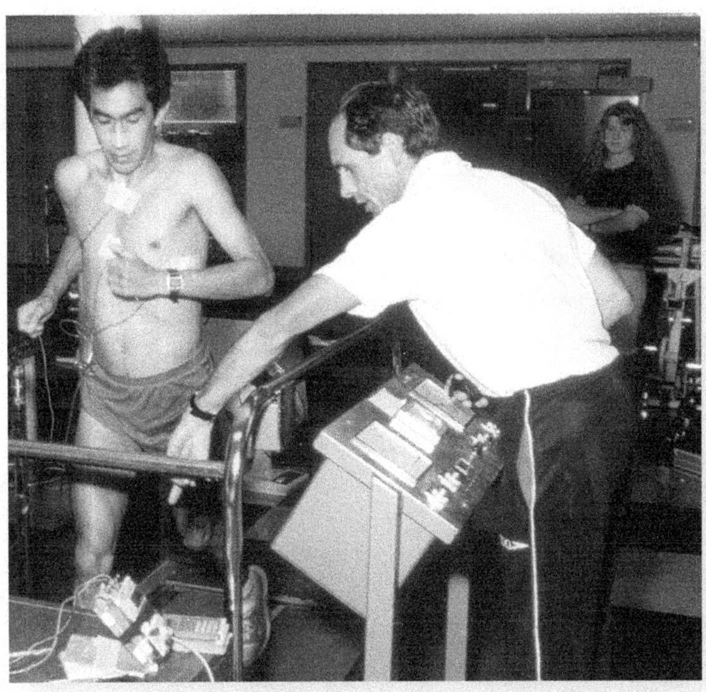

Arturo Barrios completes a $\dot{V}O2$ max test at the AIS.
Image: Australian Sports Commission

Altitude training: is it worth the effort?

In short, yes, benefits to sea-level performances are likely to be obtained from living and training at moderate altitude or simulated altitude, but there are a few 'ifs.'

If training has proceeded well; if you are an accomplished runner where any small gains in performance are critical; if you have the funding and the time; if there is good sports medical back-up; and if the weather is good.

However, as you will glean from stories to follow, benefits are not always evident, and there have been times where I have advised my athletes to remain at sea-level in their home environment. After all, great world-record holders like Elliott, Landy, Clarke, Doubell and Snell had been on top of the world without living in rarified air for extended periods, during most if not all of their most successful preparations.

The benefit moderate altitude training affords to sea-level performance are not all that obvious. For many years, while there was little doubt that altitude training improved performance at altitude, scientists were undecided as to whether or not it improved sea-level performance. In several studies blood measurements and performance changes were non-existent, so small or so variable among individuals that scientists couldn't draw firm conclusions. In recent times though, with more sophisticated measurement tools, it is generally agreed that training at moderate altitude (2000-2500m) for four weeks or more can increase total circulating blood haemoglobin mass. Because oxygen delivery to the muscles is generally considered one of the main factors limiting an athlete's aerobic power, this should lead to improved middle and long-distance running performance—all other things being equal.

But other things don't remain equal, at least not for a while, because on arrival at altitude one of the first things that happen is a decrease in plasma volume, which in turn increases haemoglobin concentration. When blood thickens like this blood viscosity is increased; it doesn't flow as freely, making more work for the heart to pump it around. Just like low grade motor oil it doesn't get into the cracks and crannies as easily, hampering oxygen exchange in the capillary bed. So in the early stages of altitude acclimatization, the net effect might assist performance at altitude but not at sea-level. The good news is that within a week or so of altitude adaptation, haemoglobin concentration tends to decline back toward its pre-altitude value, indicating a compensatory increase in blood plasma volume and to a lower blood viscosity.

Haemoglobin mass, the key measure

It's important to distinguish total body haemoglobin mass and haemoglobin concentration. It's the mass that makes a more significant contribution to oxygen transport at sea-level, not the concentration.

Haemoglobin concentration is easily and routinely measured from a blood sample at any pathology lab, but total body haemoglobin mass is a more complicated procedure and can't be determined from a single blood sample. It requires a couple of small blood samples, one before and another after rebreathing a known, very small, amount of carbon monoxide. The carbon monoxide clings to haemoglobin like glue, even better than oxygen, and by measuring how much of it is absorbed into the bloodstream we can estimate the amount of haemoglobin in circulation. It seems that an altitude of at least 1800m is required and a period of at least 3 weeks before our current measuring sticks detect any worthwhile increase in haemoglobin mass, but my guess is that training at lower heights, say 1500m to 1600m will still elicit an effect, but just harder to detect.

A pioneer of altitude training

The pioneer of altitude training for runners in Australia was a gentleman called Jack Pross (1919-2006), a thoughtful and studious coach of great influence in the NSW coaching scene. Worried about the altitude to be faced by our athletes at the 1968 Mexico Olympics he began exploring the Kosciuszko National Park. Jack gathered literature on altitude acclimatization from all around the world, but as it turned out, to little avail. He was bitterly disappointed the camps weren't attended by our best runners, writing 'I have done everything I can to encourage athletes and coaches to join us on the camps, even offering to subsidize the airfares. No takers—no interest—no future.'

I suspect part of this apathy was due to the time the runners would need to spend away from home and more importantly work, as running was a purely amateur pursuit in those days.

In the very early days of my running coaching in the 80s Jack told me about a letter he'd received from one of his club runners who happened to be in Europe at St Moritz a few months before the Mexico City Olympics. The Europeans had set up an altitude training camp in Switzerland, at a place called St Moritz, to prepare for altitude of Mexico City. There were runners and rowers from several countries, Germany being well represented. The European runners and coaches over there seemed pleased to hear that the Australians' altitude preparation was confined to just 3 weeks prior to the Olympics in the Village at Mexico City. Jack's European correspondent was sure they knew much more about competing at altitude than the Australians.

Even in those days, the seeds of altitude training for sea-level performance were well and truly sown in the European running scene. There were plans for St Moritz to continue to develop as an altitude training venue after the Olympics to prepare their athletes for sea-level races. These plans certainly eventuated and St Moritz is still one of the most popular altitude training venues in Europe. It's interesting that while coaches and athletes were convinced about the benefit of altitude training for sea-level performance it took another 40 years before more sophisticated haemoglobin mass testing convinced scientists.

Let me tell you about the first altitude training study carried out at the AIS because although we presented at conferences we never got around to publishing it internationally. My priority at that time, and one shared by colleague Dr Allan Hahn, was information for coaches rather than journal publications.

The first Australian altitude training controlled trial

It was 1994 and we wanted to know whether training at moderate altitude in the Australian Alps was of benefit to sea-level performance. I asked Shaun Creighton, an Australian Institute of Sport athlete and scholarship coach with Pat Clohessy at the time to help set this up. He made use of his many friends around the athletic world to invite a group of international runners to take part in one of the first, if not the first randomized controlled altitude training studies on elite athletes.

Acceptances were received from many highly respected distance runners, including a Moroccan contingent brought over by Said Aouita including, Brahim Boutayeb, Rachid El-Basir and Abdel Sahere; Englishmen Mark Rowland, Tom Buckner, Adrian Passey, Dave Buzza and Jon Brown;, and Americans Terence Herrington, Greg Whitely, Brad Hudson, and Danny Lopez. Our Australian contingent included internationals Shaun Creighton, Andrew Lloyd and some of the most promising 18 to 20 year-olds in the country. In all we had about 30 runners and divided them up into three venues.

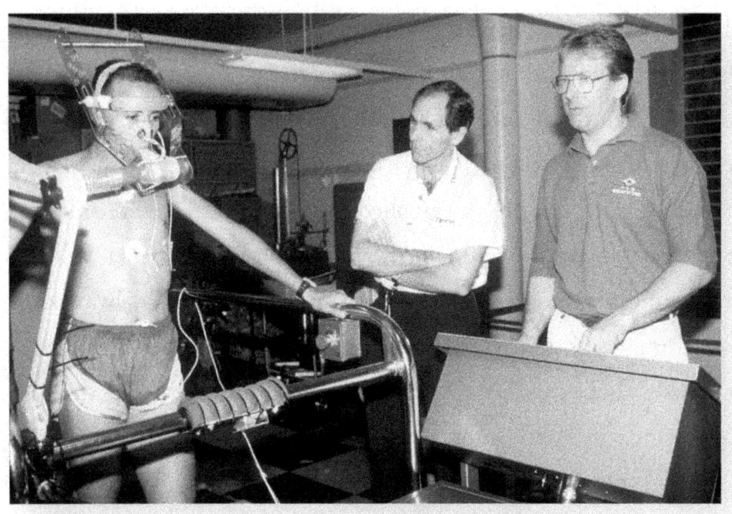

With Said Aouita at the AIS and physiologist Kenneth Graham.

Image: Australian Sports Commission

There were two altitude venues up in the Kosciusko Mountain ranges. Charlotte Pass is at around 1750m and the main runs are at 1600 to 2000m. Thredbo Village is at 1300m with the running around 1200 to 1500m. Our main study group was located at Charlotte Pass with which we matched a 'control' group right at sea-level in Sydney at Narrabeen, former site of the NSW Institute of Sport. The groups trained for three weeks, all with similar training programs and food plans prepared by AIS nutritionist Dr Louise Burke. Each group did one session on the track every week; the altitude group travelling either back to Canberra or doing a session on a track at Jindabyne, a town at the foot of the mountains at 1000m.

We investigated their performance three ways. Firstly by a 3km running time trial at sea-level (right by the sea near Bateman's Bay); secondly by a treadmill run to exhaustion during about 10 minutes of graded treadmill running where $\dot{V}O2max$ was measured as well; thirdly by an all-out anaerobic test on our big wide treadmill at 18 degrees elevation (as described in Chapter 6) that produced exhaustion in somewhere around 2 minutes. We also measured their blood haemoglobin mass and concentration.

All proceeded well, but not everything went exactly to schedule.

One day my wife and I were visiting the group at Charlotte Pass, and to my surprise, in the summer month of December in Australia, running was curtailed by a heavy snowfall and particularly nasty cold weather. And as we drove back down the mountain, my mobile phone signalled that I had received three messages. This was not unusual as we drove down the mountain into Perisher Valley, because there was no mobile phone reception at Charlotte Pass, and it always kicked in as we drove through Perisher. This time however, the news was astounding.

In remarkable contrast to the snow still falling around the car, it was 40 °C and windy in Sydney and fires were raging around the outskirts of the city. Although our control group of athletes at sea-level Narrabeen was not considered to be at risk, I was advised to get to Sydney straight away to assess the situation. So, in the one state, NSW, and on the same day, we had a snow blizzard and a bush fire!

When we got to Sydney, smoke had darkened the skies; skies which began to glow an eerie red as we crossed Harbour Bridge on our way out to Narrabeen. On arrival we looked toward the skies and listened for the radio reports. The fires were a long way off but a change of wind direction could whip a fiery fury with the potential to travel at surprising speed towards our athlete's residences. We were hiring out rooms from a local landlord and I asked him what he thought. He assured me that everything would be okay, and if the wind did change we should consider staying to help protect the accommodation. That comment sealed it for me. I had not brought international athletes here to fight fires! My response was immediate.

'Okay boys, pack your bags. We're out of here'. I'll give you 30 minutes!' I booked accommodation in the safety of the city. Within an hour and a half the group were checked in. Our Narrabeen landlord wasn't impressed, telling me there was no sense in panicking. I agreed, and told him that's why we were getting out of there.

No sooner had we got to our new accommodation, there was a report that the wind had changed unexpectedly, and heading straight toward the coast, to the Narrabeen residence. I was worried for the landlord and called his mobile. I got a short reply, '... can't talk, have to run.' The news the next day was that the athlete's accommodation block was now a smoking shell of blackened bricks. Fortunately, there were no casualties.

The blizzard and the raging fire put paid to the quality sessions that day but at least a training balance between the groups prevailed! Surprising for many, although probably unsurprising for distance runners, was that every runner, whether freezing in the mountains, or frying in the city got a run of some sort in that day. That's distance running mentality for you!

Anyway, we hardly missed a beat in terms of the training during the three weeks. The groups were highly competitive; each eager to show the other that their venue produced superior results, so testing was taken very seriously indeed. The altitude and sea-level athletes even took it upon themselves to have special racing shirts made up, and some close camaraderie developed within each group.

Following the final testing sessions, and after the athletes had departed, we set about the analysis. We looked at the pre- and post-intervention for the Charlotte Pass group first and were excited to find an average improvement of approximately 6 seconds in the time trial. In the lab it was even better. They had improved their average time on the all-out treadmill test about 6 percent, Physiological $\dot{V}$O2max was up 3 percent and when they ran at the submaximal speeds, their average heart rate and lactate levels were lower. Effects in the same direction, although not as decisive were obtained from the Thredbo group. We were very pleased. This altitude training certainly has something going for it. Athletes who were fit to start with had made some exceptional gains following just 3 weeks of their altitude camp at 1750m.

Then we looked at the sea-level group's results and we all came down from altitude with a thud.

Our Narrabeen sea-level group had improved just as much as the altitude group, very close to an average of 6 seconds in the 3km road circuit. And again similar to the altitude group, they improved their time to exhaustion on the treadmill by around 5 percent, although there wasn't any evidence of a change in their $\dot{V}$O2max. In other words, our trial had produced no evidence to support the premise that training up in the mountains for three weeks at around 1750m was of any additional benefit to training at sea-level.

This doesn't necessarily infer that training our moderate altitude regime wasn't effective, just that similar improvements can occur in a sea-level camp. The improvements may have occurred through different mechanisms, and if they complemented each other, perhaps training at altitude then at sea-level may produce better improvements than either method alone. This is the Eastern Bloc method, 3 weeks up and 3 weeks down before competing. But in our case there was no evidence of increased haemoglobin mass following the altitude exposure to support the notion that the small increase in V̇O2max was a real one, and not just a chance occurrence. In those days, though, our measures of haemoglobin mass by carbon monoxide rebreathing weren't as precise as they are now, and it's possible we might have missed a small increase.

But then again, let's keep an open mind. We might consider that an advantage of training at sea-level is its greater oxygen pressure, higher oxygen delivery to the muscle cell. Training consistently at, higher aerobic power, may in turn develop more powerful mitochondrial activity. There were other benefits of training at Narrabeen sea-level which may have helped the 'control' group. They appeared to enjoy their training experience more in this vibrant Sydney beachside suburb, with its variety of training venues and surfaces, including bush and coastal trails and beautiful sunny weather (except for the bush fire day!). Although the pristine surrounds of Charlotte Pass and the mountains had a lot going for it, living on the side of a mountain begins to wear a bit thin after a week or two, not helped by the often cool and blustery weather.

The 'group effect'

The over-riding conclusion we arrived at from this study was as follows. When athletes get together in a training camp situation, where there is friendly competition in training, ample time for rest and recovery, and where training and performance is carefully monitored, then this is likely to stimulate an improvement in fitness even in elite level athletes, no matter where you train. The 'group effect'.

The belief in altitude

The altitude-born athletes I've known have all been keen to train and live at altitude venues when abroad. For example, those in the USA choose venues such as Flagstaff (2300m) or Boulder (1600m). I remember world record holder Arturo Barrios going back to Mexico City to recharge his batteries after racing form had slipped away during an extended stint of racing and training at sea-level in Europe.

Clearly these altitude residents believe in altitude training. 'It is harder to run fast at altitude, so training there makes running at sea-level easier' seems to be their simple rationale. While this may not be a particularly scientific or convincing explanation of why altitude training can benefit sea-level performance it is a belief based on experience. Such belief, coupled with the belief that being born and raised at altitude has an additional advantage may in themselves contribute to better performances of runners born and raised at altitude.

The success of the Kenyans and Ethiopians, and the Moroccans who certainly used altitude training to prepare for races, led to most endurance coaches and their athletes supporting the concept of altitude training for better sea-level performance. Exceptional performances following altitude training by non-altitude raised athletes such as US prodigy Jim Ryan in the early 80s provided further support.

But uncertainty still prevailed, coaches remembering that Herb Elliott, Roger Bannister, John Landy, Ron Clarke, Peter Snell, John Walker, Seb Coe, Steve Ovett and Steve Cram, Derek Clayton, Rob de Castella and Steve Moneghetti (just to name a few runners whose whereabouts were known) may have trained in the mountains at various times in their careers, but certainly didn't train in thin air before some of their most historic performances. And a few years ago New Zealander Nick Willis Olympic 1500m bronze medallist and his coach Ron Warhurst made it clear that training at altitude was not part of their program. It's difficult to believe, but does remain possible, that the remarkable performances of these runners may have been even better had they utilized moderate altitudes.

Rob de Castella is an interesting case study. For several years he trained in the summers of the northern and southern hemispheres, in Boulder at 1600m, running up to around 1900m regularly and Canberra at 600m, spending only a few weeks of summer up in the mountains at Falls Creek, Victoria at 1600m. He ran at his very best following training at both venues, including winning the World Championship Marathon from an extended training period in Canberra, well before he had ever been to Boulder.

One argument sometimes levelled against altitude training is that it changes training regimes; that runners can't train with the same average speed at altitude during standard sessions. For similar speeds to be attained recovery intervals need to be increased or the distance of repetitions reduced. During altitude training, $\dot{V}O2max$, maximal heart rate and even maximal lactic acid concentration, don't reach the levels attained at sea-level. And if achieving the highest flux of oxygen through the working muscles and adaptations at the mitochondrial level are important parts of distance running training then sea level may have an advantage in this respect. This would suggest that the most successful altitude training regimes, especially for faster track events, might include periods of training and racing at sea-level before the major competition.

The best of both worlds

It's here that coaching science becomes important at the individual elite level, as optimal matching of altitude and sea-level training is likely to be related to both event and individual athlete; to get the 'best of both worlds.' Some well-organized runners might move camp from higher altitude venues to lower venues, making use of a range of atmospheric oxygen tensions.

Certainly that was what US physiologists Jim Stray-Gundersen and Ben Levine had in mind, when they combined both worlds into a training week. They investigated the effect of living at altitude but training at lower altitudes (in the AIS altitude training study in 1993 we thought similarly, the altitude group training once a week at 630m or 1000m). However, sleeping high and training low for some more intense sessions requires a suitable location and driving down a mountain for training every day, or every other day is not all that enjoyable on winding mountain roads. In any case, the effort seemed to be worth it, with evidence eventually emerging from the US research team that this regime improved haemoglobin mass and performance.

Faking altitude

An important upshot of the USA studies was that several countries without suitable high country training venues decided to simulate altitude training venues, called 'altitude houses'. These were rooms in which to sleep or train or both. Air pressure is not reduced as it is up in the mountains; instead the proportion (concentration) of oxygen in the air is lowered. This is achieved by passing the incoming air through an oxygen absorbent. A particular oxygen concentration at sea-level air pressure can be dialled up to coincide with the number of oxygen molecules in reduced air pressure at a given altitude in the mountains. For example an O2 concentration of 15 percent is equivalent to training at 2500m, which is about the altitude of Aspen. Simulating altitude not only simplified the procedure of 'sleeping high and training low' but provided the added advantage of allowing athletes to continue on with their normal daily routine as students or in the workforce.

The convenience of altitude training in a laboratory lent itself to investigation, but early studies of the effect of simulated altitude at the AIS were not all that convincing. Some minor improvements in performance were noted but nothing to write home about. With more trials and some good detective work, it was soon realized that a more potent dose had to be applied to elite athletes, maybe because their aerobic systems were already finely tuned. That extra dose came in the form of increasing the simulated altitude to 2800-3000m, together with longer exposures every day than provided only by sleep time. More than 12 hours a day seemed to be required. With more convincing evidence of a beneficial effect to endurance athletes, the small altitude chamber at the AIS was converted into a large multi-room apartment where athletes have their own bedrooms and comfortably spend extra time in normal ways, watching TV, reading, studying, and eating. It took a while but the much sought after evidence of a statistically significant increase in haemoglobin mass following simulated altitude exposure was finally demonstrated.

Are some athletes 'non-responders'?

Every time an altitude study is conducted there is individual variation in response, 'response' referring to making new red blood cells. Some athletes seem to respond more, some less and some not at all. Could it be that altitude training is of no additional benefit to some runners; that some athletes' haemopoeitic systems simply don't respond to reduced oxygen availability?

It's possible, but there are many factors with potential to impact upon an athlete's response to altitude on one occasion but not on another, such as current fitness, training histories, nutrition, previous altitude exposure, the training undertaken at altitude, age, injury or infection.

For example, prior to altitude training, an athlete's sea-level training may have already developed his or her haemoglobin mass to a point where any further increase is difficult to achieve or at least detect. Endurance training itself can itself lead to substantial haemoglobin mass increases at sea-level. An example was marathoner Michael Shelley who resumed training after a 4 week post marathon break. During the next 5 weeks of training at sea-level his haemoglobin mass increased 3 percent; as large an increase as we had ever seen in this athlete during any hypoxic exposure.

To determine whether an athlete is indeed a non-responder we need to investigate their response to repeated exposures, at the same time using a 'control' group of responders to demonstrate that positive responses were actually achievable in that situation. I haven't seen any solid evidence of this type, and remain open-minded, but based on recent experience I'm swayed towards believing that some athletes don't respond. Two of my Australian representative female marathon runners Lisa Weightman and Melanie Panayiotou failed to register any increase in haemoglobin mass on repeated exposures to hypoxic conditions.

Lisa spent 7 weeks and 9-10 hours per day in an altitude tent at the equivalent of 3000m on one occasion and on another occasion she was in Boulder, Colorado for about 4 weeks at around 1600m. With haemoglobin mass measured at the AIS in Australia and at the US Olympic Training Centre in Colorado Springs before and after each stint of hypoxic exposure there was absolutely no hint of any increase in in haemoglobin mass on either occasion. So both sleeping high and training low; and then sleeping high and training high had made no difference to Lisa's haemoglobin mass. To give you a better idea of the sorts of measures we got from Lisa, see Table 22-1.

Secondly Mel Panayiotou had two stints of 7 weeks and 9 or 10 hours a night in a hypoxic tent set at around 3000m. Like Lisa she registered no increase in haemoglobin mass, on either occasion.

It's natural to ask whether the tents were working correctly. They were; regular checks of the oxygen concentration confirmed that. Secondly, was the exposure long enough and intense enough to elicit a positive response? Yes it was, on each occasion the runners were accompanied in the tent by their partners, also athletes (Lisa's husband Lachlan, and Mel's partner Tom) who both recorded substantial (3-5 percent) increases in haemoglobin mass.

It was of course so annoying, to say the least, for Lisa and Mel not to respond twice in a row, while their partners had been measured with increased red cell production on each occasion.

But why? One obvious difference was that the partners were male, but over the years of altitude chamber observation at the AIS responses any differences in hypoxic response of males and females has not been obvious. Body size was another clear difference. Our female runners were both very small and light, less than 50kg, while the partners were about 20kg heavier, but there seems little connection between stature and response to hypoxia.

What about change in body weight during the hypoxic stint? On the first occasion, unlike her male 'control' Lisa lost a little weight, as did Mel, and it occurred to us that perhaps this slightly negative energy balance may have interfered with the erythropoiesis, but on the second occasion there was no loss of weight in either runner but again a lack of response. Diet quality is another factor to consider. Perhaps the diet of the females was a little more disciplined than their partners as it normally is in female runners, but in both cases, diet was sensible and varied, included iron supplementation of 100mg per day, and maintenance of general health was vindicated by their excellent race performances to follow exposure to both altitude per se or simulated altitude.

	Lisa Weightman			Lachlan McArthur		
	24/4	29/6	percent Change	24/4	29/6	percent Change
Haemoglobin mass (g/kg)	12.7	12.3	-3.8 percent	13.3	15.3	15.1 percent
Speed at $\dot{V}O_2$max (km/h)	18.0	18.4	2.5 percent	19.3	19.9	3.0 percent
Speed at lactate 4 mmol/L (km/h)	16.5	16.6	1.0 percent	18.0	18.9	5.0 percent
Max Test Time (min)	7.5	8.0	6.7 percent	6.0	7.0	16.7 percent
Body mass (kg)	45.0	43.1	-4.2 percent	67.2	64.1	-4.6 percent
$\dot{V}O_2$max (ml/kg/min)	70.5	70.2	-0.4 percent	68.4	69.8	2.0 percent
$\dot{V}O_2$max (L/min)	3.18	3.02	-5.0 percent	4.60	4.48	-2.6 percent
Heart Rate max (bpm)	180	177	-1.7 percent	181	183	1.1 percent
Max Lactate (mmol/L)	10.8	10.8	0.0 percent	8.3	9.6	15.7 percent
$\dot{V}O_2$ (ml/kg/min) @ 16km/h	61.2	60.1	-1.7 percent	53.4	55.8	4.4 percent
Heart Rate @ 16km/h	162	155	-4.3 percent	156	149	-4.8 percent
Lactate @ 16km/h	3.1	2.9	-6.5 percent	1.7	1.7	0.0 percent

Table 22-1: Blood and Treadmill performance for Lisa Weightman and Lachlan McArthur before and after 7 weeks of sleeping in the hypoxic tent

Then there is the training to consider, but it's difficult to point the finger at variation in training as the reason for the different responses, because all four athletes were training with high intensity and volume. Lachlan was Lisa's running training partner and Tom was a cyclist racing for a professional team, training intensively and with high volume every day.

Anecdotally, yes it seems we may have a case that some runners don't respond to hypoxia by making new red cells following a stint of hypoxia. But I'll be convinced only with a properly designed controlled trial.

Abandoning the tent

In marathoner Lisa Weightman's preparation for the World Championship marathon in Berlin she and her husband and training partner Lachlan slept in the tent for an average of 9 hours per day for 7 weeks. Physiologists at the AIS, Dr Laura Garvican and Dr Philo Saunders measured their haemoglobin mass and $\dot{V}O_2$max before and after the hypoxic tent exposure and VIS physiologist Danielle Stefano monitored Lisa's blood haemoglobin concentrations and hydration along the way. Training progressed as planned with no injuries, no illness, sleep was satisfactory and a sensible diet was accompanied by regular iron supplementation.

As shown in the accompanying table, Lisa's time to exhaustion with the standard treadmill protocol improved 30 seconds during the hypoxic tent exposure period, and there were reductions in Lisa's heart rate, blood lactate and oxygen consumption at submaximal running speed. However, her $\dot{V}O_2$max was unchanged. Training partner Lachlan also improved. His time to exhaustion on the treadmill improved by a minute and like Lisa this was accompanied by a reduction in submaximal heart rate and blood lactate, again with little change in $\dot{V}O_2$max.

As outlined in the previous section, the blood results took us by surprise. While Lachlan's haemoglobin mass had increased around 10 percent, Lisa's post-tent haemoglobin mass was slightly lower! With no improvement in haemoglobin mass or $\dot{V}O_2$max, we had no evidence of any positive tent effect for our marathoner. Her improved treadmill performance and improved responses at submaximal speeds were likely to have been achieved by training alone. In Lachlan's case his haemoglobin mass increased, but there was no corresponding increase in V̇O2max; so what was the physiological significance of his increase in haemoglobin?

On the basis of these results I had no hesitation in discontinuing the hypoxic sleeping from the Berlin World Champs campaign. This was a typical warm weather summer marathon, so over the next 6 weeks we concentrated on training in simulated warm conditions to combat Melbourne's cool winter climate. Lisa went on to run an excellent World Championships race, finishing 18th, a personal best on a very warm Berlin morning. Her heat acclimation process was likely to have been a contributing factor to her punching above her pre-race ranking on times.

A perfect place to train?

Most runners believe in altitude training. Naturally, these runners enjoy training in good weather, but it's possible that warm weather training might offer its own advantages apart from training comfort. Training in warm conditions increases plasma volume and reduces blood viscosity, so enhancing blood flow properties, and at the AIS in the 1990s we carried out and published a study which showed that performance of our elite Australian rowers was better when their blood viscosity was lower.

So the perfect place to live and train might be at moderate altitude of 1800-2800m in a moderate climate where temperatures during the day are consistently in the mid 20°s. Perhaps not by coincidence, these characteristics are close to those experienced along the Rift Valley running through Kenya into Ethiopia and in other eastern African countries renowned for their distance runners. Supplement warm moderate altitude training with periods of training and racing at close to sea-level then we may have the ideal way to maximize middle and long-distance running performance.

When even altitude doesn't provide enough

There have been reports of illicit drug taking by runners in many parts of the world, including the Africans. The thought of revered runners taking banned ergogenic substances is not a welcome one, so this section is brief.

Why, one might ask would any runner of great ability take this sort of risk? The answer is money. There are very large sums of money riding on race records, world records and places in big city marathons as well as championship races. And there is big competition between runners, even within some countries, let alone between. Cheating amongst managers, coaches, and athletes has a sordid history. For many it seems the only real deterrent is the risk of being caught; numerous athletes have been caught over the years and will continue to be caught. Unscrupulous managers, coaches, scientists and medicos continue to convince athletes that, 'if you do it our way, you won't be detected, and anyway, everybody else is doing it so you'd be silly not to ... '. The most obvious methods of cheating would include small sequential blood reinfusions or of erythropoetin (EPO) with plasma volume enhancement, urine sample substitutions with all sorts of deviant techniques. And let's face it, only an eternal optimist would assume that all drug detection authorities are not susceptible to turning a blind eye for a dollar. Corruption within the governments of some countries seems to be a way of life. And it wasn't all that long ago that performance enhancing drugs and methods were simply considered unethical rather than illegal and part of the 'all's fair in love, war and sport' of the Eastern bloc countries. Some habits are hard to break.

And let's not be coy about this, drug cheats aren't just limited to the also-rans desperately trying to make the grade. Drug cheats have been exposed at the pinnacle of world sport, especially in events relying on power output, aerobic or anaerobic. In distance running, athletes of African heritage set the standards and are hugely admired (as they are by the way in the sprints). The answer to the question as to whether there are any drug cheats among the champion Africans is exactly the same as the answer to the question of whether there any drug cheats in distance runners in general around the world. Perhaps that's being kind to the Africans, considering the Kenyan Government has never used in-training blood tests for the detection of the two most potent and infamous distance runners' ergogenic aids of all time, erythropoietin (EPO) and blood doping (extraction and re-infusion of the athlete's own blood to increase blood volume and haemoglobin mass). We see the huge rewards for these runners and their management teams and all we coaches can do is shake our head in disbelief that world track and field is run so haphazardly. Even if proper testing existed in countries such as Kenya and Ethiopia, cheats may still be a step ahead of drug testing regimes. Continued research and development of drug detective work is desperately needed. Only then will suspicions regarding the legitimacy of the world's best runners be resolved. Thoroughly appreciated are the efforts of my former colleagues at the AIS, Michael Ashenden and Rob Parisotto, whose tireless work with WADA (World Anti-doping Agency) in weeding out the cheats plays a vital role in the ongoing health and wellbeing of our sport.

Altitude training in Australia

During the mid-80s I wanted to explore altitude training with distance runners Andrew Lloyd and Carolyn Schuwalow as we worked toward their international careers. Like most distance coaches, sports scientists and endurance athletes around the world, we perceived altitude training as likely to provide an edge, but we were wrestling with the questions as to whether it was worth disrupting normal lifestyle where training was progressing well, and whether it was worth the expense of living away from home.

In Australia, we have the choice of two or three villages situated above 1500m. Our highest village is in NSW, Charlotte Pass Village at 1830m, and down the road a few kilometres there's Perisher Valley at around 1640–1700m. From Charlotte Pass there is a well-used track, not excessively steep, that takes us to the highest peak in Australia Mt Kosciuszko, 2228m. Then there is Falls Creek in Victoria, at 1540m is a bit on the low side, but provides some of Australia's best running trails at altitudes of 1600–1700m.

These villages are fine for a few weeks of a training camp atmosphere and a relaxed lifestyle, but for runners looking to reside at altitude, town living is by far preferable to life on the side of a mountain. In the USA, Boulder, Colorado and Flagstaff, Arizona have become second, or even first homes to elite distance runners from all parts of the world, including the Africans. They are at moderate altitude with all the social advantages of medium size town living, with variety of running terrain, including synthetic athletic tracks and plenty of flattish trails.

An early experience 'altitude must make a difference!'

I hadn't been up to mile-high Perisher, and Andrew Lloyd and Carolyn Schuwalow took the 2 hour drive up from the AIS in Canberra a few days before me. My first indication that life a mile up from the sea was a bit different arose when I phoned the two runners soon after they had arrived at Perisher to talk about training for the week. The phone rang for a couple of minutes and I was just about to hang up thinking I must have mis-dialled, when Andrew picked up the phone noticeably out of breath.

'Hey, Andrew, have you just got in from a run? I didn't think you were having a run this afternoon.'

'No, Dick, we didn't go for a run ... I was just making the bed, and ran up from downstairs to get the phone.'

I laughed. Here we have one of the best endurance athletes in Australia, and he's puffing after making the bed and running up a short flight of stairs. Well, at least it showed that the altitude was having some effect.

A week later I arrived in Perisher Valley to join my two runners. I was reasonably fit, and it was around 4 pm and they were heading out for an easy 8 km, having done a quality session earlier in the day. I looked around and thought how fortunate we were to have access to Cooma Hut, a beautiful lodge whose owners included some of Australia's best performed cross-country skiers, including Anthony Evans, the Australian Champion at the time whom I'd met at the AIS.

'Hang on a bit, I wouldn't mind a run' I said as I got my running shoes out of my bag.

Out we went and it was a bit chilly as we set off at a good clip, probably at a bit better than 4 min/km. After about 3 or 4 minutes I became very much aware that the air was indeed, a bit different. I was puffing at a pace I would normally handle easily. Andrew and Carolyn were chatting about how good it was up here, but I didn't take too much notice, as I was having difficulty hanging on to their recovery run pace. Then I developed a headache which amazed me as the last headache I'd experienced was right back in my Australian Rules football days after copping a whack behind the ear whilst playing football for the Preston Bullants.

I swallowed my pride and told the others to keep going. I'd walk back. Thankfully, I never experienced a headache up there again which was interesting, as during future visits to the mountains I had plenty of runs soon after arriving. It might be that I may not have run quite as quickly so soon in those later visits, but, there does seem to be a 'physiological memory' of altitude where we respond a bit quicker in successive visits, even if many months apart. A bit like the memory of our immune system improving its capacity to respond more rapidly to a previously encountered pathogen—the basis of vaccination.

The visitor and altitude training

It was about 1990, and I was busy in my AIS Physiology Department office with a grant application to submit by 5 pm that day. I had asked our receptionist to explain my situation and to hold all calls and to ask any unscheduled visitors if they'd mind dropping back the next day. No sooner had I made this request than a middle-aged gentleman unusually dressed in a well-worn grey suit and a collegiate tie of some description opened my door.

'Are you Dick Telford ... would you mind discussing a couple of questions I have on altitude training?'

He took a seat in a lounge chair opposite my desk. I was taken aback at this intrusion, as I knew full well that failure to get this application in could cost my department a valuable piece of research funding. And I was fully aware how keen these veteran (or masters) distance runners were, and how they loved to discuss their training. After all I was one.

So I thought it better to stand as my guest sat, as a suggestion that time was at a premium for me that afternoon.

'Let's take a top runner like Sebastian Coe for example' the gentleman in the grey suit continued in a pleasant English accent, 'if Coe was to do altitude training, what altitude you think he should train at? And how long do you think he should train there for, and then how long before racing should he return to sea-level?'

These questions intrigued me as they were precisely the questions we were trying to decipher for our own runners. But I had to get my grant application finished, and without going into too much detail, explained that I had no reason to doubt the regime undertaken by the Eastern Bloc countries of 3 or 4 weeks up then 3 weeks down before racing, but I did add that it all probably depended on the individual athlete, his event and his physiological response to training at altitude.

I was moving toward the door in thinly veiled demonstration that we'd better finish up, when in came Simon Doyle, a remarkably talented middle-distance scholarship holder at the AIS.

'Oh Dick, I see you've met Sir Roger.'

I sat down, lost for words, realising Sir Roger Bannister was in my office! I would have ditched that grant application for an opportunity to talk on with the great man. I would be the interviewer, not the other way round. But Sir Roger got up, 'Thanks for the brief chat Dick, I've a plane to catch so must be off'.

The next time I saw Sir Roger was a few years later. He placed a ribboned medal around my marathon runner Lisa Martin's neck after her second placing in the London Marathon. After the ceremony, he was surrounded by dignitaries and admirers. I'm sure he would have been too busy for a chat, so I didn't approach him ... We live and learn.

When I got it wrong again

It was 1995. David Evans and Julian Paynter were two talented young 5000m runners in the AIS squad and I was keen explore the purported benefits of 3 weeks of altitude training in Flagstaff, Arizona. The only problem was that for this particular trip we only had funding for 6 weeks.

Our accommodation next to a golf course in Flagstaff was ideal as we could run on the grass for all the recovery runs. Training went well. The sessions were varied, of good quality but well controlled at 2500m to ensure an uninterrupted 3 weeks of consistent work. We were careful not to overdo training during the quality sessions, bearing in mind that a period of racing in Europe was only a few weeks away. The quality of the track work was restricted as it normally is at altitude, with all interval sessions accompanied by longer recovery. The theory was that the altitude effect would more than compensate for the easier training. Julian did tell me he thought the recovery runs were a bit too quick but the boys seemed to be coping well enough.

Our limit of three weeks in Europe meant we didn't have the luxury of a stint of solid sea-level training to back up the altitude work. Taking this into account we eased back on the training intensity at Flagstaff in preparation for a couple of races 7-10 days after arrival in Europe. If they went well, then there might be some ongoing support from meet directors to stay on for more racing.

On arrival at sea-level in Europe, both Dave and Julian told me they didn't feel sharp at all on the track. I put this down to jet-lag but the change in altitude may also have had something to do with it. Just a few days after arriving, European based Australian manager Maurie Plant rang to tell us he'd been able to get the boys into a race sooner than we expected, 5 days after arriving. I wasn't enthused about this given the boys weren't feeling on top of things, but with the difficulties of getting into good races in Europe, we decided to have a go.

That race didn't go well, both boys running 5000m in a sluggish looking 14 minutes; all the more disappointing given that both had personal best times of close to 13:30. Adding to the disappointment, Dave came down with a virus, no doubt his immunity affected by the stresses of change of altitude, international travel, and now the stress of wondering whether Flagstaff training had done the trick. Dave's health didn't improve over the next three days and racing in the next week was out of the question, so we decided that returning to Australia was his most sensible option.

Julian's confidence needed a boost if he was to turn that 5km time around in a week or so. On reviewing the training we had done in Flagstaff the only thing we didn't fit in over the last two weeks was his long run; we had concentrated more on pre-competition race-pace work. With the next race anticipated to be 6 days away, I set him a medium long run of an hour and a half, running at a comfortable pace. Not long after Julian had returned from his run, Maurie called to tell us that Julian had been accepted into the Stockholm Grand Prix. I should have been delighted, but we were preparing for a lower key race in a week and that long run two days before wasn't the best way to prepare for a big meet 5km. Again, we had got this opportunity out of the blue; Maurie had obviously worked hard to get that entry; so we decided again to take advantage of the opportunity, hoping that the previous race and a few days had turned Julian around, and that the long run had not left any residual tiredness.

Unfortunately even the magic of the Stockholm stadium didn't make any difference and Julian, despite a strong-minded effort to stay as long as he could at 13'30" pace, trailed off in the latter laps to come in with no zip in his legs in around 14 minutes again. We were due to leave in 5 days, and with no form on the board after two chances, Julian and I went home with our tails between our legs.

The magic of altitude hadn't worked, the training regime we adopted in the hypoxic conditions had not provided sufficient benefit, if any, to compensate for the stress of travel, restricted budget and time away, and the reduction in training quality. In retrospect we would have been far better off training in Australia to achieve the highest level of fitness possible and going straight to Europe, racing a couple of lower key races while getting over jet-lag and then having a real crack at some fast times. I wondered whether the recovery runs between the quality efforts at Flagstaff might have been too taxing. My first trip overseas to an altitude venue as a coach had not been a success. I felt for my two runners who had deserved success. But as I've not stopped doing in this game, again I lived and learned.

PS. Interestingly, a decade later, I set marathon runner Lisa Weightman a 2 hour run two days before she was to run the Gold Coast 10km as just a steady training run. However, on lining up for what was supposed to be a steady training run, she met some unexpected opposition from a couple of triathletes who showed no fear or respect for Lisa in going out hard to take an early and rather substantial lead. Weightman's competitive juices were stimulated. In contrast to the Julian Paynter experience she surprised everyone by running superbly in a personal best time. But then again, there was no expectation, no stress, no long travel and no altitude training; and she was a marathon runner.

Chapter 23
Ultramarathons and veteran runners

'You're entirely bonkers. But I'll tell you a secret. All the best people are.'

Lewis Carroll

A runner can be justifiably proud of averaging 65km a week for 9 months; ultra-marathoners have been known to average 65km a day.

Ultramarathoners are often older, more experienced runners, perhaps reflecting enhanced anatomical or psychological endurance. It might also reflect an undying desire for personal achievement and athletic recognition, something no longer within reach in shorter events. Perhaps the challenges of time and distance incomprehensible to youth require the mindset of a veteran athlete seeking the meaning of life at the halfway mark.

I've known a number of champion ultra-distance runners over the years, and still find it difficult to comprehend firstly what drives these characters and secondly how the hell they do it. There are those runners who compete in 100km races, and running more than twice as far as Pheidippides without stopping is certainly quite a feat in itself. Then there are the extremists who treat a 100km day like any other day at the office; they refuel, sleep and do it again the next day, then do it again, and again, and again.

Discovering ultra talent

I was in Frankston shivering a bit from a mix of morning chill and nerves at the start of my first marathon, the Big M Melbourne marathon of 1978. Running a marathon for the first time is a daunting experience to which many a reader will attest. But being shoulder to shoulder with a mob of similarly uncertain characters was of some comfort, although nervous chatter accompanied by nervous smiles and nervous movements aren't all that reassuring.

The bloke next to me looked a bit different. He was about 50 I reckoned; and conspicuous. His faded grey suit pants were a bit too short to be stylish but I liked the nice cuffed hems; the same style I remember my high school PE teacher used to wear every day. I looked down to make sure the laces of my state-of-the-art three-week old pair of well-padded running shoes were still tied up properly. I couldn't help notice the off-white circa two year-old Dunlop Volleys (the ones with a touch of green on the side) and grey socks under the little bit too short strides of my distinguished fellow marathoner. One thing's for sure, the chap was thoroughly enjoying the excitement of the start … I remember thinking how nice it would be if he could get 5km up the road with the pack.

A politician spoke for 5 minutes, about 4 min 50 seconds too long, and the gun cracked. The wave rippled down towards us and my section moved off. We'd travelled about a mile when to my amazement my suited running companion moved up to my side. He was clearly enjoying himself, and the spectators were enjoying him. They cheered and he waved with a big grin. I couldn't resist.

'Are you running the full marathon? Are you trying to get right into the Town Hall?'

'Yeah mate, no worries' was the gravelly reply.

'I'd love a bit of your confidence' I replied 'where does that come from when we've got 25 miles to go?'

'Well, mate, let me tell you', he said with a grin I'll never forget but did see many years later.

'I'll make it for sure, no worries mate. Last night my mate was supposed to pick me up from my motel near the end of the marathon in Melbourne and drive me down here to Frankston. He couldn't make it, so I had to run down ... got it done easy. So I reckon running back won't be a problem.'

'Are you having me on?'

'No, mate' he smiled. See you at the Town Hall'.

I laughed and told him he might have to look for a longer race next time.

The next time I saw this chap's easily recognized craggy face was some 4 years later. His picture was all over the newspapers as he was leading the inaugural Melbourne to Sydney ultra-marathon. Cliff Young was the name all over the paper, a potato farmer from Colac in the Western District of Victoria. It's the stuff of legends that he went on to win that race.

I was to boast about that interchange with Cliff some 15 years later, tongue in cheek, telling my colleagues tasked with talent identification at the Australian Institute of Sport that I may have trumped them. After all, I did tell Cliff that day at the Melbourne Marathon that the marathon might be too short a run for him!

As fate and good fortune would have it, I was to meet him again, in my lab at the AIS in Canberra.

Who needs sports science?

Cliff became a celebrity in 1982 when he won that inaugural 875km Melbourne to Sydney race in such grand style. For the potato farmer from Colac, money was never an issue. Both helping others and the thrill of the race had higher priority than a fist full of dollars. Cliff reckoned that with all the training and the huge efforts of his competitors, they deserved to share his prize-money.

'I didn't run any faster than they did' he was to tell me later 'I just slept less'.

This was typical of the laconic and self-deprecating humour of a Cliff Young interchange. As one who'd never sought riches and lived and loved a simple bucolic life, his winnings must have represented a windfall. Nevertheless, 'Cliffy' as he became affectionately known around the country had no hesitation whatsoever in distributing the winner's bounty among his competitors, and in so doing captured the heart of the nation. He epitomised the Australian sporting hero, gifted, gutsy, unassuming, generous, and all at the age of 61.

So here were Cliff and I meeting up again in 1982, four years after our fleeting meeting out of Frankston, 42.195km from the Melbourne Town Hall. This time we were at the AIS where Cliff was the focus of attention of a television documentary. My role was to assess Cliff physiologically to 'discover' what made him tick.

The TV cameras were all set. I asked Cliff to get up onto the treadmill. It was a big unit with a big step up onto the belt. Cliff posed me a question we all thought rather curious at the time, but we sort of expected curious questions from this man.

'Why can't I just run on the floor, Dick?'

'Cliff' I replied 'We are going to measure the power of your engine and to do that you need to breathe through this valve, and most importantly you have to run at different speeds, not just run on the spot on the floor. That's why you have to get up on the treadmill'.

I can still remember the quizzical look on Cliff's face.

'Well ok Dick, you're the boss, but I still reckon it'd be better running down here on the floor'.

Up he hopped onto the treadmill, and to measure his V̇O2max, we fitted him with the respiratory valve and its associated headgear. Cliff for once was speechless. He had no option.

Our technician signalled that all was ready to begin the treadmill running test. Cliffy's eyes were as big as his Colac cows, glancing nervously sideways from under the head gear.

'Ok, Graham, let's go' and our technician pressed the big red button that started the belt rolling, slowly at first to get Cliff walking then jogging.

Cliff looked down to me and the TV crew in amazement as the treadmill mat started rolling. He started the obligatory walking then jogging as the belt gathered a little speed. Looking down at the moving treadmill mat, he loosened the valve a little and muttered, much to the delight of his laboratory audience, 'This's a bloody good idea Dick!'

Clearly, a treadmill with a moving mat had not featured in Cliff's life on the farm. Who said champions need sports science?

The Cliff Young guide to winning

Cliff survived the laboratory test, efficiency of the 'Cliffy shuffle' showing up well and his $\dot{V}$O2max of just over 50ml/kg/min was pretty damn good for a 61 year-old. He certainly didn't train to increase his aerobic power, never raising a puff in training or racing, and at the speed he ran all day and half the night in his ultras he cruised at around half that power.

That night, my wife Sue and two children Nerilee and Rohan, aged 9 and 6 at the time, were really looking forward to having dinner with Cliff. We discovered the deceptive wisdom of his humour; his broad Aussie bush accent and disregard of conventional English grammar tended to disguise the wisdom of his words. The kids loved the little drawings of the running man with the happy face on the card he had specially prepared for them.

I was intrigued as to how a chap his age was able to run for hours upon hours day after day. Sure there was that famous, efficient Cliffy Young shuffle, but to keep that going all day and most of the night is remarkable to say the least. If I asked my athletes, even my marathoners, to get out each day for more than 2 hours for a few days in succession, I would be inviting injury, even mutiny.

'How do you manage to stay in one piece with all this time on the road Cliff? Don't you suffer from any injuries?'

'Well, Dick, as a matter of fact I did suffer an injury in that Melbourne to Sydney race. I fell over on that bloody shoulder of mine. Don't really count that as a running injury though because I first hurt it quite a while back ... Yeah, 50 years ago about, I fell out of a pine tree and broke my collar bone. I didn't tell Dad because my sister had fallen out of the same tree, and Dad told us not to climb that tree again. So I didn't tell 'em. After about three weeks, I had to because it just got too bloody sore. At least with that extra time up my sleeve, I didn't get into as much trouble.'

That recollection tells us something about the Cliff Young character. Along with his efficiency and robust chassis, he could ignore pain and discomfort. But there was one more human trait he was able to overcome to his racing advantage. Sleep.

Rather than the speed at which he moved, Cliff Young's ability to go without sleep was a key factor in that Melbourne to Sydney triumph; an uncanny ability to continue on running, day and night, with only a catnap here and there.

'Just how is it possible to stay awake for a start, let alone continue running?' I asked. 'And what do you think about as you churn out these hours on the road?'

'Nothing much, Dick' was the now expected simple and straightforward answer 'I just keep concentrating on where I'm going ... Hurt my hip 30 years ago chasing a couple of stray cows, not looking where I was going and put my bloody foot in a rabbit hole. Not going to let that sort of thing happened again, all sorts of holes on the side of that bloody highway. Worse than the farm.'

And Cliff had another simple explanation for his ability to keep on going like that proverbial TV battery commercial.

'I didn't want to sleep. Bad dreams came when I tried, haunted by the sound of footsteps of the other runners!'

That told us something else about the real Cliffy Young character. Underneath the laid back happy-go-lucky potato farmer exterior was a man who really wanted to win, one who was well aware of his limitations and was prepared to do what was required to overcome them.

Time had ticked away, and we were finishing up dinner. There was one banana crème dessert left on the table. Cliff had really enjoyed his dinner but a man who runs 100km in a day has to make sure the tank is refuelled properly every night.

'Anyone want this?' he asked, his already well-employed dessert spoon directed at the lonely dessert. Without waiting too long for an answer, with a 'Oh well, I'd better do the right thing by the cook', that banana crème was no longer lonely.

I noticed a breakfast menu on the next table. I asked Cliff if he wanted breakfast in his room. 'That'd be nice' he said 'I'll be out for a run around 5, and back around 7 ... have to leave for the airport about 9. Dick, this light's not that good, would you mind filling the menu out for me?'

'No worries Cliff, they've got individual packets of Corn Flakes, Sustain, Weetbix, toast and vegemite or honey and fruit compote. What would you like?'

'Yeah, that's fine, what you read out'll do' he said with that Cliff Young look in his eye, 'and can you ask them to throw in a couple of eggs on toast and a cuppa please? No milk with the tea, too fattening. '

I ticked all the boxes, and gave it to the night porter, who took it and casually looked at the all the ticked boxes, then looked up at me again. 'Don't worry it's not a mistake' I explained 'This is the guy who won the Melbourne to Sydney footrace and he's got a real big fuel tank!'

My family and I really enjoyed that dinner with Cliff.

Pat Farmer–mind boggling

Over 9 months, 65km a week is good; 65km a day is difficult to comprehend.

Sue and I live only a few dropkicks from Parliament House. We're so close, that when Parliament is sitting, we can see a shimmer of hot air just above the big flag, even in the winter. It's around 10.30 pm and I hear a knock on the door. Pat Farmer MP has dropped over after a big day in the House in his role as Parliamentary Secretary to the Minister for Education, Science and Training. We regularly discussed politics over a late night cup of tea, sometimes over dinner, but mainly we discussed ways to improve the health of Australian kids and quality of life of older Australians. And of course, distance running.

A year or so post his politicking days, Pat rings to tell me about a run he has in mind.

'I'm going to run from Pole to Pole, Dick. I need to average 65 kilometres a day for nine months and 40 kilometres a day when I'm on ice and snow. I reckon I can raise a couple of million dollars for Red Cross if I get things right'.

Pat loves to run long and hard, in fact ridiculously long and dangerously hard, and he loves to help people in need. With this run he had all that covered.

And run Pole to Pole he did. He did average the 65 kilometres a day, and ran up to 100 kilometres on some days, other around 30km a day pulling a sled across the ice. This type of assignment is extreme, and risky.

'I have to admit there was one stage I wasn't sure I would pull through'. Pat wasn't just talking about whether he would finish or not, but whether he would actually survive. It's hard to imagine, but this Pole to Pole venture nearly cost Pat's family and friends his life, all for the sake of a run.

But of course this wasn't just a run, just as climbing Everest wasn't just a climb. Pat was hell-bent on achieving something no man had done before; it was the kind of super-human challenge that extreme sports people seek.

As Pat spoke to me about his intentions, I thought about my two current Olympic marathoners, Lisa Weightman and Michael Shelley. Setting that sort of distance for even one day would provoke an unprintable response from Michael and even Lisa would have serious thoughts about my state of mind! Now imagine Pat repeating this feat every day for 10 months and 13 days, except when pulling a sled across the ice in temperatures as low as -40°. His diarized published account of his epic journey, *Pole to Pole*, has our best marathoners shaking their heads in disbelief.

Marathons are mere sprints in comparison with extreme ultra-marathons, and the specific fitness requirements vary accordingly. The elite marathon runner has a big engine compared to chassis weight, yet has to be fuel efficient and develop a big fuel tank.

It's different for the ultra-marathon runner. Engine size assumes less importance as the lower running speed places a correspondingly lower demand on power output.

And while efficiency is important to the extreme ultra-marathoner, it's in a different way to the marathoner. Unlike the elite marathoner, if fuel is running a bit low the extreme ultra-marathoner can re-fuel properly at pit-stops or even on the run. Mechanical efficiency is the key to ultramarathon performance, with emphasis on 'mechanical,' referring to reliability of the engine and chassis rather than fuel economy. The ultra-runner has to back up long distances day after day, and move in a way such that 100,000 ground reaction shock waves each day are absorbed without mishap. Stress to joints, bones, and muscles, immune and endocrine systems is not just imposed by the repetition of the physical exercise but by the harshness of the environment. In Farmer's case the temperature of his running environment that ranged from a cool –40°C to warm +40°C!

And resilience above the shoulders is just as important as below. The Central Governor Model of fatigue has it that the brain will prevent the body from self-destruction by sending signals to the muscles that turn them off, which we sense as 'fatigue'. Should this view of fatigue prove to be true, a hypothesis to follow might be that the extreme ultra-marathoner is able to down-regulate this central protective mechanism which would be downright dangerous.

'The fat padding on the soles of my feet is depleted and it is just skin and bones hitting the tarmac. Any strength that I do have is coming from my heart not my legs. This whole journey is about will-power, perseverance, stubbornness and will-power, none of which you can measure in a laboratory' (Pat Farmer, *Pole to Pole*. One man, 20 million steps).

Pat might not have been measuring 'will-power, perseverance, stubbornness and will-power' with the tools of a physiologist or pathologist, but he did so through his diarized reports of his body and mind responses. This is qualitative research at its finest and his laboratory was spread over half the circumference of the Earth.

But he did provide us with some numbers. Big ones, such as the 20 million steps and not so big ones like 10, the number of kilograms that Farmer lost, starting at the North Pole at 68 kg. Some might view this as a large reduction in body muscle and fat, but in reality it was a remarkably small reduction for a man who had run the equivalent of a couple of marathons nearly every day for close to a year. To have dropped only 10 kg during a period of unimaginable physical and psychological stress is testimony to the Farmer team, and brother Bernie's organizational capacity in pulling off this amazing accomplishment.

Pat Farmer and Cliff Young demonstrate to us all that passing what is generally considered the prime of life need not dampen the desire or the physical and psychological strength to carry out feats of endurance at the upper limits of human capability.

Racing against time

I'm hoping this little piece of my own late-coming and limited running career isn't interpreted as self-indulgence, but instead as a modicum of motivation to anyone suspecting they might be over the hill when that magic number of 40 is approaching.

I ran seven marathons and didn't debut until until my 34th year on the planet, following a football and cricket background. I suppose I was always of better than average fitness through my football career. There was good reason for this. I was one of the little guys on the paddock and the only way I could get a kick was by running into an unoccupied space and hoping someone would kick it to me. This worked pretty well, especially in the last half when my opponents got sick and tired of running around after me. In those days, we all stayed on the field for the whole game, none of this soft stuff we see nowadays where players are 'subbed' off the ground for a rest when you start to puff a bit! So I was used to running a lot, even on the footy field and more often than not, just like a long-distance runner, out by myself!

My maiden marathon was the 1978 Melbourne City marathon, known as the Big M marathon in those days, and it remains my most memorable. It took me 3hr11' minutes, the slowest of the seven I was to run. My last marathon was in Canberra 5 years later and my best one at 2hr27' (forget the seconds, I do) but I often do things in groups of 7, and it was time to move on.

At 38, I realized that in dedicating my youthful fitness to Australian Rules football and cricket, I had very limited experience of what it was like to train specifically for running. I 'd had a good taste of marathon training, luckily training with (on the recovery runs) with Rob de Castella and Pat Clohessy's elite group at the AIS, but my feeling for middle-distance training was lacking. In coaching or consulting as a physiologist to these athletes in these distances, I wanted to know exactly what it felt like to train and race in intensively 'lactic' conditions; a huge turnaround from the marathon, where almost all my training was geared toward the opposite – training to exclude the lactic system and rarely trying to running fast.

That I was approaching 40 was not coincidental as I had an eye on the 1500m event in the Veterans (Masters) athletics scene. I knew a few runners who competed nationally and internationally in Veterans events and age certainly hadn't dampened their enthusiasm. It was about time I put my foot on the start line at the track with these chaps. Already in the marathon, I had had some ding-dong battles with competitors in the 35-39 age bracket but I didn't rate that as veteran class. After all, Carlos Lopes was 37 when he won Olympic marathon gold in Atlanta, and Priscilla Welsh was 2nd in the London Marathon in 2hr26'51" in her 43rd year!

I planned out a new training program to regain a bit of the kind of speed I vaguely remembered possessing on the football field. Running plenty of miles in my marathon build-up with very limited track work, along with fartlek type repetitions at not much faster than 5km or 10km pace at best, I found myself struggling to run 200m in 32 seconds and 400m in 66 seconds. Marathon training specificity had certainly done its best to convince my 'fast twitch' fibers that they should be helping out more in the aerobic side of things. At least I had trained up for some 10km fun runs along the way, and my last *Canberra Times* 10km run of 31'46" on a not so flat course wasn't too bad. But I was far too pedestrian to compete in the M40 1500m where they are running 4:05 at the Nationals. I struggled to run one lap at this pace.

The question was 'Can I get faster as I get older?' I looked forward to finding out.

Building into that summer I introduced some 200m, 300m and 400m reps to try to regain some feeling of fluency at around anticipated race speed. I reduced the length of the long Sunday run to about 20–25km and cut back on my weekly volume to around 100 km. I seemed to be getting more comfortable at faster speeds, and was moderately encouraged that at 39 the anaerobic power of my youth was not totally lost. I then introduced some longer speedier work over 600m and 800m to develop better tolerance of that lactic feeling of which I was beginning to becoming more aware as my speed improved. Soon came the summer season and time to test myself out.

I was nervous lining up with a pair of spikes in a race over 3 ¾ laps. Ridiculous really—why would I be nervous? No-one expected me to run fast; I didn't expect to run fast, and who cares anyway? Well, I cared, I suppose. I learnt that even approaching so-called middle age, competition nerves don't age and fade away. The very thought of an all-out effort to utter exhaustion, even in a race as short as 4 or 5 minutes, was stirring up the 'fight-or-flight' response.

As I stood on that curved start line, a question went through my mind. 'Why am I standing here with a churning stomach when I could be home watching the cricket?' A very good question indeed, and as it turned out I was to ask it of myself many a time over the next four years of Veteran class middle-distance running. But we humans have relatively short-term pain memories, even after events more painful than half of us will ever know; but most woman do. Perhaps it's the post-race psychological high and intense satisfaction of going through the ringer but still doing our best that not only blurs both pre-race emotional distress as well as post-race lactic distress. In any case, on completing the warm down run, I was always eager to conjure up how I was going to run faster next time. I don't think I'm on my own on this count.

In that first year I ran a 1500m in 4:11 early in the season and got down to 4:07 by the end of the season. My 800m time started at 2:09 and was 2:05 at the end of summer. As that season progressed I could feel my marathon-modified muscle fibers rediscovering their true identity and recovering a bit of contractile speed.

In the following winter and a year older my track work continued to improve and come summer the races followed suit. By the end of that next season I had a 4:03 1500m and a 2:02 800m under my belt. The thought of getting older but getting faster and running PBs was a source of motivation unavailable to my close competition in the 40+ age group who had been athletes for decades and running a PB was a distant memory.

In the next year, my 43rd, I was pleased that adaptation to my faster training kicked in once again. For the 1500m and 800m races I ran spot-on 4' and 2' and my form was good enough to win the National 1500m title in Adelaide.

When would a progression of age beat a progression of training? Motivation wasn't a problem. There was the thought of another PB against the tide of time. There was the lure of the sub 4' 1500m and sub-2' 800m. There was the terrific competition from two local Canberra runners John Bell and Garry Hand in the

M40 bracket. Finally the World Masters Track and Field Championships were to be held in Melbourne that coming year which seemed like a fitting way to finish off a mid-life middle-distance career (I nearly wrote 'crisis').

The World Masters Track and Field Championship would be my last serious race. Furthermore, with the personal learning experience of racing middle-distance, there comes a time where that kind of personal endeavour compromises the energy and attention required for my work with young athletes at the AIS. And there is the consideration of just how long could, or should a fellow push himself to the limits of lactic exhaustion time and again?

To make things even a bit more challenging at the upcoming Masters World Track and Field Champs, I arrived back from conference in India just a few days before the first heat of the M40, 1500m. Apart from a bit of usual 'Delhi belly' all was fine. I flew straight to Melbourne and headed down the Tullamarine Freeway to my usual little Melbourne motel haunt, the Albany, close to my long-time favourite Royal Botanic Gardens, and a short jog from Olympic Park.

Given my late entrance to the scene, I had run a PB in the last race I ever ran over each of the 800m, 5km, 10km, 'City to Surf' 14km, half-marathon (I only ran one) and the marathon. Now this was not only my last 1500m it was my very last race. It turned out well. I was equal third with fellow Australian Tony Murray as it turned out, in a PB of 3'57' something.

That completed the suite. That's enough I thought. I never ran another race. At least physically.

Veterans, as competitive as ever and even feistier

I was at the weekly cross-country run as part of the ACT Veterans Athletic Club to launch Jack Pennington OAM's book *The Evolution of Veteran Athletics 1966-1981*. About 100 veteran runners had gathered at the aptly named Horse Paddock's Rd after racing around the foot of the not so aptly named Mount Taylor, one of the many of what I'd call 'hills' around the ACT. I guess Taylor's Hill just didn't have that ring of lofty importance commensurate with national, capital status..

I love the spirit among the veteran runners. It's 25 years since I competed in the Vets (40+ years) scene, which in itself constitutes a bit of a worry, but the atmosphere hasn't changed. I look around and see many faces I used to see week in week out back in 80s, and, although those faces are now more clearly defined by lines radiating in a variety of interesting directions, it is obvious that physical activity has agreed with this group. They are lean, fit and loving life.

The winners names are read out and they are presented with their medals in front of an attentive and appreciative group. Whenever the Veteran cross-country runners get together stories are exchanged, probably not for the first time, and probably nicely embellished with age. This gathering was no exception. Jack Pennington, a veteran's veteran and a very successful local coach in his own right, loves to tell Percy Cerutty and Arthur Lydiard stories and I'm all ears.

I've no doubt that veteran athletes are as feisty and competitive as in their younger days; maybe even feistier and more competitive. I experienced a bit of this some months before this book launch at the foot of Mt Taylor when I was asked to speak at the ACT Veterans Athletic Association Annual General Meeting. The president was introducing me to the gathering when a voice from near the back boomed 'Point of order! The invitation for Dick Telford to speak here contravenes AGM policy; the AGM has the specific purpose of dealing with administrative affairs.'

The president listened to the point of order, turned to me with a part puzzled part embarrassed kind of expression, thought for a minute, then turned to his audience.

'I put the motion that invited speaker Dick Telford be permitted to speak at this AGM', 'Those in favour?' I didn't dare look around but heard a rustling of a sea of hands rising round the room. 'Those against?' I didn't look around then either but there had to be at least one.

'Thank you' said the president 'I now welcome Professor Telford to the podium.'

I half-expected one or two to get up and leave, but they didn't. Afterwards a couple of people came over. 'Gee that was a bit embarrassing, but don't worry about it Dick. That guy was a thrower and he's never liked distance runners!'

About a year later I was invited to share the podium with my long term good friend and academic colleague, statistician Professor Ross Cunningham to speak at another AGM; this time that of the Australian Statisticians Society (ACT branch). I suspect no one realized the significance of my deep inhalation as I was introduced, nor the exhalation of relief when no point of order emerged from up the back.

Running out of sight

Thirty-nine year-old Roy Daniel and I were on an easy run through the Left Bank of Paris during his lead-up to the biggest marathon of his life, in Athens 2004, where he would join his coach, former AIS Scholarship Coach, Robbie Bolton. Just for fun, we had confined our conversation to French, but for me, unlike Roy, each slowly produced sentence required a concentrated effort. So much so that I made an error I will never forget.

Running ahead of Roy, I spotted a picturesque little park across a small roadway and asked Roy (in slow Australian French) to follow me. But with my intense focus on the French grammar I completely forgot to mention the small step we had to negotiate. You see ... but Roy couldn't. Roy went down with a thud as his foot caught the curb.

Roy is a partially-sighted runner and was on his way to the Athens Paralympics. Fortunately his remarkable physical and mental resilience showed through. He just picked himself up, dusted himself down and on we went. I was so relieved no real damage was done, and dismayed with my loss of concentration. Any minor injury could have undone six months of preparation. It didn't, though, and Roy went on to win silver.

Running with Yannis Kouros, Shaun Creighton and local runner John Gilbert while on a visit to the AIS.

Chapter 24
Children and running

Children yet, the tale to hear
Eager eye and willing ear

Lewis Carroll

Physical activity is vital to a child's physical and mental development. It's also the key to producing champions in later life.

Generally speaking

There are three main considerations when it comes to physical activity for children: Health, happiness and sporting aspiration.

On consideration of health and happiness, there is the undoubted positive aspect but also a very real negative aspect. On the positive side, there is plenty of evidence, including that of the Australian Lifestyle of our Kids (LOOK) longitudinal study in Australian children, to show us that a child needs to use his or her muscles regularly and vigorously for healthy growth and development. And that physical activity and being fit leads to a child feeling happier.

In specific terms the LOOK study demonstrated that children who are insufficiently active during primary school are more likely to proceed into secondary school with undesirably elevated insulin resistance (a precursor to Type 2 diabetes), and higher cholesterol (a risk factor for cardiovascular disease). The more sedentary a child, the greater the likelihood of being overweight or obese, and that is often accompanied by lower self-confidence and lower academic achievement. That should be a huge incentive for policy makers, teachers, coaches and parents to create an environment where kids are taught how to move and are given the opportunity and incentives to move. The word is out, only time will tell now whether the forces of common sense in schools and the community outweigh the sendenterophilic forces of modern technology.

Early specialisation

Nowadays children are commonly introduced into sporting squads which involve training for many hours a day at very young ages. In such circumstances, parents and coaches are no longer just thinking about the important role physical activity plays in health and general development. Instead they are thinking about the possibility of their child becoming a champion. The assumption is that early specialisation of training and practice from a young age is necessary to achieve elite status in adulthood or even earlier. Such an assumption is, unfortunately, a reasonable one in many sports; swimming and gymnastics for example require years of training at early ages to develop elite level motor skills and specific fitness.

I slotted in that 'unfortunately' as the cons of a radically changed lifestyle may outweigh the pros. It's typical for a targeted 8 year-old to spend 12 hours a week training for gymnastics here in Australia; and progress to 24 hours a week by the age of 10. Why? Because the countries who dominate the world scene are doing it, and it's reasoned, if we want to do well in the Olympics we have to start early too. Hard to argue with that, but in 2004 Chinese 4 year-olds were undertaking gymnastics training for 12 hours week and who knows what they're doing now.

Most would agree that the sensible approach is for children to engage in a variety of active sports and pursuits and to specialize in a chosen sport, if that is their wish, in their mid-teens. But then again my preference is based more on developing a happy and well balanced child, teenager and young adult, not on producing world champions. Maybe I'm biased, because smart parents and smart coaches of runners can get the best of both worlds. Prospective champion runners don't have to specialize early. In fact it's counterproductive and an overuse injury risk for children to train for running for even a quarter of the time required of swimmers and gymnasts as they seek elite status.

To introduce and encourage children to train for any sport several hours every day in their primary school years is a big decision; a lifestyle changer for both child and parent. But we should be careful about being judgmental on this issue. Serious young athletes lead a disciplined life of before or after-school training and vital aspects of happy healthy growth and development requires careful parental attention to nutrition, homework, sleep, as well as engagement in non-active recreation and social interaction. Given the problems of modern society, with insufficient physical activity, high incidences of obesity, addiction to screen-gazing and recreational drugs, there is a very good argument for the disciplined lifestyle required of early specialisation, especially in the teenage years. The added value of the team-work and close relationship that develops between parents and a child who trains for many hours a week is sadly lacking in many, if not most families these days.

Decisions we make as parents are based on individual circumstances, our family traditions and culture, and there is no right or wrong way. If we believe our child has special aptitude for a particular sport that requires early specialisation, then sensible, sensitive parenthood is crucial to ensuring the child does embrace and enjoy the challenges of working toward excellence at an early age. Sure, the 'pushy parent' syndrome does exist, but I've also heard children explain how much they love to practise the piano for hours each day, practise ballet and train for swimming and gymnastics (one girl telling me how much she enjoyed pratice for all four disciplines!); and these children told me they'd be absolutely miserable if they weren't allowed to continue.

But if that fire in the young belly and the enjoyment is missing or if expectations overwhelm outcomes then a sensible and sensitive parenthood needs to step in to balance life up.

Here's a typical example of a young fellow who loved to train for running.

Earlier in 2010 my wife and I were in Europe, and former World triathlon champion and Commonwealth Games marathon bronze medallist (now sadly deceased) Jackie Fairweather (nee Gallagher) kindly looked after my female running group in Canberra. When I returned Jackie pointed out a new member of the group, a wisp of a boy aged 12 who had been running with the girls doing track work on Tuesday evening. I introduced myself and he asked me what the girls were doing tonight.

'8 to10 times 400m on 2 minutes tonight' I replied.

'Oh that sounds fine' he said 'I'll do them in around 75 seconds ... but you do mean a full 2 min recovery and not a 2 min cycle, don't you? If it's the 2 min cycle I'd have to do them in about 80.'

The girls were listening and laughed. 'Yes, Dick, while you were away we've realized that Joel has it all well under control. He loves running and if we want the latest news on distance running in Australia, we just ask him.'

This sort of super keenness is usually reserved for the ball sports in Australia, because the football codes and cricket dominate our media. As I found out Joel Findlay had finished 18th in his age group, the 11 year-old group in the National schools cross-country. He was pleased with his placing as he pointed out to me that nearly all the kids were head and shoulders taller than him and he should catch up in the next few years. I smiled—this young fellow really did have it all worked out.

This book has been long in development, progress sandwiched in between research and coaching. It's now 2015, and apart from programmed-in rest periods, and the odd injury (often from falling off a bike, or miskicking a football) Joel has hardly missed a training session in five years. He's grown of course and catching up to his peers. Last year in the National Championships on the track, he was second in the 3000m, and has run PBs each year in the, 800m, 1500m, and 3000m. He's still really enjoying his running training and competition. And it's pleasing that he's matched his running progress with success at school and with his music, which I'm always interested to hear. Balance in life makes is important. And anyway it makes a better runner.

The middle road

The majority of well-informed parents take the middle road when it comes to sport, opting to introduce their children to a variety of early sporting experiences, allowing the children themselves to discover where their sporting talents and preferences take them. And for most sports, but not all, this pathway of least resistance is entirely compatible with excelling in a sport in the teenage and adult years.

Running, jumping, throwing, hitting and kicking are fundamental skill requirements of numerous sports and transferable from sport to sport. Early proficiency in these fundamental skills, together with good fitness and a good sprinkling of vigorous physical activity through the week during the primary school years sets a child up to be a good performer in a wide variety of sports and active recreational pursuits, and for some to go on to achieve elite level status.

How much training to be an elite runner?

As mentioned above, specialized running training at an early age isn't necessary, and in contrast with some other sports, a 'normal' lifestyle is compatible with optimal running development right through to the mid-teenage years. For example a champion adult 1500m runner doesn't have to train specifically for running races during the prepubescent years. As outlined in the 'thought' experiment in Chapter 4, participation in games which require plenty of running is sufficient, but also necessary, to facilitate optimal growth and development; and so prepare a mid-teenager for the more demanding specific training of a senior 1500m runner. Of international runners I have been associated with over the years I can't think of one who wasn't a very active youngster, but many didn't train for running at an early age.

Playing football was common for the males. Australia's current leading marathoner runner, Michael Shelley, played football (called soccer in Australia) in his early teens. Simon Doyle, a former highly world-ranked 1500m runner also played soccer as his main sport, and well into his teens. Some runners have simply loved running from an early age. Olympic 10,000m finalist Carolyn Schuwalow was running 5km for fun in primary school and longer distances in her early teens. Lisa Weightman was another to proceed on from Little Athletics. My ex-Ethiopian runners and Australian Olympians Sisay Bezabeh and Mizan Mehari were training with a large squad of elite runners early in their early teens. Paris Marathon winner Nickey Carroll was a terrific young tennis player. Olympic medallist Lisa Martin (Ondieki) was a keen young runner in primary school but was keen on hurdling and the shorter running events. World championship cross-country winner Benita Willis (Johnson) played competitive hockey and liked to compete in Little Athletics competitions all through her school days. Australian mile record holder and Olympian Lisa Corrigan has always loved running and competed in Little Athletics along with the traditional school ball sports involving running in her early school days.

The wealth of anecdotal information and experience over the years sends a clear message. Children who have done plenty of running, usually within running-related sports, are more likely to become good runners in later life. The same could be said for youngsters growing up in a seaside environment who are involved in regular swimming training and the paddling associated with surf life-saving and surfing. These children are more likely to develop the fitness and 'feel' for moving efficiently in the water, vital for elite swimming and canoeing competition later on.

Whatever path is decided upon it all boils down for parents and coaches to realistically and sensitively guide the course of training for their child; to draw the line when the normal physical and/or psychological stresses of training and competition show signs of developing into physical and/or psychological distress. Training with a happy group and coach who loves a laugh and to have fun is a very important consideration. Training with an over-serious 'win at all costs' type of coach, who views each youngster only as his or her potential Olympian, is not enjoyable and likely to be counterproductive in the long term. Being matched up at training and in competition week after week against children of superior ability (usually earlier developers) is not enjoyable either.

But the bottom line is Mum and Dad's influence. Show me a mum or dad who loves to take their child out for a run or walk in the bush, for a backyard game of cricket, a kick of the footy, or a swim, row or paddle on the river and I'll show you a happy child; one who is well prepared to decide for themselves where they put sport on the list of things to do in life.

So how much running?

'My daughter just loves running ... how much should she be doing?'

Not a particularly easy question to answer. Perhaps we might be guided by the age-old real estate agent's response to the three most important considerations in selecting a property to buy; 'position, position and position'. The coach's response to the three most important considerations in a youngster's training program might well be 'enjoyment, enjoyment and enjoyment'.

Making it a bit easier for us to tell when children are enjoying their running is that they usually know when enough is enough. Kids will usually stop running or other strenuous physical activity when they're 'too tired', 'puffed out', or have 'a stitch' or 'sore legs.' But that's when the child is in control of the situation. Sometimes in formal sporting venues amidst serious coaching ambitions of the adults running the show, the child may not be in control. That's where we need to be a savvy of potential consequences, particularly those psychological, of doing too much too early.

But it's not uncommon for youngsters to fall into the trap of doing too much. Keen young runners know full well that, all other things being equal, training longer, faster, and more frequently is going to result in improved performances, and a better chance of winning. As is often the case, all other things won't be equal, and with increased training stress in a growing child comes an increased risk of injury and even early signs of joint degeneration.

It makes no sense for children and early adolescents to train hard with high volume and/or exhausting intensity unless your priority is to develop a child prodigy rather than an accomplished senior. I've seen many a case of athletes who have trained with great intensity and/or volume through early adolescence, won national junior championships, only to succumb to persistent injuries in early adulthood, probably the result of years of premature training stress.

But what are the limits? Here are some general guidelines, based only on anecdotal evidence and personal experience.

Pre-adolescence

Age 0-5: Facilitate play and games that may involve the two gears typifying physical activity at this age group, flat-out and stop. Our kids will know when to stop and start.

Age 6-10: Encourage participation and practices in games that require plenty of movement and skills practice; and ball games are great as they can incorporate both. Little Athletics is a good option too because it encourages variety of movement experiences including running. An important aspect of a budding young runner's preparation is going for a jog along the beach or along a bush trail, making sure it's enjoyable, and unforced. But other forms of activity are valuable as well, whether they be in the form of cross-country skiing, cycling, swimming, paddling, rowing, skating, gymnastics, climbing or hiking.

Who needs toys, when you can get to mum's shoes?, Lisa Weightman's baby Peter Richard keen to get an early start.

Training volumes for runners at adolescence

11–17: Some boys and girls have found they excel at running, win in the school carnivals and are keen to join an Athletics club. That's great but this is a time to hold back that little bit to protect the joints of a growing body from excessive shock waves of footstrike.

In general, but with wide individual variation, usually down, the volume of running training for keen young middle-distance runners might build gradually to 20km/week at age 11; 25km/week at age 12; 30km/week at age 13; 35km/week at 14; 40km at age 15; 45km at age 16; 50km/week at age 17. Running can take place once every day, with one obligatory running rest day every week, where some swimming or cycling or just a normal day throwing some baskets with friends.

Quality training sessions for young adolescents in my group takes place together with the senior group on Tuesday, Thursday and Saturday. On the other days some of my 14 year-old runners go for a bike ride or swim, or some other form of recreational activity, or nothing at all. Others combine other sports such a football (usually soccer) cricket, hockey or netball with running training.

It makes sense for young runners to train mainly on grass or bush trails and hills. We do a lot of fartlek work, where I set tasks for the group such as 'running to that tree and back' or 'running a solid lap of the oval' followed by a series of efforts of various distances and various recoveries. I often instruct all the runners doing an out and back repetition to 'turn when the first runner reaches the tree'. In this way every runner gets back to me at the same time, the faster runners of course having run further. The 'out and back' fartlek training is group training at its best. Runners run at their own level, and the faster runners turn to have the pack in front of them, and try to chase it down before they get back to me.

It's important to adjust the intensity and duration to avoid overdoing things. On the synthetic track, which we use sparingly during the winter preparation, and more often a grass track, the young (13–14 year old) runners would do sessions like 4–6 x 400m (1 minute walk recovery) and 4 x 200m (1 minute walk recovery), this being a subset of my senior runners' 'master session'. We do hill sessions on most Thursdays where the juniors run up a hill that takes about 2 minutes and down the other side and then do it again. This is followed by a shorter faster 30 second hill which we'd do 4 times with a slow jog down. On Saturday our youngsters might run a 4km cross-country or a grass or bush trail run of similar length or one broken up into 1km or 2km repetitions. We often finish with a few shorter faster efforts of 150 to 200m with emphasis on good posture and technique.

By the time the runners are age 15 they're doing about 40km running a week, building 5km on average next year, although that all depends on how they are coping with their growth spurt. A period of rapid growth can impede the progress of young runners, both male and female. In this period it's not unusual for boys in particular to develop soreness in joints around the knee, hip and lower back. These are commonly referred to as 'growth pains'. They seem to me to be mismatches in the rates of growth of ligaments, bones, muscles and tendons pain often amplified by the running. Training often has to be reduced with periods of running rest periods. Sometimes a few days, sometimes a few weeks, and on occasions months are required to ensure the aches and pains resolve. Coaches need to re-assure children that indeed this is part of growing up and that their time for more consistent training will come.

An exception to the rule, at least for a speedster

The Patrick Johnson story

It's 1996 and I've just begun a stint of full-time coaching at the AIS, eager to experience the challenge of such a position following my previous role in Sports Science. My new AIS office overlooks the track and is not all that conducive to working when a track meet is on, especially as I have a good line of sight across the finish line. It's a warm, sunny Spring afternoon, and with the University Games

100m heats underway, my powers of concentration on this administrative report I was writing are challenged to say the least. The first couple of heats were interesting with a couple of runners looking quite good. The gun fires to start the third heat, and inadvertently letting my work distract me from the race momentarily, I look up from my papers to get quite a surprise. One runner is so far out in front at the 40m mark that I wait to see why they aren't recalling the field after a false start. I realise that there was no false start as the runner surges past the line even further in front.

I didn't see the time (but later found it to be around 10.5" or 10.6") but this chap looked so good that I had to do something about it. Not coaching sprinters, my immediate reaction was to contact my friend Esa Peltola who had recently left his AIS post in sports science, as I had, to resume a sprint running coaching career which he had initiated in his former home country of Finland. 'Esa, there's a chap out there in the Uni games who to me looks something special' I told him. 'I'd like you to cast your eye over him in the final.'

This he did. Our runner was a bit slow out of the blocks in that final, in fact he didn't have much of a clue as to how to get out of the blocks at all. It didn't matter. By 30m he'd caught the field, by 60m he was a metre in front and by 100m second place was daylight. Esa didn't say much but his eyes told the story. A few days later he was coaching this fellow and Esa told me his new runner's name was Patrick Johnson and he was 24 years old. He also told me that the race I watched from my AIS office was Patrick's 3rd race in 10 years. Esa introduced me to Patrick when he came on board the AIS as a scholarship holder and I found out that the young man had an indigenous Australian mother and an Irish father. I smiled when he told me that he'd spent most of his adolescent life out on a fishing boat and he'd done no running at all. Here was I working out ways to ensure that our kids are physically active and into sport for their health as well as their future sporting careers and this chap had done the opposite. I suppose this is consistent with the premise that sprinters have either got it or they haven't. Of course training for speed and power and improving technique will improve a sprinter. But it does seem that genetics might play a more decisive role in determining an individual's outright running speed in comparison with an individual's distance running capability.

Aerobic dominated performance seems to be more responsive to, and indeed may rely on an extended period of endurance activity as a child followed by years of specific middle and long-distance running in adulthood.

In any case, a couple of years later Patrick ran the 100m in 9.93 and became the first Australian, and, I believe, the first man of non-African descent to break 10 seconds. Not bad for someone who'd spent most of his early life fishing. Hats off to Esa, Patrick and the AIS.

Running literacy

I like to talk to the youngsters about this period of growth and how patience is required in terms of waiting for personal best efforts. It's not uncommon for runners, and teenage boys in particular, to listen more intently to their coaches than to their parents. I'm sure my son did. However, it's obvious to me as a coach (well backed up by research) that parental attitudes to competition and physical activity in general are the strongest influences on youngsters' attitudes and participation in sport and physical activity in general. I've been fortunate to coach youngsters, both male and female, whose parents were and are supportive to their child's training and competition, success from year to year being sensitively gauged from personal improvement, not necessarily from winning or losing.

A typical week of a keen adolescent runner

Here's a typical week for one of my 14 year-old boys who have chosen running as their primary sport, but loved to be active and loved to cycle and swim. As it turns out it happens to be Joel, the 11 year-old who I mentioned turned up to training while I was overseas. Now he is just on 17, indicating the longitudinal nature of my writing! When he was 14, Joel mapped out his preferred weekly schedule of cross training to supplement the running training I had set. My comment to him was that if at any stage he feels he is getting a bit too tired, or hasn't got enough time for homework, or has a family or school function then he simply takes a day off training. It seemed to work out well and he went on to improve his time the following track season. Here's a typical week in that program.

Monday AM: 1.5km swim; **PM**: 25km cycle

Tuesday PM: Grass track, warm-up 3km, 6 x 400m (1' walk recovery) warmdown 2km

Wednesday: AM or PM: 30km cycle

Thursday, PM: Bush trail 10' warm-up, 3x 1km (2' walk recovery), 10' warmdown

Friday AM: 1.5km swim; **PM:** 25km cycle or a rest day every second Friday

Saturday AM: 15' warm-up, 3km solid 'threshold' run on grass trails, 15' warmdown

Sunday AM: 10km run on bush trail over hills

If a cross-country race was planned on Saturday, we might 'freshen up' a bit by cutting back Thursday to 3 x 600m. More often than not a local cross-country race would be run as a Saturday training session as part of a usual training week.

Joel has always enjoyed his training, and enjoys discussing how modifications might best suit him at any stage.

We might call this as being 'running literate'.

The kid I remember in the 50s and 60s

My athletic exploits pale in comparison with the runners whose stories punctuate this book, but I wondered at secondary school why I always won my age-group cross-country events or school athletic carnival mile races. And in later life, after enjoying plenty of running around on the football and cricket grounds, I wondered why making a mark on the veterans running scene came relatively easily.

I now look back and think about the runs my father encouraged me to do around, but not into Camp Pell, a slum-like area adjacent to our rented Victorian-era two story villa in Park Street Parkville, an inner suburb of Melbourne. Camp Pell was full of army huts, home to the otherwise homeless after World War II, a large eye-sore of grassless dirt, and dogs that bit anything with meat on it.

Camp Pell was later to be cleaned up and transformed into Royal Park, which Melbournians now know as a beautifully expansive area of trees and sporting facilities. I used to walk up Story Street past University High School to the little primary school I attended at the far corner of Melbourne University, a distance of around 2 km. Because I was often running late, literally, I needed to jog to school, bag on back. Being driven to school, as most kids are nowadays, never ever crossed my mind, or, presumably, the minds of my parents.

I then attended Northcote High School, because it was midway between Parkville and the brand new cream brick house my parents were going to buy in Reservoir, a new northern suburb of Melbourne. In Reservoir, we lived about 1.5km from the Reservoir train station, so here I was again, usually running late, with my brown kit bag full of books and a couple of sandwiches. Running with a bag and puffing solidly seemed the normal thing to do. It saved time.

It was at Northcote High School and with a team called the Broadway Rovers that I played my first football match at the age of 12; the little school I had attended in Melbourne Uni didn't have enough kids to field a team of sufficient age to play against other schools. Not having played sport at primary school didn't make much difference as I spent a lot of time behind our house on the grass kicking a footy, playing makeshift cricket or belting a tennis ball against the side wall of the house (I reckon the marks on the wall are still there 6 decades later).

We had Interhouse sport at Northcote High and interschool sport. We had 'house spirit' and 'school spirit' not experienced in many public schools these days. Sport and physical activity wasn't in short supply but it didn't finish there. I'd get home from school and spend an hour or two hour kicking a footy in the street or playing cricket in the driveway with my mate and next door neighbour John Hindmarsh (we would in later years exploit our teamwork profitably on the football field playing for the Preston Football Club).

So that goes a long way to explaining why I won those cross-country races when I got to High School; running and plenty of physical activity formed part of the daily routine from grade one!

Why middle-distance runners are rare

A 13 year-old boy called Juach saw my group training in a park and asked if he could join in. He told me he arrived here in Canberra from Sudan 4 months ago. One of the runners in my group, promising middle-distance runner Josh Johnson, asked, 'Are you a distance runner or a sprinter?'

The boy said shyly that he liked both but he was pretty fast.

'Ok then' Josh said 'Race me to that gum tree.'

When someone called out 'Go!' the kid took off like a cut cat, and beat Josh to that gum tree by a whisker ... and Josh was the quickest middle-distance runner in my group!

Juach kept coming to training. I soon formed an opinion that he could be a very good 800m runner, as he told me he had won his school cross-country. 'Ok Juach' I said 'We have National Junior Championships in Sydney this year, but they're only 10 weeks away. How would you like to have a go at qualifying to run for the ACT?',

'Ok' was his typically understated reply, which I interpreted as 'I'd love to.'

Not long later Juach was identified as a good young soccer player and had been selected to train in a junior squad in the ACT. When he told me I said, 'That's terrific Juach, soccer's a great game and we can easily work out your running training around your soccer practice, so one helps the other. Actually we've had some great runners who played soccer in their teens, and some great soccer players who were really good runners in their teens. Later on you'll have to make up your mind which sport you really want to concentrate on.' Juach was pleased about that.

So Juach would come to training, never missing a chance to run with the group, whom he had got to know well. Sometimes he would come after soccer training, and I would ask what he did, complementing the soccer training with some training that didn't overtire him. He loved the running training and our group. With only two races under his belt, we went up to Sydney for the Junior Track and Field Nationals. This fellow was a very quick learner, and soon found out how best to run two laps in the quickest time possible. He made the final and running within the boundaries of his limited preparation, produced a remarkably mature race to take the silver. In his fourth ever 800m race, two in the ACT, and the heat and final in Sydney, he was now second in his age group in Australia!

His schoolteachers were overjoyed at his success and one of his teachers rang to ask if I could send a photo, and I did, as Sue, my wife had got a good one of him on the podium first time ever and in the Nationals! This was a happy experience for the talented young refugee. It also pleased my more senior runners, including marathon runner Alex van der Meer (soon to become my assistant coach) who took Juach under their wings and made him feel at home at all times, teaching him about running and the Australian way of life. That's what running groups are all about; comradeship and support.

So it was with some disappointment when one of Juach's teachers came over to see me at training to tell me that the ACT junior squad soccer coach did not want the 13 year-old boy from Sudan to continue running. He wanted Juach to concentrate solely on soccer, and incentives to train and travel with the ACT squad secured the deal. Of course, Juach loves soccer and was tickled pink to be selected in the squad, so all turned out well for him. National sporting associations receive government funding directly proportional to their success and soccer football can't really be blamed if they put pressure on their junior coaches to secure paediatric talent early and ensure they don't lose it. That's modern sport, competition to reel in that special fish is getting more intense in a relatively small pool. Nevertheless, track and field coaches can't help being disappointed when the powerful professional sports, the ball sports, nip potential Olympic talent in the bud with appealing offers of support not able to be matched by a minor sport like Athletics.

In the interest of our kids and the country

Our sporting leaders would do well to develop a national code of practice that fosters the development of young talented sportspeople, putting aside single-minded interests of a coach. Granted, in the modern competitive world of sport, and particularly in lowly populated Australia, this might be a hard ask.

It would certainly help if coaches tasked with developing our children's skills and attitudes to sport had a thorough understanding of child development and in particular how to develop what many now refer to as 'physical literacy' (see below) in every child. In Australia, senior sport coaches enjoy greater status and financial rewards than coaches of our juniors; and even in our less professional sports, taking athletes to the World Championships is more prestigious than taking youngsters to World Junior Championships. Consequently the best coaches migrate to the senior ranks. That this happens is one very good reason the monetary rewards and status of junior coaches should approach those of the senior coaches. After all, expert junior coaching, and properly taught physical education at school is vital in developing the fitness and a general love of physical activity which underpins the development of champions.

In further support of coaches of junior athletes receiving more credit and support, coaching young athletes through their developing years is arguably a more complex task than coaching adults. One coach who certainly knows his trade here is Brett Green who lives on the Gold Coast. A very successful throws coach, his broad knowledge of developmental coaching was shown in how he brought a young Michael Shelley through to World Junior representation in the steeplechase. Most importantly, he brought his young athlete through injury free, and full of motivation. Brett's coaching was an essential aspect Shelley's success on the track then as a Commonwealth champion and Olympic 16th place-getter in the marathon.

Physical literacy

The term 'physical literacy', coined by Margaret Whitehead, an academic from the UK and recently appointed adjunct professor at the University of Canberra, has crept into sporting and educational terminology in recent years. A physically literate child is one who has achieved an appropriate development of a variety of gross and fine movement skills, fitness, and motivation to enjoy a physically active lifestyle in areas of their liking for years to come. Parents, school teachers and coaches in particular are responsible for creating an environment in which children can develop physical literacy.

If we can pave the way for a nation of physically literate children through the vitally important developmental pre-adolescent years, sporting organizations would no longer have to jostle so intensely to gain the services of a talented child as the numbers would soon far exceed those who could be offered sporting opportunities and scholarships.

More importantly to most parents, a physically literate child is more likely to embark on a lifetime of physical activity, and so enjoy its proven benefits to health and happiness into old age.

Some 12 year-olds are 10 and others 14

One complicating issue in children's sport is that physical maturity occurs at different times and rates. Children grow and get stronger and faster at different rates. Consequently we parents, teachers, coaches (and children) need to recognize and account for the variation in biological (developmental) age that is obvious at any given chronological age. We have little alternative to classifying children according to chronological age, but in terms of physique, and therefore, sporting prowess, this advantages children who are early developers and disadvantages those who develop late.

I looked back on some individual data from a study conducted with post-graduate student Lindsay Ellis at Phillip Institute of Technology (now part of RMIT, Melbourne) in the late 1970s. We measured 12 year-old children participating in Little Athletics competition. (Lindsay by the way went on to work as a physiologist at the AIS and then became Director of the Northern Territory Institute of Sport). In those days we measured wrist X-rays to estimate physical maturity and biological age. Some of the chronologically 12 year-old boys were of biological age 14 years and others 10, and among the girls there were even larger discrepancies in biological age. No-one expects a 10 year-old to match the physical capabilities of a 14 year-old, so how do we ensure late developers get the kind of, enjoyment and reward that encourages them to continue in organized sporting competition?

The most sensible way to devise ways to measure and recognize success in children's sport is through individual improvement. Coaches, parents, teachers and the children themselves need to be in full agreement that success comes not just by winning or placing in a race or competition, but making a personal performance progression. In the case of running, it is a lifetime or seasonal PB. Wise counselling is required, especially for the late developing children, to ensure their sporting satisfaction. It's important they understand that their time in the sun will come, but that the sun may rise a little later in the day for them personally.

The wise coach and parent will point out the many cases among our elite athletes where patience and consistency of training has produced the best rewards in the end, not necessarily along the way.

Role models

We often hear debates as to exactly what inspires youngsters to do their best at sport, and what motivates them to seek physically active lifestyles. For me personally as a child, and later as a researcher in the role of physical activity on child health, it has become clear that parents, sporting heroes, PE teachers and sports coaches all play highly influential roles. Active parents have active kids; primary school teachers who love sport and who are fit themselves develop fitter students. And, by the way, as we've demonstrated, these teachers are rewarded further with classes that achieve better academically.

I was 15 and like nearly every kid in Victoria a keen Aussie Rules footballer and cricketer. In between football and cricket we had the school 'House' athletics competitions. My PE teacher at Northcote High School was a chap called Alec Weston, and like many PE teachers, he left a lasting impression on me.

A dapper little bloke with a cheeky grin and neatly brylcreemed hair and, muscular arms, he was always dressed impeccably in freshly ironed light grey slacks, spotless Dunlop volley shoes, and a white open neck shirt. PE was good fun but obviously lowly rated by the academic staff, because the school had no gymnasium in those days and we used to get changed in what we called the 'long room', which doubled as the entrance to the tuck shop. When it was raining we'd do exercises in the long room or boxing with big spongy gloves.

Alec didn't go to university or Teachers' College and I think he got the job at Northcote High because of his interest in kids' sport and his role as a trainer and masseuse to some top cyclists. He was a trainer and masseur to Russell Mockridge, an Olympic cycling gold medallist. Mockridge was killed in a car accident. Alec was distraught and never really recovered as far as my young mind could work out. Alec lived for sport and the school. When I look back I realise he was one of those significant influences, along with my father, on my love of sport through a lifetime. He loved running nearly as much as cycling and it rubbed off on me.

Before the inter-school sports he'd take a few of us off in his big Chevrolet to do some training down at the beach on the sand dunes and in the forest up and down the hills. One school term Alex didn't turn up at school. We heard that the Victorian Education Department made formal teaching qualifications mandatory and Alex was no longer employed.

Sporting heroes

I've heard it said that our top athletes do little to inspire youngsters. I beg to differ.

Kids are strongly inspired by their sporting heroes. Overwhelmingly this is positive, but it has to be admitted on occasions, not so positively. Here are two positive instances.

A grade 5 girl was asked to write an assignment of her favourite sportsperson. She chose marathon runner Lisa Weightman.

'Lisa Weightman has taught me that you can have a big amazing dream and although you might think it's unachievable, with persistence you can achieve it. So someone with a positive attitude and a will to never give up can do anything, all you have to do is try. Lisa is that kind of person that keeps trying and never gives up. She has made me think that I can do lots of things even something as great as hers just if I keep trying.'

And here's how Ron Clarke, one of the greats of Australian distance runners helped to produce another fine Australian distance runner. Chris Wardlaw relayed this story in a tribute to Clarke after his death in June 2015.

'... Clarkie profoundly influenced my life. Late 1964 or early 1965. I was in year 9/10 as a 15 year-old at Melbourne High School and Clarkie visited as an alumnus to speak to our weekly assembly. He brought along Bob Schull, USA, who had won the 1964 Tokyo Olympic 5000m and who had come to Melbourne to race Clarkie and others. Clarkie said there was an Olympian sitting before him in the Hall. He knew this because when he had sat where we students were as a student himself in the late 50s, he had no idea of the possibility ahead of him; yet here he was returning as an Olympian. I have taken that story with me. In the days after listening to him in the Melbourne High Hall, when running to the local milk bar at night to fetch the milk, I WAS Ron Clarke!'

Role models at home

It's now November 8, 2015. I'm at the NSW 3000m championships in Sydney, at the old TS Marks track. I haven't been here for 15 years, Homebush Olympic Park having ruled the roost for major events in Sydney since 2000. It's good, because we're allowed down to the edge of the track and the atmosphere surpasses that of big brother Homebush. Two of my new squad of runners, Jordan Gusman and Josh Johnson, together with a teenage local ACT runner of great promise, Josh Turley, are having a run. My daughter Nerilee and son-in-law Brent have brought their youngsters Bronte, Braiden and Jamie down to add some vocal support from trackside. They must have cheered well, because Jordan and Josh J finish 1 and 2, with all three runners recording big PB's, setting up a promising summer of racing.

As I drove into the track I heard a chap repeat what seems to be the currently fashionable statement that our new breed of children aren't likely to live as long as their parents. Well, some mightn't, but as I watched my grandchildren sprint out to the high jump mat I thought how lucky these kids were to have their family as role models; parents who take them to netball, football, dancing and surfing, with an ex-footballer Dad and Uncle Rohan who both love to coach football, and a Mum and grand-mum who love to keep fit. The chances of these children leading a physically active lifestyle and enjoying their sport is high, and as might be gleaned from Chapter 4, so are their chances of spending more, not less time on this planet than their parents.

Chapter 25
Running for Health

'In my youth' said his father, 'I took to the law, and argued each case with my wife; And the muscular strength, which it gave to my jaw has lasted the rest of my life.'

Lewis Carroll

Our health is intimately linked to our physical activity; and what we did in our youth may well have set us up for life.

We human beings, despite, or even because of millions of years of evolution, have many faults. Not just in the way we think, which is pretty obvious, but in our design, which I suppose is also pretty obvious. One basic architectural flaw lies within our ability to control our own biochemistry, in particular the concentrations of sugar and fat in our bloodstream. In recent centuries and especially during the last century this flaw has created havoc to the extent that we have now an epidemic of poor blood sugar and fat control which in medical language is Type 2 diabetes.

We only function properly within a very narrow range of blood glucose concentration. If it gets too high or too low for too long, vital organs including the brain just can't cope, and in an unresolved situation it's coma and death.

Good old Mother Nature certainly saw the need to keep blood glucose levels up, as it allowed us to 'fight or flee'. Even the thought of combat or competition can trigger off signals to the pituitary, adrenal, and thyroid glands and pancreas to secrete an array of hormones which elevate blood glucose and prepare us for action.

On the other hand we have only one hormone tasked with lowering blood glucose. If that hormone is dysfunctional or absent we are in real trouble. The hormone is insulin, and it operates by opening up pathways through the membranes of muscles and liver so that glucose can be extracted from the bloodstream. But if our brain and life itself are so dependent on maintaining blood glucose within a narrow range, why is it that we only have one hormone to reduce blood glucose when we have many hormones to increase it? How could we have survived as a species without any sort of hormonal back-up for insulin?

The answer is because Mother Nature never envisaged that we'd ever be a sedentary species. Muscular activity has a powerful insulin-like outcome on blood glucose, lowering blood glucose (and fat) with little or no help from insulin. With muscular activity having become a rarity in the 21st century we have a problem, because insulin has lost a very important collaborator in blood glucose control.

Hats off to Homo Sapiens ingenuity; we've done a remarkable job in avoiding manual labour, and saving human energy and time. But it's happened so quickly that we've taken Mother Nature completely by surprise. Unfortunately she has never owned a crystal ball, and is an abysmally slow thinker (at least in our perception of time), and possesses no semblance of creativity, all efforts confined solely to reactivity. So Mother Nature had no chance of anticipating that we humans would ever lead such sedentary lifestyles and suffer from too much fat and sugar rather than the opposite!

Typical of our physiology if we don't use it we do lose it. Muscles lying dormant don't require glucose (or fat). What's more, unused muscles even lose their sensitivity to insulin, meaning that more and more insulin is required for a muscle to take up blood glucose. We become 'insulin resistant', a precursor to developing full blown Type 2 diabetes, where specialized cells in our pancreas become worn out, having been asked to work overtime for so long without the help of active muscles. Glucose and fat accumulates in the bloodstream, and although it is buffered to a certain degree by the liver and fat tissue, in time leads to fatty liver and obesity, conditions known to make us even sicker. Many Type 2 diabetics can turn things around to a degree by introducing physical activity, controlling dietary fat and sugar intake, and in advanced cases by regular insulin injections; but there may be a lot of collateral tissue damage.

One particularly damaging complication of a slothful lifestyle is the one we can all see; obesity. Over-filling our fat stores has some problems of its own, but a major one is that obese people are less able to move comfortably, so less likely to move and we have a vicious cycle. But if you are extra-large don't despair. There are several excellent studies which provide some good news for those who really struggle with their weight. Firstly even one bout of physical activity will have a small, but measurably positive effect on coping with blood sugar, so any effort is not wasted. Secondly physical activity, even very slow walking can lead to better health even if there is no weight loss. Thirdly, an overweight active individual is often healthier than a thin inactive one. Fourthly, carrying a bit of extra body fat might even be of assistance to longevity so you don't have to be as skinny as a rake. Finally, regular physical activity, no matter what you've been told is a vital aspect to controlling body composition, by making it easier to balance energy intake and output. An inactive overweight person is likely to eat less than an active lean person, yet still put on weight.

So can you be fit and fat? Yes, sort of, but in this instance being 'fit' means being in reasonable metabolic shape, not fit for running your best 10 km. Moreover, running itself is great medicine. In a recently published, study of more than 55,000 people over a 15 year period, a team including former highly performed marathon runner, now researcher Russell Pate showed that running, even slow running for 5 or 10 min/day is associated with a markedly reduced risk of premature death. But note the words 'reduced risk'. There are plenty of other risk factors like family history, smoking, poor diet, obesity, chronic psychological stress so don't get complacent.

Don't think being physically active and lean automatically means low risk. Being active will certainly reduce the risk of succumbing to chronic disease and premature death and dampens the effect of other risk factors, but it certainly doesn't immunize you.

Should running be fun?

Isn't it strange that nowadays we have to conjure up ways to be active to avoid getting sick? Given that we've evolved to preserve energy, it's no great wonder that many of us seek ways to avoid wasting it. In general, evolution encourages us to engage in activities which increase the possibility of reproducing by making such activities enjoyable.

It's a bit tricky with running, and physical activity in general. On the one hand, it should be enjoyable because in the face of predators or famine it can save our very lives. And for youngsters, playing develops the body and mind. But then again it shouldn't be encouraged, so perhaps not too enjoyable, because we need to save energy and store body fat in preparation for hard times. This is consistent with the tendency for older beings to lose their youthful interest and zest for physically active games. And physical activity in general. The adult mindset is programmed to get more enjoyment from eating and sexual activity, both of which, indirectly and directly respectively, help pass on our DNA. While there have been suggestions that the energy expenditure involved in sexual activity is of a similar magnitude to that of an easy training run, the literature is not at all clear. There's a paucity of observational data, and anyway, as I've stressed throughout this book individual variation has to be taken into account.

When all is said and done, we all know that physical activity is important for our health. Our policy makers have a dilemma as to what to do about the modern absence of obligatory physical activity in developed affluent countries. If individuals decide not to find ways to include physical activity in their daily lifestyle, we can ignore it on the premise that it's purely an individual choice. Fair enough but it's been estimated that even in Australia, failure to meet recommended guidelines of physical activity is costing literally billions of dollars in hospital care, pharmaceuticals, and lost revenue. That's a lot of money tax payers have to fork out.

Big brother

We've outlawed smoking in public places because blowing out carcinogens for others to breathe in is worthy of a legislative preventive approach. At home or during pregnancy smoking isn't outlawed but there are strong arguments that it should be. Might some sort of argument be applied that outlaws an extreme sedentary lifesyle in an able-bodied person? Sounds ridiculously Orwellian, and anyway we'd argue that slothfulness is a lot different to smoking because it can't be transmitted like smoke or a virus to our neighbours or family ... but is this really true?,

We know that physical inactivity is transmitted socially to children through parental behaviour, and while this is a potent transmitter, perhaps there is more to it than that.

It's a good bet that, in time, a gene or set of genes will be isolated which directly influences our propensity to move; a set of genes perhaps related to those promoting storage of energy and obesity. But more pertinent to our consideration of a legislative approach to physical inactivity, another reasonable bet is that this DNA is influenced epigenetically. The physical activity of our mothers, or even our grandmothers, through its profound neuroendocrine and biochemical influence, not just during pregnancy but leading into it, is likely to modify the expression of our own genes; in particular those genes which influence how much (or little) we seek out physically active lifestyles, how readily we produce energy or save energy, how easily we move, and our size and shape. Should this be the case, then at least educating our families as to the benefits of an optimal level of physical activity in a prospective mother would appear be well worthwhile.

A parallel argument applies to our diet. Inducing childhood addiction to high density sugary, salty, fatty foods of low density micronutrient value might also be considered offensive behaviour. Childhood obesity and childhood physical inactivity are closely linked. One causes the other, in both directions. An irresponsible parent who provides an obesogenic environment, caring little about the body composition of their child might reasonably be considered negligent.

Especially when early neglect of diet and physical activity can set-up chronic problems for a lifetime. So how rediculously Orwellian is the suggestion of a policy outlawing inactivity as we have for smoking? Rather rediculous yes, but raising it served my purpose.

To you joggers or in other ways regular physical activity seekers, thank you. You are not only setting up our youth for a physically active and more enjoyable lifestyle but extending the duration of your quality time on this planet as well.

With his dog Zac relaxing on Chapman Ridge after a run together.

Running to relax

Pat Clohessy, best known for his coaching role from the very start to the finish of Rob de Castella's career, is famous for his expressions of encouragement to his athletes. 'Looking good' and 'You're on the rise' made many a runner smile. But a key ingredient in Pat's training practice was ensuring that his athletes did not train with more intensity than was necessary and that relaxation was an important ingredient of a training program.

'Shute!' he'd say. 'I reckon he's overdone it now ... gone off the boil.'

Pat would never hesitate adjusting a program down if an athlete was under any form of stress, physical or psychological. He'd witnessed countless injuries and sickness in athletes, much of which he would ascribe to attempting too much in training, and not enough relaxation of mind as well as body.

That makes a lot of sense, given the intimate relationship between mind and body. For a start, a happy athlete will respond to training more thoroughly than an unhappy one. There are all sorts of reasons for this, a major one being that psychological stress can upset our neural and hormonal control, increasing our susceptibility to fatigue and adaptation to training. It works the other way as well. An athlete who doesn't over-reach in training and so maintains good control of those circulating hormones is likely to be a more psychologically stable, happier athlete. Coach Clohessy may not have put it these terms but knew this well.

So did other successful coaches. It's interesting that such coaches are often acknowledged by their charges; referred to by their athlete as 'a friend' (Steve Ovett of Harold Wilson) or 'a father figure' (Ralph Doubell of Franz Stampfl) or 'making sense of life' (Herb Elliott of Percy Cerutty). It is no coincidence that most of our best athletes have enjoyed a strong bond with their coach.

A more relaxed, happier athlete is a healthier one as well. And that applies to us all. Enlightened health practitioners view relaxation alongside physical activity as playing an important role in the prevention of chronic disease.

State of mind or 'mood' if you like, has a direct autonomic nervous system influence on the secretion of the very same set of 'fight or flight' hormones which make such a big impact on energy production. However, danger looms when there is a steady stream of secretion of these hormones brought about by sustained 'stress'. It might be ok to get the 'butterflies in the stomach' reaction prior to a race now and then, but it's certainly not all right to have that 'uptight' sort of feeling persist day and night. Chronic secretion of stress-related hormones can produce a toxic environment and inflammation and cellular damage not dissimilar to processes associated with failure to control blood sugar and fat in Type 2 diabetes.

Athletes have recognized the intimate relationship of mind and body for many decades, and sports psychology evolved to fine tune this interaction. The ancient Greeks, through the likes of Plato and Aristotle, were way ahead of the game; they recognized the important interaction of mind and body eons ago and were clearly competent 'sport psychs'. No wonder the Greeks won all the medals in those early Olympics! Ironically it's taken a new set of threats to health, mediated through lack of physical activity that has led all of us, not just athletes, to take more notice of the wise men of ancient Greece. The mind-body interaction was also well recognized the 'far East'. The age-old practice of yoga makes use of freeing the mind from confounding influences and exploits mind-body interaction to induce whole person relaxation.

Interestingly runners can induce similar states of mind during running, especially when surrounded by the beauty of natural flora and fauna. For me it's eucalyptus, wattle trees, kangaroos and parrots. Like yoga, it doesn't come straight away and requires practice. The Bluearth Foundation with headquarters in Melbourne deserves to be acknowledged for the role it plays in developing, physical literacy in children throughout Australia. It's well-designed physical activity program, which makes use of may types of movement challenges, including yoga is unique around the world in that a four-year randomized control study has clearly demonstrated its benefit to the health and happiness of children from an early age.

The way we move affects the way we think; and the way we think affects the way we move. The way we move and think is who we are and how we are.

We are all runners at heart, if we are allowed to be.

Words mean more than we mean to express when we use them:
so a whole book ought to mean a great deal more than the writer meant.

Lewis Carroll

References

Chapter 4

Perez-Pastor EM, Metcalf BS, Hosking J, Jeffery AN, Voss LD, Wilkin TJ 2009, *Assortative weight gain in mother-daughter and father-son pairs: an emerging source of childhood obesity. Longitudinal study of trios,* (EarlyBird 43)', International Journal of Obesity, vol. 33(7), pp. 727-35.

Telford RD, Cunningham RB, Fitzgerald R, Olive LS, Prosser L, Jiang X, Telford RM 2012, *Physical education, obesity, and academic achievement: a 2-year longitudinal investigation of Australian elementary school children,* American Journal of Public, Health, vol. 102(2), pp.368-74.

Telford RD, Cunningham RB, Telford RM, Daly RM, Olive LS, Abhayaratna WP 2013, *Physical education can improve insulin resistance: the LOOK randomized cluster trial,* Medicine & Science in Sports & Exercise, vol. 45(10), pp. 1956-64.

Chapter 5

Brooks GA 2000, *Intra- and extra-cellular lactate shuttles,* Medicine & Science in Sports & Exercise, vol. 32(4), pp. 790-9.

Telford RD, Minikin BR, Hahn AG, Hooper LA 1989, *A simple method for the assessment of general fitness: The Tri-level profile*, Australian Journal of Science and Medicine in Sport, vol. 21 (3), pp. 6-9.

Telford RD, Minikin BR, Hooper LA, Hahn AG, Tumilty D McA 1987, *The Tri-level fitness profile*, Excel, vol. 4, pp. 11-13. This publication was produced by the Australian Institute of Sport and is available from the Australian Sports Commission National Sports Information Centre.

Telford RD 1982, *Specific performance analysis with air-braked ergometers. Part II: Short duration work and power*, The Journal of Sports Medicine and Physical Fitness, vol. 22(3), pp. 349-57. PubMed PMID: 7162191.

Telford RD 1982, *Specific performance analysis with air-braked ergometers. Part I: Aerobic measurements*, The Journal of Sports Medicine and Physical Fitness, vol. 22(3), pp. 340-8. PubMed PMID: 7162190.

Wallman K, Goodman C, Morton A, Grove R, Dawson B 2003, '*Test-retest reliability of the aerobic power index component of the tri-level fitness profile in a sedentary population*', Journal of Science and Medicine in Sport, vol. 6(4), pp. 443-54.

Chapter 6

Astrand PO, Rhyming I 1954, *A nomogram for calculation of aerobic capacity (physical fitness) from pulse rate during submaximal work*, The Journal of Applied Physiology, vol. 7(2), pp. 218-21.

Billat V, Renoux JC, Pinoteau J, Petit B, Koralsztein JP 1995, *Times to exhaustion at 90, 100 and 105 percent of velocity at V̇O2max (maximal aerobic speed) and critical speed in elite long-distance runners*, Archives of Physiology and Biochemistry, vol. 103(2), pp. 129-35.

Clarke R 1966, *The unforgiving minute*, Pelham Books, London.

Ferri A, Adamo S, La Torre A, Marzorati M, Bishop DJ, Miserocchi G 2012, *Determinants of performance in 1500m runners*, European Journal of Applied Physiology, vol. 112 (8).

Lenton, B 1981, *Off the Record: Running Interviews with Ron Clarke, Rod Dixon, Herb Elliott, Jack Foster, John Landy, Arthur Lydiard, Albie Thomas and Chris Wardlaw*, Brian Lenton Publications.

Morgan DW, Daniels JT 1994, *Relationship between V̇O2max and the aerobic demand of running in elite distance runners*, International Journal of Sports Medicine, vol. 15(7), pp. 426-9. Erratum in: 1994, International Journal of Sports Medicine, vol. 15(8), p. 527.

Saunders PU, Telford RD, Pyne DB, Peltola EM, Cunningham RB, Gore CJ, Hawley JA 2006, *Short-term plyometric training improves running economy in highly trained middle and long-distance runners*, The Journal of Strength and Conditioning Research, vol. 20(4), pp. 947-54.

Slawinski JS, Billat VL 2004, '*Difference in mechanical and energy cost between highly, well, and nontrained runners*', Medicine & Science in Sports & Exercise, vol. 36(8), pp. 1440-6.

Smith D, Telford RD, Peltola E, Tumilty DA 2000, '*Protocols for the Physiological Assessment of High-performance runners*', in C.J. Gore (ed), Physiological Tests for Elite Athletes, Human Kinetics Publishing, Champaign, IL.

Chapter 7

Cerutty P 1973, *Schoolboy Athletics*, Hutchinson of Australia.

Clarke R 1966, *The unforgiving minute*, Pelham Books, London (as told to Alan Trengrove)

Lenton, B 1981, *Off the Record: Running Interviews with Ron Clarke, Rod Dixon, Herb Elliott, Jack Foster, John Landy, Arthur Lydiard, Albie Thomas and Chris Wardlaw*, Brian Lenton Publications.

Stampfl F 1955, *Stampfl on Running*, Macmillan.

Chapter 8

Bandschapp O, Soule CL, Iaizzo PA 2012, *Lactic acid restores skeletal muscle force in an in vitro fatigue model: are voltage-gated chloride channels involved?*, American Journal of Physiology - Cell Physiology, vol. 1, pp. 302-7.

Lane N 2002, *Oxygen: the molecule that made the world*, Oxford Uni Press.

Gladden LB 2008, *A lactatic perspective on metabolism*, Medicine & Science in Sports & Exercise, vol. 40(3), pp. 477-85.

Noakes T 2003, *The Lore of Running*, 4th edn, Oxford University Press.

Robergs RA, Ghiasvand F & Parker D 2004, *Biochemistry of exercise-induced metabolic acidosis*, American Journal of Physiology Regulatory Integrative and Comparative Physiology, vol. 287, R502–R516.

Shokolenko I, Venediktova N, Bochkareva A, Wilson GL, Alexeyev MF 2009, *Oxidative stress induces degradation of mitochondrial DNA*, Nucleic Acids Research, vol. 37, No. 8 2539–2548

Chapter 9

Lawrence A, Scheid M 1987, *The Self-coached Runner*, Little Brown and Co.

Chapter 16

Thompson, K 2014, *Pacing. Individual Strategies for Optimal Performance*, Human Kinetics.

Chapter 19

Murray B, Stofan J, Eichner ER 2003, '*Hyponatremia in athletes*', Sports Science Exchange, vol. 16, pp. 1-6.

Olsson KE, Saltin B 1970, '*Variation in total body water with muscle glycogen changes in man*', The Scandinavian Physiological Society, vol. 80, pp. 11-18.

Chapter 20

Garvican LA, Lobigs L, Telford R, Fallon K, Gore CJ 2011, *Haemoglobin mass in an anaemic female endurance runner before and after iron supplementation*, International Journal of Sports Physiological Performance, vol. 6(1), pp. 137-40.

Telford RD, Cunningham RB 1991, *Sex, sport, and body-size dependency of hematology in highly trained athletes*', Medicine & Science in Sports & Exercise, vol. 23(7), pp. 788-94.

Telford RD, Sly GJ, Hahn AG, Cunningham RB, Bryant C, Smith JA 2003, *Footstrike is the major cause of hemolysis during running*, Journal of Applied Physiology, vol. 94(1), pp.38-42.

Chapter 21

Brian Lenton Interviews 1997, Brian Lenton publications.

Gray AB, Smart YC, Telford RD, Weidemann MJ, Roberts TK 1993, *Anaerobic exercise causes transient changes in leukocyte subsets and IL-2R expression*, Medicine & Science in Sports & Exercise, vol. 24(12), pp. 1332-8. Erratum in: 1993, Medicine & Science in Sports & Exercise, vol. 25(4), p. 535.

Lenton, B 1981, *Off the Record: Running Interviews with Ron Clarke, Rod Dixon, Herb Elliott, Jack Foster, John Landy, Arthur Lydiard, Albie Thomas and Chris Wardlaw*, Brian Lenton Publications.

Pyne DB, Smith JA, Baker MS, Telford RD, Weidemann MJ 2000, *Neutrophil oxidative activity is differentially affected by exercise intensity and type*, Journal of Science and Medicine in Sport, vol. 3(1), pp. 44-54.

Sandler RD1, Sui X2, Church TS3, Fritz SL4, Beattie PF4, Blair SN5 2014, *Are flexibility and muscle-strengthening activities associated with a higher risk of developing low back pain?*, Journal of Science and Medicine in Sport, vol. 17(4), pp. 361-5. doi: 10.1016/j.jsams.2013.07.016. Epub 2013 Aug 8.

Smith JA, Gray AB, Pyne DB, Baker MS, Telford RD, Weidemann MJ 1996, *Moderate exercise triggers both priming and activation of neutrophil subpopulations*, American Journal of Physiology, vol. 270(4 Pt 2): R838-45.

Stuber KJ, DC, Bruno P, Sajko S, Hayden JA 2014, *Core Stability Exercises for Low Back Pain in Athletes: A Systematic Review of the Literature*, Clinical Journal of Sport Medicine, vol. 24(6).

Chapter 22

Telford RD, Kovacic JC, Skinner SL, Hobbs JB, Hahn AG, Cunningham RB 1994, '*Resting whole blood viscosity of elite rowers is related to performance*', European Journal of Applied Physiology and Occupational Physiology, vol. 68 (6), pp. 470-6.

Saunders PU, Garvican-Lewis LA, Schmidt WF, Gore CJ 2013, *Relationship between changes in haemoglobin mass and maximal oxygen uptake after hypoxic exposure*, British Journal of Sports Medicine, vol. 47, pp. i26 -i30.

Chapter 23

Farmer P 2012, *Pole to Pole*, Allen and Unwin Publishers.

Chapter 24

Whitehead M 2001, *The concept of physical literacy*, European Journal of Physical Education vol.6,(2).

Telford RD, Cunningham RB, Fitzgerald R, Olive LS, Prosser L, Jiang X, Telford RM. *Physical Education, Obesity, and Academic Achievement: A 2-Year Longitudinal Investigation of Australian Elementary School Children.* American Journal of Public Health. 2012 102:368–374.

Telford RD, Cunningham RB, Telford RM, Abhayaratna WP. *Schools with fitter children achieve better literacy and numeracy results: evidence of a school cultural effect.* 1. Pediatric Exercise Science. 2012 Feb;24(1):45-57.

Chapter 25

Lavie CJ, McAuley PA, Church TS, Milani RV, Blair SN 2014, '*Obesity and cardiovascular diseases: implications regarding fitness, fatness, and severity in the obesity paradox*', Journal of the American College of Cardiology, vol. 63(14), pp. 1345-54. doi:10.1016/j.jacc.2014.01.022. Epub 2014 Feb 12.

Lee DC, Pate RR, Lavie CJ, Sui X, Church TS, Blair SN 2014, *Leisure-time running reduces all-cause and cardiovascular mortality risk*, Journal of the American College of Cardiology, vol. 64(5), pp. 472-81.

Telford RD, Cunningham RB, Telford RM, Riley M, Abhayaratna WP. *Determinants of childhood adiposity: evidence from the Australian LOOK study.* Public Library of Science One. 2012;7(11)):e50014.

The Author.
Image: University of Canberra

About the Author

Melbourne born Dick Telford has a PhD in metabolic physiology and he played and coached Australian Rules football and cricket at high levels in sport crazy Melbourne. Winning became familiar. At Northcote High School in his final year the school cricket team (which he captained) and the school football team were all-school champions. As a senior player, Dick won Best Player at the Preston Football Club in the Victorian Football Association (now VFL) in successive years as the club won successive premierships; and Dick won the Liston Trophy for Best and Fairest Player in the VFA in that first year. He later coached Preston Cricket Club to a premiership in the Victorian Sub-district Cricket Association, and was the Coaching Coordinator and Manager of the Victorian Cricket team which enjoyed Sheffield Shield wins in successive years.

Then he was invited out of the blue to move to Canberra as the inaugural sports scientist at the Australian Institute of Sport, the first professional full time position of its kind in Australia, tasked with setting up an Australian philosophy for sports science. The AIS soon developed a prestigious reputation around the world, and Dick's role coincided with a remarkably successful period in Australian sport leading to the Sydney 2000 Olympics. Four medals in Montreal had blossomed out to 58 in Sydney. In the mid 80s he began coaching runners, and his international record in coaching distance runners mirrored the success of his sports science achievements.

Our records indicate that Dick has been personal coach to more Commonwealth games medalists than any other Australian distance coach, having coached 4 gold medalists (Andrew Lloyd, Lisa Ondieki, Kate Anderson and Michael Shelley); 2 silver medalists (Kylie Risk, Michael Shelley) and 2 bronze medalists (Jackie Gallagher (nee Fairweather), Lisa Weightman). He has also coached Australia's only Olympic marathon medallist, (Lisa Martin (Ondieki)), and was physiologist to former world champion Rob de Castella throughout this runner's illustrious career.

And just for the record (as distance runners delight in personal records) at the time of writing, a check of the all-time listings of Australian distance running from 10km through to marathon reveals Dick's directly coached male athletes make up 6 of the 18 Australians who have run a sub 28 minute 10 km; 4 of the 12 10km female runners who've gone under 32 minutes; 3 of the 10 male sub 62 half-marathoners; 5 of the 12 female sub 72 minute half-marathoners; 4 of the 21 sub 2:12 marathoners, and 3 of the 6 female sub 2:30 marathoners. Overall that's 32 percent of these all-time Australian running performances and on top of this, Dick has been a personal physiologist, consultant or involved in the early development of several others in these all-time ranking categories.

Dick has continued to combine coaching with his scientific research in nutrition, immunology and physiology and over the last decade his research focus turned to the physical and psychological development and well-being of children. His work has been recognised at the highest levels by his peers in both sport and science.

He is a Fellow of both the American College of Sports Medicine and Sports Medicine Australia.

In 1992 his work was recognised at the highest level, being awarded the Medal of Australia (AM).

He was inducted into the Australian Sporting Hall of Fame in 2014. In 2014 Athletics Australia awarded Dick the Australian Athletics Coach of the Year.

Dick Telford is currently Professorial Fellow in the University of Canberra Research Institute for Sport and Exercise, an adjunct Professor in the Medical School at the Australian National University, and he continues to coach and advise athletes throughout Australia.

The Canberra based training group has grown over the years and continues to expand.

Index

A

B

G

H

I

J

K

L

T

www.ingramcontent.com/pod-product-compliance
Lightning Source LLC
Chambersburg PA
CBHW070440100426
42812CB00031B/3344/J

* 9 7 8 0 9 9 4 3 5 5 8 9 8 *